I0585216

Friedrich Delitzsch, Archibald R. S. Kennedy

Assyrian Grammar

With paradigms, exercises, glossary and bibliography

Friedrich Delitzsch, Archibald R. S. Kennedy

Assyrian Grammar
With paradigms, exercises, glossary and bibliography

ISBN/EAN: 9783337227791

Printed in Europe, USA, Canada, Australia, Japan

Cover: Foto ©Andreas Hilbeck / pixelio.de

[redacted] N GRAMMAR

[redacted] PARA[redacted]

[redacted] SARY A[redacted]

BY

[redacted] ICH DE[redacted]

[redacted] ATED FROM TH[redacted]

BY

[redacted] K [redacted]

BERLIN,
H. REUTHER'S VERLAGSBUCHHANDLUNG.

LONDON,
WILLIAMS & NORGATE
14, HENRIETTA STREET,
COVENT GARDEN.

NEW YORK,
B. WESTERMANN & Co.
838, BROADWAY.

PARIS,
MAISONNEUVE
& CH. LECLERC
25, QUAI VOLTAIRE.

1889.

DEDICATED

AS A TOKEN OF RESPECT AND INDEBTEDNESS

TO MY FRIEND

PAUL HAUPT.

AUTHOR'S PREFACE.

The present work is intended to be of use not only to Assyriologists but to Semitic scholars generally, by presenting them, in as brief compass as possible, with a summary of the latest results of research in the department of Assyrian grammar. In return, it appeals not merely or chiefly to Assyriologists but to every Semitic scholar for their co-operation in the solution of numerous unsolved problems, some of which, at least, are of the utmost importance for comparative Semitic philology. Its aim is thus the same as that of my "Assyrisches Handwörterbuch" (Leipzig, Hinrichs 1889) the compilation of which has become possible by the appearance of this grammar. My larger dictionary, which is also of the nature of a concordance, will be continued without interruption and with renewed energy.

The brevity of the Chrestomathy may appear strange. But even had I extended it to many times the size, it would still have been practically useless. For acquiring familiarity with Assyrian literature, even as represented by the so-called historical texts, and with the monuments of the Old and New Babylonian empires, not to speak of the so-called Sumerian texts, it is indispensable to have a much more comprehensive table of characters on the one hand, and on the other, a more extended chrestomathy such as my "Assyrische Lesestücke". By-and-by it will be possible to recommend simply the first or fifth volume of Rawlinson's "Inscriptions of Western Asia", supposing, that is, that one or other of these volumes will again be obtainable. I have accordingly selected only a couple of historical texts, an easier and a more difficult one, furnishing these, however, with footnotes and a glossary in such a way that they will, I trust, afford the student his first lesson in the reading and interpretation of Assyrian, and introduce him to the use of this grammar.

I am well aware of the many defects incidental to this first essay but I intend to continue with unwearied diligence the investigation of such problems as have not yet been satisfactorily solved — among which I partially include the discussion in §§ 12—14. It shall be my earnest endeavour to bring this manual abreast of the newest results of Semitic philology in general and of Assyriology in particular, and to maintain it thenceforth in that position.

Leipzig, Easter 1889.

Friedrich Delitzsch.

Note by Translator.

It was the intention of the publishers that this English edition should appear almost simultaneously with the original. The delay has been caused by the demands of my own work during the winter.

I shall consider myself amply rewarded for my labour of love in translating and editing Professor Delitzsch's book, if in its English dress, it should prove a boon to the aspiring student in this country and America to whom the German original is a sealed volume.

Aberdeen, 12th June, 1889.

A. R. S. K.

TABLE OF CONTENTS.

Grammar.

Introduction (§§ 1—5).

The Written Character (§§ 6—25).

Page

Phonology (§§ 26—52).

A. Vowels.

B. Consonants.

Page

Morphology (§§ 54—118).

A. Pronoun.

B. Noun.

C. Verb.

Syntax (§§ 119—152).

A. The individual Parts of Speech.

ABBREVIATIONS.

ABK *vid.* Litteratura 134. — **AL**[3] *v.* Litt. 127. — **ASKT** *v.* Litt. 110. — **Assurb. Sm.** *v.* Litt. 169. — **Assurb. S. A. Sm.** II *v.* Litt. 123. — **Assurn.**: Large Alabaster Inscription of Assurnasirpal I R 17—26. — **Assurn. Balaw.**: do. Slab Inscription from Balawat V R 69. 70. — **Assurn. Mon.**: do. Monolith Inscription III R 6. — **Assurn. Stand.**: do. so-called Standard Inscription, Layard 1 (with variants 2—11). — **Beh.**, **NR** and the other Achaemenian inscriptions, **D**, **K**, etc. are cited in the usual way: for **Beh.** *v.* III R 39. 40, for the rest Bezold's "Achaemenideninschriften" (*v.* Litt. 113). — **C**[a], **C**[b]: Assyrian Eponym Canon, published in the second edition of my "Lesestücke" (AL[2]). — **Desct.**: Legends of Ishtar's Descent to Hades IV R 31. — **Dict.** *v.* Litt. 211. — ***E. M.*** II *v.* Litt. 84. — **Esarh.**: Six-sided Prism of Esarhaddon I R 45—47. — **Hamm. Louvre**: Inscription of Hammurabi, *v.* Ménant's "Manuel etc." (Litt. 143), pp. 306—312. — **K.**: Tablets of the Kuyunjik collection in the British Museum; for the books etc. in which they have so far been published, as also for the tablets indicated by **S.** (**Sm.**) or **M**, see Bezold, Kurzgefasster Überblick über die babylonisch-assyrische Literatur nebst einem chronologischen Excurs, zwei Registern und einem Index zu 1700 Thontafeln des British-Museums. Leipzig 1886. (XV, 395 pp. 8). From the third edition of my "Lesestücke" (AL[3]) are quoted: **K. 3437** (p. 97 ff.). **K. 4378** (p. 86 ff.); also **Fragm. 18** (p. 95 f.) and **Sm. 954** (p. 134 ff.); from ASKT: **K. 56** (= II R 14. 15, p. 71 ff.). **K. 101** (p. 115 f.). **K. 133** (p. 79 ff.). **K. 246** (= II R 17 f., (p. 82 ff.). **K. 3927** (p. 75). **K. 4350** (= II R 11, p. 45 ff.); — from Pinches' *Texts:* **K. 196. K. 823. K. 831**; — from Assurb. S. A. Sm. II: **K. 95. K. 359. K. 509. K. 538. K. 562. K. 2867.** Note also: **K. 64** = II R 62 No. 3. **K. 245** = II R 8. 9. **K. 4341** = II R 36 No. 3. **K. 4386** = II R 48. — **Khors.** *v.* Litt. 106. — **Lay.** *v.* Litt. 104. — **I Mich.**: Caillou de Michaux I R 70. — **Nabon.**: Cylinder inscription of Nabonidus I R 69. — **Neb.**: Slab

Inscription of Nebuchadnezzar I R 53—58 (50—64). **Neb. Bab.** or **Bors.** or **Senk.**: do. Cylinder Inscriptions from Babylon (I R 52 No. 3), Borsippa (51 No. 1), and Senkereh (51 No. 2). — **Neb. Grot.**: do. Cylinder Inscription, first published by Grotefend, I R 65—66. — **Nerigl.**: Cylinder Inscription of Neriglissar I R 67. — **Nimr. Ep.**: *v.* Litt. 116 (Nimr. Ep. XI. XII. denotes the eleventh and twelfth tablets of this epos as copied by me; for the former see AL³ p. 99 ff. Tablet XII is now edited by P. Haupt in Delitzsch-Haupt's "Beiträge zur Assyriologie und vergleichenden semitischen Sprachwissenschaft", I, 1889, 48—79). — **NR** *v.* **Bch. Pinches,** *Texts* *v.* Litt. 112. — **Proll.** *v.* Litt. 210. — **IR, IIR,** etc. *v.* Litt. 105; the numerals after R denote the page and the line, the letters the columns. — **S.** or **Sm.** (tablets of the Smith collection of the British Museum) *v.* K. — **Sᵃ, Sᵇ, Sᶜ**, syllabaries published in AL³ pp. 41—79. — **Sarg. Cyl.** or **Bull Inscr.**, cited as in Lyon's "Sargontexte", *v.* Litt. 115. **Sarg. Cyp.**: Inscription of Sargon on the monolith found in Cyprus III R 11, cf. Schrader's new edition of the text mentioned in Litt. 111. — **Senhb.**: Six-sided prism of Sennacherib I R 37—42. — **Senhb. Bav.**: do. Rock inscription of Bavian III R 14. — **Senhb. Bell.**: Lay. 63—64 (my numbering of the lines omits the heading and consequently differs by one line from Layard's). — **Senhb. Const.**: do. Slab inscription, now in Constantinople I R 43. 44. — **Senhb. Kuy**: do.: Inscription on the Kuyunjik bulls III R 12—43. — **Senhb. Rass.**: Sennacherib Cylinder in Rassam's collection. — **Senhb. Sm.**: *v.* Litt. 175. — **Shalm. Balaw.**: Inscription of Shalmaneser II on the bronze gates of Balawat, *v.* Litt. 109. — **Shalm. Co.**: do. Two inscriptions on colossal bulls, published Lay. 12—16, 46—47, cited according to my own arrangement. — **Shalm. Mo.**: do. Monolith inscription III R 7—8. — **Shalm. Obv.**: do. Obelisk inscription Lay. 87—98. — **Shalm. Throne Inscr.**: *v.* Litt. 121, 191. — **Shams.**: Obelisk inscription of Shamshi-Rammân I R 29—31 (32—34). — **Strassm.** *v.* Litt. 208. — **Str. I. II.** *v.* Litt. 118. 125. — **Tig.**: Eight-sided prism of the elder Tiglathpileser I R 9—16. — **Tig. jun.**: Tablet inscription of the younger Tiglathpileser II R 67. — **Zurich Voc.** *v.* AL³ p. 84 f.

Familiar abbrevations such as cf. = compare (**confer**), **v.** or **vid.** = see, etc. call for no further notice.

INTRODUCTION.

Assyro-Babylonian or simply *Assyrian* is the § 1.
name given to the language of the Semitic literary monuments in Babylonian or Assyrian wedge-writing. Though known to us for only a few decades, in a literature of surpassing richness, Assyro-Babylonian was the tongue of Semitic empires on the Euphrates and the Tigris, which reach back into the fourth millenium B. C.—the Old Babylonian, the Assyrian, and the Neo-Babylonian. After the destruction of Nineveh (c. 608) and the fall of Babylon (c. 538), it continued to be spoken in Babylonia during the period of the Achæmenian kings (cf. the Persian cuneiform inscriptions of the so-called third species), till at last, in the second century B. C., it had gradually to give way before the Aramaic dialect, leaving behind it its last important monuments from the times of the Seleucidæ.

It is almost exclusively to *excavations* that we § 2.
owe our possession of an Assyro-Babylonian literature. The following are the principal dates:

Assyria. Final identification of Nineveh with the two mounds Kuyunjik and Nebi Yunus by Rich in 1820. Excavation of *Dûr-Šarrukên*, the city of Sargon, in the mound of Khorsabad by the Frenchmen Emil Botta (1842—1845) and Victor Place (1852). Excavations in Nimrud (Kelach) and Nineveh by the Englishmen Austen Henry Layard (1845—1847; 1849—1851), Hormuzd Rassam (1852—1854), George Smith (1873; 1874; 1876, † 19. Aug. 1876), Hormuzd Rassam and those under his direction (Nov. 1877—July 1882): discovery of the palaces of Assurnazirpal, Shalmaneser, Esarhaddon and others in Nimrud, the South-West Palace of Sennacherib and the North Palace of Assurbanipal (Sardanapalus) in Kuyunjik; discovery, among the ruins of the latter, of the library of clay tablets belonging to Assurbanipal by Rassam 1854 (several thousand literary works, partly of Assyrian origin, partly copies of Babylonian originals; hitherto only a part recovered—c. 30000 (?) fragments, hidden away in the British Museum). Beginning of the excavations in Kileh Shergat (Assur) by Layard and Rassam 1853. Rassam's discovery of "The Bronze Gates of Shalmaneser II" in the mound of Balawat 1878.

Babylonia. Exploration of the extensive ruins, Babil (Babylon), Birs Nimrud (Borsippa), Niffer (Nippur), Warka (Erech), Senkereh (Larsam), Ur (Mugheir, *al-Muḳayyar*), Abu Sharein (Eridu), by the Englishmen Loftus and Taylor under Sir Henry Rawlinson's superintendence (1849—1855) and by the French expedition (sent out under the leadership of Fulgence Fresnel and Jules Oppert 1851—

1854; loss of the collection in the Tigris May 23, 1855). Discovery by Arabs in the mound of Jumjuma (Babylon) 1874 of more than 3000 tablets (1″—1′ square) containing records of private business transactions; the collection was secured by George Smith in 1876 for the British Museum, and is being added to from year to year. Rassam's Babylonian expeditions (1879—July 1882), which resulted in the discovery of Sepharvaim in the extensive ruins of Abu Habba 1881; the excavation of the temple of the Sun, and the finding of the temple archives, consisting of clay cylinders and (acc. to Rassam's calculation) c. 50,000 unfortunately very badly burnt, clay tablets; exploration of the two largest mounds of Babylon, Babil and Kaṣr, and of Tel Ibrahim, the site of Kutha; discovery of the palace of Nabonidus in Borsippa. E. de Sarzec's excavations of the ruins of Tello or Tel Loh (1875 to 1880; 1882 purchase of the collection for the Louvre). North American (Wolfe's) expedition 1884—1885. Systematic excavations are at present being continued only in Tello; in stead of which there has been for years an active trade in Babylonian antiquities, especially in clay tablets and cylinders, often of the highest scientific value, which have been dug up by the Arabs *in situ*, and purchased in the East or in Europe, for the museums in London, Paris, Berlin and elsewhere.

Of *rock inscriptions*—apart from those of Darius on the rock-hewn graves of Naksh-i-Rustam (near Persepolis) and on the face of the rock at Behistun (Media)—the following are the most notable: Inscriptions and sculptures of Tiglath-pileser I and of three of his successors at the entrance to the fountain grotto of the Sebeneh-Su, the left parent stream of the Tigris; Sennacherib's Bavian inscription (Assyria) of 60 lines; two inscriptions of Nebuchadnezzar in the Wady Brissa (Lebanon), together comprising 19 columns. — Details as to excavation and editions of the text *v.* Litteratura A, b. and C.—*Museums* with Assyro-Babyl. antiquities: *British Museum*, London; *Louvre*, *Musée de Clerqc* and Bibliothèque nationale, Paris; Museums in *Berlin*, Constantinople, New York, Liverpool, the Hague, St. Petersburg, Zurich (Vatican in Rome, Leyden, Brussels, Graz and others).

§ 3. The *decipherment* of the Assyro-Babylonian wedge-writing, *i. e.* of the wedge-writing in the third column of the Achæmenian inscriptions, is based on the deciphering of the Old Persian wedge-writing in the first column, a work of genius on the part of Georg Friedrich Grotefend (who made out the names Darius, Xerxes, Hystaspes; 14. Sept. 1802, translation of the first two Achæmenian inscriptions), Eugène Burnouf, Christian Lassen (both 1836; first employment of the Darius inscription J with its list of satraps) and Henry Rawlinson, who copied (1835—1837) and (in 1846) explained the Behistun inscription. After the Old Persian alphabet of 40 signs had been fully deciphered, Hincks and Jules Oppert, Benfey and Spiegel carried on and completed the thorough investigation of the Old Persian language.

The observation made by Botta and others, that the characters on certain monuments excavated in Assyria and deposited in the Louvre, notwithstanding manifest differences, were identical with those of the third column of the trilingual inscriptions, was the starting-point for the decipherment of this third species. The Old Persian monuments with their phonetically written proper names, especially since the number of those clearly made out had been raised from ten to ninety by Sir Henry Rawlinson's publication of the Babylonian part of the Behistun inscription, were, in this connexion, what the Rosetta stone with its Greek text was to the decipherers of the hieroglyphics.

Moreover it was soon remarked that, in the Babylonian translations of the Old Persian texts, all the names of countries, cities, deities and persons were indicated by a particular sign (the so-called determinative) placed immediately before them, a discovery which resulted in fixing, without much difficulty, a considerable number of signs with their approximate values. While, however, the proper names above referred to would have been tolerably sufficient for the decipherment of inscriptions in alphabetic characters, it soon became apparent that the Babylonian wedge-writing was not alphabetic. One difficulty surmounted, the decipherer found himself face to face with another. Sir Henry Rawlinson, who arranged the signs occurring in the Babylonian Text of the Behistun inscription, to the number of 246, was the first to detect the polyphony of the Babylonian signs (Sept. 1851), while Hincks, with equal acuteness, first detected the syllabic character of the Babylonian writing (1849—1852), and thereby put an end to the grand mistake of supposing that the Babylonian writing was alphabetic, with several signs for each individual letter (de Saulcy, and, for a considerable period, Rawlinson). The work of decipherment was brought to a close by Jules Oppert (1859) with the aid of Assyrian sign-lists or "syllabaries", which had meanwhile been discovered. These lists, *inter alia*, explained the signs representing so-called compound syllables, that is, syllables containing two consonants with a vowel between, by the signs for the corresponding simple syllables, *e. g.* No. 162 of the table of signs by *da-an*, *ka-al*, *ri-ib*, No. 206 by *ḫa-ab*, *ki-ir*, *ri-im*; and alongside the signs representing whole words, the so-called ideograms, they gave a phonetic reproduction of their meanings, *e. g.* No. 165: = *a-ḫu* and *na-ṣa-ru*. All Assyriologists of note (Ménant, Norris, Talbot, George Smith, Sayce, Schrader and others) have been, and still are, active gleaners in this rich and fruitful field, removing old and false, and discovering new syllabic and ideographic values. A new task —perhaps the last—was undertaken in the increasingly successful deciphering of the archaic signs on the oldest bricks, clay cones, and cylindrical seals, and especially on the monuments discovered by de Sarzec at Tello, a task which, thanks to the labours of Amiaud and others, is, like its predecessors, gradually approaching completion.

For details see Litteratura B, a and b.

§ 4. The beginnings of *grammatical investigation* coincide with the early attempts at decipherment, notably those of de Saulcy, who was the first to read the personal and possessive pronouns, and to recognise the relative and a few verbal forms. The same scholar made a number of observations regarding gender and number which still hold good, and led the way (1849) in the analysis and explanation, as Semitic texts, of such Achæmenian inscriptions as were then accessible. Sir Henry Rawlinson, thereafter, in his translation of the Babylonian Behistun text, succeeded in referring words and phrases to Semitic forms. The first to elaborate on a firm basis a system of the pronoun and verb, and consequently of the elements of the grammar was Hincks (1854—1856); he even thus early compared the Assyrian verbal inflexions with those of Hebrew, Syriac, Arabic and Ethiopic, and sought in this way to determine more precisely the position of Assyrian in the group of the Semitic tongues. It is, however, to Jules Oppert (1860), that we owe the first connected presentation of Assyrian grammar; he it was who, aided by the results obtained by other Assyrian scholars, noted the various parts of speech, and discovered the mimation, the pronominal inflexion, the formation of the derived verbal stems, the feminine forms in the inflexion of the verb, and the general features of the syntax and composition of words. Oppert and Hincks continued their grammatical investigations, while Schrader tested the reliability of the decipherment, and the results it had yielded for the Assyrian grammar and lexicon. Among younger Assyriologists Pognon substituted the only admissible reading *ma* for the false reading and supposed copula *va*. It is, however, Paul Haupt in particular who, in a series of papers distinguished by observations of great acuteness, has not only freed the grammar of Assyrian from numerous errors, more especially in the department of phonology and morphology, but has roused grammatical research to new life by his breadth of view, and the originality of his suggestions.

Details in Litteratura D. For the foundation of Assyrian Lexicography and the carrying on of the work *v. ibid.* E and F.

§ 5. The *literature* preserved in the Assyrian tongue occupies on the score of age the first place among the literatures of the Semitic peoples. The oldest of the longer, phonetically written, Semitic texts known up to the present time are, in Babylonia, those of Hammurabi (c. 2200), in Assyria the large stone inscription of Rammannirari I (c. 1350) containing eighty lines. These are followed by the inscriptions on the octagonal clay prisms of Tiglathpileser I (1110 B. C.), each containing eight hundred lines, and by the bulk of the Assyrian and Neo-Babylonian literature, from Assurnazirpal to Assurbanipal, from Nebuchadnezzar to Nabonidus, and later from Cyrus to Artaxerxes and even to Antiochus I. Soter— comprising, therefore, a period of more than two thousand years. Engraved on bricks, prisms and cylinders of clay (the latter usually built into the corners of palaces and temples), on slabs of marble and alabaster, on statues, obelisks and colossal bulls, and, above all, on clay tablets of every shape, a literature has been récovered which already far exceeds in compass the whole of the O. T. scriptures, and which, as now from year to year, will doubtless continue to increase for an indefinite period, till at length the wealth of material shall become inexhaustible. Texts of many hundred lines record the wars of Assyrian and Babylonian kings, their buildings, their deeds at the chase and elsewhere, and unfold a lifelike picture of the politics, culture and geography not only of Babylonia and Assyria, but also of all the neighbouring peoples of Western Asia. In addition to these, chronological lists and records of every sort (eponym-lists, chronicles, synchronous histories, tables of kings) render it possible to fix the dates of individual dynasties and monarchs, and afford unimpeachable chronological data reaching back into the fourth millenium B. C. Prayers and psalms, legends of the gods, stories of the creation, lists of the gods and exorcisms of varied content, a great epic in twelve books, along with a great number of astrological tablets, curious lists of secret remedies, oracular deliverances and calendars afford a profound insight into the religion, mythology and superstition of those nations. As companions to the tablets of purely scientific, astronomical, and mathematical contents, we may place long lists of words from the same or a similar stem or having the same or a similar ideogram, lists of synonyms, of the names of occupations, persons, stars, animals, plants, clothes, wooden instruments and utensils, paradigms, collections of signs, all well adapted to lead us, as they led the pupils in the priestly schools of Babylonia and Assyria, to a more and more thorough understanding of the Assyrian language as it was written and spoken. Numberless letters and contract tablets, finally, reports of generals and astronomers, proclamations and petitions, deeds of purchase and sale of every description, marriage certificates, bequests, wills, house inventories, receipts and so on reveal the social life of the Assyrians and Babylonians even to its most secret recesses.

THE WRITTEN CHARACTER.

The characters in which the literary monuments § 6.
of Assyria and Babylonia are written have the form of wedges—the writing running from left to right. Under the name of wedge-writing are comprised all the species of writing in which the fundamental element is a so-called wedge (Latin *cuneus*, whence the now usual name *cuneiform*). This wedge may be described as a stroke proceeding in a straight line from a hollow three-sided pyramid, or, as it appears when graphically reproduced on paper, from a triangular head, the stroke being attached to the apex of the triangle, opposite the initial base. In addition to the horizontal (𒀸), perpendicular (𒁹) and sloping (𒀺, 𒀹, 𒀹) wedges, there is the double wedge (𒌋), or arrowhead with the opening always to the right. The latter has arisen either from a single triangle by lengthening the sides, or from the union of two sloping wedges (or lines) with their heads joined so as to form an angle (𒌋, <).

The sloping wedges  and  occur in only a few Babylonian signs, *e. g. ki, di, libbu.*

§ 7. The Assyro-Babylonian wedge-writing was originally a straight-line picture-writing. The original pictures, giving, mostly by means of straight lines, a rough outline of the objects to be represented, are, it must be confessed, only with difficulty recognizable even in the oldest (the so-called archaic) literary monuments. In these the characters when unabbreviated approach the oldest forms and, if not exclusively at least in the main, still employ the straight line. The same remark applies to the early Babylonian and Assyrian texts, in which lines and wedges occur side by side. Finally, in the later Babylonian and Assyrian the straight line has almost entirely given place to the wedge, and the characters have undergone systematic simplification owing to the ever increasing popularisation of writing and the tendency to adopt shorter forms, the result being that the original pictures have become entirely unrecognizable. Nevertheless some of the characters, more particularly in the form in which they appear on the monuments of Tello, present the original picture with sufficient clearness to remove all doubt as to the pictorial origin of the oldest Babylonian writing (see one or two illustrations in No. 3 of addenda to the table of characters). To this we must add that the native scholars themselves testify to this origin of the cuneiform writing, and have even given a pictorial representation of it in their tablets. The union of two or more of these simple pictorial signs or ideograms, either to a single new sign—the one being inserted in or placed above the other—or to a group of signs, rendered it possible to represent in writing a further series of objects and ideas. Thus, for example, the union of 'mouth' (table of characters, No. 39) and 'food' (No. 84 has also this meaning) produced 'eat' (224); 'fence' (206) and 'ox' (250), written twice, gave 'cattle-pen', 'herd' (271); 'water' (1) and 'heaven' (60), 'rain' (1); 'water' and 'eye' (86), 'tear' (1). To understand the compound ideograms, we must, of course, go back, in most cases, to the oldest forms of the component signs: thus the formation of the ideogram for 'month' out of 'day' (26) and 'thirty', and of that for 'wild ox' by means of 'ox' and 'mountain' (176), is no longer recognizable in the later Assyrian form of these signs (227, 53), but easily enough in the early Babylonian (*v.* § 9 addendum 3).

Each of the simple or compound ideograms could, as a matter of course, be employed to express several words having the same or a cognate signification; improperly, however, to denote words having the same or a similar sound but an entirely different signification: thus 'star' (60, *v.* § 9 Add. 3) could also symbolize 'heaven' (*šamû*) and 'the god of heaven' (*Anu*, עֲנוּ), then 'god' in general (*ilu*); and since the idea of 'high' was associated with heaven in the Semitic mind, it might be employed, over and above, to express 'to be high' (*elû*). The picture of a drop of water (1) could also serve to represent a drop of the seminal fluid and thereby express 'beget' 'begetter' (father), 'begotten' (son, *aplu*) and so on. We can easily understand, further, how the symbol for 'eye' should comprise all the meanings given under No. 86, 'see' (*amâru*) 'glance' (*dagâlu*), and other synonyms. Equally intelligible is the fact that the sun's disk (26) might denote not only the 'sun', but also 'day', 'be bright', 'shine', 'light' and similar ideas.—The groups of signs could be treated in the same way, and 'tear' (the water of the eye, No. 1), for example, employed to express the ideas of weeping, sighing etc.

According to the above, the wedge is not, at bottom, an essential characteristic of the Assyro-Babylonian writing. There exist many ancient texts in which the writing is still more or less line-writing. It was only with the increasing employment of soft clay as writing-material and the use of a wooden stylus, that the head of the former simple line assumed the shape of a hollow three-sided pyramid—the writing gaining thereby in firmness and clearness.

§ 8. Notwithstanding its more than four hundred ideograms, and its almost numberless sign-groups, a mode of writing so exclusively confined to ideograms could not accomplish its object; not only was it ambiguons, but it was either entirely unable to exhibit the component parts of words, or could do so only in an extremely unsatisfactory way. This necessitated a further step in advance: ideograms for phonetic combinations consisting of a consonant and vowel (*mu*), or of a vowel and consonant (*an*), or even of the form: consonant, vowel, consonant (*nab*, *tim*, *mul*), were set apart as signs for the syllables in question. Out of the ideographic writing there was gradually developed, in this way, a *syllabic* writing, ideograms and sign-groups (the latter almost exclusively employed to denote nouns) being, however, retained. It is to be expected that anterior to and contemporaneous with this system, there were other attempts to improve the method of writing; the system just described, however, was the only one that came into general use. This it did in spite of obvious imperfections: the ideograms, for example, that had been employed as syllabic signs were still retained as ideograms, and even two or more syllabic values were derived from a single ideogram, in cases where the latter was rendered by a number of short words. Thus from the symbol for 'head, chief, beginning etc.' (131) were taken *riš* (cf. *rêšu* 'head') and *šaḳ* (cf. *šaḳû* 'be high', *šâḳû* 'officer'); from the sign (101) uniting 'skin' (67) with 'water, liquid' (1) were taken *šun* (cf. *šunnû* 'wash') and *ruḳ* (cf. *ruḳḳû* 'anoint'); from the ideogram for 'wild ox' (190) *rim* (cf. *rîmu*) 'wild ox' and *it* (cf. *lêtu* 'wild cow'). The further step—to give up altogether the signs for the compound syllables, and (even with the retention of ideograms) to be content with the signs for the simple ones—was never taken. It was not till the Neo-Babylonian period that a growing preference was shown for the signs representing the simple syllables (consonant and vowel, or vowel and consonant), but even then they were not exclusively employed, and in any case the preference came—too late.*) The Assyro-Babylonian writing, then, is a script capable of expressing both words and syllables, the individual characters of which can express not only a single word and a single syllable, but even several words and syllables. Details may be gathered from the follg. table of characters.**)

*) The representation given in the foregoing section of the development of the Assyrian writing is in great part dependent on one's attitude towards the "Sumerian" question. The latter is treated at length in § 25.

**) I transcribe ז *z*, ח *ḫ* (خ), ט *ṭ*, ס *s*, צ *ṣ*, ק *ḳ*, שׁ *š*.

Table of Characters. §9.

A. Signs for the simple Syllables.

Sign. Syllabic and Ideographic Values. — Groups of Signs.

 a — mû Pl. mê (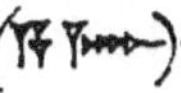) water. mâru, aplu
child, son. —  zunnu rain. 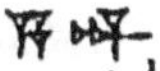,
 determinative after numbers
and measures.  tâmtu sea.
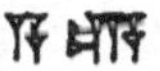 milu flood. 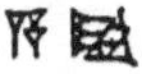 ugaru mea-
dows, fields.  eḳlu field. 
dimtu tear, bakû weep. 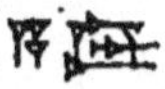 nâru
river, canal; determ. before names of rivers
and canals (also before ênu fountain, a-
gammu marsh). 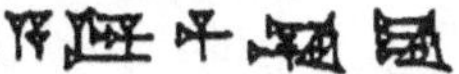 or
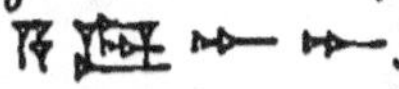 Idiḳlat, Diḳlat Tigris.
 Purâtu Euphrates (s. also
No. 26). 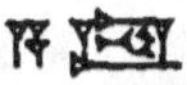 iddû pitch, with 
kupru do. () 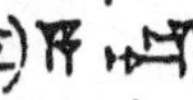 âsû physician
(bârû seer, magician).

 i — ṇa'âdu (Perm. na'id) to be exalted. — ()
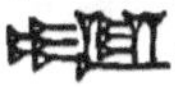 askuppu, askuppatu threshold.

 e

Sign.	Syllabic and Ideographic Values. — Groups of Signs.	
4. 	ú	šam. — measure of length: ammatu (אמה). Determ. before names of plants. — 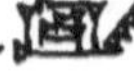 u s. No. 271.
5. 	u	()  Rammân, god of thunder.
6. 	û	s. also No. 38. —   the „water-country" Umliâš.
7. 	'a/i/u, a/i/u' ; '	s. also No. 271.
8. 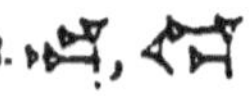	bu	ḳâšu to present.
9. 	bi	k/gaš, kas. — šikaru intoxicating drink.
10. 	be	bat/d; mit/t/d; b/pit; (mut); til; ziz. — bêlu, enu lord. labâru be old, labiru old. ()  mîtu a dead man, pagru corpse. naḳbu subterranean spring.
11. 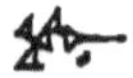	b/pu	sir; g/ḳit. —  () arâku be long, arku long, šadâdu draw.
12. 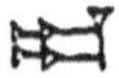	ab/p (ab)	
13. 	ib/p	
14. 	ub/p; ár	kibratu region.
15. 	ya	(taḫ). — 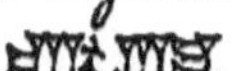 našû lift up.
16. 	yi	ḳanû reed. —   kênu true, faithful.   apparu rushes, sea-wrack.
17. 	gu	
18. 	ag/k/ḳ	

No.	Sign.	Syllabic and Ideographic Values. — Groups of Signs.	
19.		ig/k/ḳ	bašû be.
20.		ug/k/ḳ	
21.		d/ṭa	
22.		d/ṭi	šalâmu be complete, II1 preserve uninjured, šulmu completion, setting (of the sun). — dânu judge. = the god Šulmânu.
23.		du	k/ḳ/g ub/p; (kin). — alâku go, or, with the syllabic value laḫ, itallu-ku go. kânu II1 establish, kênu firm, true.
24.		ad/t/ṭ	abu (abû) father.
25.		id/t/ṭ	idu hand, side, might. — našru eagle. le'û powerful. rêṣu helper, narârûtu help.
26.		ud/t/ṭ; tú	tam; pa/ir; la/iḫ; ḫiš/s. — ûmu day; šamšu sun, piṣû white. — aṣû go out, rise (of the sun). urru light. siparru bronze. the city of Larsam. Sip(p)ar; with prefixed: Purâtu.
27.		z/ṣa	
28.		zi	napištu soul, life. — imnu the right; s. also No. 163.

Sign.	Syllabic and Ideographic Values. — Groups of Signs.	
29.	zu.	idû perceive, know. — apsû abyss.
30.	az/s/ṣ	
31.	iz/s/ṣ	gis. — iṣu wood, tree. Determ. bef. names of trees, woods and utensils of wood. — daltu door. a-bu thicket of bulrushes. sik(k)ûru bolt. kirû plantation, park. burâšu cypress. ( ) ḫaṭṭu staff, sceptre. ašagu thorn (similar is). ušû a valuable wood. ṣillu shadow, shade. eršu (iršu) bed. ḳaštu bow. tukumtu attack, fight. (also) narkabtu chariot. tukultu assistance, kakku weapon; -karînu a valuable wood. er(i)nu cedar. nîru yoke. (also , ( )) kussû throne. ( ) paššûru dish, bowl.
32.	uz/s/ṣ	
33.	ḫa	nûnu fish. Determ. after names of fishes.

Sign.	Syllabic and Ideographic Values. — Groups of Signs.	
34. [cuneiform]	ḫi; ṭi	(šar).  — [cuneiform] ([cuneiform]) ṭâbu good, gay, ṭubbu joy, health. 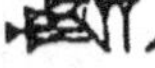 — [cuneiform] [cuneiform] kuzbu extraordinary magnificence.
35.  [cuneiform]	ḫu	pag/k, bag/k. — iṣṣuru bird. Determ. after names of birds.
36.  [cuneiform]	aḫ	 [cuneiform] is special sign for uḫ.
37. 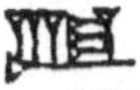 [cuneiform]	ṭu	šiḳlu shekel.
38. 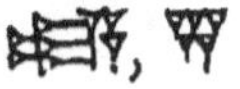 [cuneiform], [cuneiform]	ia	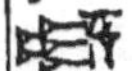  often merely a; hence  [cuneiform] [cuneiform] and [cuneiform] [cuneiform] change with [cuneiform] [cuneiform] (No. 6).
39.  [cuneiform]	ka	pû mouth. šinnu tooth, in partic. ivory.   — [cuneiform] [cuneiform] [cuneiform] suluppu date.
40.  [cuneiform]	ki	     also for ḳi. — erṣitu (irṣitu) earth; ašru place. itti with.  — [cuneiform] [cuneiform] šaplu, šupâlû lower, low, šapliš Adv. beneath.  [cuneiform] [cuneiform] (or [cuneiform]) [cuneiform] Šumêr Sumer. [cuneiform] [cuneiform] kinûnu coal-pan. 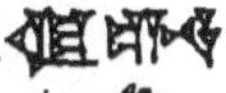 [cuneiform] [cuneiform] karâšu camp. [cuneiform] [cuneiform] šubtu dwelling. — Determ. after names of cities and countries.
41.  [cuneiform]	ku	also for ḳu. dur; tuš; (ub/p). — tukultu assistance. ṣubâtu robe, garment; Determ. before names of garments. ašâbu dwell.
42. [cuneiform]	la	
43.  [cuneiform]	li	
44.  [cuneiform]	lu	ṭib. — ṣabâtu take. etêḳu I1.2 advan-

Sign.		Syllabic and Ideographic Values. — Groups of Signs.
		ce, march. ṣênu small cattle, flock (often prefixed to this word as determinative). — [cuneiform] [cuneiform] tame sheep. [cuneiform] [cuneiform] niḳû (?) sacrificial lamb.
45. [cuneiform]	al	
46. [cuneiform]	il	
47. [cuneiform]	ul	
48. [cuneiform]	el	
49. [cuneiform]	ma	[cuneiform] [cuneiform] mâtu country.
50. [cuneiform]	mi	mûšu night. ṣalmû, [illegible] black. hence image.
51. [cuneiform]	me	šip/b, sip.
52. [cuneiform]	mu	šumu name. zakâru name, speak; zikru name. In proper names also nadânu give. — [cuneiform] ([cuneiform] [cuneiform]) šattu year.
53. [cuneiform]	am	rîmu wild ox. — [cuneiform] [cuneiform] pîru elephant. ([cuneiform] [cuneiform] [cuneiform] ivory).
54. [cuneiform]	im	šâru wind, region. — [cuneiform] [cuneiform] [cuneiform] šûtu southwind, south; [cuneiform] [cuneiform] [cuneiform] ištânu, iltânu north; [cuneiform] [cuneiform] [cuneiform] aḫarrû west; [cuneiform] [cuneiform] [cuneiform] šadû east. [cuneiform] [cuneiform] urpatu, erpitu (irpitu) clouds. [cuneiform] [cuneiform]-zû hurricane. [cuneiform] [cuneiform] na'idu exalted.
55. [cuneiform], [cuneiform]	um	
56. [cuneiform]	na	

Sign.		Syllabic and Ideographic Values. — Groups of Signs.
57. 𒉌	ni	z/ṣ al. — šamnu fat, oil, also [cuneiform] oil. — [cuneiform] ḫimêtu cream. [cuneiform] ilu god. [cuneiform] the city Dilmun.
58. 𒉈	ne; ṭe	b/p il, k/ḳ um (Babyl. also bi). — išâtu fire (also [cuneiform]). eššu new. [cuneiform], also, has the syllabic value b/p il and the meaning eššu new.
59. 𒉡	nu	lâ, ul not. ṣalmu image. — [cuneiform] niššakku governor, prince, etc.; cf. No. 68.
60. 𒀭	an	ilu god, determ. bef. names of deities. šamû Pl. šamê (genly. written with phon. complement 𒀭 [cuneiform]) heaven. — 𒀭 [cuneiform] ([cuneiform]) Nergal, also the plague-god. 𒀭 [cuneiform], 𒀭 [cuneiform] ([cuneiform]), with ligature [cuneiform], Bel; whence (𒀭) [cuneiform] city of Nippur. 𒀭 [cuneiform], 𒀭 [cuneiform] Adar. 𒀭 [cuneiform] parzillu iron. 𒀭 [cuneiform] išâtu fire (orig. the fire-god). 𒀭 [cuneiform], usually 𒀭 [cuneiform], also 𒀭 [cuneiform] ([cuneiform]) [cuneiform] Nergal. 𒀭 [cuneiform], 𒀭 [cuneiform] Ištar (Nanâ), usually 𒀭 [cuneiform] (with ligature [cuneiform]) and 𒀭 [cuneiform] Istar. 𒀭 [cuneiform], 𒀭 [cuneiform] Igigê, the spirits of heaven. 𒀭 [cuneiform] ([cuneiform]), 𒀭 [cuneiform] Nabû Nebo. 𒀭 [cuneiform], 𒀭 [cuneiform]

Sign.		Syllabic and Ideographic Values.—Groups of Signs.
		the moon-god Sin; do., also called Nannaru. Gibil the fire-god. Nusku. , usually or (rarely) Maru(u)-duk Merodach. lumassu protecting genius; (also with following) šêdu bull-god. , also (i.e. bêl ni-me-ḳi) und Ea (Ἀος). , also Šamaš. () the god Ašûr, whence Aššûr Assyria. Rammân (in the west Daddu, Addu = הדד); s. also No. 5. Adar, Nergal (both written in same way as âlik maḫri). Bêlit. Mâlik (but also the wife of the sun-god).— Ni-sa-ba barley (? or millet ?); aš-na-an wheat. anaku lead. elû upper. opp. elat (height) opp. išid (depth) šamê (south opp. north ?). ṣalûlu shadow, shade. adâru, atalû eclipse (e.g. of sun and moon).
61.	in	also .

Sign.		Syllabic and Ideographic Values. — Groups of Signs.
62.	en	bêlu, enu lord. adi unto. — kuṣṣu cold (acc. to Jensen). s. No. 60. kêpu ruler of a city.
63.	un	nišu people, nation, Pl. nišê ( ) people, persons. zikrêti women.
64.	sa	
65.	si	ḳarnu horn. — šigaru lock of a door. šutêšuru (ישׁר) guide.
66.	se	(šum). — nadânu give, present.
67.	su	kus/ẓ; (ruḳ). — mašku skin. zumru body. erêbu increase. — ḫušâḫu famine.
68.	pa	ḫaṭṭ. — iššakku plenipotentiary, ruler, prince, etc.; cf. No. 59.
69.	pi	(me; ma, also ; a; tu; tal). — uznu ear, mind; also .
70.	pú	(ṭul). — bûru well, cistern.
71.	ṣi	
72.	ṣu	rik; (zum).
73.	ḳa	a measure (subdivision of).
74.	ḳi	k/ḳin. — šipru missive, letter.
75.	ḳu	ḳum.
76.	ra	raḫâṣu "overflow," flood.
77.	ri	t/ṭal.

	Sign.		Syllabic and Ideographic Values. — Groups of Signs.
78.		ru	šub/p. — nadû throw, lay.
79.	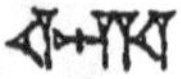	ar	cf. No. 14.
80.		ir	
81.		er	âlu city, town; determ. bef. names of towns.
82.		ur	lik/k; taš/s, das; tiš/z; (tan). — 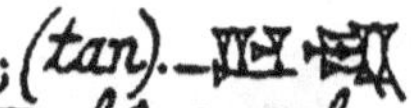 nêšu lion.  aḫû jackal. 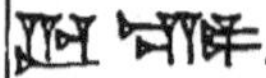 kar(ra)du strong, brave. 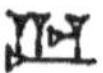  kalbu dog.
83.	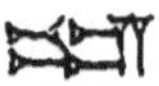	úr	išdu basement, legs, loins.
84.		ša	gar. — šakânu set, make; šitkunu placed, made; 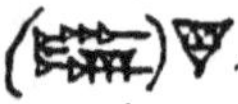 šaknu viceroy. šarâḳu to present. —  ḳâšu to present (cf. No. 8).  kudurru boundary, territory. 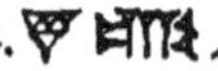 bušû one's goods; treasure.
85.		šá	
86.		ši	lim; (ini). — ênu (înu) eye. pânu countenance, pâni before. maḫru front; maḫri before. amâru see. — 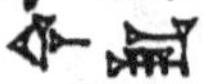 barû see.
87.		še	šê'u corn.  magâru, magiru (be) favourable; šemû obedient, devoted. —  šamaššammu sesame. 

Sign.		Syllabic and Ideographic Values.—Groups of Signs.
		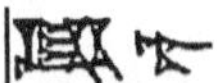 eṣêdu to harvest.
88. 	šu	kiššatu host, totality.. šanîtu time (e.g. three times).
89. 	šú	ḳat, ḳut.—ḳâtu hand; also .—  Bâbilu Babylon. 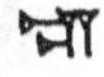 ubânu (point of) the finger, peak.  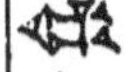 šuklulu perfect.  šêbu old man, elder.
90. 	aš	a measure.
91. 	áš	rum; dil.—ina in. Contraction for Aššûr Assyria: ; in names of persons also for the god Aššûr, nadânu give and aplu son.
92. 	iš	mil.—epru dust.
93. 	eš	ṣin.—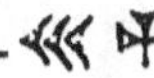 purussû decision.
94. 	uš	nit.—zik(a)ru male. šuššu the number 60.
95. 	ta	ištu, ultu out of, also: itti with; ina in, in the company of. Often written .  s. No. 1.
96. 	ti	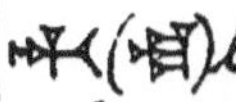 balâṭu, balṭu live, living
97. 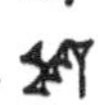	te	ṭaḫû approach.—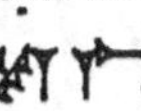 gallû devil.
98. 	tu	cf. No. 26.—erêbu enter.  summatu dove.

B. Signs for the compound Syllables

with the exception of those given under A.

Sign.	Syllabic and Ideographic Values. — Groups of Signs.
99.	ḫal. — a class of priests (šêbu magician?).
100.	muḳ/k; (puk).
101.	šun, šin; ruḳ/g.
102.	b/pal, b/pul. — palû year of a king's reign, reign. nabalkatu cross. enû bend. naḳû pour out, offer (in sacrifice). — Aš-šûr city of Assur.
103.	gir, more frequently ád/ṭ. — paṭru dagger. — zuḳaḳîpu, aḳrabu scorpion. ( ) birḳu lightning.
104.	b/pul.
105.	tar (ṭar); ḳ/kut, ḳud, šil, ḫaṣ; (gug). — naḳâsu cut off, down. parâsu decide. sûḳu street. — rêbitu square, market-place.
106.	naḳ/k/g.
107.	(ḳal).
108.	šaḫ (šiḫ). — šaḫû swine (acc. to Jensen).
109.	maḫ (miḫ). — ṣîru exalted; rabû, maḫḫu great.
110.	b/pab/p, ḳ/kur. — naḳru hostile, enemy. In the

Sign. | Syllabic and Ideographic Values. — Groups of Signs.

names of persons also aḫu brother, naṣâru protect, the „total" (of an addition), same meaning as .

111.  kat/d. — Cf. No. 121. (naṣâru preserve).

112.  šir.

113. 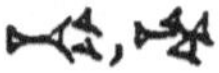 k/q/g ul, zir. — zêru seed, descendants.

114.  bar (par), maš/s. — ašaredu first, highest (in rank). parâsu decide. — ṣabîtu gazelle.

115.  k/q un. — zibbatu tail.

116. 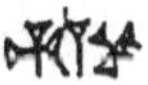 nam, sim. — šîmtu fate, decision. — sinûntu swallow. () bêl paḫâti, pâḫâtu, šalaṭ viceroy, ruler.

117.  mut/d.

118.  zat/ṭ/d.

119. 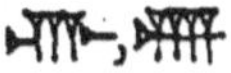 nun, z/ṣ/s il. — rubû (rabû) great, noble; () rubûti magnates. — abkallu he that has to decide, leader.

120.  kab/p, gap, rarely ḫup/b, for which is used. — šumêlu the left.

121.  kat/d (also); cf. No. 111; gat, k/q/g um. — kitû ( ) a dress stuff.

122.  t/d im.

123.  mun, also . — ṭâbtu good, well-doing (but also dâbtu with various meanings).

No.	Sign.	Syllabic and Ideographic Values. — Groups of Signs.
124.		š/s ur.
125.		suḫ.
126.		kar; (kan).
127.		tik/ḳ. — kišâdu neck; bank (of river), also aḫu. — … Kûtu Kutha.
128.		ṭ/t/d ur.
129.		g/k ur. — târu return, II 1 carry off, bring back; make.
130.		ṭar; (dir).
131.		šaḳ/k; riš/s. — rêšu head; beginning. ašaredu, rêštû first, highest in rank. — … ḳaḳḳadu head. … ašaredu. (…) … šaḳû, rêšu officer, … (…) rab-šaḳ(ê) chief officer.
132.		d/t/ṭ ir.
133.		tap/b, ṭab, dap.
134.		tak/g; šum. — lapâtu overthrow.
135.		nab/p.
136.		mul. — kakkabu star, determ. before star-names.
137.		dup. — ṭuppu tablet. šapâku, tabâku pour out.
138.		k/g an; (kam). — Determ. after numbers. — … ḫêgallu superabundance.
139.		tur (ṭur, dur). — ṣaḫru, ṣiḫru small. mâru child, aplu son. — … aplu son. … mâr-

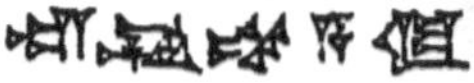

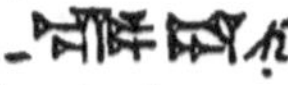

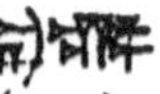

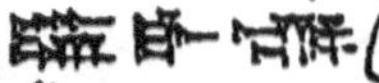

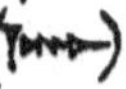

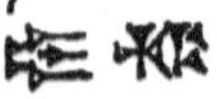

Sign.	Syllabic and Ideographic Values. — Groups of Signs.
	tu, bintu daughter.
140.	rap/b.
141.	š/s ar; šir; ḫir. — šaṭâru write.
142.	kas; raš/s. — ḫarrânu street, campaign. šinâ two. — space of two hours, two hours' march. illatu might, armed forces.
143.	gab/p, ḳab(kap); d/t aḫ, d/t uḫ. — paṭâru cleave, dissolve. irtu breast. — (?) mâḫiru, šâninu rival; miḫru (maḫru?) copy.
144.	t/d aḫ.
145.	zik; (ṣip).
146.	gaz/s, (kas). — dâku kill; dîktu fallen warriors; tidûku killing, murder.
147.	ram. — râmu to love.
148.	t/d um; (ib).
149.	šim; rik/k. — rikku incense.
150.	k/ḳ ip/b.
151.	tak/ḳ, (dak). — abnu stone; determ. bef. names of stones. — narû table of stone. parûtu (?) alabaster (?), white marble (?). kunukku seal. ugnû crystal (?).
152.	k/ḳ ak/ḳ; dá. — epêšu make, banû create; binûtu creature. kalû all. — kalâma

Sign.	Syllabic and Ideographic Values.—Groups of Signs.
	all sorts of, various.
153. 	mal.
154. 	dak/ḳ/g, (tak); (par).
155. 	šab/p, sap.
156. 	sib/p.— rê'û shepherd.
157. 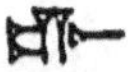	mar.—  mât aḫarrê Westcountry.
158. 	duk; lut/ṭ/d.— Determ. before names of vessels.
159. 	k/ḳ/g it, kid; saḫ, siḫ; lil.
160. 	rit/d; šit/d; lak/ḳ; mis/ṣ/z; (kil).— minûtu number. 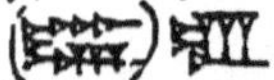 šangû priest.
161. 	la/u ḫ; riḫ.— sukkallu messenger.
162. 	kal; rib; lab/p; (lib/p); d/t/ṭ an.— dannu mighty. 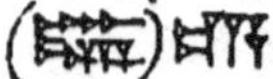 edlu lord.—  or 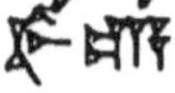  batûlu and batûltu young man, virgin.
163. 	bit/ṭ/d, pit; (e).— bîtu house.— 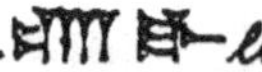 ekallu palace.  traditional orthography (e-sag-ila) of the temple of Merodach in Babylon,  traditional orthography (e-zi-da) of the temple of Nebo „bîtu kênu" in Borsippa.  kallâtu bride.  igâru wall.
164. 	nir.

	Sign.	Syllabic and Ideographic Values. — Groups of Signs.
165.		šiš/s, sis — aḫu brother. naṣâru protect. —   Ûru city of Ur.
166.		zak/ḳ. — imnu the right. pûtu side, access.
167.		ḳar (gar)
168.		lil.
169.	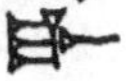	g/ḳal — rabû great.
170.		b/piš, k/gur
171.		mir — agû crown. ezzu fearful.
172.		b/pur.
173.		d/tub.
174.		lul; lib/p; lup; paḫ; nar. —  musician (zammêru?).
175.		g/ḳam; gur.
176.		kur; mat/d; šad/t/ṭ; lat; nat — mâtu country. šadû mountain. Determ. bef. names of countries and mountains. kašâdu capture, conquer. napâḫu rise, mount up (of the sun).
177.		šud/t; sir. — rûḳu distant.
178.		ṣir; muš. — ṣêru serpent.
179.		tir. — ()  kîštu forest.
180.		kar (ḳar). — kâru stronghold.
181.		liš/s.
182.		ṣab/p, zab; b/pir; lap/ḫ. — ṣâbu warrior, Pl.

Sign.	Syllabic and Ideographic Values. — Groups of Signs.
	people. — … (…), also … (…) ummânu Pl. ummânâti army, forces. … narâru, nirâru helper.
183.	zib/p, ṣip.
184.	kam; ḫam. — Determ. after numbers, esp. the ordinals. ummâru, diḳâru large drinking-cup.
185.	(ḫuš; ruš. — ezzu fearful.)
186.	(ṣun). — ma'adu much.
187.	b/pir.
188.	ḫaḫ/ur, mur, kin.
189.	muḫ. — eli upon, over.
190.	lit/ṭ/d; rim.
191.	kiš/s, ḳiš. — kiššatu host, totality.
192.	g/k/ḳul, sun.
193.	ni/um; (tum, also …). — (…) … Elamtu Elam.
194.	lam.
195.	z/ṣur.
196.	b/pan, bam. — For … s. No. 31.
197.	kim. — kîma like, as.
198.	ḫul. — limnu evil.
199.	tul. — til(l)u mound, heap of ruins.
200.	d/tin. — balâṭu live. — … Bâbilu.

Sign.	Syllabic and Ideographic Values. — Groups of Signs.
	s. No. 209.
201. 	dun; š/s ul.
202. 	pad/t/ṭ; šuk.
203. 	man; niš. — šarru king. Šamaš sun.
204. 	d/ṭiš, tiz/s/š. — and to. Determ. bef. masc. proper names.
205. 	lal; (la). — šaḳâlu weigh. ṣamâdu to harness; ṣimittu team.
206. 	k/g il; rim; (rin); ḫab/p; kir.
207. 	z/s ar.
208. 	b/p ul.
209. 	zuk/ḳ, suk.
210. 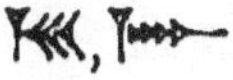	miš. — Sign of the plural.
211. 	šik. — Determ. before dress stuffs.
212. 	s/ṣ al; rak/g. — Determ. bef. fem. proper names. Before adjectives it forms neuter nouns, e.g.  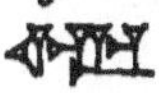 limuttu the evil. Hence used as ideogr. for the neuter, and also the personal, indef. pronoun:  (phon. compl.), genly. 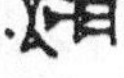 mamma any one, mimma anything.
213. 	nin. — bêltu lady (bêlu lord). aḫâtu sister.
214. 	d/ṭam. — aššatu, ḫîrtu woman, wife.
215. 	nik/ḳ.
216. 	lum; ḫum; (kuš; gum).

Sign.	Syllabic and Ideographic Values. — Groups of Signs.
217.	tuk/k :— išû be, have.
218.	gug.
219. ,	sik, zik, šiḳ, (pik/k)

C. Ideograms

with the exception of those given under A and B.

Sign.	Ideographic Values. — Groups of Signs.
220.	(contracted from and). () the god Aššur (No. 60), , city, land Aššur.
221. ,	šaptu lip.
222.	taḫâzu battle. Also
223.	lišânu tongue, speech. — Šumêr.
224.	akâlu eat.
225.	puḫru totality.
226.	zikaru, ardu man, servant, slave.
227.	arḫu month. — Nîsânu, — A-a-ru, — Simânu, — Du'ûzu, — Âbu, — Ulûlu, — Tišrîtu, — Araḫ-šamna, — Kislîmu, — Ṭebêtu, — Šabâṭu, — Addaru.
228.	ebûru fruits of the field.
229.	uššû bottom, foundation. (Syllab. value pin). — () nartabu irrigation works.
230.	ṣibtu income, property. — bûlu cattle. šuttu dream.

Sign.	Ideographic Values.— Groups of Signs.
231.	in , also eribû locust.
232.	biltu tribute. talent.
233.	genly. elippu ship. (Syllab. value má).— () malaḫu boatman, sailor.
234.	arba', erbitti (irbitti) four.
235.	erû copper.
236.	bâbu gate. (Syllab. value ka(n)).— abullu city gate. ()() Bâbilu Babylon.
237.	followed by Ninua, Ninâ Nineve.
238.	also šarru king.
239.	dûru wall.
240.	ṣêru, edinu plain, field; wrongly used for ṣîr against.
241.	šîru flesh, body; determ. bef. parts of the body. Also sign, omen.
242.	followed by Uruk (Arku) Erech.
243.	išdu foundation.
244.	imêru ass (also); also a measure (חֹמֶר ?).— atânu she-ass. purîmu wild ass. sisû horse. parû bullock. gammalu camel. mule? is prefixed as a determinative in gam-mal; uduru dromedary; murnisḳu steed, etc.
245.	arkû later, following; arki prep. behind, after.
246.	karanu wine.

Sign.	Ideographic Values. — Groups of Signs.
247. 	rapâšu be wide, rapšu wide, broad. ummu mother.
248. 	kisallu floor. Cf. also No. 57.
249. 	also with determ.  gušuru beam.
250. 	alpu ox, bull.
251. 	târu return. (Syllabic value gi).
252. 	ezzu fearful. Cf. also No: 60.
253. 	amêlu human being, man. Determ. (also , ) before names of tribes and professions.
254. 	ḳablu midst, encounter, fight.
255. 	parakku most holy place, throne-chamber. (Syllabic value bar).
256. 	bêltu lady, mistress.
257. 	ṣalmu image.
258. 	preceded by  or followed by , Akkadû country of Accad.
259. 	libbu heart, midst. —  (also ) city of Assur. —  great-grandson (also grandson), descendant.
260. 	niḳû drink-offering, offering.
261. 	šêpu foot, also , prep. at the foot of athg., under. —  bones.  šaknanâku governor.
262. 	kabtu heavy, honoured. Cf. also No. 54.
263. 	marṣu ill, bad, difficult. murṣu illness.

Sign.	Ideographic Values. — Groups of Signs.
264. ([cuneiform]	nabû announce. Syllabic value pá).
265. [cuneiform]	tukultu assistance, helper. — [cuneiform] abarakku grand vizier. [cuneiform] concubine.
266. [cuneiform]	damku gracious, favourable; dumku grace.
267. [cuneiform]	Copula u (û) and. (Syllabic value u).
268. [cuneiform]	û ditto; sign of repetition.
269. [cuneiform]	ellu shining, pure. — [cuneiform] hurâṣu gold. [cuneiform] kaspu silver.
270. [cuneiform]	imnu the right. Cf. also No. 60.
271. [cuneiform]	(Syllabic value u). — [cuneiform] ṣênu flock (sheep etc.).
272. [cuneiform], [cuneiform]	šarâpu burn. ḳilûtu burning.
273. [cuneiform]	libittu sun-dried brick. — [cuneiform] agurru burnt brick.
274. [cuneiform]	The cypher 2 (šinâ). Often written after ideograms for parts of the body occurring in pairs, as [cuneiform], [cuneiform]. Sign of repetition, like No. 268.
275. [cuneiform]	šumêlu the left.

Appendices.

1) Cyphers: [cuneiform] 1 ([cuneiform] ištên one); [cuneiform], [cuneiform], [cuneiform], [cuneiform], [cuneiform] (syllabic value aš), [cuneiform], [cuneiform] or [cuneiform], [cuneiform], [cuneiform] 10, [cuneiform] 11, [cuneiform], [cuneiform], [cuneiform], [cuneiform], [cuneiform] 1 šûšu or soss = 60, [cuneiform] 70, [cuneiform] 80 (or [cuneiform]), [cuneiform] 100, [cuneiform] 200, [cuneiform] 1000, [cuneiform] 2000.

2) *Neo-Babylonian forms of a few common signs*: 2. . 7. .
8. . 14. . 15. . 18. . 25. . 29. . 39. . 40. . 43 .
44. . 61. . 78. . 95. . — 103. . 105 . 122. . 131. . 151.
. 158. . 161. . 163. . 165. . 176. . 178. . 179. .
187. or . 196. . 197. . 200. , . — 226. . 227. . 236.
. 238. . 244. . 253. . 259. .

3) *Archaic and Old Babylonian forms of certain signs*: 23. arch. (to be supposed written vertically). 60. arch. , O.B. . 89. arch. , O.B. . 175. arch. . 87. . 206. . 250. . — 53. arch. , O.B. . 227. O.B. .

How the Vowels are written.—In Assyrian the vowel of a syllabic sign may, *per se*, be regarded as long or as short. Even the breaking up of shut syllables like *kar*, *kir*, *kur* into *ka-ar*, *ki-ir*, *ku-ur* does not necessarily imply that the vowel is long. When it is intended to indicate expressly that a vowel is long, this is done, in the case of open syllables in the middle and end of words (*Wortin- und -auslaut*), by adding the sign for the vowel in question (*a*, *i*, *e* or *u*): thus we find either *li-ša-nu* or *li-ša-a-nu* 'tongue', *ni-ru* or *ni-i-ru* 'yoke', *be-lu* or *be-e-lu* 'lord', *nu-nu* or *nu-u-nu* 'fish'; so *la* and *la-a* 'not', *ma-ḫa-za* 'cities' and *še-la-ša-a* 'thirty', *ki-i* 'like, as', *mal-ke* 'princes' and *mu-u'-di-e* 'multitudes'. The verbal endings *î* (2 f. sg.), *û*, *â*, of the present, preterite, permansive and imperative, when standing at the end of a word, and therefore to all appearance unaccented, are never written *plene*: we may write *ik-šu-du-u-ni* but never anything but *ik-šu-du*, *ik-ka-lu*, *šit-ku-nu*. On the other hand the long vowels discussed in § 38 *a*, which are the result of contraction, are but rarely found written defectively at the end of a word, as in *kus-si* for *ku-us-si-e* 'of the throne'; *ḳa-bi* for *ḳa-bi-e* 'speak' (Nimr. Ep. 48, 178). In shut syllables in the middle and end of words, *î*, *ê*, *û* are practically never expressly indicated (*ši-im-tu* 'fate', *i-šim* 'he appointed'; § 10.

be-el-tu 'lady, mistress', *i-be-el* 'he ruled'; *pu-ur-tu* 'wild cow', *i-du-uk* 'he killed'); with *â* alone do we find side by side e. g. *tam-tu* and *ta-a-am-tu* 'sea', *da-an* and *da-a-an* perm. 'he is judge', etc. In both open and shut syllables in the beginning of a word (*Wort-anlaut*), the length of the vowel may be indicated in the same way if the breath (*Hauchlaut*) is expressed: cf. *'a-a-ru* 'go out'=*'âru*, *'u-ú-ru* 'send'=*'ûru* (= *urru*) —cf. also *tu-'a-a-mu*=*tu-â-mu* 'twin'—. This method was, however, seldom employed. In general the indication of the breath was dispensed with at the beginning of a word (*v.* § 20), consequently all indication of the length of the vowel had also to be dispensed with: thus *a-ši-pu* 'conjurer', *i-nu*, *e-nu* 'eye', *ú-ru* 'nakedness'. It is worth noting, in particular, that the prefixing of the simple vowel sign, which takes place not unfrequently with shut syllables in the beginning of a word, does not necessarily imply that the vowel of the initial syllable is long. It is their etymology, not their orthography, that tells us that the vowel of the construct forms *a-ar* (from inf. *âru* st. איר), *a-al* 'city', *i-in* 'eye' is long, = *âr*, *âl*, *în*; for in spite of such orthographical forms as *i-iš-ta-lal* 'he plundered' (VR 55, 43), *a-a i-in-nen-na-a* 'let not be oppressed', *e-en-tu* 'lady', *u-uš-ziz* 'I set up', *u-ul* 'the highest', also 'not', and in spite of the fact that

Nebuchadnezzar and his successors were extremely fond of writing *e-eš-ši-iš* 'anew' (adv.), *e-ek-du* 'strong', *e-ep-ti-iḳ* 'I built', the initial vowel of all these words is short. Also in *ki-a-am* 'thus', *ti-a-am-tu* 'sea', the vowel sign *a* seems to be inserted far more for the purpose of emphasizing the breath or the hiatus, than of indicating the length of the vowel. Strangely enough, *â* is the only long vowel for whose expression there is special provision in the Assyrian system of writing; for details see §§ 13 and 14.

Very frequently a vowel may be recognised as long from the fact of the following consonant being doubled. In spoken language the length of a vowel is often compensated for by such a sharpening of the immediately following consonant (cf. Hebr. Article ·הַ = הָ; ·שֶׁ = *šâ*; צִבִּים plur. of צִבִּיץ); syllabic writing, moreover, was specially adapted to the reproduction of words according to their actual pronunciation. Hence *ru-uḳ-ḳu* 'far' = *rûḳu*, *ur-ru* 'light' = *ûru*, *Ṣi-du-un-nu* = צִידוֹן, *Lu-ud-du* = לוּד, *ḳurbannu* קָרְבָּן, *ba-ba-at-te* 'the gates' = *bâbâti*, *pa-nu-uš-šu* 'his face', *ṭa-ba-aḫ-ḫu* Inf. 'sacrifice' (IV R 68, 33 a), *i-na-ar-ru* 'they subjugate' = *inârû*, *mu-ni-iḫ-ḫa* Shams. III 29 and *mu-ni-ḫa* ibid. IV 23. Instances like *iṣṣanundu* = *iṣṣanûdu* (§ 52) show that we have not to do here with a mere orthographical freak. § 11.

Considerable caution is necessary in dealing with the doubling of a consonant, in so far as such doubling is not demanded by the grammatical form, inasmuch as it may have its *raison d'être* not only in the length of the preceding vowel, but also in the accentuation of the latter (§ 53); or it may be due simply to inaccuracy of the orthography, or to a desire to reproduce more exactly the ordinary pronunciation (§ 22).

§ 12. When the two vowels *i* and *a* come together, which happens most frequently when a genitive sing. takes the pron. suff. of 1. pers. sing. (*i-a*), they are generally expressed by a single sign *ia* (*v.* § 9 No. 38): cf.: *aḫi ta-lim-ia* 'of my full brother' (VR 62 No. 1, 22. 26). When *ia* is joined to an ideogram, the *i* may at the same time do duty as a phonetic complement (§ 23): *zêr-ia* 'of my family' (Beh. 3) = *zêri-a*. If, however, the *i* vowel is already expressed in writing, as, for example, in *bi-ti-ia* 'of my house', then the *i* of *ia* is purely pleonastic; in other words, the sign *ia* represents the simple *a* vowel. Perhaps this method of writing the pronominal suffix of the 1. pers. sing. is the cause of what, at first sight, appears sufficiently striking, namely that the sign *ia* is in many other cases employed to express the vowel *a*, nothwithstanding the fact that—at least in the first of the forms given in § 9, No. 38—it may easily be recognised as made up of *i* + *a*. Thus always after plural forms in *ê*: *ûmê-ia* = *ûmê'a* 'my days'; cf. also *ir-ba-'a-ia*, var. *ir-ba-'-a*, certainly *irba'â* (*erba'â*) 'forty';

rê'-ia 'shepherd' = *rê'-a* (Tig. I 34); *ka-ia-an* (IV R 45, 42), perm. from כון, certainly = *kân*, like *da-a-ri* perm. from דור; *ia-u* and *ia-nu* 'where?' the latter = *ânu*, Hebr. אָן, *ia-um-ma* 'any one' = *â'umma*. See also § 14 and cf. § 41.

An exceptional position in the representation of the long vowels is that of *â* (*v.* end of § 10), inasmuch as for this vowel a special sign, a double *a* (*v.* § 9 No. 6), is usually employed, without, however, superseding the methods discussed in § 10. Examples of initial *â*: †*a-a-u*=*â-u* name of the sign *a*; †*a-a-ši*=*âši* 'for my part', pron.; *a-a-nu* = *ânu* 'where?' (*v.* end of § 12).—Medial and final: †*ta-a-a-ra* (V R 33, 11) 'compassion' (pronounce *târa*) alongside of *ta-a-ru* (V R 21, 54a); †*ta-a-a-ar-tu* 'return' (pron. *târtu*) alongside of *ta-a-ar-tu*, *ta-ia-ar-tu*, all = *târtu* st. cstr. *ta-rat*; †*na-a-a-lu* and *na-a-lu* i. e. *nâlu* name of an animal; †*ka-a-a-nu* 'firm', †*ka-a-a-ma-nu* 'everlasting', †*da-a-a-nu* 'judge' alongside of *ka-ia-nu*, *ka-ia-ma-nu*, *da-ia-nu* (pron. *kânu*, *kâmânu*, *dânu*); †*ṣa-a-a-i-du* 'hunting', also *ṣa-i-du*, both = *ṣâ'idu*, showing that *da-a-a-i-ku* 'killing', fem. *da-a-a-ik-tu* and similar forms are to be read *dâ'iku*, *dâ'iktu*; †*ba-a-a-ar-tum* part. Qal (same form as *râmtu*, IV R 57, 46 a); †*ka-a-a-an* perm. of כון, also *ka-ia-an* (§ 12); †*u-ka-a-a-an* alongside of *u-ka-a-an*, *u-ka-an* all = *ukân* 'he established'; †*ḫa-* § 13.

za-ḳi-a-a-u, 'Hezekiah' (Lay. 61, 11); country of †*Na-ba-a-a-ti*=*Naba'âti* (נְבָיוֹת) and then *Nabâti*; the tribe-name *Ḫa-a-a-ap-pa-a* also *Ḫa-ia-pa-a* = *Ḫa'âpâ* (Hebr. עֵיפָה), *Ḫâpâ*; †*u-ḳâ-a-a* = *uḳâ* 'he waits' (*u-ḳa-a-a-ki* = *uḳâki* 'he waits for thee', *u-ḳa-a-a-u* = *uḳâ'û* 'they wait'); camels *ša*†*šú-na-a-a*, i. e. *šunâ* (*šunnâ*) *ṣe-re-ši-na* 'with double back' (Lay. 98, I. III); the river *U-la-a-a* and *U-la-a* = *Ûlâ* (אוּלָי); goddess *Na-na-a-a* and *Na-na-a* (even *Na-na*) = *Nanâ* (Ναναία); hence it would seem that *Ma-da-a-a* and *Man-na-a-a*, which are the names of two countries and their inhabitants, should —nothwithstanding the Hebr. מָדַי, מִנִּי—be read *Madâ* (*Mâdâ*) and *Mannâ* (= original *Mâdâį*, *Mannâį*?). Further, having regard to such orthographical forms as *Za-za-a*—cf. also *šal-ša-a-(a)* Assurb. Sm. 130, 1— nomina relationis ending originally in *âį*, like *Ṣi-du-un-na-a-a*, *Za-za-a-a*, should be pronounced simply *Ṣîdûnâ*, *Zâzâ*. In the same way, perhaps, the plural forms in *â* with pron. suffix of the 1. pers. sing. e. g.: *še-pa-a-a* 'my feet' simply *šêpâ*; at all events *šêpai* is a monstrosity, and uncontracted forms like *šêpâ'a* are at variance with the elsewhere usual fusion of two contiguous vowels (cf. §§ 38 and 47). Proper names like †*Apla-a-a* 'my son', †*Šu-ma-a-a* 'my name' were certainly pronounced *Aplâ*, *Šumâ*, as is proved by the fact that they are often written *Ap-la-a*, *Šu-ma-a*.

In all the words and forms denoted by †, it seems to me impossible to regard *a-a* as equivalent to *ai*, as is done by so many Assyriologists; it appears to me, further, that even elsewhere there is not a single instance where it is necessary to read *a-a* as *ai* (*v.* especially § 31). Some of the words written with *a-a* far rather suggest *a'a* (*â'a*, *a'â*), though even in these cases contraction to *â* must very soon have taken place.

Since, according to § 12, the sign *ia* has very frequently the syllabic value *a*, we find not only *a-a* but also *a-ia* and *ia-a* (even *a-ia-a*) written for *â*, apparently at hap-hazard. Examples of the *anlaut*: *ia-a-bu* (e. g. Assurn. I 28), even *a-ia-a-bu* (I R 27 No. 2, 68), alongside of *a-a-bu* st. cstr. *a-a-ab* (pronounce *âb* Esarh. II 43), all = *âbu* 'enemy'; *a-ia-ru* and *a-ru*, both = *âru* 'child, offspring'; *a-ia-ši* (Assurn. II 26) and *ia-a-ši* alongside of *a-a-ši*, all = *âši* 'as for me'; *a-ia-um-ma* (Shalm. Bal. V 3), *a-a-um-ma* and *ia-um-ma* all = *â'umma* 'any one'; *ia-a-nu* 'it is, or was, not' = *ânu* perm.; *ia-a-ri*, also *a-ar* = *âru*, *âr*(*i*) 'forest' (יַעַר);—*inlaut*: *ta-ia-a-ru* 'merciful' (I R 35 No. 2, 7) alongside of *ta-a-a-ru* (IV R 66, 42 a), = *târu*; hence *za-ia-a-ru* must = *zâru* (זָר); — *auslaut*: *Ar-ma-a-ia* (Tig. V 47), also *Ar-ma-a-a*, both doubtless to be read simply *Armâ* (*v.* end of § 13). § 14.

The fact that the vowel is included with the consonant in the Assyrian characters is to the advantage of the otherwise complicated Assyro-Babylonian wedge-writing. This advantage is not impaired by § 15.

the fact that about twelve signs admit two different vowels (*a* and *i* Nos. 26 *bis*, 108. 141. 159. 162. 182; *a* and *u* Nos. 102. 143; *u* and *i* Nos. 10. 101. 174. 193; cf. 199), and that four signs may be pronounced with as many as three different vowels (*a*, *i* and *u* Nos. 7. 36. 161. 188), inasmuch as the grammatical form and variants scarcely ever leave us in doubt as to the proper selection. Still the provision made for distinguishing graphically the *e* and *i* vowels is, we must admit, very unsatisfactory. There are, it is true, twelve signs (viz. those for *e*, *be*, *ṭe*, *me*, *ne*, *se*, *še*, *te*; *el*, *en*, *er*, *eš*), which were specially intended to represent the *e* vowel, but in practice the same sign was used indiscriminately for syllables containing *e* and *i*. We advise the beginner to remember that all the syllabic signs given in the table with *i*, such as *ki*, *piš*, may also be pronounced with *e* (*ke*, *peš*), and that some of them, in fact, *must* be so pronounced (*e. g. reš* No. 131). This lack of precision is less felt with long *e*, since the sign specially coined for *e* is pretty frequently added (*v.* § 10): the manifold variations *bi-lu*, *bi-e-lu*, *be-e-lu* 'lord', or orthographical forms like *ri-e-šu* 'head', *ri-e-mu* 'grace', *ṣi-e-nu* flock (sheep and goats), point assuredly to *bêlu*, *rêšu*, *rêmu*, *ṣênu*. It is quite otherwise, we regret to say, with short *e*, inasmuch as the forms with this vowel, which almost always arises by modification from an original *a*, completely coincide in their graphic representation with those forms, of which *i* is the characteristic vowel. For this reason it is extremely difficult, or even impossible, to pronounce with certainty regarding a number of complex problems presented by Assyrian morphology, especially as regards the formation of the noun. For the transliteration of Assyrian we may lay it down as a rule, that the above twelve *e* signs should in all cases be transcribed with *e*, the corresponding twelve *i* signs (*i*, *bi*, *ṭi* and so on), on the other hand, with *i*; with the other signs, e. g. *li*, *ir*, we may make the choice of the vowel (*e* or *i*) depend on the form of the word in each individual instance.

For the reason of this misplaced parsimony as regards the indication of the vowel *e*, see the appendix to the orthography (§ 25), which we have devoted to the Sumerian problem.

Of the two signs for *u* (§ 9 Nos. 4 and 5) the first § 16.
is practically never used for the copula *u* (*û*), while the second practically never serves as a syllabic sign in the beginning of a word (an exception is found in Esarh. VI 24). The third sign for *u* (*ù* No. 267) was originally ideographic. — The accents (mostly acute) over the vowels of certain signs, *ú*, *tú* etc. are not meant to indicate the position of the tone or the quantity of the respective vowels; they merely serve,

in the transcription of Assyrian words, to distinguish a sign for a simple syllable from another and more frequently occurring sign for the same syllable. Besides *u*, cf. *bu*, *pu* Nos. 11. 70; *da* 21. 152; *da* 24. 103; *la* 42. 205; *ma* 49. 222; *pa* 68. 264; *ar* 79. 14; *ur* 82. 83; *ša* 84. 85; *šu* 88. 89; *aš* 90. 91; *tu* 98. 26. In the case of certain so-called composite syllables, represented by two or even three different signs, a similar distinction would be of use only if universally adopted; it is better, meanwhile, to help ourselves by the addition of another value of the sign in question, or by some other device.

§ 17. In general it is a law that every consonant with its accompanying vowel shall form a single syllabic sign. Thus we find *a-šib*, 'dwelling', fem. *a-ši-bat* or *a-ši-ba-at*, but not *a-šib-at*. There are, however, a large number of exceptions to this rule; e. g. *i-ša-ka-an-u-šu* 'they make it', *u-šat-lim-u-ni* 'they gave up', *iṣ-bat-u-nim-ma* 'they siezed and', *ad-iš* 'I trod down', (= *adiš*), *ir-a-mu* 'they love' (= *irâmû*), *Tab-a-la* 'country of Tabal', *ḳur-us-su* 'his bravery'; *âšibat* itself is written *a-šib-at* in II R 66 No. 1, 9. An important exception, further, is the verbal suffix of the 1. pers. sing.: we find, it is true, *ub-bi-ra-an-ni* 'he banished me', but in most cases the orthography is *šûzib-an-ni* 'deliver me', *ûlid-an-ni* 'she bare me'.

How the Consonants are written. — We are still uncertain as to the reason why each of the pairs *da* and *ṭa*, *di* and *ṭi*, *za* and *ṣa* should be represented by only a single sign; also as to why *bu* should be systematically used for *pu*, when a special sign for the latter already existed. Otherwise the parsimony manifested in the elaboration of the signs, especially the orthographical assimilation of syllables distinguished from each other only by the varying degrees of hardness possessed by their initial and final consonants, must be signalised as an altogether wise, and, in fact, necessary step on the part of the inventors of the written characters. On the contrary we can only regard as an unnecessary luxury — however agreeable they may be to us — the creation and preservation of double signs for *ar* and separate signs for each member of such pairs as *bat* and *pat*, *gam* and *kam*, *gur* and *kur*, and so on. Although this orthographical fusion, so to speak, of the syllables *ag*, *ak*, *aḳ*; *mad*, *mat*, *maṭ*; *ḳib*, *ḳip*, *gib*, *gip* may have for us temporary inconveniences, yet there is never any permanent uncertainty, inasmuch as our doubts are removed either by the immediately following sign, or by other forms of the same stem (e. g. *ab*(*ap*)-*ti*, but *pi-tu-u*; *ad*(*aṭ*, *at*)-*bu-uk*, but *tu-bu-uk*). Still less were the Assyrians ever in any doubt or difficulty on that § 18.

account. The beginner should note that the syllabic values given in table B, so far as regards labials, gutturals, and dentals, are not the only possible values. — As regards the sibilants, we find that a clear distinction was made between *š* on the one hand, and *z ṣ s* on the other, in the *auslaut* of simple syllables, but not in that of compound syllables. In the *anlaut* of compound syllables we have, in most cases, two distinct sets of signs, one when the first letter is *z* or *ṣ*, another when it is *s* or *š*: cf. *zab, ṣab* (No. 182); *zag* (166); *zal, ṣal* (57); *zar, ṣar* (207); *zib, ṣib* (183); *zig* (145); *ziz* (10); *zil, ṣil* (119); *zum* (72); *zun* (186); *zur, ṣur* (195); but *sab, šab* (155); *sag, šag* (131); *sal, šal* (212); *sar, šar* (141); *sib* (156); *sig, šik* (219); *sis, šiš* (165); *sil, šil* (105); *sum, šum* (135); *sun, šun* (192); *sur, šur* (124). Exceptions are: *zin, sin* (93); *zuk, suk* (209) on the one hand, and *šin* (101), *šuk* (202) on the other. Add to these the series of syllables *zir, sir* etc. with six signs in all: *zir* (113), *ṣir* (178), *sir* (177 and 11), *šir* (112 and 141); finally *saḫ* (159) and *šaḫ* (108). For the signs containing *m* note § 44 of the phonology.

§ 19. The fact that *ḳi, ḳu* are frequently written *ki, ku* (*e. g. ki-ni,* 'nests' alongside of *ḳi-in-ni, iš-ku-lu* 'they numbered' and, without exception, *kirbu* 'interior') is doubtless owing to the circumstance already referred to in § 11, that the syllabic, as opposed to the consonantal, method of writing readily tempted a scribe to adapt his orthography more to the every-day pronunciation of the consonants or words in question. Nevertheless the orthography required by the history and etymology of the words continued in regular use. The employment of *ka* for *ḳa* is far more rare: *ḳa-lu-u, ḳa-mu-u, ḳa-ra-bu* is much more frequently written than, say, *ša-ka-šu* (שקש). On the other hand, the frequent rendering of *ḳa* by *ga* is certainly due to a peculiarity of the Babylonian pronunciation, and accordingly falls to be treated of under phonology (*v.* § 43); for analogous phenomena in Assyrian see the same section. In cases like *e-bi-e-šu* 'make', written instead and alongside of *e-pi-e-šu* (and that in texts where the special sign for *pú* is employed by preference), *bi* 'mouth' (Neb. Grot. III 46), and *vice versâ ru-ku-pi* 'carriage, vehicle' for and alongside of *ru-ku-bi, ip-pa-áš-ši* 'it is' (st. בשה) and others, as also in cases like *zu-ba-tu* 'dress', *a-zu-u* 'going up', *zi-i-ru* 'exalted', *er-zi-tu* 'earth' written for and alongside of *ṣubâtu, âṣû, ṣîru, erṣitu*, we may be uncertain as to whether it was the orthography or the pronunciation of the respective scribes — this at least, in the first place — that was inexact, careless and bad; but forms like *tu-um-ku* for *dumḳu, tu-ub* for *ṭu-ub*, *aḫ-tu-u* for *aḫ-ṭu-u* (חטא) are simply to be regarded as orthographical mistakes, of which, in any case, there are many and varied specimens in the Assyro-Babylonian cuneiform texts.

§ 20. The spiritus lenis or א in the beginning, middle, or end of a word may be expressed by a special sign (*v.* § 9 No. 7). In the beginning (*anlaut*), however, orthographical forms like *'a-a-ru* 'go out', *'-ab-tu* 'he perished', *'i-il-tu* 'curse' are extremely rare (see above, § 10); the usual way was to write *a-ḫu* 'brother', *i-nu* 'eye', *e-mu* 'father-in-law', *u-nu* 'utensil', *ab-du* 'servant', *ir-tu* 'breast', etc. In the *inlaut* we find *ša-'a-al* (i. e. *ša'âl*) 'request, ask', *la-'a-bu* 'flame', *ri-'a-a-šu* 'creeping thing', *Ha-za-'i-ilu* חֲזָאֵל, *Sir-'i-la-a-a* יִשְׂרְאֵלִי, *ú-ma-'i-ir* 'he, I sent', *na-'i-id* 'he is exalted', *re-'u-u* 'shepherd', *mu-'u-ur* 'present', *ir-'u-ub* 'he, she was enraged', but also without the breath: *iš-al* 'he asked', *im-id* 'he increased', *ra-i-mu* 'loving'. For the *auslaut* cf. *i-ba-a'* 'he comes' (בוא), *uš-bi-i'* (from same stem); see also § 47.

Orthographical forms like *u-ma-'a-ru*, *u-ma-a-ru* on the one hand, *u-ma-'-a-ru* on the other (Prs. II 1 from מאר) equally with *iš-'-a-lu*, *li-šam-'-i-da*, *bu-'-u-ru* 'catch', *'-a-bit* 'he was destroyed' and many others point to the fact that the sign for the breath was employed for the latter *per se*, without an accompanying vowel; for if we were to transliterate thus: e. g. *u-ma-'a-a-ru*, we should then have to read *uma'âru*, which would be false, and if we were to write *u-ma-a'-a-ru*, we should have an exception to the rule in

§ 17. The breath also serves to indicate a mere hiatus, e. g. *ḫa-'-iṭ* alongside of *ḫa-a-iṭ* (part. from חרט). The sign of the breath seems to represent the vowel *a* in *ia-'-nu* 'where?' (V R 40), *ia-'-nu* 'it was not' (cf. §§ 12—14). — Numerous examples of a breath at the end of words are found in the Achæmenian inscriptions, but the origin and purpose of this orthography is as yet obscure: e. g. *it-tal-ku-'* 'they went'.

Of the two signs for *šu* (Nos. 88 and 89), the former, apart from the pronouns *šu-u* and *šu-a-tu*, is practically never used in the beginning of a word; thus we find e. g. *šu-zu-ub* 'save' only Shalm. Ob. 166, elsewhere always *šú-zu-ub*. § 21.

The doubling or the sharpening of a consonant is expressed by writing the consonant twice: *addin* 'I gave', *uparrir* 'I broke in pieces'. Often enough, however, this rule was not observed—another consequence of the desire to reproduce with greater exactness the popular, but less accurate, pronunciation: *madattu* 'tribute', *a-din*, *li-du-ú* 'let them throw', *li-mir* 'let shine', *u-lil* 'I purified, cleansed' (Shalm. Ob. 28), *i-ḳal-la-pu* Nif. 'it is peeled' (IV R 7, 51 a), and many others. In revenge, simple consonants are often found written twice: *ad-du-ku* 'I had killed' (I R 7 No. IX, A, 2), *ez-zi-bu* 'they forsook' = *êzibû*, *u-šat-bu-niš-šum-ma* = *ušatbûnišú'ma*, etc; here belong also *abbûti* 'fatherhood', *aḫḫu* 'brother' (in addition to the usual *abû*, *aḫu*). § 22.

§ 23. Reading-signs. — In connected texts the Assyrian writing has no means of separating either words or sentences; but instead, the rule is strictly observed of ending every line with a complete word. Examples of a word being divided at the end of a line are extremely rare. When it is intended, in vocabularies or elsewhere, to indicate expressly that two words or sentences are not connected with each other, the sign ⩓ is put between them. — A great help to the reading and understanding of Assyrian texts consists of the so-called determinatives, i. e. written signs which, remaining themselves unpronounced, indicate to what category the word they accompany belongs. Most of these determinatives are prefixed to their words, and this prefixed determinative is, properly speaking, never wanting before the names of deities (No. 60), of persons, male and female (204. 212), of countries and mountains (176), of towns and rivers (81. 1) and before the names of tribes (253). Exceptions occur only with names of male persons written more or less ideographically. Much less frequent is the determinative before the names of trees, woods and utensils (31), as also before the names of stones (148) and occupations (253), when the latter are written phonetically, e. g. like *ni-ru* 'yoke', *ṣu-um-bu* 'cart' — and the words with determinatives are, for the present, understood to be everywhere so written. The same remark holds good of determinatives with the names of birds (35) and fishes (33), which take their determinatives after them. Assyro-Babylonian names of towns and districts — whether written ideographically or phonetically — are determined by a postfixed *ki* (40), not excluding, at the same time, a prefixed *mâtu* (176) or *âlu* (81). All the determinatives just given (with the exception of 176 and 81), with the addition of a few others, as, e. g., those before the names of garments (41) and vessels for holding liquids (158), when they constitute the first or last member of words written purely ideographically, render the same service as before phonetically written words. In this case, however, they are rarely mere determinatives to assist the eye, so that they might in certain cases be dispensed with (as e. g. *iṣu* 'wood' before the ideogr. for *ellipu* 'ship' *v.* under No. 31), but are in most cases necessary elements in the written representation of the idea conveyed by the words in question; we might also say that they are simply the ideographic equivalents of the first member of a compound Assyrian name, as, e. g. *aban išâti* 'fire-stone', *karpat šikari* 'wine-pot', and many others. — A valuable help in reading ideographically written words is found in the so-called phonetic complements. These consist usually of one, rarely of two syllabic signs, which, by giving us the final syllable of the word, enable us to obtain the correct reading of the ideogram, both as regards the choice of the proper equivalent and its grammatical form. The ideogram for *erêbu* 'enter' (98), or, as it is usually transcribed, TU with phon. compl. *ub* is *êrub* (*êru-ub*) 'I entered'; TU-*ab*=*etárab*. ŠA(84)-*un* is = *iškun* or *aškun*, ŠA-*an*=*aštakan*. If ideograms like *šarru* 'king' are followed by *tu*, *ti*, or *ta*, or by *ú-tu*, *ú-ti*, or *ú-ta*, this points to the abstract noun *šarrûtu* (or *-ti*, *-ta*): *ni* after an ideogram provided with the sign of the plural (210) indicates the plural form in *âni*: AN^{pl}-*ni* = *ilâ-ni*, ER^{pl}-*ni* = *âlâ-ni*. There is no law compelling the use of a phon. complement; there are, however, certain words that are written with a phon. compl. in the great majority of the cases where they occur, so especially AN-*e* i. e. *šamê* 'heaven', and KI-*tim* i. e. *erṣitim* 'of the earth'; cf. also the ideogram for the 'Euphrates', No. 1 in the table of characters. These complements are specially useful when an ideogram may be read in two different ways. Take, for example, the ideograms KUR (176) and UD (26): KUR-*ú*, KUR-*a*, KUR^{pl}-*ni*, KUR^{pl}-*e* must be read, *šadû* (*šadu-ú*), *šadâ* (*šada-a*), *šadâni*, *šadê* but KUR-*ti*, KUR^{pl}-*ti* *mâti*, *mâtâti*; UD-*mu*, UD-*mi* = *ûmu*, *ûmi*, but ^{ilu}UD-*ši*=*Šamši*.

Forms which look as if a phon. compl. had been added to a syllabic sign, as *ak-šud-ud* = *akšud* 'I captured', (Senhb. I 36 and oft.), *ša-nin-in* = *šânin* (Assurn. Balaw. 6), *ke-niš-eš* = *kênêš* 'faithfully' (ibid. 39), must be regarded as little other than freaks of the scribe. Another sort of freak is to write *mu-šak-li-lil* (V R 65, 4 a), *ab-lu-lul* (V R 10, 83), *li-ir-mu-muk* (III R 43 col. IV 18) = *mušaklil*, *ablul*, *lirmuk*; still another *tab-rat-a-ti* (V R 65, 9 b), and such like.

Practical Hints. The reading of the 55 selected signs — each, as a rule, with only one ideographic value — given under C in § 9 presents no difficulty. § 24. Of the 98 signs for simple syllables (A) there are 70 which stand for one syllable only, and of these 70, there are 30 which are not once used as ideograms; of the 120 signs for compound syllables (B), there are more than 70 which represent one syllable only, and of these, there are about 39 which are not once used as ideograms. In other words: out of a total of 278 written characters or signs, there are about 125 (55+30+40) as to whose reading there is never any doubt. — In the case of signs with several syllabic values, the beginner should be guided by the immediately preceding or immediately following sign, choosing that value which begins with the same vowel or consonant with which the preceding sign ends, and *vice versa:* thus he should read *al*-160 not, let us say, as *al-miš*, or *al-šit* but *al-lak*; in the same way *al*-82 is not *al-ur* but *al-lik*; *ma*-14 not *ma-ub*, but *ma-dr*; *ú*-174-188 not *ú-lib-ḫar* or *ú-paḫ-mur*, but *ú-paḫ-ḫar*. He should also avoid all phonetic combinations and word-forms which his acquaintance with Hebrew tells him to be impossible in Semitic. The most valuable assistance, however, in arriving at the proper value of signs with numerous syllabic values, is rendered by the thousandfold variations in the Assyrian texts themselves (here sign 160, there *la-ak*; here 162, there *ka-al* or *ri-ib* and so on), and by knowing as many as possible of the different forms of one and the same stem (e. g. *il-li-ku, al-lik*, *il-lak*). Familiarity with both of these aids can, of course, only be acquired by continued and extended reading of the cuneiform, especially of historical texts. — The much rarer difficulty, as to whether a sign is to be read as a syllable or as an ideogram, may, in many cases, be overcome by the beginner, if he will first inform himself from the table of characters, whether a sign, that does not appear to him to be syllabic, may not be joined to the immediately following sign or signs to form a single ideographic sign-group. — As aids to the beginner in the proper division of the words, the following hints may prove useful: let him single out the prepositions *a-na* and *i-na*, and set down the simple horizontal wedge always as the prep. *ina*; he should always look out for the determinatives mentioned in § 23; he should especially make a search for the verbal, or more precisely the preterite, forms of the 3. and 1. persons, which are easily distinguished by their vocalic *anlaut* (*i*, *a*, *e*, *ú*; *il*, *al*; *ib*, *ab* etc.) from the other words of the sentence; the sign *miš* (210) must always be taken as the sign of the plural — the word *a-ḫa-miš* excepted — and consequently the sign immediately preceding should always be read as an ideogram.

It is self-evident that all these hints are given with the utmost reserve, and without any guarantee that they will hold good on all occasions.

Who invented the cuneiform writing? The important question, whether the Assyro-Babylonian wedge-writing (which was the parent of the Susian, Armenian and Old Persian wedge-writing) is an invention of the Semitic Babylonians, or of a non-Semitic race settled alongside of the latter in Babylonia, that is, of the so-called Sumerians or Accadians or Sumero-Accadians, will probably be answered more and more in favour of its invention by a Semitic race. If such is the case, then Joseph Halévy and his school will have to be acknowledged as the victors in the scientific warfare which they have been carrying on for many years with Jules Oppert and his followers. The Semitic origin of the following syllabic values is admitted by all: *u* (5) and *ù* (267), *id* (25), *iṣ* (31), *el* (47), *er* (81), *ša* (84); — *mit*, also *mut* (10), *kin* (23), *ḫaṭ* (68), *in*(*i*) (86), *ḳat* (89), *zir* (113), *sim* (116), *raṭ* (118), *šaḳ* and *riš* (131), *rap* (140), *ram* (147), *riḳ*, *šim* (149), *dan* (162), *bit* (163), *mat*, *šad* (176), *kar* (180), *ṣab* (182), § 25.

lit, *rim* (190), *kiš* (191), *kim* (197), *tul* (199), *lib* (259) To the same category, moreover, belong the following values for simple syllables, which the Assyrians themselves testify to have been derived from Semitic: *az*, *as*, *aṣ* (30) from *a-su* (S[b] 2, 12), *us* (32) from *usû* (S[b] 2, 4), *la* (42) from *lalû* 'plenty' (S[b] 2, 10; same root as *lulû*), *al* (45) from *allu* (S[b] 226), *ul* (48) from *ullu* 'rejoicing' (S[b] 98; from root *alâlu*), *um* (55) from *ummu* 'womb, mother' (S[b] 118): nothing in the world justifies us in calling such words as *usû* or *allu* "loan-words". In addition to these, the following assuredly will yet be proved to be good Semitic Babylonian: *α*) of simple syllabic values, *ub*, *up* (14), with the meanings as ideograms of 'side, quarter of the heavens', from *uppu* 'side, enclosure' (cf. S[b] 257); *ig*, *ik*, *iḳ* from *iḳḳu* 'door' (II R 23, 62*e*); *ud* (26 from *uddû* 'bright, clear'); *mu* (52) meaning as ideogram 'name', and *me* (51) as ideogr. 'speak, name' from *mû* 'name'; *an* (60) as ideogr. 'heaven, god', from *anu* 'heaven, god of heaven, god in general'; *en* (62) as ideogr. 'lord' from *enu* 'lord' (cf. *entu* 'lady, mistress, *enûtu* 'lordship'); *še* (87) from *šê'u* 'corn'; *β*) of compound syllabic values, *šam* (4) from *šammu* 'plant'; *šar* (34) from *šâru* 'superabundance'; *šip* (51) from *šiptu* 'conspiracy' (אשׁפה); *tal* (77) from *talâlu* 'throw' (cf. IV R 30, 24a); *šun* and *ruḳ* (101) v. p. 16; *bal*, *pal* (102) from *pulû*; *nak* (106) from *nakû* 'pour out, give to drink' (the phonetic value *šaḳ* had been already taken from *šakû* 'be high'); *šaḫ* (108) from *šaḫû*; *bar* (114) as ideogr. meaning 'decide' from *barû* 'decide'; *nun* (119) cf. Dict. p. 116; *dim*, *tim* (122) from *timmu* 'rope'; *tap* (133) from *tappû* 'companion', a Semitic word as is shown by the bye-form *tappîu*; *dup*, *tup* (137) from *tuppu*; *šer* (141) as ideogr. 'vegetation' from *šêr'u* with the same meaning; *gaz*, *ḳaṣ* (146) from *ḳaṣâṣu* 'cut off, tear, crush to pieces'; *kit* (159) from *êktu* 'end'; *rit* (160) from *rêtu* 'superintendence' (stem ר־א$_4$־ח); *bur* (172) meaning, as ideogr., a 'hollow vessel' from *bûru* (st. ב־א$_1$־ר); *nar* (174) from *nâru* (נֵּבֵר); *ṣir* (178) as ideogr. 'serpent' from *ṣir'u*, same meaning (st. צ־ר־א$_4$); *tir* (179) as ideogr. 'forest' from *tirru*, same meaning (II R 23, 56*e*); *ḫuš* and *ruš* (185) from *huššû*, *ruššû*; *zun* (*ṣun* 186) from *zunnu* 'throng, abundance'; *ḫar*, *ḫir*, *hur* (188) from st. *ḫarâru* 'gird closely round', whence *ḫarru, ḫartu* 'ring', *ḫarrânu* 'narrow way', and others; *kil* (206) as ideogr. 'enclosure, cattle-pen' and such like, from *kalû* 'shut in' whence e. g. *bît ki-li* 'prison'; *suk, zuk* (209) from *sukku* 'defence', also 'hut, tent'; *lal* (205) as ideogr. 'be full' from *lalû* 'fulness'. It belongs to the dictionary to show more fully the grounds for the Semitic origin of these syllabic values and of many more, such as *uḳ* (20), *im* (54), *nu* (59); *bat* (10), *ḳub* (23), *laḫ* (26), *tib* (44), *ḳum* (58), *pû* (70), *mil* (92), *ḫal* (99), *gir* (103), *ḫaṣ* (105), *maḫ* (109), *maš* (114), *dir* (132), *kan* (138), *tur* (139), *gal* (169), *šud* (177), *bir* and *laḫ* (182), *muḫ* (189), *šul* and *dun* (201), *ḫab* (206), *sal* (212), *niḳ* (215), *siḳ* (219) as ideogr. 'hem in, oppress; hemmed in, pressed down, weak, small etc.' (cf. סיק 'hem in, oppress'; *sîḳu* 'hemmed in, oppressed weak' S^c 6). It is not, however, the number of examples that is the main point — even three such syllabic signs as *an, mu, šag* (*šak, šaḳ*) with the meanings as ideograms of 'heaven', 'name', 'head' suffice to determine one's position for or against the Semitic origin of the Assyro-Babylonian wedge-writing. Whoever is of opinion that the Assyr. *anu* 'heaven', *Anu* 'god of heaven, god in general' (fem. *An-tu*, abstr. noun *Anûtu* 'deity') is a thoroughly Semitic word,*) that on account of its ע in Hebr. עֻנַּת מַלְכֵּךְ, it must even be regarded as common to all the Semitic tongues and not an exclusively Babylonian word; whoever, again, is convinced that *mu* (*mû*) 'name' can be only a Semitic word,— if for no other reason than because of its interchanging with *me* (*mê*) and *ma* (*mâ*) — and, without prejudice, looks fair in the face the fact that in genuine Assyro-Semitic texts *mû*, Gen. *mê* really appears as synon. of *šumu* (*v.* my Dict. p. 140 and cf. p. 275); whoever, finally, cannot bring himself to regard the Assyr. stem *šaḳû* 'be high' (*šuḳḳû, šušḳû* 'raise') as borrowed from the Sumer. *sag* 'head', or to consider as purely fortuitous the phonic coin-

*) Cf. the stem ענה 'be opposite', whence also the prep. *ana*, related to عَنْ; the sky or heaven was so named as being that opposite the upward glancing eye; cf. de Lagarde's combination of אֵל with the stem אלה, whence the prep. אֶל with the same meanings as Assyr. *ana*.

cidence of Assyr. *šaḳû*, 'person of rank, officer' (syn. *rêšu*) and the above *sag*, *šag* 'head, pinnacle, chief', such an one must admit the Semitic origin of the Assyro-Babylonian wedge-writing from beginning to end, for he requires these phonetic values at every step when reading the so-called Sumerian texts. All other proofs for the Semitic origin of the Babylonian cuneiform have only a secondary value, in so far, at least, as it is always possible to weaken their force by all sorts of sophistical arguments. One fact, however, deserves to be emphasized, namely that the phonetic system graphically represented by the Babylonian writing is practically identical with that of the Semitic Babylonian tongue. Thus the writing indicates the spiritus lenis (א) after the characteristically Semitic manner, and is without ע only because Semitic Babylonian does not possess this sound. It has, moreover, *ḫ*, and special signs for *ḳu*, *ḳi*, *ḳu*, *ṣi*, *ṣu*, *ṭu*. And were we to take offence at the fusion of *ṣa* with *za*, of *ṭa* with *da*, and of *ṭi* with *di*, and, starting from these, to declare the other signs just given (*ḳa*, *ḳi* etc.) as only a later Semitic adaptation of signs with, originally, quite other phonetic values, then the question involuntarily presents itself, why the Semites did not carry out the same adaptation for *ṣa*, *ṭa*, and *ṭi*; three signs more or less would have been of no consequence. On the other hand we regard the follg. facts as almost incontrovertible arguments against the so-called "Sumerian" origin of the Babyl. wedge-writing: first, the language of the supposed Sumerian inventors, like that of the Babylonian Semites, has no *h*, no *y*, and no *v* (*w* or *u̯*); secondly, in complete accord with the language of the Babyl. Semites, it is ignorant of the diphthongs *ai* and *au*, as well as of the vowel *o*; and finally, the Sumerian inventors confused the vowel *e* with *i* in pronunciation (hence the extremely defective distinction between these two vowels in the written character) in precisely the same way as the Semitic Babylonians are proved to have done.

With the acceptance of a Semitic, therefore of a non-Sumerian, origin of the Babylonian wedge-writing, a fatal blow is dealt to the existence of a Sumerian tongue and Sumerian texts.

For not only is it the case that with the syllabic values above set aside as Semitic there disappear very many of the words supposed to be most genuinely Sumerian, without which it is impossible to read a single so-called Sumerian text, but it is also true that the apparent development in the meaning of such Sumerian words as *an*, *ana* — whose supposed original signification 'be high' is certainly due to the fundamental idea implied in *šamû*, the synonym of *anu* — bears the unmistakeable stamp of artificial manufacture, and that by Semitic hands. The same is true, in a still higher degree, of the delightfully heterogeneous mass of meanings so often united in many 'Sumerian' words: cf. *bal* 'axe' and 'spindle' (*pilakku* and *pilakku*), *bar* 'wicked, jackal, side', even 'brother' (owing to *aḫu* and *aḫû* uniting these meanings in Assyrian), *mu* 'name' and 'man' (*zikru* and *zikaru*) *šun* 'wash' and 'quarrel, fight' (*šunnu* and *šanânu*) *u* 'and' and 'or' (*û* copula, and *û*=*au* אוֹ 'or') and hundreds of others. The fact just noted has, for a considerable period, awakened suspicion in regard to 'Sumerian'. In fact, no other alternative will be left us but to bid farewell for ever to those words in their character of 'Sumerian', and to acknowledge them as the conventional readings, based on Semitic words, of certain ideograms*), — no matter whether the latter serve to express a single word, or a whole bushelful of

*) To establish with increasing accuracy the connexion between ideograms and their conventional renderings or—what often comes to the same thing—their syllabic values, must be one of the principal lines of future investigation. We would, however, even here emphasize the fact that the conventional readings or syllabic values need not necessarily be taken from the proper signification, so to say, of the ideogram—from the object, let us suppose, represented by the original picture. The picture of a star, for example, does not signify a star, but is a symbol for heaven, whence it derives its syllabic value *an* (60); the picture of the leg does not signify the leg, but symbolizes the idea of walking, going bare-foot and hence may have the syllabic value *du* (23). In the same way the picture of a reed might serve to give symbolical expression to the idea of bending, turning; a picture of a fish might denote excess, crowd, enormous numbers of anything, and hence they might receive respectively the syllabic values *ge* and *ḫa*.

Babylono-Semitic words, connected with each other by sense or sound (*e. g. erû* 'chest' and 'bronze', *libittu* 'brick' and *lipittu* 'enclosure'). The extraordinary number of significations belonging to many signs and their conventional pronunciation must not be overlooked. Thus for the sign *u* with the reading *buru*, VR 36, 37 gives no fewer than 52 Assyrian equivalents; for the sign *te* VR 40 gives more than 18; for the sign *a*, VR 22 gives more than 10, among which we find *mû* 'water', *banû* 'beget', *ruṭbu* 'wet', *lubšu* 'garment', *anâku* 'I' and *atta* 'thou'. These facts alone are sufficient proof of the impossibility of recognising in *buru*, *te*, *a* words of human speech. Equally convincing is the argument from the fact that these supposed 'Sumerian words' are entirely innocent of any distinction between the noun and the verb, as well as between the transitive, intransitive and causative meanings of the latter: the 'Sumerian word' *bur* signifies *šapâlu*, *suppulu*, *šuplu* and *šupalû* 'be deep or low'; 'deepen or lower'; 'deepening, a hollow'; 'deep, low'. The truth will be that the sign *u*, with its conventional reading *bur*, taken from the Assyrian *bûru* 'hole' (Hebr. בְּאֵר), served as graphic symbol for the idea 'to be deep' in all its concrete embodiments. Such multiplicity of meaning attaching to the individual ideograms, and the extreme uncertainty and obscurity of long ideographically written texts occasioned thereby, were bound to lead to this, that texts written entirely with ideograms were accompanied by a phonetic reproduction of the pronunciation as handed down by oral tradition. In productions of the higher, poetical style, above all, where great importance attaches to the finer shades of meaning, it was simply indispensable that the pronunciation of the original should be added in some such clearly intelligible fashion. It is becoming increasingly evident that the so-called bilingual texts are simply Semitic texts with a twofold orthography: the one form being the ancient and sacred ideographic writing of the priests, which, however skilfully conceived and cleverly elaborated, remained enigmatical to the last; the other, the ordinary syllabic writing. We are led to the same conclusion, with almost greater certainty by a consideration of the groups of ideograms. It is manifest that combinations of signs like SIG. DUB. SIG. DUB. BA. *i. e.* clothes-rending-clothes-rending' or LU. SAG. BI. DUL. LA. *i. e.* 'man-head-be-cover' cannot possibly be 'Sumerian words' for 'bitter mourning' (*ublu malû*), 'mourning of a man' (*amêlu adir*), but are purely ideographic and ingenious representations of the idea of mourning. Were these and the hundreds of ideogram-groups contained in the so-called vocabularies and bilingual texts real compound words, Sumerian must have been a tongue which was practically unable to express ideas and objects by a single word. Supposing, however, that we were to have recourse to the daring assertion that these groups of ideograms are the equivalents of single Sumerian words with which we are still unacquainted simply because the necessary glossaries are wanting, we should, when we came to draw the consequences, land ourselves in a veritable quagmire of impossibilities. These groups of ideograms can be nothing more than groups of ideograms, more precisely ideographic equivalents of Semitic words, conceived by Semites and the offspring of the Semitic mind. The symbolical reproduction of mourning by 'covering of the head', and of bitter mourning by 'complete rending of one's raiment' bears on the face of it its Semitic origin, and so it is with the groups of ideograms, one and all, — they are graphic equivalents of Semitic words, sometimes ingenious, sometimes clumsy, not unfrequently punning, but also, at times, with no meaning at all. The vocabularies—the subscriptions to which, by the way, do not breathe a whisper of any other tongue alongside of the Assyro-Babylonian—like the so-called bilingual texts serve the purposes not of comparative philology but of comparative orthography and comparative editing (*nicht vergleichend-linguistische, sondern vergleichend-graphische, vergleichend-redactionelle Zwecke*).

The glosses, which in the vocabularies here and there accompany simple ideograms and groups of ideograms, and lists of which are found in syllabaries of the species S^b, are still in need of more thorough investigation as regards the manifold ends they serve; we know, however, that they contain, for the most part, the conventional readings of the above-mentioned signs and sign-groups, readings which are either identical with the Assyrian equivalent of the signs referred to, as given in the column to the right, or borrowed from one of its synonyms. Certain of these glosses are still obscure; others, as *pisan* 'reservoir', in particular, 'water-reservoir', are being proved, with ever increasing certainty, to be genuinely Semitic words. Moreover when the ideogram for *ṣûmu* 'thirst', made up of 'mouth' and 'day, sun etc.', is accompanied in VR 31 by the gloss *im-ma*, we may have been justified formerly in regarding it as a 'Sumerian' word, but now, when we read in Babylonian Semitic texts the words *emmu* 'hot', *immu* 'heat', and at once recognize them as derivatives of the Semitic stem חמם, it is clear that the gloss owes its existence to a synonym of *ṣûmu*, the genuine Semitic *immu*. In the same way, as our acquaintance with the lexicon of Assyrian increases in extent and depth, the result will be the clearing up of all the other glosses that as yet remain obscure. Thus even the characteristic 'Sumerian' word *dingir* 'god' has been shown to be good Assyro-Semitic by the equation *di-gi-ru-u* = *ḫi-li-bu-u* = *ilu*, quite recently found in a vocabulary by Bezold!

That the so-called Sumerian connected texts of volumes II, IV and V, the exorcisms, hymns etc. have, one and all, passed through Semitic hands, and from beginning to end present traces of Semitic influence, revision, transposition or whatever one may choose to call it, is an admission which has likewise been gaining ground for a considerable period and may at all events be put down as a support of the anti-Sumerian view. In fact, to admit the existence of a 'monkish' or 'dog Sumerian' swarming with compounds, phrases, arrangements of words etc., even transitions of meaning*) either common to all the Semitic dialects or

*) The cases in which whole Semitic words with their terminations have passed over into 'Sumerian', as, *e. g. za-ba-lam-a-ni* 'their offering', and the still more repulsive cases in which the Semite, when writing 'Sumerian', mixed up two Semitic words with totally different meanings, *ašris* 'humble' (ישר) and *ašriš* 'in its place', are intentionally disregarded above. For here there

peculiar to the Semitic of Babylonia, be these the medium of the speech, poetry and writing of Semites or of Sumerians or of both, to admit this is, at bottom, the beginning of Anti-Sumerianism. For, not to speak of other impossibilities, this admission, on the usual hypothesis of the contemporaneous existence of the two peoples and tongues, leads to consequences that are absolutely alarming, for they mean that the Sumerian 'language' must simply cease and determine. Moreover it will never be possible for any one to draw a hard and fast line between 'dog Sumerian' and pure classical Sumerian; for the presumably purest Sumerian, that of the unilingual texts of the old kings of Ur, Larsam and Tello (*Lagaš*) is 'dog Sumerian'. Apart altogether from such plays upon words as, for example, *da-er* 'lasting, eternal', which clearly betray their Semitic origin (st. *dâru*, 'last', part. *dâ'ir*, *dâ'er*), we meet at every turn, even in these texts, those Semitic forms of thought and speech, with which we are all familiar from the Assyrian monuments and other sources: cf. in the royal titles such expressions as 'the called one of the true heart, object of the lifting-up of the eye, etc.' of such and such a deity.

How is it, finally, with the grammatical forms of Sumer-

---

can be no question of any linguistic principle being at work: they are simply examples of most regrettable negligence and disregard of the old rigid ideographic principles, allied, in part, with thoughtlessness and ignorance. A similar declension from the old methods of writing appears also in the so-called 'dialectic' texts, in which the old ideograms are confused (*e. g. tug* 'be' for *dug* 'speak') and Semitic words and forms admitted with increasing recklessness (*e. g. še-ib* 'enclosure' from Assyr. *šibu*, syn. of *lipittu*; *šu-li-li* = *šûlula* IV R 20 No. 1, 15/16). As for the 'dialectic' phonetic changes between 'Accadian' and 'Sumerian', the change of *g* and *d*, of *n* and *š*, of *dug* and *zib*, I regard them as simply impossible from the point of view of the physiology of sound; in all probability, we must look for the explanation rather in Babylono-Semitic synonyms. The change of *m* and *g*, however, — which, by the way, must have been present in Sumerian as early as the time when the Semites 'borrowed' the cuneiform writing, cf. the syllabic values *mi*, *mir*, *mal*—seems to have its analogy in the Semitic tongue of Babylonia (*v.* phonology § 49, a, note).

ian, which still continue to be put forward, along with the phonetic syllabic values, as the leading argument for the existence of a Sumerian language? These, too, are open to suspicion in many ways. At the very outset we are struck by the singular fact that in the midst of the most genuine Semitic Assyrian texts, where there can be no question of 'Sumerian' originals of any sort, we find such 'Sumerian word-forms' as *dam-na* 'his wife', *al-tur* 'he will be diminished', *ni-gal* 'it will be' *ba-bad* 'he will die', *na-an-bal-e* 'let no one transgress'. Did the Semitic scribes of Babylonia and Assyria really go so far as to use full-fledged Sumerian words, with their formative elements, as ideograms to represent their own proper Semitic word-forms? Did they — to use a simple illustration — write: 'the master *mourra*', wherein *mourra* simply represented an ideogram for 'he will die'? Or is it not infinitely simpler to regard orthographical forms like these as wholly and solely attempts at writing the ideographic equivalents of Semitic words? More important, however, than the above is the circumstance that Sumerian grammar reminds us so very often of Babylonian Semitic. 'Sumerian' employs the characteristically Semitic mechanism of the construct state, distinguishes precisely the same tenses as Assyrian, and has, in the Verb, a *šu*-stem and a *ta-an*-stem. Its adverbial ending in *eš* e. g. *ul-le-eš*= *elṣiš* (*elṣeš*), *zi-de-eš*=*kêneš* corresponds exactly to the Assyrian, *e. g. mûšiš* 'during the night', *šamâmeš* 'heavenwards', *dabû'eš* 'like a bear'. The correspondence is rendered all the more complete by the express statement in VR 37, 57—59 that *eš* or, as it is customary to say, the 'Sumerian' *eš* is equivalent to *i-na* as well as to *a-na* and *ki-ma*. It is suspicious that the 'Sumerian' *ḫe*, like the Assyrian *lû* (from לאה 'wish, decide'), is not only the precative particle, but like the Assyr. *lû* — *lû*, also signifies 'whether — or' (*ḫe-a* — *ḫe-a*), not to mention the use of *ḫe* for the emphatic *lû* with preterite forms (VR 62 No. 2). We have lists (cf. that published by Bertin in the Journal of the Roy. Asiat. Socy. XVII, part 1.) in which the elements of so-called Sumerian inflexion are subjected to a most thorough analysis and set down as preformatives, informatives or afformatives e. g. *ne* and *bi-i* = *ana šu'ati*, *bi-ne* and *ne-e=atta šu'ati*, *bi-in* and *in=šû šu'ati; i-ni-ni* and *mi-ni-ni* — *i-ni-e* and *mi-ni-e* — *i-ni-in* and *mi-ni-in=anâku* — *atta* — *šû šu'ati šu'ati*; *in-na-ni-ni=anâku šu'ati šu'ati û anâku šu'ašum; mu=iâ'um šapliš* etc. How very strange that the Babylonians should be thus familiar with the structure of the Sumerian tongue in its minutest details! Were the Sumerians themselves such thorough masters of their language that they could thus instruct the Semites in its deepest mysteries? Or did the Semites themselves discover all those significations by comparative study of the Sumerian texts? It is infinitely more credible that lists like these were drawn up solely for the convenience of the scribes; they were meant to show what meaning was attached to the multifarious syllables and groups of syllables which were employed as the ideographic equivalents of the Semitic forms. There is at present no reason to doubt that what appear above to be elements in the composition of words will turn out to be ideograms artificially designed by the Semitic inventors of the wedge-writing. Here, as elsewhere, we may apply the saying: dies diem docet. Bertin's list already proves this much, that in 'Sumerian' words such as *innanlal*, *baninlal* 'he weighed it' (*iškulšu*), *nan*, *nin* do not, as is universally assumed, correspond to the pronominal suff. *šu*, thus giving us, in 'Sumerian', an incorporated pronoun, but rather that *an-lal*, *in-lal* are equivalent to *iš-kul*, and that *inna* and *bani* symbolize the object, which in Assyrian, as is well known, precedes the verb (= Assyr. *šu'ati šu iškul* 'it, itself, he weighed'). In this wise another support of the 'Sumerian' theory falls away. I do not deny that, especially as regards these supposed Sumerian forms, there are enigmas still awaiting solution, but there is not one among them that can seriously affect the line of argument which we have hitherto pursued. The Semitic Babylonians will be found entirely justified when they ascribed the invention of the art of writing to their god Nebo, and that besides the Cossæans, they never anywhere make the slightest mention of a third, a Sumero-Accadian, people will in the long run be explained by the fact that such a people was never in existence.

Phonology.

A Vowels.

I. Vowel Sounds.

§ 26. Assyrian has the following vowel sounds: *a*, *i*, *u*, *e*; *â*, *î*, *û*, *ê*. Of diphthongs it has perhaps *ai*.

§ 27. Examples of short and long *a*, *i*, *u* (to which the beginner may mentally add the corresponding Hebrew words and forms):

ă: amtu 'maid', *šarru* 'king', *kallâtu* 'bride', *naḫlu* and *naḫallu* 'valley, wady', *malkatu* 'princess', *šamšu* 'sun', *daltu* 'folding-door', *narkabtu* 'waggon, chariot', *ašṭur* 'I wrote'; *iṣbatû* 'they siezed'; *aḫu* 'brother', *ḳanû* 'reed'; *tašrup* 'thou didst burn'.

ĭ: ilu 'god', *bintu* 'daughter', *ṣillu* 'shadow', *parzillu* 'iron'; *šipru* 'mission'; *timâli* 'yesterday', *libittu* 'brick', *imêru* 'ass'. (For *i* = *ia*, e. g. *išrup* 'he burned', *v.* § 41; for *i* from an older *a*, e. g. *šêlibu* 'fox' *v.* § 35).

ŭ: mutu 'husband', *šumu* 'name', *ummu* 'mother'; *uznu* 'ear', *išrup* 'he burned'; *išrupû* 'they burned', *Purât* 'Euphrates', *Ulûlu* 'the month Elûl'.

â: sâsu 'moth', *attâ* 'thou'; *lâ* 'not', *atânu* 'she-ass', *alâku* 'go', *pâḳidu* 'superintending', *bâmâti* 'high places'. (For *â=a'*, e. g. *râdu* 'storm'=*ra'du*, *v.* § 47; for *â=i-a, i-â* etc. *v.* § 38, a).

î: šî 'she', *ittî* 'with me', *maḫîru* 'purchase price'. (For *î=i'*, e. g. *zîbu* 'wolf'=*zi'bu*, *v.* § 47; for *î= ai, ai̯ v.* §§ 31 and 30; for *î* as compensation for *i* with sharpening of the following consonant, e. g. *zîmu* 'splendour'=*zimmu, zimi̯u, v.* § 41, b).

û: šû 'he', *atûdu* 'he-goat', *imûtû* 'they died'. (For *û=au, au̯ v.* § 31; for *û=u'*, e. g. *bûru* 'well'= *bu'ru, v.* § 47; for *û=i(e)-u, i(e)-û, â-u, â-û, ê-u* etc. *v.* § 38, a.; for *û* as compensation for *u* with sharpening of the following consonant, e. g. *bûnu* 'child'= *bunnu, buni̯u, v.* § 41, b).

Assyrian *ĕ* (*ä*) has in every case, practically, arisen § 28. by phonetic change (*umlaut*) from an original *ă* (*v.* § 34); *ê* is sometimes *ai* or *ai̯* reduced to a monophthong, e. g. *ênu* (*înu*) 'eye' (=*ain*), *têr* 'make, do'(= *tair, ta'ir*), *dêkat* 'she was killed' (=*daikat, da'ikat*), *bikêtu* (*bikîtu*) 'weeping' (=*bikai̯tu*), *ibrêma*, 'he looked and' (=*ibrai̯ma*), and sometimes modified *â*, e. g. *imêru* (see for the latter § 32). Whether these two species of *ê* were also distinguished in pronunciation, cannot now be determined.

For an *e* which has perhaps arisen from an original *i* under the influence of a following *r* or *ḫ* *v.* § 36.

§ 29. From the law of vowel change discovered by Haupt and discussed in §§ 32—34, we learn that Assyrian must be assumed to have had, for a certain period at least, the vowels *e* and *ê*: in very many cases to explain Assyrian *i* and *î*, comparative Semitic phonology and morphology require us to assume an *e* and an *ê* as half-way between *a* and *i*, *â* and *î*. That the Assyro-Babylonians, further, still pronounced *e* and *ê*, we know, in the first place from the Hebrew and Greek reproductions of a number of Assyro-Babylonian words: note especially *Bêlu* בֵּל, Βῆλος, *Belos* (cf. *Bêl-šar-uṣur* בֵּלְשַׁאצַּר, *Bêl-ibuš* Βήλιβος); *Bêltî* 'my mistress' = Βῆλθις (Hesychius), cf. בַּלְתִּי Isa. 10, 4 (Lagarde); *Nêrgal* נֵרְגַל (cf. Νηριγλίσσαρος); *ištên* עַשְׁתֵּי; *Ṭebêtu* (written *Te-bi-e-tu*) טֵבֵת; *êlamu* אֵילָם Ez. 40.—There is much against הֵיכָל being taken as a loan-word from *e-kal-lu*, but from עֵילָם we may reasonably conclude that in Babylonia and Assyria *Elamtu* was pronounced with the vowel *e*. Compare also *neru* 'the number 600' νῆρος and the gloss of Hesychius σαύη· ὁ κόσμος Βαβυλώνιοι, doubtless = *šamê*, pronounced *šaṿê* 'heaven' *v.* § 44). We are taught the same, in the second place, by the fact that many words and inflexions are uniformly written with *e*. Cf. the substantives *ri-e-šu* 'head', *ṣi-e-nu* 'small cattle', *ṣi-e-ru* 'field' as distinguished from *ṣi-i-ru* 'exalted', *še-e-ru* 'morning' as distd. from *ši-i-ru* 'flesh', *ri-e-mu* 'mercy' as distd. from *ri-i-mu* 'wild ox'; also verbal forms like *ušêzib* 'I saved', *ušêṣi* 'I brought out' (cf. Aram. שֵׁיזֵב and שֵׁיצִיא), *uštêšir* 'I led aright', the middle syllables of which are always written *še* and *te*, never *ši* and *ti*. Not less convincing are the plural forms in *ê*, where such frequent forms as *mu-u'-di-e* 'crowds', *ša-di-e* 'mountains', *ni-ḳi-e* 'offerings', *ḳu-ra-di-e-šu* 'his warriors', *ik-ri-be-šu* 'his prayers', *kul-ta-ri-e-ša* 'her tents', *bi-e-li-e-a* 'my lords', and the frequently occurring addition of the phonetic complement *e* to ideographically written plurals like *amê-lu*^{pl}*-e* 'men, people' (Shalm. Mo. rev. 34. 85), *aplu*^{pl}*-e* 'sons' (ibid. 38), *bêlu*^{pl}*-e* 'lords' (Assurn. I 19 and oft.) *ilu*^{pl}*-e-a* 'my gods' scarcely leave room for doubt as to the reading *mu'dê, bêlê'a, amêlê, aplê, ilê'a* etc. See also § 32, *a*, note. And even if it is insisted on that orthographical forms like *ri-i-mu* 'womb, mercy' (S^b1), *us-si-bi-la* 'I caused to bring' (=*uštêbila*; these and similar forms often in letters), *šad-di-i* 'mountains' (in Sennachb.), *re-e-ši-i-šu* 'its summit' (V R 62 No. 1,

18), *ik-ri-bi-šu* 'his prayers' and others prove that the *ê's* above adduced were pronounced as *î*, still the illustrations in the first series given above, with their decidedly persistent orthography, retain their character and value, like many similar cases in English, as specimens of historical orthography and testify that in former times the *ê*, demanded by the laws of phonology and morphology, was really so pronounced and was thus distinguished from *î*. The same holds good of short *ĕ*: infins. like *epêšu* 'make', *erêbu* 'enter' will scarcely ever be found written *ipêšu*, *irêbu*, either because they were pronounced with *e* for a very long time—and may then be regarded as examples of historical orthography—or, as is more probable, because they were so pronounced down to a late date. We may, indeed, gather from such favourite modes of writing as *e-ep-še-ti* 'deeds', *e-eš-ši-iš* 'new' (*v.* § 10) that *e* was known down even to Neo-Babylonian times. A third unquestionable proof of the existence of a vowel *e* in Assyrian is afforded—assuming the purely ideographic nature of so-called 'Sumerian'—by the lists giving the ideographic equivalents of the Assyrian grammatical forms, as mentioned above on p. 70: they show us that between *e* on the one hand and *i* on the other a clearly marked distinction was drawn, cf. sets of preformatives like *un*, *an*, *in*, *en*; *ub*, *ab*, *ib*, *eb* etc.

While accepting the conclusions reached in the foregoing section, we must, nevertheless, keep two facts in mind: the first, that even in the earliest period *ê*, in particular the *ê* having its origin in *ai* or *ai̯*, must have had a strong leaning towards the pronunciation *î* (cf. § 25 above, p. 64). Thus e. g. *bîtu* 'house' (extremely seldom *bêtu*), *îši*, *tîši* 'I had, thou hadst' (so written without exception) would seem to have been never pronounced otherwise than with *î*, and in the case of *ênu* and *înu* 'fountain', the double pronunciation must go back to a very early period. Thereafter, in the course of time, the tendency to pronounce *e* as *i* increased in favour, especially, perhaps, in every day speech, so that *anînu* 'we', *îmur* 'he saw', *inu* alongside of *enu* 'time', *amîlu* alongside of *amêlu* 'man' must not only have been so written but so pronounced (note *Amêl-Marduk*=אֱוִיל־מְרֹדַךְ); in the inscriptions of Rammânnirârî I. it is already quite a common thing to find forms like *lu-ti-ir* (IV R 45, 13. 43) — cf. *Šamaššum ukîn* Σαοσδούχινος. In this way is explained the early uncertainty, fatal even to the historical orthography, in the graphic representation of the *e* and *i* vowels. Even from the very first these two vowels, as we have just seen, were confused to a considerable extent in the Assyro-Babylonian writing, and afterwards a further step was § 30.

taken and the special sign for *e* used also for *i:* thus, e. g. *at-ti-e* 'thou' (fem.); *še-e-ru* 'flesh, blood relation'; *šú-me* 'my name' (V R 62 No. 1, 24. 27); *aḳi-eš* = *aḳîš* 'I presented' (I R 8 No. 3, 7); genitive singulars like *šul-me* (Sams. II 21. III 68), *ḳa-te* (ibid. IV 43); *me-iṭ-ru* 'rain', *me-iṣ-ru* 'territory' (IV R 44, 8. 21 and often), *mešiḫtu* 'measure, extent'; *e-mit-tu* fem. of *imnu* 'to the right'; *ba-be-lat* 'bringing' (I R 27 No. 2, 6), *ḳa-eš-še* 'presenting' part. (II R 60 No. 2, 32); *e-me-du* pret. I 1 of אמד$_4$, *u-še-bu* 'I sat down' (Shalm. Mo. Obv. 15), *ra-am-me-ik* 'pour out', the king's name *Bêl-du-me-ḳa-an-ni* (V R 44, 46 d) etc. Note especially the interchange of *ne-mi-ḳu* and *ni-me-ḳu* 'wisdom' (Neb. Grot. I 4, Neb. I 7). The necessary remarks as to the transliteration have been made in § 15 (end). It will be the task of future investigators, putting aside the occasional varieties of pronunciation, to decide with increasing accuracy as to each individual form, whether on grammatical grounds we should set it down as having been originally pronounced with *e* or with *i*, always keeping in mind the possibility that accent and analogy may have also their say in the matter. I refer here, by way of illustration, to the genitive sing. of nouns in *û*, such as *šadî* and *šaddê*, *šaḳî* and *šaḳê*, *nadê*, *palê* (always), *akkadî* (often), *apsî*, *reš-ti-i* (IV R 33, 38 a) from *šadû* 'mountain', *šaḳû* 'high', *nadû* 'throwing' etc. (cf. § 66); to the feminine plurals in *âte, ête,* as *re-še-ti-e* 'summits', (Shalm. Mo. obv. 7), *ta-ma-a-te* 'seas', *Ištârâ-te* (II R 66 No. 1), *mâtâti* and *mâtâte* passim, *ep-še-ti-e-šu, ep-še-te-ia* 'his, my deeds'; to the cases mentioned in §§ 34, *α* note and 36, and others. It will be not less necessary to prepare statistics of all the cases in which, in spite of the existence of as many as twelve signs for *e*, we find *i* used, in order to ascertain whether, and if so to what extent, words and forms like *šú-mi-lu* 'left', *si-bu-u* 'the seventh', *iš-mi* 'he heard', *imur* 'he saw', *îli* 'he came up' were pronounced with *i*. We must, however, at the outset give up hopes of discovering lines of demarcation as regards either time or place, of the nature, for example, of those which separate eastern from western Syriac.

D i p h t h o n g s. The diphthong *au*, *au̯* is always in Assyrian reduced to *û*, hence e. g. *rûḳu* 'far' (= *ra'uḳu, rauḳu*), *minûtu* 'number' (=*minautu, minau̯tu*), *ûšib* 'I sat down' (=*aušib, au̯šib*). For this reason words like *šûru* 'ox', *mûtu* 'death' become to the eye identical with *nûnu* 'fish', *šûmu* 'garlic'—when written at least, and most probably also in pronunciation. It is, *per se*, a possible hypothesis that the Babylonians and Assyrians had in reality a vowel *o* which became identical with *u* only when written § 31.

(as in the case of *e* and *i*); cf. for this supposition σῶσσος = *šuššu*. We must, however, in any case — be the Semites the inventors or the borrowers of the wedge-writing — admit that even in the earliest period *o* and *u* were in most cases interchangeable in pronunciation. Moreover the confusion of the ideograms for *û* 'and' and *û* (*ô*) 'or' is an undoubted proof that in the historical period *o* was pronounced as *u*. The circumstance that the *o* of Hebrew proper names is rendered in Assyrian by *u* e. g. אַשְׁדּוֹד *As-du-du*, יָפוֹ *Ja-ap-pu-u*) cannot be accepted as proof that the latter was pronounced as *o*; the explanation rather is that *u* was written as approaching most nearly to *o*, as may be gathered from the various renderings of מוֹאָב, — sometimes *Mû'âba*, sometimes *Mâ'âba*.

It is also probable that *ai*, like *au*, was always reduced to a monophthong (*ê*, *î*), cf. *bi-i-tu* 'house'. *mâmîtu*, *maškîtu*, *nabnîtu*, and *v.* §§ 28 and 30. For this reason, if for no other, it appears suspicious to class certain forms like *a-a* 'not', *a-a-u* 'which?' as exceptional forms. Even as regards the written form it would be very strange both that *â* and *ai* should be so completely identified, and that the diphthong *ai* should be graphically rendered by a double *a*. Just as it is most probable from the graphical point of view, that *a-a* represented long *â* (*v.* § 13), so, from the point of view of grammar and lexicon, there is no consideration which compels us to read *ai, aiu, ainu, ailu* instead of *â* 'not', *â'u* 'which?', *ânu* 'where', *âlu* 'ram, stag'. For fuller treatment see the relevant sections in the chapters on the pronoun, noun, and adverb, viz: for the interrogative stem *â* § 59, for nouns like *âbu* 'enemy', *dânu* 'judge' § 64, for the negative particle *â* § 78.

II. Phonetic Changes affecting the Vowels.

Change of *a* to *e* (*ä*).

Change of *â* to *ê* (frequently alongside of the original forms with *â*).*) § 32.

a) *With preceding i, e or ê: ši-ni-ti* (i. e. *šinêti*) alongside of *šinâti* 'they', verbal suffix, plur. fem.; *imêru* 'ass' (=*imâru*); *girrêti* 'ways', *mi-iṣ-re-ti* 'borders'. —*emêtu* 'mother-in-law' (=*emâtu*); *ištênu* (prop. *eštênu*, ground-form *aštân*) alongside of *ištânu* 'sole, one', *erênu* 'chest'; *epšêti* 'deeds', *ešrêti* 'temples', *edlêti* 'bolted (doors)'; *en-di-ku* (i. e. *endêku*=*emdâku*) 'I stand' perm.—*rêmênû* 'merciful' (=*rêmânû*); *bêlêti* 'mistresses', *rêšêti* 'summits', *tênišêti* 'human beings'.

*) All the words written by me in continuous transliteration with *e* or *ê* are found with the special sign for *e*. The subdivisions of §§ 32—34 have been suggested, in the first place, by practical considerations: thus the emphasizing of a neighbouring *i* or *e* does not necessarily mean that this *i* or *e* has occasioned or favoured the change from *a* to *e*. For an undoubted motive for the change of *a* to *e* see § 42.

Alongside of these feminine plural forms, such as *šiprêti, zikrêti, limnêti, bêlêti* (all written expressly with *ê*; *ni-ri-bi-ti* forms an exception) and others, we find quite frequently forms with *â*: *gimrâti, libnâti, niklâti, ṣimdâti*; *elâti* (*u šaplâti*); *šar kênâti* 'king of justice' (V R 55, 6). See also under γ.

β) *With following i: a-ni-ni, ni-nu* 'we' (i. e. *anêni, nênu=anâni, ana'ni*); *têdištu* 'renewal', *têbibtu, têliltu* 'brilliancy' alongside of *tâdirtu* 'fear'; 1. pers. sing. pret. Qal of Verbs primæ $א_1$, with *i* in the second syllable: *êsir* 'I imprisoned' (but *âkul* 'I ate'); participles I 1 of verbs primae $א_{4.5}$: *êpišu* 'making', *êribu* 'entering'; of verbs med. $א_4$: *rê'û* 'shepherd' (=*rê'i-u*); of verbs tertiæ $א_{3-5}$: *šêmû* 'hearing'. In the same way *ri-bu-u* 'fourth', *si-bu-u* 'seventh', *pi-tu-u* 'opening', *li-ku-u* 'taking' are doubtless to be read *rêbû, pêtû* etc. Stray examples are also found with other stems, cf. especially *šêššu* 'sixth' (=*šâdšu, šâdišu*); pret. and pres. of the Shafel and Ishtafal of verbs primæ $א_{4.5}$ and primæ י: *ušêbir* (pres. *ušêbar*), *ušêrib, uštêrib* and *ušêšib, ušêṣi, uštêšib* 'he caused to dwell', alongside of the rarer *ušâliṣ* 'I caused to rejoice', and *ušâšib, uštâbil* 'he brought'.

γ) *Not in proximity to i, e or ê.*

â, in which an ' quiesces: mêsiru 'enclosure', *mêdilu* 'bolt', *mêtiḳu* 'course, way' (= *mêsaru, mâsaru* etc.); *nêribu* 'entrance, pass' (= *nêrabu, nârabu*); *rêšu* 'head'

(= *râšu, ra'šu*), very rarely *râšu, ṣênu* 'flock, small cattle', *ṣêru* (*ṣi-e-ru*) 'back', *rêmu* 'womb, mercy', *šêru* 'morning', *bêlu* 'lord', but also *râdu* 'storm'; *šumêlu* 'left', *šêlabu, šêlibu* 'fox'; *nap-ti-e-tu* (*naptêtu*) 'key' (= *naptâtu, napta'tu*), *tašmêtu* 'hearing, granting (of a request)'; 3. pers. m. sing., m. and f. plur. pret. Qal of verbs primæ א: *êkul* 'he ate' (= *iêkul iâkul*), *êsir* 'he imprisoned', *ênaḫ* 'he sank', *êpuš* 'he made', *êzib* 'he left', *êrub* 'he entered'; with $א_{4.5}$ also 2. pers. sing. and plur. and 1. sing.: *têpuš, êpuš, têzib, êrub* (contrasted with *tâkul, âkul*, 'thou atest, I ate'; for *êsir* 'I imprisoned' *v.* β); forms of the sing. pret. Qal of verbs tertiæ א with *ma* appended enclitically: *abbê-ma, ipté-ma, išmê-ma, ašmê-ma* 'I called', 'he opened', 'he, I heard'; also without *ma*, but shortened, in pres. as well as pret. of verbs tertiæ $א_{3.4}$: *lu-up-te* 'I will open', *liš-me-u* 'let them hear', *i-pe-te-šu* 'he opens it', *i-še-me, a-šem-me* 'he will, I shall hear'; this *e* is then further shortened to *i*, *v.* § 39.

â, in which an ' does not quiesce: šurmênu 'cypress' from an older *šurmânu, râmênu* and *râmânu* 'self'; *ku-dur-re-ti* 'landmark', *rûḳêti* 'those at a distance', *ma-di-e-tum* 'many' *i. e.* lands (H. 6), cf. *a* above; infs. of verbs primæ $א_{4.5}$: *epêšu* 'make', *erêbu* 'enter', also in verbs primæ $א_1$, such as *erêšu* 'choose, wish', *amêru* 'be deaf'. Examples are found even with strong verbs:

namêru 'shine' (Tig. VII 101), *pa-ṭi-ru* 'open' (1 Mich. III 14), *ša-gi-mu, ra-mi-mu* (IV R 28 No. 2) and many others; these, however, are doubtless = *paṭêru*, *šagêmu*, *ramêmu*; infs. of verbs mediæ $א_4$ *bêlu* 'rule', (= *be'êlu*). The same intermediate forms must be assumed for the infs. of verbs tertiæ $א_{2-5}$, such as *petû* 'open', *šemû* 'hear' (= *petê'u, šemê'u*), see further § 34, β. The change of *â* to *ê* in the 3. pers. fem. plur. of the pret. is rare, *e. g. uṭṭammê* for *uṭṭammâ* (V R 47, 9 b). On the other hand we must place here *ê* 'not', alongside of *â, êkâ* 'where?' alongside of *a-a-ka,* i. e. doubtless *âkâ* — cf. *ak-ka-a-a*, *a-ki-i* 'how?' and *ânu* אָן 'where?'

§ 33. *b*) Change of *a* to *ê* — the doubled consonant originally following the *a* being now written singly.

zêṛu 'seed' (= *zâru, zarru, zar'u*), *bêru* 'glance' (= *bâru*, *barru*, *bariu*). — Pret. of the Piel and Iftaal (exclusively in Tiglathpileser I and Assurnaṣirpal?): *u-na*(*k*)-*ki-ir* 'I changed' and *u-ni-ki-ir* (I R 28, 9 b), *urappiš* 'I extended' and *u-ri-pi-iš* (Tig. I 61), *unappiṣ* and *u-ni-pi-iṣ* (Assurn. III 53), *unak*(*k*)*is* 'I cut off' and *u-ni-ki-is* (Tig. III 99 and often), *u-ki-ni-iš* 'I subdued' (Tig. I 54), *u-ri-ki-is* 'I covered' (I R 28, 11 b), *u-na* (var. *ni*)-*ki-is* 'I struck off' (Assurn. I 117), *lu-pi-ri-ir* 'I broke in pieces' (Tig. V 90), *u-ba-an-ni* and *u-been-ni*, 'I caused to shine' (Tig. VII 98), *lup-te-ḫir* 'I collected' (Tig. I 71), *uš-te-pi-il* 'he has bent'. The second form of each pair just given (cf. also *u-te-im-me-iẖ* 'he took' I R 28, 20a) favours the reading of *u-ni-ki-is* etc. as *unêkis*, (or *unékis?*), *urêpiš*, and so on.

c) Change of *a* to *e*. § 34.

α) *With i or e following:* the syllable *ša* in the pret. and part. of the Shafel and Ishtafal of strong verbs (likewise confined to Tig. and Assurn.?): *ušakniš* 'I subdued' and *u-še-ik-ni-iš* (Tig. VI 38) i. e. *ušékniš*, as also *u-šik-ni-ša* (Assurn. I 23), *u-šik-lil* 'I completed', *mu-šik-ni-šu* (also *mušaknišu*) 'subduing' (Tig. VII 43) and others, which must be read with *e*, *u-še-eš-kin* 'I caused to make' (Tig. VI 46), *u-še-ik* (var. *šak*)-*ši-du-šu* 'he helped him to conquer' (Assurn. I 39); *uštasẖir* and *ulteshir*. — The *a* of the present of verbs tertiæ י: *išási* 'he speaks' and *i-šis-si* i. e. *išési* (IV R 5, 37b); of verbs tertiæ $א_{3.4}$: *i-pe-te-šu* 'he opens it', *te-liḳ-ḳi-e* 'thou acceptest' (K. 101), = *teléḳî*, *i-še-me* 'he hears', *i-še-im-ma-'-in-ni* 'they obey me', (Beh. 7), *išémû* 'they will hear'; more rarely with strong verbs: *ta-pi-is-si-nu* 'thou wilt conceal' (Beh. 102), *te-ḳib-bir* i. e. *teḳé-bir* 'thou shalt bury'. — The *a* of the pret. of the Ifteal: *aḳṭérib* 'I advanced', *iptéḳid* 'he handed over', *iḳtérâ* (= *iḳtéri-a*) 'he summoned', *itéli* 'he went up', *itébir* 'he crossed', *etétiḳ* 'I marched' (but also *etátiḳ*), *iltéḳi* 'he took', *altéme* 'I heard', *artédi* 'I marched'. But note also *itérub* 'he entered', *etépuš* 'I made' (alongside of *etárub* 'I entered', *etápuš* 'I made'). — For the nominal form فِعَل *v.* partly under γ, partly under δ. — A few 1. perss. sing. of the pret. Qal and Ifteal: *iḳ-bi* i. e. certainly *eḳbi* 'I spoke' (I R 49 col. III 19), *e-ip-ti-iḳ* i. e. *eptiḳ* 'I built' (Neb. IV 24 and oft., Nerigl. I 26), *e-ip-ti* i. e. *epti* 'I laid bare' (Nabon. III 31); *e-ir-te-it-ti* (pronounce *ertéti*) 'I set up' (Neb. VI 38), *e-ir-te-id-di-e-ma* (pron. *ertedê-ma*) 'I went' (Neb. II 23).

From the forms just given, which are few in number and seemingly confined to later times, with אֶ for אַ in the preformative, are to be distinguished the 1 pers. sing. pret. Ifteal (and Iftaneal) of verbs primæ $א_{4\cdot5}$, e. g. *etêli* 'I went up', *etêpuš* 'I made': like the 3 pers. e. g. *etêli* pl. *etêlû* 'they went up' (V R 8, 82), *etabrû* 'they crossed' (Assurn. III 28), *etêpuš* 'he made' (Khors. 7) and *etenêpušû* (also *etanápušû*) 'they made' (V R 3, 111), these forms seem to owe their *e* to the intimate connexion of the reflexive stem with the Qal (*êbir*, *têbir*, *êbir*). In the 3. pers. they interchange with the regular forms after the manner of *itâmar* (i. e. *ittámar*), viz: *itêtiḳ*, *itêli* and so on, while *atâpaš* (Shalm. Balaw. II 5) is the solitary example of the 1 pers.

β) *With ê or é following:* the first syllable of the infs. of the verbs mentioned in § 32 γ: med. $א_4$: *bêlu* 'rule' (= *be'êlu*, *ba'êlu*), primæ $א_{4.5.1}$: *epêšu*, *elû* 'go up', *erêbu*, *erêšu* (but also *epâšu* e. g. Tig. VII 74); tertiæ $א_{2-5}$: *šebû* (= *šebê'u*) 'be satisfied', *šemû* 'hear', so too *ni-gu-u* 'shine' (נגה), *pi-tu-u* 'open', *li-ḳu-u* 'take', *ḳi-bu-u* 'speak' are to be pronounced as *negû*, *petû*, *leḳû*, *ḳebû*.

The older forms *patû*, *laḳû*, *ḳabû*, *ḫarû* 'dig' are still found alongside of those just given, and that not unfrequently. A few examples occur even with strong verbs, cf. e. g. *si-ki-ru*, certainly = *sikêru*, *sekêru* 'bolt' (alongside of *sanâḳu* II R 23, 43 c).—*teléḳî* 'thou takest' (= *taléḳî*), *teḳébir* 'thou shalt bury'.

γ) *Initial (anlautendes) a* ($א_{1-5}$) in various nominal and verbal forms.

$א_1$: *erṣitu* (= *erṣatu* § 35, *arṣatu*) 'earth', but *anbatu* 'plants'. — *erû* 'chest'.—*enšu* 'weak', *eširtu* 'temple' (فِعْل).—*alallu* and *elallu* 'cistern' (فَعَّل).

$א_2$: *erîtu* 'pregnant' (فَعِل).—*erû* 'be pregnant' (فَعَال).

$א_3$: *emu* 'father-in-law'.—*im-mu* (i. e. *emmu*) 'hot', also *annu* 'favour, grace'.—*eḳlu* 'field' (st. cstr. *e-ki-el*), *eklitu* 'darkness'.—*ebru* 'friend' (st. cstr. *e-bi-ir*), *eššu* 'new' = *edšu*, *edišu*, *adišu* (فَعِل).

$א_4$: *enu* 'lord, master', *ezzu* 'fearful'. — *enzu* 'goat', *ešrâ* 'twenty'.—*eli* 'upon', *elamu* 'high' (فَعَل).—*edlu* 'bolted, barred', *epištu* 'deed' (فَعِل).—*endêku* 'I stand', perm. = *amdâku*.—*epuš* 'it is made', perm. (فَعُل)—*erub* 'enter', *ebir* 'go across', (but *akul* 'eat').—*emûḳu* 'might', doubtless for *amûḳu*. Cf. with these *abdu* 'servant', *adî*, *adi* 'unto', *agalu* 'calf', *atûdu* 'he-goat'.

δ) *Other miscellaneons cases*: the *a* of the nominal stem فَعِل and of the permansive of the Qal of stems tertiæ $\aleph_{3-5}$: *pi-tu-u* (i. e. *petû*, same formation as *edlu*) 'opened'; *tebâku*, *tebûni* 'I come, they come'.—*šelaltu* 'three' alongside of *šalaltu*, *narâru* and *nerâru* (Khors. 113) 'helper', *ṣerritu* (*ṣirritu*) 'concubine' (צָרָה).—*taṣlîtu* and *teṣlîtu* 'prayer', so too *teṣbîtu* 'wish, request = *taṣbîtu*, and *tašrîtu* as well as *tešrîtu* (*tišrîtu*) 'consecration; beginning, the month Tishri'.

On §§ 32—34: certain groups of ideograms, as well as many glosses, still present the equivalent Babyl.-Assyr. words, even when the latter have *e*, in their original form with the vowel *a*: cf. A. SI. GA = *esigû*, A. DE. A = *edû*, A. GUB. BA = *agubbû* and *egubbû*, ŠUR. MAN = *šurmênu*, *epinu* (gloss *apin* S^b 291), *šênipu* or *šînipu* (gloss *šânabi* S^b 52), etc.

2. Transition of unaccented short *a* to *i*.

§ 35. The transition of unaccented short *a* to *i* under the influence of an *ê* or *e* in the preceding syllable is found in the follg.: *šêlibu*, more rarely *šêlabu* 'fox'. Cf. also the above-mentioned *šênipu* 'two thirds' contrasted with the gloss *šânabi*.—*mêsiru*, *mêtiḳu* and others from *mêsaru*, *mâsaru*, so too *nêribu* = *nêrabu*, *v.* § 32, β.—*bêlit*(*u*) 'lady, mistress', rarely *bêlat* (III R 7 col. I 3; see for the ground-forms *bêlatu* and the still older *ba'latu* II R 36, 65. 62 a), *rêbitu* 'street, market-place' (= *rêbatu*, *râbatu*).—*ezzu* fem. *ezzitu*, *ellu* 'shining' fem. *ellitu* (as opposed to *dannu*, *dannatu*), *erṣitu*, *eklitu* (§ 34, γ) from *erṣatu*, *eklatu*, so *irpitu*

(i. e. *erpitu*) 'cloud' from *erpatu;* for this reason in § 34, δ *ṣirritu* 'concubine' was given as *ṣerritu.*—*ešrit* 'temple' (st. cstr. originally *eš(i)rat,* from *eširtu*).—Accented *a* is more stable: *mêtaḳtu*, *mêkaltu* 'small stream'; *elamtu* fem. of *elamu*; but cf. e. g. *ni-bar-tu* and *ni-bir-tu* 'crossing'.

In close connexion with the two vocalic sound-changes just given, let us mention the transition, suggested by Haupt, of *i* to *e* under the influence of an immediately following *r* or *ḫ*: *i* seems to have partially assimilated itself to these two consonants as in Hebr. יֶחְבַּשׁ for יִחְבַּשׁ. Take, for example, extremely frequent orthographical forms—in certain cases occurring almost without exception—such as *u-nam-me-ra* 'I caused to shine', *u-ma-e-ru* 'they sent', *u-maš-še-ir-šu* 'I sent him away' (Tig. V 29), *uš-še-ru* 'they tore down', *lu-maš-še-ru* 'they left' (Tig. III 67), *mu-gam-me-ru* 'carrying out, completing', *uš-te-eš-še-ra* 'I set right', *za-e-re-šu* 'his enemies' (IV R 44, 25), *mêšaru* and *mêšeru* 'righteousness' (but surely = *mêširu*) and many others; to these add *u-te-im-me-iḫ* 'he caught', *lu-šat-me-ḫu* 'they caused to hold', (Tig. I 51), *ta-me-iḫ* 'holding' (Tig. VI 56) and others. Now forms like these should really compel us to see in the *e* more than a mere inaccurate way of writing *i*, from which it must follow that these forms are not, like *u-šaḫ-* § 36.

me-ṭu-ni or *mu-ša-ak-ni-eš* (Assurn. III 111), for example, to be classed with the cases discussed in § 30.

3. Syncope of short (and long) Vowels.

§ 37. We distinguish the following cases of syncope:

a) *Syncope of unaccented short a and i after a long syllable.* (1) The *a* (*i*) of the feminine termination: *ti'âmtu* = *ti'âmatu*, *bêltu* = *bêlitu*, *bêlatu*; *šimtu* 'decision', *siḫirtu* 'circuit' st. cstr. *siḫîrat*; *batûltu* 'virgin', *šubûltu* 'ear (of corn)' = *šubûlatu*, *uṣûrtu* (*uṣurtu*) 'curse' st. cstr. *uṣûrat*. *Rabîtu, šaḳûtu*, also, stand for *rabî-atu, šaḳû-atu*.—(2) The *i* of the participle فَاعِل: *âšibu* and *âšbu* 'dwelling', fem. (st. cstr.) *âšibat* and *âšbat*.—(3) *i* in the preterite Qal of Verbs primæ ו: *ûbilûni* and *ûblûni* (*ublûni*) 'they brought', *ûbila* and *ubla* 'he brought', *ûridûni* and *urdûni* 'they went down'.

b) *Syncope of unaccented short a, i, u after a short syllable.* (1) In many nominal forms, both inflected and uninflected: *šantu* 'year' (= *šanatu*), *rapšu* 'far, wide', fem. *rapaštu*, st. cstr. *rapšat*, pl. *rapšâti* (for *rapašu, rapašat, rapašâti*); *ṣiḫru* 'small', fem. *ṣiḫirtu*, st. cstr. *ṣiḫrat*; *pulḫu* 'fear', fem. *puluḫtu*, st. cstr. *pulḫat*;—*maliku* and *malku* 'prince', *kabtu* 'heavy', fem. *kabittu*, st. cstr. *kabtat*, *erinu* and *ernu* 'cedar' (*labiru* 'old' is never syncopated);—*zikaru* and *zikru* 'male';—*limnu* 'wicked', fem. *limuttu*.—(2) In many verbal forms:

the *i* of the permansive of the Qal in almost all the forms except the 3. pers. sing. masc.: *ašbat* 'she dwells', *ašbâtu* 'I dwell', *ašbû* 'they dwell' instead of *ašibat* etc.; the vowel of the second radical in the imp. Qal: *uṣrâ* 'help' (=*uṣurâ*), *erbî* fem. 'enter' (=*erubî*);—the vowel of the second radical in Ifteal and Nifal: *imtalkû* (=*imtalikû*) 'they took counsel together', *iptaḫrû* 'they assembled (themselves)', *ittaklû* 'they confided', *iterba* 'he entered' (=*itéruba*), *itepšû* 'they made' (also *itépušû*), *iktanšuš* 'they prostrated themselves before him' (=*iktanašû-š*) alongside of forms like *iptálaḫû*;—*ša i-da-bu* 'who will speak' (=*idabbu*, *idábubu*), *âli aštallum* 'the city which I carried away (captive)' (=*aštálalum*, K. 257 obv. 32).

c) *Syncope of unaccented short a after a doubled consonant*, the doubling being, at the same time, dispensed with: *altu* 'wife'=*aštu*, *aššatu*, *maṣrâti* plur. of *maṣṣartu* instead and alongside of *maṣṣarâti*, *u-gal-bu* 'they flog'=*ugallabû*, *u-na-ak-ru* 'they make enemies of' (=*unakkarû*), etc.

Examples of the rare *syncope of a long vowel* are: *râmânu*, *râmênu* and *râmnu* 'self'; *rêmênû* and *rêmnû* 'merciful'; *âl narmišu* 'his favourite city' (Neb. III 36) for *âl narâmišu*; *ušziz* 'I set up' from and alongside of *ušêziz*.—A case of syncope must also be assumed in *kî us-ba-ku(-ni)* 'during the sojourn' (in Assurn. and Shalm.); see my Assyrian dictionary p. 29.

4. Contraction of two Vowels.

§ 38. Two very different sorts of contraction of two contiguous vowels may be discussed together in the present section:

a) Contraction of two contiguous vowels in such a way that the first vowel loses itself in the second, lengthening the latter when it is short, is especially frequent in verbs tertiæ infirmæ, where it is found in the most varied forms. Examples of the contraction of *i-u* (*û*) to *û*, and of *i-a* (*â*) to *â*: *bânû* 'building', *pêtû* 'opening' (=*bâni-u*, *pêti-u*), *mušamṣû* 'causing to find' (=*mušamṣi-u*); also *imṣi* 'he found', *ipti* 'he opened', *išmi* 'he heard', *ibni* 'he built'; but with the frequent ending *a* of the sing., the *â* of the 3. pers. plur. fem., the *u* of the relative clause and the *û* of the 3. pers. plur. we have *imṣâ*, *imṣû*; *iptâ*, *iptû*; *išmâ*, *išmû*; *ibnâ*, *ibnû*. In the case of *i-u* (*e-u*), however, we still not unfrequently find the uncontracted forms e. g. *e-li-u-ni* 'they went up' (Assurn. II 82), *il-ḳi-u-ni* 'they took, fetched' (I R 28, 27a), *iḳ-bi-u-ni* 'they command', *liš-me*(*mi*)-*u* 'may they hear' (Tig. VIII 26). Contraction of *â-u* to *û*: *našû* 'carry', *banû* 'build' (= *našâ'u*, *banâ-u*, *banâịu*); also in the adjectives of relation in *â* with the *u* of the nom. sing. and the *û* of the plur. masc.: *Aššûrû* (=*Aššûrâu*, *Aššûrâịu*) 'the Assyrian, Assyrians'; Exx. of *ê-u* to *û*: *petû*, *šemû*.

Note, further, (for the *inlaut*) §§ 55, b and 57, a. A large field for the contraction of two vowels is also afforded by the declension of nouns formed from verbs tertiæ infirmæ: *rubû* 'great' (= *rubâ-u*?), gen. *rubî*, acc. *rubâ*, plur. *rubê*; *rabû* 'great' (= *rabî-u*), gen. *rabî*, acc. *rabâ*; *šurbû* 'great' (= *šurbû-u*), gen. *šurbî*, acc. *šurbâ*; *namsû* 'washing-place' (= *namši-u*); *rabâti* 'great' (fem. plur.), *tabrâti* (= *tabrî-âti*), cf. *e-ri-a-ti* (also *e-ra-a-ti*) 'pregnant women', *nam-zi-a-ti*; so too *unâti* = *unû-âti* (not = *unaṷâti*), etc.

b) Contraction of two contiguous vowels in such a way that the first vowel is preserved, while the second is suppressed, giving up, at the same time, its accent to the first vowel and sharpening (doubling) the immediately following consonant, if the latter is not already sharpened: in verbs primæ א in the pres. of the Qal and in the pret., pres. and part. of the Piel; cf. *i-'a-ab-ba-tu* i. e. *i'ábatu* 'he will destroy' (I R 27 No. 2, 57), usually, however, *ibbatu*, *immar* 'he sees' (= *i'ámar*), *illak* 'he goes' (= *i'álak*); *u'abbit* 'he destroys', pres. *u'abbat*, part. *mu'abbit*, but usually *ubbit*, *ubbat*, *muddiš* 'renovating' etc. (The pres. Qal of verbs primæ $א_{4.5}$: *ezzib*, *tezzib*, *ippuš* (*eppuš*), *irrub* (*errub*) is formed directly from the preterite; for details *v.* § 90, a, note).

For the contraction of the precative particle *lû*

and the vocalic preformatives of the verb *i, u, a* see § 93.

5. Complete Loss of Vowels.

§ 39. Complete loss of vowels, together with the loss of the א which accompanies the vowel as first radical or of the א or י as third radical, which has been absorbed by the vowel, is found, on the one hand, in both nominal and verbal formations from stems primæ ו (*anlaut*) and, on the other hand, in those from stems tertiæ א and י (*auslaut*). As examples of the *anlaut* we may cite here nominal stems formed like *biltu* 'offering', *šiptu* 'conspiracy', *šubtu* 'dwelling', *šuttu* 'dream', also *lidu, lidânu* 'child' (from stems primæ ו or א), = *ibiltu, ušubtu* etc.? Observe *ilittu* alongside of *littu* 'shoot'. To these we must add the imperative Qal of stems primæ ו; *rid* 'come down', *ṣî* 'go out' etc. Other, more isolated, examples of the loss of an initial vowel are: *anîni* and *nîni* 'we', *timâli* 'yesterday' from and alongside of *itimâli*; *têziz* (= *itêziz*) 'he provoked' (Nimr. Ep. XI, 162), *âbur* instead and alongside of *â îbur* in the Babylonian street-name *A îbur ša-bu-um* (Neb. V 15), *lâši* instead and alongside of *lâ îši* 'he was not' (cf. *la-aš-šú* Tig. VII 25); *dûku, balliṭ* (= *adûku, uballiṭ*, Assurn. I 81) doubtless belong to the speech of the common people. Before we give examples of this loss in the *auslaut*, there is a preliminary to it which must be mentioned here. This is the extreme shortening of the final vowel produced by the short vowel of the second radical and the vowelless third radical, in verbs where the latter is a weak letter. This shortening takes place in every case where the final vowel is not retained by an appended *ma*: thus we find *ibbêma* 'he announced and', *išmêma* 'he heard and' (*ê* = *â*, *v.* § 32, γ), also *ibrêma* 'he saw and' (*ê* = *ai*, *ai*), but elsewhere with short *e* (cf. *ipéte* 'he opens', *išéme* 'he hears'), and usually short *i*, *ibbi*, *ipti*, *išmi*, *ibni* 'he built' (*tabni*, *abni*). In such preterital and presential forms this short *i* is now and then completely suppressed: *lu-uṣ* 'I will go out' (= *lûṣi*, in prop. names), *i-ta-am* 'he thinks' (= *itámi*, Neb. III 26), *i-še-im* 'he will hearken to' (= *išéme*, Shalm. Throne Inscr. 5), *i-te-il* 'he goes off' (= *itéli*, V R 25, 45 d), etc.; cf. וַיִּבֶן. Among nouns we find a completely analogous case in *matê-ma* 'whensoever' (*ê* = *ai*, *ai*), but *mati* 'when?' and still further shortened *mat*, e. g. *adi mat* '(till) how long?'; in the same way we have *eli* (from *elî*) and *el* 'upon'. Cf. also the permansive forms of the Qal: *mali* 'he is full', *malat*, *mal-â-ta*; *ba-ni*, *ban-at*, *ban-â-ta* etc.; participles like *nâši* 'carrying', *bâni* 'building': st. constr. *nâš*, *bân*, fem. *bân-tu*, st. cstr. *bânat* 'mother', so *lêḳat* 'accepting', *šêmat* 'hearkening to', *mušamṣat* 'causing to find'; the same applies to the const. st. of the nominal stem فَعِل: *rab* (from *rabû* = *rabî-u*) etc. Even long vowels are completely dropped within verbs tertiæ י: observe *šurbû* fem. *šur-bûtu*, perm. 2. m. sing. *šurbâta*. For the passages where the above mentioned feminine forms are to be found see § 68, and notice the remarks in § 62 concerning points discussed in the present section.—Other, isolated, cases of the vowel being dropped in the *auslaut* are e. g. the suffix *š* (for *šu*, *ši*), and the permansive forms *kašdât(a)*, *kašdâk(u)*.

B. Consonants.

I. Consonantal Sounds.

§ 40. Assyrian has the following consonants: ', *b*, *g*, *d*, *z*, *ḫ*, *ṭ*, *k*, *l*, *m*, *n*, *s*, *p*, *ṣ*, *ḳ*, *r*, *š*, *t*.

§ 41. Assyrian lacks the two semi-vowels *u̯* and *i̯* and it is only from the inflexion of words that we can gather that they once existed in the language even as radical letters.

a) Verbs primæ ו uniformly appear in Assyrian as verbs primæ $א_1$, hence *ašâbu* 'sit', *âšibu* 'sitting', (')*aldû* 'they are born', *ušâšib* and *ušêšib* 'I caused to sit', cf. also *u'allid*; only the pret. of the Qal *ûšib* (i. e.

i̯ûšib, *i̯au̯šib*) and the pres. still betray the original *anlaut* (for details *v.* under verbs primæ ו, § 112). Hence also *âru* 'forest' (=وَعْر; for the orthography of the word *v.* § 14), *arḳânu* 'vegetables' (written *ia-ar-ḳa-nu*), *a'elu* (*a'ilu*) 'wild goat' (written *ia-e-le* plur. I R 28 col. I 20); for the sign *ia*=*a* see § 12 (whoever reads *iarḳânu*, *ia'elu* must assume them to be borrowed from Hebrew or Aramaic). For the ו of stems tertiæ ו, which is treated quite like the י of stems tertiæ י, and, like י, is no longer retained as an independent consonant, *v.* the close of this §. For verbs med. ו, as well as for those med. י *v.* § 115.

b) In Assyrian the Semitic semi-vowel *i̯* is always dropped in the *anlaut* before *i*, *u*, *û*, *î* and *ê*: thus we have *immu* 'day', *upaṭṭira* 'he cleft, opened', *ûrid* 'he went down', *ûmu* 'day', *îši* 'he had', *êkul* 'he ate' not *i̯immu*, *i̯upaṭṭira*, *i̯ûrid*, *i̯ûmu*, *i̯îši* (=*i̯ai̯ši*) *i̯êkul* (from *i̯âkul*). Assyrian had also a dislike to the phonetic combination *i̯a*. It was employed, it is true, to express יַ and יָ of foreign, especially Hebrew, names, e. g. *Ia-û-du* יְהוּד, *Ia-ap-pu-u* יָפוֹ, *Ia-u* יָהוּ; in such foreign words, however, the initial *i̯* was only pronounced with difficulty, and was, by preference, entirely suppressed (cf. *Ialmân* and *Almân*, *Iatnâna* and *Atnâna* 'Cyprus', always supposing that these words really have *i̯* for their initial vowel). In the same way the pronunciation of *ia-a-me* 'of the sea' (II R 41, 45 a. 43, 59 a) was not *i̯ami* but *âmi* (*v.* § 14); still less did they pronounce *i̯âši* instead of *âši* (*v.* §§ 14, 55 b). Initial *i̯a* appears in Assyrian sometimes as *a*, e. g. *anaḳâti* 'she-camels' (III R 9, 57. st. ינק), sometimes as *i*—the latter, perhaps, in *išû* 'be, have', (but cf. § 112) and in *idu* 'hand, side'? (the orthography of the form *ia-du* I R 7 No. F, 8, by the way, it to be explained acc. to Assurn. II 60). *i̯a* always appears as *i* in the prefix of the 3. pers. m. sing. and m. and f. plur. of the Qal, Ifteal, and Nifal: *ikšud* 'he captured' (=*i̯akšud*), *illik* 'he went' (=*i̯a'lik*), *iktašad* (=*i̯aktašad*) etc. The only exception is the pret. Qal of verbs primæ ו, י and, excluding אלך$_2$, primæ א, cf. the beginning of *a* and *b* of the present section. *i̯*, in Assyrian, is likewise dropped between two vowels: hence the pronom. suff. of the 1. pers. sing.—only, of course, where it would be *i̯a* and not *i*—after *â*, *û*, *ê* and *a* always appears as *a*: *še-pa-a-a* 'my feet', doubtless pronounced *šêpâ* (§ 13), *abû-u-a* 'my father' (Beh. 1), *ga-tu-u-a* 'my hands', *maḫ-re-e-a* 'before me' (also written *maḫ-re-ia*—read *maḫ-re-a* § 12—), *bi-e-le-e-a* 'my lords', *ap-la-a(-a)* i. e. *aplâ* 'my son'. Judging from these facts, to assume Assyrian forms like *a-i̯a-lu*, *da-i̯a-nu* is open to very grave suspicion (cf. § 13). In the same way the above mentioned suffix appears as *a* after a short *i*: *šarru-ti-a*, *ina ta-a-a-ar-ti-a* 'on my return' (Shams. III 37) i. e. *šarrûti'a*, *târti'a*; on orthographical forms like *šarru-ti-ia v.* § 12. This omission of *i̯* between two vowels must be assumed for the original ending in *âi̯* of the so-called adjectiva relationis, when a case-sign is appended: *Aššûrû* 'the Assyrian' (=*Aššûrâi̯u*). When no case-sign is attached, the ending referred to is probably in *â* (*v.* § 13): *Ṣîdûnâ* 'the Sidonian'; the original semi-vowel, however, is still distinctly recognizable in the two feminine endings, *â-i-tu*, where it appears as a vowel, and *îtu*, where *âi̯* or *âi* is reduced to a monophthong. Loss of the semi-vowel *i̯* seems also to occur in the pronoun *â'u*, *â'umma*, *â'amma* (*v.* § 59). It is, however, especially the *i̯* of stems tertiæ י that, has completely lost its independence in Assyrian. After a long vowel it is dropped, cf. inf. *banû*= *banâi̯-u̯*, *amâtu*, *kinâtu*, *rubû* (=*rubâi̯-u*). With a preceding *a* the semivowel *i̯* unites to form *ai̯*, *ai*, *ê* or *î* (cf. *bikîtu*), which is frequently shortened to *e* or *i* when standing at the end of a word (*matê*, *mati* 'when?', *adî* and *adi* 'until', *ibni*) and afterwards dropped altogether (*mat* 'when', *elî*, *eli*, *el* 'upon'), *v.* § 39; with a preceding *i*, it becomes *î* (cf. *rabîtu*, part. fem. *pâdîtu*), which is also shortened, when standing at the end of a word (*rabi* 'he is great'), and afterwards dropped altogether (*ban-at*, *rab*), *v. ibid.* In forms like *zimu*, *bûnu*=*zimịu*, *bunịu* the semi-vowel has assimilated itself to the preceding consonant, whereon the doubling has been compensated for by the vowel being lengthened (cf. other cases of this sort in §§ 33 and 53). All that has been said concerning the *ị* of stems tertiæ י holds good *mutatis mutandis* for the ו of stems tertiæ ו: hence inf. *manû*, *minûtu* 'number', *imnu* 'he numbered', *mînu* 'number'.

§ 42. In the aspirate or breath, ' or א, are united the Hebr. א, ה, $ח_1$ (i. e. ح), $ע_1$ (ع) and $ע_2$ (غ); there was certainly no difference in the pronunciation of the initial *a* of *aḫu* 'brother', *alâku* 'go', *alîbu* 'sweet milk', *adi* 'unto', and *aribu* 'raven'. From an etymological point of view, however, these various ' must be clearly distinguished according to their five-fold source; this is all the more necessary from the fact that there are unmistakable indications, in the morphology of Assyrian, of the original diversity of '. Thus, in most cases at least, *â*, *tâ*, *a* etc., when $א_{4.5}$, corresponding to a Semitic ע (ع, غ), immediately precedes, follows or quiesces in one of them, have a far greater tendency to pass into *ê* and *e* than when in the neighbourhood of $א_1$ (Hebr. א): thus we have *âkilu*, but *êpišu*, *êribu*, *râ'imu*, but *rê'û* (*v.* § 32, β); *tâkul*, *âkul*, but *têpuš*, *êpuš*, *têrub*, *êrub* (§ 32 γ); *ušâkil*, *âkul*, but (usually at least) *ušêbir*, *ušêrib* (§ 32, β); *ma'âdu* 'be many' (also *râmu* 'love'), but *bêlu* 'rule'; *akul* 'eat', but *ebir*, *erub* (§ 34, γ); *innamir* 'he was seen', but *innemid* 'he was placed'. Even when at a greater distance, $א_{4.5}$, as compared with $א_1$, makes its influence felt in Assyrian morphology in favour of the change of *a* and *â* to *e* and *ê*; thus we find *akâlu*, but *epêšu*, *erêbu* (§ 32, γ, p. 83), *maṣû* 'find', but *šemû* 'hear' (p. 84); *nâšû* 'carrying', but *šêmû* 'hearing' (§ 32, β). Cf. further *nitámar*, but *nitépuš*; *attábi* 'I named', but *attéme* 'I heard'. The conjugation of the verb *alâku* 'go', deviating as it does from that both of verbs primæ $א_1$ and of verbs primæ $א_{4.5}$, would be inexplicable were there contained in it an א, radically different from those just mentioned.—Assyrian *ḫ* in the great majority of cases corresponds to the Arabic خ ($ח_2$), e. g. *aḫu* 'brother' *ḫaṭû* 'to sin', while ح ($ח_1$), as already remarked, has been, in most cases, reduced to א, e. g. *emu* 'father-in-law', *šêru* 'morning', *leḳû* (*liḳû*) 'take'.

With regard to the pronunciation of the explosives *b*, *g*, *d*; *p*, *k*, *t*; *ḳ*, *ṭ*, we would offer the following remarks, keeping in mind what has been already said in § 19. The Babylonians were accustomed to pronounce *ḳ* quite like *g*: they pronounced and wrote *ga-ga-du* 'head', *ga-ga-ru* 'ground', *ga-tu* 'hand', *ga-* § 43.

ar-du 'strong', *i-ga-ab-bi* 'he speaks', while the Assyrians spoke and wrote *ḳaḳḳadu*, *ḳaḳḳaru*, *ḳâtu*, *ḳardu*, *iḳabbi*. Examples of similar orthography are met with in Assyrian vocabularies and so-called 'bilingual texts', since these go back, in most cases, to Babylonian originals. Moreover, from the point of view of the physiology of sound, *g* and *ḳ*, as is well known, are so nearly related, that one cannot be suprised at meeting even in original Assyrian texts—those, for example, of Tiglathpileser I and Sargon—the mode of pronouncing and writing the *ḳ* just referred to: *gurû-nâti*, *ugarrin* from the st. קרן, etc.—Recently the question has been raised by Haupt, whether or not in Assyrian, as in Hebrew and Aramaic, the בגדכפת between two vowels were pronounced as spirants. Haupt answers the question in the affirmative. He appeals, *inter alia*, to the Babylonian reproduction of the name Artaxerxes by *Artakšatsu*, and the relation of the latter to the Hebr. אַרְתַּחְשַׁשְׂתְּא; also to the equations Ταυθέ (Damascius) = *Tâm(a)tu*, *Tâv(a)tu*, Βῆλθις (Hesychius) = *bêl(a)tî*, Σαοςδούχινος (Berossos) = *Šavaš-šum-ukîn* (the reproduction of the names of the king *Šarrukîn* and of the god *Nêr(u)gal* by the Hebr. סַרְגוֹן, נֵרְגַל seems less convincing, although it is now regarded as most probable that the pronunciation of the above six consonants as spirants in Hebrew dates from an early period). Haupt further refers to the fact that the historical orthography of words containing one or more of the בגדכפת appears now and again to be departed from in favour of the every-day pronunciation: thus (acc. to Pinches) in V R 14, 10 d Assyr. *na-ba-su* interchanges with the Babyl. *na-ba-ti*,—the *s* thus appearing to represent ת̄—and, in particular, the fem. *ma'attu* 'much' (=*ma'adtu*) is, in Assurbanipal, repeatedly written *ma'assu*: cf. *ṭâbtu ma'assu* 'much good' (Assurb. Sm. 170, 93); *dîkta ma'assu adûk* 'many did I kill' (ibid. 291, m), interchanging with *dîkta ma'attu adûk* (V R 7, 115); *itti tirḫati ma'assi* 'with much dowry' (V R 2, 71), interchanging with *itti nudunnê ma'adi* (ibid. 78). These examples, for which it is difficult to find another explanation than that just given, really afford material for reflexion in regard to this important question of the בגדכפת. The frequently observed interchange of *g* and *ḫ* in ideograms and glosses, as we find it in the ideographic system of writing—cf. among others the quite usual form *laḫ-ga*=*laḫa*—might also, from the anti-Sumerian standpoint, be brought forward in favour of pronouncing *g* as a spirant.

The labial nasal *m* was, in general, pronounced as in Hebrew, especially at the beginning of a word, cf. *Mar(u)duk* מְרֹדַךְ, Μολοβόβαρ (Hesych.) = *mulu-* § 44.

bab(b)ar, etc. In loan-words from the younger Babylonian and in foreign words learned through that medium, *m* after a vowel, in the middle and end of words, is repeatedly given by the Hebr. or Aram. ו: cf. *Araḫšâmna* מַרְחֶשְׁוָן, *Kis(i)lîmu* כִּסְלֵו, *Si-ma-nu* סִיוָן, *Amêl-Marduk* אֱוִילמְרֹדַךְ ('Αμιλμαρούδοκος, Berossos), *zîmu* 'brightness' זִיו, *argamânu* 'red purple' Aram. אַרְגְוָן (Hebr. אַרְגָּמָן). The above is confirmed by the glosses of Hesychius, according to which the sun was called among the Babylonians σαώς (=*Šamaš*, *Šavaš*; cf. also Σαοςδούχινος), the world σαύη (*v.* § 29), as well as by Damascius' rendering of *Tâmtu* and of *Damkina*, the wife of Ea, by Ταυθέ and Δαύκη. From these facts, taken in connexion with the Babylonian and Hebrew rendering of Persian words like *Dârayavaush* by *Dâriâmuš* i. e. דָּרְיָוֶשׁ, it is quite evident that the Babylonians in later times pronounced the labial nasal *m* as the labial spirant *v*. That *m*, however, at a much earlier period, both in Babylonian and Assyrian, was in many cases pronounced as *v*, in the *inlaut* at least, is proved by the Assyrian transliteration of foreign *v* and Semitic *u̯* in names like *Jâmanu*=יָוָן 'Ionia', *Arma-da* (in Tiglathpileser I, Assurnazirpal, Shalmaneser) alongside of *A-ru-a(d)-da*, *Ar-u-a-da*=אַרְוָד (cf. *Ḫa-u̯-ra-a-ni* 'Hauran'). Note also the Assyrian *Ḫal-man*= حَلَب (with the nunation), just as, *vice versâ*, *šurmînu* 'cypress' appears in Aramaic as שורבינא (alongside of שורוינא). We are led to the same result—namely, that even in the Assyrian period *m*, in the *inlaut*, was in many cases pronounced as *v* (not universally, however, cf. *Sulmân*=שַׁלְמַן in the name of Shalmaneser) —by the name of the planet Saturn, Hebr. כיון (Am. 5, 26), Arab. كَيْوَان in its relation to Assyr. *ka-a-a-ma-nu* (i. e. *kâmânu*, *kâvânu* § 13; acc. to Haupt we should read *ka'âvân*, from which we should have Hebr. כַּיְוָן like מְיָוֹת alongside of מְנָאוֹת).—For the complete omission of the *m*, after it has become *v*, *ꟻ*, see further § 49, a; see also the same section for an occasional *v* (*u̯*), a secondary development from an intervocalic א.—For the pronunciation of *m* as *n* before dentals and gutturals, as also for the rare interchange of *m* and *g*, see the same section. Finally for further treatment of *m* see § 52.—For the pronunciation of the dental nasal *n* as *m* before labials, see § 49, b. For *n* see also § 52.

For the liquids *l* and *r*, in so far as they have been developed from sibilants see § 51, 3.—We may further, in passing, call attention to the various ways in which a shewa-like vowel, with a leaning to syncope, is treated and written when following *r*, thus: *Aramu* and *Armu* 'Aram', but also *Arimu* and *Arumu*; *Arabu*, *Aribu*, *Arubu* and *Arbu* 'Arabian'; § 45.

ni-ri-bu, *ni-ru-bu* (Assurn. II 24) and *nirbu* 'pass'.— On *r* and *l* as the second radical in quadriliteral stems *v.* § 61.

§ 46. On the pronunciation of the two sibilants *z* and *ṣ* there is nothing to be said: it is the same as in Hebrew and, just as there are etymologically two ז's and three צ's in Hebrew, so there are two *z*'s and three *ṣ*'s in Assyrian. Cf. *irzu* 'cedar' אֶרֶז, أَرْز, ܐܪܙܐ (z_1), *uznu* 'ear' אֹזֶן أُذْن, ܐܕܢܐ (z_2); *ṣûbu* 'finger' אֶצְבַּע, أُصْبَع, ܨܒܥܐ ($ṣ_1$), *ṣupru* 'claw' צִפֹּרֶן, ظُفْر ܛܦܪܐ ($ṣ_2$), *erṣitu* 'earth' אֶרֶץ. أَرْض, ܐܪܥܐ, ($ṣ_3$). Of the two sibilants *s* and *š*, the former corresponds to the Hebrew ס; the latter, *sh*, is also etymologically of three kinds: *ša'âlu* 'ask' שָׁאַל, سَأَلَ, ܫܐܠ ($š_1$), *šûru* 'ox' שׁוֹר, ثَوْر, ܬܘܪܐ ($š_2$), *karšu* 'belly' כְּרֵשׂ, كِرْش, ܟܪܣܐ ($š_3$). In Babylonian both *s* and *š* never, we may say, ceased to preserve their original pronunciation. This is best shown by the names of the months, which the Hebrews borrowed from the Babylonians during the exile: *Tišrîtu* תִּשְׁרִי, *Araḫšâmna* מַרְחֶשְׁוָן, *Šabâṭu* שְׁבָט on the one hand, *Ni-sa-an-nu* נִיסָן, *Si-ma-nu* סִיוָן, *Kis*(*i*)-*limu* כִּסְלֵו on the other. Cf. further *Bêl-šar-uṣur* בֵּלְשַׁאצַּר (also *ištên* עַשְׁתֵּי) for the one sibilant, *Sippar* סְפַרְוַיִם, *Sinuballiṭ* סַנְבַלַּט for the other, as also the Babylonian names of the winds which have found their way into the Aramaic of the Babylonian

Gemara: *šûtu* 'South' שׁוּתָא and *šadû* 'East' שַׁדְיָא. (Also שִׁנְעָר, if = *Šumêr;* here belong further the Aramaic שֵׁיזֵב, שֵׁיצֵא, and perhaps the Hebrew-Aramaic אשׁף). In accordance with the above, the Babylonians render the *sh* of a foreign tongue, as we should expect, by *š: Kûšu* 'Ethiopia' like כּוּשׁ, *Dâri-âvuš* (דָּרְיָוֶשׁ), *Kûraš* (כּוֹרֶשׁ) = Pers. *Dârayavaush*, *K'ur'ush* etc.; a foreign *s*, on the other hand, is rendered by *s*, cf. Babyl. *Aspašina* and Pers. *Aspacanâ*, Babyl. *Uštaspa* and Pers. *V'ishtâspa* etc. בֵּלְטְשַׁאצַּר is no exception to the rule, for this name in Babylonian may have been equally well *Balâṭašu-uṣur* as *Balâṭsu-uṣur*; it seems, in any case, to be strongly influenced by the similarly pronounced בֵּלְשַׁאצַּר. A real exception, however, is a word which is repeatedly found in Nebuchadnezzar written *ḫursaniš* 'mountain-like', while 'mountain, mountain range' is, in its original form, *ḫuršu*. The exception has perhaps been caused by the coming together of two sibilants and the effort to obtain greater case of pronunciation by means of dissimilation. Compare, however, *usannû* (III R 43 col. III 21) instead and alongside of *ušannû* (1 Mich. II 14), אִסְתְּנָא 'North' = Babyl. *ištânu*, and a few others.

The two pairs *Šu'âlu* שְׁאוֹל and *Ištâr* עַשְׁתֹּרֶת have been intentionally disregarded, since their explanation as loan-words from Babylonian is both uncertain and improbable.—The name of the Old Babylonian king *Samsu-i-lu-na*, the son of Hammurabi, and that of the Old Assyrian king *Samsî-Rammân* (1 R 6 No. 1) render it probable that even in the earliest period the word for 'sun' fluctuated between *šamšu, šamsu* and *samsu.*

In Assyrian, on the other hand, *š* has given up, more and more, its pronunciation as *sh* and has gradually become identical with *s*. For Assyrian words and forms, it is true, the historical orthography was faithfully adhered to (although after *s* and *š* had become identical in pronunciation, they could not fail to get mixed up in writing, cf. *išḫup* 'he cast down' Tig. II 39, *išpunu* Shalm. Ob. 21, *našḫuru* 'a turning to' I R 35 No. 2, 7 for *isḫup*, *ispunu*, *nasḫuru*; also *askup* and *iškupu* Tig. VII 24. 22, and again *isruka* 'he gave' Assurn. II 26 for *išruk*, and many others) but the employment of the signs containing *š* was confined to genuine Assyrian words, while the *š* of foreign words was rendered simply by *s*, it being, of course, pronounced like that letter. An Assyrian *š*, on the other hand, naturally appears as a simple *s*, when reproduced by foreigners, since these heard only an *s*. As illustrations of the latter statement cf. *Tukultî-pal-ešara* תִּגְלַת־פִּלְאֶסֶר, *Šarrukîn* סַרְגוֹן, *Ašûr-aḫ-iddina* אֵסַרְחַדּוֹן, *šaknu*, 'viceroy' סְגָנִים pl.; of the former, יְרוּשָׁלַםִ *Ursalimmu*, שֹׁמְרוֹן *Sa-me-ri-na*, אַשְׁדּוֹד *Asdûdu*, הוֹשֵׁעַ *A-u-si-'a*, 'Ethiopia' כּוּשׁ *Kûsu, Šašank* Σέσωγχις *Susinku* and many others. In Hebr. רַב־שָׁקֵה (=Assyr. *rab šakê* 'chief officer') the שׁ may be due to a mistaken popular etymology. In the same way the rendering of *Aššur* by אַשּׁוּר is only an apparent exception, since the Hebrews' acquaintance with the name of the country must date from a period prior to the time when *š* was universally pronounced as *s*. Such a period may perhaps be found in the reigns of Tiglathpileser II and Sargon; the ס in the sadly disfigured name of king שַׁלְמַנְאֶסֶר (Assyr. *Šulmân-ašared*) is to be explained partly by dissimilation, partly by the influence exercised by the name תִּגְלַת־פִּלְאֶסֶר. In Assurbanipal's time the rule given above, that *š*, notwithstanding its being pronounced as *s*, must not be employed to render a foreign *s*, began to be set aside, and consequently we find in a few proper names like *Pu-ši-ru* 'Busiris', *Ḫininši* (חָנֵס), *Ši-ia-a-u-tu*, *Pi-ša-an-ḫu-ru*, *Ḫa-rsi-ia-e-šu*, in Assurbanipal's prism inscription an Egyptian *s* rendered by an Assyrian *š*, pronounced as *s*. Still the only correct rendering of a foreign *s* like that just given is found, for example, in the name of Sais, Egyptian *Sau*, *Sai* (with ס), Assyr. *Sa-a-a* (with ס). Phenomena such as these would be inconceivable, had the Assyrians, as some maintain, pronounced not only *š* as *s*, but also *s* as *š*. That the name of the moon-god in Assyro-Babylonian was *Sin* (with ס), not *Šin*, is a fact which nothing can alter; the rendering of the name *Sin-aḫê-erba* by סַנְחֵרִיב proves, accordingly, that the Assyr. *s*, like the Babyl. *s*, was never pronounced and never heard otherwise than as *s*. So long as no Assyrian word can be pointed out, the *s* (ס) of which is reproduced in a foreign tongue by *š* (שׁ), we must maintain that in the pronunciation of Assyrian *s* and *š*, we have to do, not with an interchange of sounds (*Lautverschiebung*), but simply with a 'onesided softening of the broad sibilant *sh* to *s*'— for which analogies are not wanting in the other languages of the Semitic group.

For the rendering of שׁ in Assyrian cf. on the one hand שְׂנִיר = *Sanîru* (III R 5 No. 6, 45), on the other דַּמֶּשֶׂק *Di-ma-aš-ḳi* (I R 35 No. 1, 15. 21). *Vice versâ* cf. תִּגְלַת פִּלְ(א)סֶר and especially כַּשְׂדִּים, the inhabitants of the land of *Kašdu*.

II. Phonetic Changes affecting the Consonants.

§ 47. The Breath. When ' closes a syllable, either (1) it quiesces in the vowel which precedes it, lengthening this vowel when it is short, e. g. *zi-i-bu* i. e. *zîbu* 'wolf'=*zi'bu, mûru* 'young animal, esp. foal',=*mu'ru* مُهْر, *nâdu* 'exalted'=*na'du, na'idu, nîkul* 'we ate', *šûḫuzu* 'cause to take', *nâmuru* (Inf. Nif.) 'be seen'= *na'muru*—for other examples of *a'*=*â* (and then=*ê*), and for ' at the end of a word (*Wortauslaut*) v. § 32 β and γ—, or (2) it is assimilated to the consonant which follows it: *allik* 'I went'=*a'lik*; orthographical varieties like *a-lik* are to be considered in the light of § 22. Nevertheless, instances are by no means rare in which the breath has been retained: cf. *mu'du* 'multitude', *bi'šu* and *bîšu* 'wicked', *bu'šânu* and *bûšânu* 'bad smell', *na'butu* 'flee', *ibâ'* 'he comes', etc.

When ' follows a syllable ending with a consonant, it is mostly assimilated to the consonant which precedes it, and should this doubling of the consonant be dispensed with, the preceding vowel is lengthened: *labbu* 'lion'=*lab'u*, *ḫiṭṭu* 'sin', *nîbu* 'number'=*nibbu*=*nib'u*, *zêru* 'seed'=*zâru*, *zarru*, *zar'u* (*v.* § 33); *innamir* 'he was seen', *innabit* 'he fled'=*in'amir*, *in'abit* (pret. Nif.). Nevertheless instances are found, especially in the conjugation of verbs primæ א$_{1.2}$, where the ' has been preserved: *iš'al*, *ir'ub* (cf. § 20), *im'id* 'he, it increased' alongside of *i-mi-du*, *lišam'ida* 'may he increase'.

Between two *a*-vowels, ' either maintains itself or is dropped, the result, in the latter case, being the contraction of the two vowels: *ma'adu* 'much', *la'abu* 'flame', *ša'âlu* 'ask' and *mâdu* 'much', *ma-du* i. e. *mâdu* 'be much' cf. also *râmu* 'love'. ' maintains itself, as a matter of course, in cases like *ri'âšu* 'vermin', *mu'âru*, *ba'ûltu* 'subjects'; but it does the same also in *na'id* 'he is exalted' and *râ'imu* 'loving', for example, so long as the *i* is not syncopated. Loss of ' and subsequent contraction seem to occur in *rûḳu* 'distant'=*ra'uḳu*, *rauḳu*. We should naturally expect the virtually doubled or sharpened ' to be particularly persistent, and the Piel forms of verbs mediæ א$_{1.2}$, such as *uma'ir*, *mu'uru*, *mula'iṭ*, confirm our expectations. It is hard, notwithstanding, to decide whether *bu'uru* 'catch, hunt', even in cases where it is written not *bu-'-u-ru* or *bu-'u-ru*, but *bu-u-ru*, is to be read as *bu'uru* or, giving up the ', as *bûru*, the reason being that alongside of *uma'irdni* 'he sent me' we also meet with forms like *u-ma-ra-an-ni* (V R 34 col. III 1). For the contraction of *i'dšaš* and similar forms to *iššaš* *v.* § 38, b. For the loss of ' in the *anlaut*, e. g. in *timâli* 'yesterday' *v.* § 39, and for the same in the *auslaut* in consequence of the shortening of the vowel, in which ' quiesces, e. g. *nâši*, *pêti* (form فاعِل from נשׂא$_1$, פתא$_3$) *v. ibid.*

§ 48. *b*, *d* and *t*. The labial *b* readily assimilates itself to the *m* of a following *ma*; the assimilation is esp. frequent in *êrumma* 'I entered and' instead and alongside of *êrub-ma*. Cf. also *u-ši-im-ma* 'he dwelt and' alongside of *u-šib-ma* (Senhb. V 4) and pres. *uš-šab-ma* (K. 4350 col. I 6. 9). No argument, however, may be drawn from these in favour of reading *b* as *v*, and *m* as *v* (as e. g. *êrumma*), in view of other cases of a consonant being assimilated to the *m* of the copula *ma*, as e. g. *liškumma*=*liškunma* (*v.* § 49, b).

Among the dentals, *t* of the Ifteal and Iftaal is assimilated to a foregoing *z* or *ṣ*: *iz-zak-kar* 'he speaks', *aṣṣabat* 'I, he siezed'; on orthographical varieties like *a-ṣa-bat*, *a-ṣab-ta* cf. § 22. For the assimilation of the same letter to a foregoing *š*, see § 51, 2.—Vowelless *d*, further, is assimilated to a following *t*, e. g. *ma-at-tu* fem. of *ma'adu* 'much'; also to a following *š*, when the latter is the third radical of a stem containing three consonants: *eššu* 'new' (=*edšu*, *edišu*), *šêššu* 'sixth' (=*šêdšu*, *šâd(i)šu*).—After *ḳ* the *t* of the reflexive stems becomes *ṭ*, e. g. *aḳṭérib* 'I approached', after *g* it becomes *d*, e. g. *agdamar* 'I complete'. Also after *m* and *n* it is frequently softened to *d*, e. g. *amdaḫiṣ* 'I fought', *umdašir* 'he quitted', *amdaḫar* 'I received', but compare with these *amtaḫar* (for *attaḫar* *v.* § 49, a) *imtalik* etc. The same change is presented by the *t* of the feminine after *m* and *n*: *tâmtu* and (always, it would seem, in ordinary pronunciation) *tâmdu* 'sea', *sinûndu* 'swallow' etc.

N a s a l s. *a*) *m*. Of the nasals, the labial nasal *m*, § 49. before an immediately following dental, passes into the dental *n* always, we are sure, in pronunciation, and in most cases in writing as well: cf. *mundaḫṣê* 'warriors'=*mumdaḫ(i)ṣê*, *ṣindu* 'yoke (of oxen), team' (Khors. 124, צמד), *ṣandû* (V R 35, 16)=*ṣamdû*, *nakamtu* and *nakantu* 'treasure', *ḫanṭu* 'swift, active' for *ḫamṭu* etc. Frequently also before a following *ṣ* or *š*: *unṣu* 'want' alongside of *umṣu*, *ḫanšâ* 'fifty', *i-ri-en-šu* 'he presented to him' (III R 43 col. I 13, ר$_3$אם); occasionally the *n*, which arises in this way from *m*, is afterwards assimilated to *š*: *šú-un-šu* 'his name', and then into *šuššu*, *ḫânšu* and *ḫâššu* 'fifth'. Cf. also *na(m)ziâti* (Assurn. II 67). This transition of *m* to *n* must be assumed as an intermediate stage in *at(t)aḫar* 'I received' (Assurn. II 102. Shalm. Ob. 120). *m* also passes into an *n* before *ḳ*: hence *dumḳu* and *dunḳu* 'favour', *emḳu* and *enḳu* 'wise'; cf. also *iḳḳut* =*imḳut*.

m, when pronounced as *v*, seems to have been completely dropped in the younger Babylonian texts whenever it occurs in the middle of a word (*inlaut*) between two vowels: thus we find the form *ušalmâ*, *ušalvâ* 'I, he caused to hem in' written *u-ša-al-va-am* and *u-ša-al-am* (V R 34 col. I 34. 26); cf. also *u-šat-vi-iḫ* and *u-šat-iḫ* 'he caused to sieze' (V R 65, 5b, st. *tamâḫu*), *šur-i-ni* 'cypress' (2. 4b) in place of the usual *šurmêni*, *šurmîni* (intermediate form *šurvîni*, *šurƒîni*), *na-'i-ri* 'panther' (V R 46, 43b) for *namiri*, and a few other forms. Observe also *Du'ûzu*, *Dûzu* (=*Dûvûzu*,

Davvûzu?) in its relation to תַּמּוּז (and *zu-u'-ri-šu* 'his body' III R 43 col. IV 16 for *zu-um-ri-šu* 1 Mich. IV 6). When, on the other hand, a *v* is found where the etymology of the word does not lead us to expect it, as e. g. in *u-ḳa-va-an-ni* 'he waited for me' (V R 65, 27a) alongside of *u-ga-a-an-ni* (V R 63, 28a) i. e. *uḳâ'anni*, and especially in *ḫâmiru*, *ḫâviru* 'wooer, bridegroom, husband' (cf. e. g. *ḫa-me-ir* IV R 27, 2a, *ḫa-mir* Descent rev. 47) in place and alongside of *ḫâ'iru* (st. חִיר 'see, choose', as Haupt rightly assumes, *v.* V R 50, 60a), in this case Haupt regards the *v* as a secondary development from the intervening spiritus lenis. Or was it the case that the signs *ma*, *mi*, *mir* (*va*, *vi*, *vir*) etc. were simply employed for *'a*, *'i*, *'ir*, just as the sign *mur* (*vur*, § 9 No. 188), for example, was on occasion used for *ur*? This would, to a certain extent, be a parallel to the use of *i-a* for *a*.

In the Babylonian writing an interchange has been observed between *m* and *g*, on which scant light has yet been thrown. Thus *ḫuršam* 'mountain range', for example, was ideographically rendered by *ḫur-šag*, and, *vice versâ*, *ḫalâḳu* (*ḫalâgu*) 'perish' by *ḫa-lam-ma* (Haupt, ASKT 181, XII), *šaḫluḳtu* 'destruction' by *ša-ḫa-lam-ma* (see for the latter ideogram III R 60, 71, 65, 4. 22b). The name שִׁנְעָר, also, whose identity with *Šumêr* still remains probable, at least, seems to point to the conclusion that the *Semitic* Babylonians, in certain cases, pronounced *m* as *ng* or — without the nasal tone — as *g*: in writing they kept to the historical orthography *Šumêr*, but the Hebrews heard *Šungêr*.

b) *n*. The dental nasal *n*, when it is vowelless, readily assimilates itself to the immediately following consonant. Such is always the case with the *n* of the Nifal and Ittafal, e. g. *iššakin* and *ittaškan* 'it was made'; and almost always with the *n* of verbs primæ נ, hence *iššuk* 'he bit', *iššû* 'they took', *attabi* 'I named', *madattu, mandattu*=*mandantu* 'tribute' (in the Shafel we also find *ušanṣir* 'I set a watch', *ušanbiṭ* 'I made to shine'; but cf. *im-bi* 'he spread abroad' on the one hand, *ušašši* 'he caused to carry' on the other). As third radical, *n* is assimilated in *mandattu, libittu* 'brick', *šukuttu* 'rubbish, stuff'. From other cases of the assimilation of *n* we would single out the following: *lil-bi-im-ma* 'may he cast down' (viz. his countenance)=*lilbin-ma* (V R 56, 55), *liš-kum-ma* 'may she do and'=*liškunma* (III R 43 col. IV 17. 1 Mich. IV 7), but *al-bi-in-ma* (V R 66 col. I 11), *az-nun-ma* (V R 62 No. 1, 13). The converse, viz. progressive assimilation, is illustrated by the name of the moon-god *Nannaru*=*Nanmaru* (Haupt). *Ar rê'î*=*an rê'î* 'to the shepherd' is read in Pinches' *Texts* p. 15 No. 4, 9. Assimilation of *n* after a long vowel is found in *ummâtu*=*ummântu*, fem. of *ummânu* 'army', *ištâtu*=*ištântu*, fem. of *ištân, ištên* 'one' and a few others.

Before *b*, *n* passes into *m* in all cases in pronunciation and in many cases in writing as well: cf.

however *inbu* 'fruit', but *imbûbu* 'flute' (st. נבב). The same change takes place before *k*: *šumkuru* 'estrange' and 'make keen' (the glance, *v. E. M.* II, 339, l. 6), *ušamkir* (st. נכר), and even before dentals and nasals (*v.* § 52). It is to be carefully noted, however, that the Assyrian script has not in all cases developed *two* signs for compound syllables ending in *m* and *n* (e. g. *dam* and *dan*) but has in very many cases been content with a single sign (*v.* § 9 Nos. 148. 206 and cf. 138; No. 182, also, has the two values *rim* and *rin*, No. 196 *ban* and *bam*; special signs for *ḫan* (in addition to that for *ḫam*), *lan, nan, ran, šan*, *tun* (*v.* p. 138), *mam, mim* etc., not met with as yet, in all probability never existed)—For this reason, we need have no scruples in reading *šum, šam* etc. as *šun, šan.*

In the imperative Qal of verbs primæ נ, *n* is merged in the spiritus lenis, hence *uṣur* 'protect', *iši* 'lift up', *idin* 'give thou'; also in the infins. of the Ifteal *itpuṣu* (=*nitpuṣu*), *itanbuṭu*, *itanpuḫu* (=*nitábuṭu, nitápuḫu*) and Iftaal (?): *itappuṣu*; the same applies to the characteristic (Nifal) *n* in the infinitives of the Ittafal (Intafal): *itaplusu* 'see' (=*nitaplusu*), *itaktumu* 'faint' (=*nitaktumu*), etc.

For the employment of *m* and *n* as substitutes for a doubled consonant, or one sharpened by the tone, see § 52.

§ 50. Liquids. For the interchange of *r* and *l*, when both go back to an original sibilant, *v.* § 51. Assimilation of *r* to the following consonant is nowhere found: for this, if for no other, reason *ḫaṭṭu* 'staff', *annabu* 'hare' cannot be derived from older forms such as *ḫarṭu, arnabu.* That words like *ḳaḳḳaru* 'the ground' are no proof of the assimilation of *r* is shown in § 61, 1 (p. 144).

§ 51. Sibilants. 1) When immediately preceded by a vowelless dental or sibilant, the *š* of the pronominal suffixes is always changed to *s*, hence *mât-su* 'his country' (contrasted with *mâta-šu*), *aṣ-bat-su*; thereon the dental is frequently, the sibilant always, assimilated to the *s*, after which both dental and sibilant, it would seem, are entirely dropped in writing (for the accent *v.* § 53, *a*): hence *šal-la-su-nu* 'their spoil' (Khors. 47) from and alongside of *šal-lat-su-nu* (Khors. 48), *ḳaḳ-ḳa-su* 'his head' (Esarh. I 18), *ḳa-a-su* 'his hand' (=*ḳâssu*, *ḳâtsu*, *ḳât-šu*), *karassu* 'his body' (from *karšu*), *murussu* 'his sickness' (*murṣu*), *izussu* 'he parted it' (=*izûz-šu*), *u-šak-ni*(*-is*)*-su-nu-ti* 'I subdued them' (כנשׁ), *u-lab-bi-su-nu-ti* 'I clothed them, *lâ uš-ḫar-ma-si* 'he shall not destroy it, (the palace)' (I R 27 No. 2, 39 חרמט). Exceptions like *ap-pa-lis-šu* (Assurb. Sm. 290, 55), *ar-ku-us-šu* (V R 8, 12) or *bi-rit-šu-nu* (II R 65 No. 1 obv. 3a) are very rare, and in Assyr. texts may be explained by the pronunciation which we find in later times of *š* as *s*, so that they are quite as reprehensible as the rendering in Assurbanipal of a foreign *s* by *š*, (*v*. § 46 p. 109). Compare, however, in Babylonian *uṣṣabbit-šunûtu* (Beh. 87), *ḳîšât-šunu* 'their presents' (V R 33 col. V 46).

2) The radical letter *š*, which precedes the *t* of the reflexive forms Ifteal and Iftaal, and also the *š* of the causative form which precedes the *t* of the Ishtafal are able to maintain themselves in very many cases (apart from the change to *l*): *aštakan* (*altakan*), *uštêbila* etc. There is, however, a marked tendency on the part of this *št*, especially in the language of everyday life, to pass into *ss* or *s*: hence in both Babylonian and Assyrian letters the frequent forms *assapar*, *asapra* 'I sent', *isaparûni* 'they sent', *ussîbila* 'I sent for'; cf. *usamriṣ* (III R 4 No. 4, 41). Among the longer historical texts, the only one that shows a special fondness for these forms is the great inscription of Assurnazirpal, which is otherwise remarkable for its peculiarities (because reflecting the language of the people?): *asakan* 'I made' (Assurn. III 2 and often), *asarap* 'I burned' (II 21) etc., etc.

3) Before an immediately following dental, Assyrian sibilants very frequently become *l* (cf. *vilta* in certain Italian dialects, e. g. that of Pisa, alongside

of *vista*), hence *šêlalti* 'three', *ḫamilti* 'five', *rapaltu*=*rapaštu*, fem. of *rapšu, maltîtu* 'drink' from and alongside of *maštîtu, alṭur* 'I wrote' (Assurn. I 69) from and alongside of *ašṭur* (Esarh. III 48), *altanan* 'I fought' (Tig. I 55. III 77, שׁנן), *manzalti* 'stand, position' (V R 2, 43), *eldu* and *eṣ(a)du* 'harvest'; *tultêšera*=*tuštêšera* 'thou governest' (IV R 67, 12b). The same change occurs when two different sibilants come together: *ulziz* 'I set up' from and alongside of *ušziz* (=*ušêziz*), *alsi* 'I spoke, called'=*ašsi*. From *iltânu* 'North' in the Assyr. vocabulary II R 29, 2h, contrasted with the talmudic אִסְתְּנָא (Babyl. *ištânu*), from the Babyl. *kuštâru* 'tent' (V R 35, 29), in Assyr. always *kultâru*, and especially from the name for Chaldaea, hitherto found only in Assyr. texts, viz. *Kaldu* contrasted with the Hebr. כַּשְׂדִּים, which presupposes the Babyl. *Kašdu*, we might be tempted to conclude that this phonetic interchange of *š* and *l* was peculiarly Assyrian; such, however, is not the case, for forms exhibiting this particular change occur in the later Babylonian period at least, e. g. in the texts of Nebuchadnezzar. It is long since it was inferred from the Babylonian *Uraštu*, Assyr. *Urarṭu* (אֲרָרַט) that an *r* formed an intermediate stage between *š* and *l*; since then other examples of this sort have been found, especially by Pinches: thus even in the same (Neo-Babylonian) text IV R 15 we find *išdudu* (l. 5) alongside of *irdudû* (l. 10), an Assyr. duplicate having in both passages *išdudû*. Cf. the name of the plant *maš-ta-kal* (?), *mar-ta-kal* and *mal-ta-kal*.

As a substitute for the doubling of a consonant, characteristic of the stem or of the inflexion of a word, as well as for the sharpening of a consonant occasioned by the tone, a nasal sound is often given to the vowel preceding the consonant in question: *ṣumbu* 'freight waggon, cart'=*ṣubbu*; *numbû* 'scream, howl'=*nubbû*, *ḫambaḳûḳu* (=*ḫabbaḳûḳu*), *Amḳarrûna* 'Ekron' (עֶקְרוֹן); *inamdin*, *inambi*, *ittanamzaz*, *ittanamdi* (all written with *nam*, for which comp. p. 117) from and alongside of *inddin*, *indbi*, *ittanázaz*, *ittanádi*; *ittanbiṭ* and *ittanánbiṭ* (I 3) 'he shone' (=*ittábiṭ*, *ittanábiṭ*), inf. *itanbuṭu* (=*nitábuṭu*), *etanamdarû* (I 3) 'they were afraid' (=*ittanáddarû* or *etanáddarû*); *innamdarû*, *innandarû* (IV 1) 'they rage', *ittanamdar* alongside of *ittanáddar* (IV 3) 'it rages'; *iṣṣanundu* (=*iṣṣanúddu*), *aštamdiḫ*, inf. *šitamduḫu* (=*aštádiḫ*, *šitáduḫu*). For the duplicate forms *nâduru*, *nâḫuzu* and *nanduru*, *nanḫuzu*, for *ittananmar* 'it is found' (IV 3 =*ittanâmar*, *ittaná'mar*) and other cases consult § 11. There is no instance of the doubling being resolved by means of *r*. § 52.

Another substitute for the doubling of a consonant is the lengthening of the preceding vowel: note as examples *ṣûbu* 'cart' (=*ṣubbu*) and the cases mentioned in §§ 33 and 41, b, *zêru* 'seed' (=*zâru*, *zarru*), *zîmu* (=*zimmu*, *zimiu*) etc. (*ušâziz*, *ušêziz* § 101 may also come in here as being=*ušazziz*, *ušanziz*); for a similar case of compensation for the sharpening of a consonant cf. the forms with enclitic *ma* mentioned in § 53, d.

§ 53. By way of appendix we may here add a few remarks as to the place of the tone in Assyrian words. *a*) There can scarcely be any doubt that in words like *ḳárdu*, *šárratu*, *epússu* ('ei feci'), *mušákšid*, *mušákšidu*, *uttákkar*, *uštáklil*, *tušaḫḫássi*, and in those like *abû́bu*, *nakrû́ti*, *imḗrê*, *ikšudû́ni*, *narkabấti*, *idûkû́ni*, *ušamsikû́ni*, *ikšudsunû́ti* the position of the principal tone or stress is really as indicated above. Forms like *ulabbissu* 'I clothed him' (=*ulabbiš-šu*), even when written *u-lab-bi-su* must, according to the above, be accented *ulabbisu*, *ulabbissu*. The sharpening of the immediately following consonant, however, which never fails to accompany the accenting of a short vowel, and the fact already repeatedly referred to, that the Assyrian writing adapts itself to the everyday pronunciation are the causes of certain other phenomena. Thus as regards the present of the Qal, the fact that in the great majority of cases the second radical is written twice, as in *išaḳḳal*, *iballuṭ*, *inaddin*, *ilabbin*, *išemmû*, shows without a doubt that the characteristic *a*-vowel of these presents was accented.

The same is proved for the syllable *ta* of the verbal stem I 2, and for the syllable *na* of the verbal stem I 3, both in the preterite and in the present, by the extremely frequent forms which are written thus: *ištakkan*, *aštakkan*, *iltak(k)anu* (Assurn. I 30), *attaḳ(ḳ)i* 'I sacrificed' (Tig. VIII 10), *amdaḫ(ḫ)iṣ*, *mundaḫḫisê* 'warriors', *iktarrabû* 'they blessed', *iptallaḫû* 'they were afraid', *muttabbil* 'leading, ruling', *italluku* 'go to and fro', cf. *aštamdiḫ*, *ištamdaḫû* 'they drew' (§ 52);—*iḫtanabbata* 'plundered', *ištanappara* 'he sent', *imtanallû*, cf. *ittanamdi* (§ 52). The forms *aḳṭérib*, *iltéḳi* (§ 34, *a*) as alternatives of *aḳtarib* etc. render it also in a high degree probable that the syllable *ta* in I 2 was likewise accented. That in the present Nifal, further, the tone rested on the second syllable is shown by orthographical forms like *innaḳḳû* 'there are poured out', *innemmedu* (rel.) 'there is hidden', and especially *innamdarû*, *innamdû* 'they are founded' (V R 64, 27 b), cf. § 52. In the continuous transliteration of Assyrian words, forms with the consonant written twice should be given as in *išaḳḳal* or *išáḳal*, so that *išaḳal* might signify that the second radical was written only once.

b) When a consonant is uniformly written once, on the other hand, we may with certainty infer that the preceding short vowel is unaccented. Consequently, in the case of verbal and nominal forms like *iškulu* (rel.), *iškulû, iškulâ*; *ḫatanu* 'son-in-law', *labiru* 'old' etc., this much at least is certain that the tone did not rest on the middle syllable. That the tone, moreover, did not rest on the last syllable we know from the fact already mentioned in § 10 regarding the verbal forms, that the length of the verbal endings *î, û, â* is never expressly denoted in writing, when they are part of the last syllable of the word: even with verbs tertiæ י we find, though rarely, forms like *ib-nu* 'they built', an impossible orthography were the accentuation *ibnû́*. The same is proved with still greater certainty by the contraction of forms originally ending in *ê* and *î*, such as *išmê, išmî, ibnê, ibnî* to *išmĭ, ibnĭ* etc. We should therefore read: *ikšud, tákšud, tákšudî, ikšudû* etc.

c) Special attention must in future be paid to those cases in which the verbal forms now mentioned are nevertheless—in contrast to the course pursued in the overwhelming majority of cases—written with the third radical doubled. As against the supposition that these are simply cases of inaccurate and defective orthography (*v.* § 22) we have, in the first place, the circumstance that forms written in this way are, after all, not so rare as one might suppose, and, in the second place, the fact that, in some cases at least, the sentence accent is seen to be, without a doubt, the determining factor. I shall confine myself here to a few examples, in which the verbal forms in dispute are distinctly brought out by means of spaced type. 'An art, which among the kings, my fathers, none *îḫuzzu* had learned' (end of sentence). 'District and border *iškunnû* did they establish' (end of section II R 65 obv. col. I 23); 'such an one *iškunnû* they set up to bear rule over them' (end of sentence, ibid. col. II 32, supplement). 'Whirlwind and hurricane *iš́abbannû* (end of sent., Nimr. Ep. XI, 122)'; 'what I tell them, *ippuššâ* they do' (NR 24); '*ul illikkû* 'they have not come' (end of sent. K. 831 obv. 7); 'in the evening *ušaznan(n)û šamûtu kîbâti*' (Nimr. Ep. IX, 83); 'on the street *ittanamzazzû šu-nu* they tread' (IV R 2, 17b); *immalillû*, *ittanaḫlallû* (end of sent. IV R 15, 38, 40a). Examples are often found in the contract tablets: *ušzizzû* (Strass. II 13, 6); 'till the creditor *kaspa išallimmu* is paid in full' (Str. I. 118, 11), *inamdinnu* 'they must pay', and many others—all of them pausal forms. Also at the end of relative clauses: 'their landmarks which *ibṭillû* had been removed' (Khors. 136); 'where my father *ipḳiddušu* had appointed him' (Assurb. Sm. 46, 62); 'Auramazda who *iddinnu* hath created this earth (or these heavens etc.)', in D, 2f., for example; 'what I *êpuššu* have done here, and what I *êpuššu* in another land, all that I *êpuššu*' (E, 16—18); 'what I *êpuššu* and what my father *îpuššu*' (D, 14. 19. C, a, 11f. C, b, 21/23). Cf. also *iškunna* Assurn. III 110. This orthography is not unfrequently found in the second of two verbs joined by *ma*: 'Assurbanipal, on whom Nebo and Tasmet have bestowed (*išruḳûš*) great intelligence, *iḫuzzu ênu namirtum* hath received a clear-seeing eye' (often in the subscriptions to tablets); *ikbusûma ušaknišsû šêpûšun* 'they trod (them) down and made them submissive' (Esarh. IV 36); 'Sargon, who brought the king to his city of Assur and *Muski êmiddu apšânšu* (Lay. 33, 11). Cf. also I R 49 col. IV 6. Attention is even called to the position of the tone by lengthening the vowel in place of sharpening the immediately following consonant: cf. *u-ši-i-bu* K. 13 (IV R 52 Nr. 2) l. 6; and *ul-te-zi-i-bi*? (Assurb. Sm. 293, a c), also *bi-i-li* (IV R 5, 39b)? Of permansive forms the following demand a place here: 'Istar *išâta lit-bu-šat mêlammê na-ša-a-ta* (var. *našat*) was clad with fire, wore (a mantle of) radiance' (V R 9, 80) where *našâta* seems to be simply the equivalent of *našâta*. From the contract tablets cf. the phrase *ištên bu-ud šanî naši*, for which we find also *na-a-ši*, *na-aš-ši*, fem. *na-ša-a-ta*. In the same way is explained the phrase often met with in the subscriptions of tablets *šaṭirma ba-a-ri* (IV R 16, 67b).

d) The enclitic particle *ma*, including both the copula *ma* and the *ma* of emphasis, draws the tone to the syllable immediately preceding it; vowels originally long then re-appear, though often enough it is only to disappear once more in the sharpening of the *m* of *ma*: cf. on the one hand *ma-ti-e-ma*, *aḳ-ri-e-ma* st. קרא₁ (Sarg. Bull Inscr. 99), *ap-te-e-ma* (Senhb. I 27), *iš-me-e-ma* (often), *aš-me-e-ma* (V R 3, 127), *adḳêma*, *aḫrêma*, *aš-te-'-e-ma* (often), *ab-ri-e-ma* (Neb. Senk. II 3 and often), *u-maš-ši-i-ma* (Sarg. Cyl. 46), on the other hand *šanumma* 'some other one' (=*šanû-ma*), *îlamma* 'he came up and' (=*îlâ-ma*); vowels originally short remain, the tone, of course, causing at the same time the sharpening of the *m* of *ma*, cf. *amêlûtumma* (Nimr. Ep. XI, 182) *illikamma* 'he went and', *ikkisû-nimma* 'he refused and'; in some cases, however, the lengthening of the short vowel is substituted for the sharpening of the *m* (cf. § 52 note). Thus in *mi-tu-ti-i-ma* (IV R 67 No. 2, 60b), *i-ba-ru-(ú-)-ma* 'he went out and' (rel., Sarg. Cyl. 21), 'when that house *i-lab-bi-ru-(u-)ma* shall become old and', 'whoever *u-ma-a-ru-u-ma* (III R 43 col. I 32) will send a friend and', alongside of *u-ma-'-a-ru-ma*.—In many cases we may be in doubt as to whether the length of the vowel, preceding the enclitic *ma*, is to be explained by the first or by the second of the methods now exemplified. This applies, for instance, to the verbal suffix of the 3. pers. m. sing., which, united to *ma*, is often written *šumma* or *šûma*; cf. *liškunšumma* 'may he appoint unto him' (V R 56, 43); *ar-ši-šu-u-ma* (V R 3, 20), *tam-nu-šu-u-ma* (V R 3, 7), *liskipû-šu-u-ma* IV R 6, 68a. 63, 55a): does the original long vowel of *šû* make its appearance here? And how is it with *šarri eni-ia-a-ma* 'of my lord the king' (K. 823 obv. 5 etc.), *šumi-ia-a-ma* (also *šumi-a-ma*) 'of my name'? And how with *kalâma* 'all together' (declined *ka-la-mu,* gen. *ka-la-a-mi* Nimr. Ep. 1, 4)?

How far it may be safe to draw conclusions of a more general nature in regard to the position of the tone from orthographical forms like *ina bi-ri-in-ni* 'between us' (V R 1, 126), is a question which, on the one hand, it is difficult to decide, and which, on the other hand, it is better to reserve for the future (cf. § 74). In general, neither nominal nor verbal suffixes draw the accent of the word to the syllable immediately preceding them: *kin-na-aš-šu gabbi* 'his whole family' (IV R 52 No. 2, 8) like *ab-bi-e-šú* 'I addressed him' (V R 64 col. III 11) is evidently influenced by the sentence accent. It would be of special importance if we could infer from *nam-kur-ri-šu-nu* (e. g. Tig. III 3) contrasted with *na-am-ku-rum* (II R 47, 49d), that the stress could not, in Assyrian, fall upon the fifth syllable from the end of a word (e. g. *nâmkurišunu*) as is possible in Arabic, but that, in cases like these, the stress was laid upon the syllable nearer the end of the word.

MORPHOLOGY.

Merely mentioning in passing the only interjections as yet met with, viz. the exclamations of pain, *a-a* (doubtless=*â*) and *û'a*, we proceed at once to the pronominal stems, and to the pronouns developed therefrom. The former consist either of the vowels *â* and *û* simply, or of one of the consonants *t*, *n*, *k*, *g*, *š*, *l*, *m*, with a short or a long vowel, **The latter are to be learned from the paradigms A, 1—6;** §§ 55—60 are meant to be nothing more than observations supplementary to the paradigms. § 54.

A. The Pronoun.

1. Independent personal pronouns: *a*) To express the nominative: sing. 1. c. *anâku*.—2. m. *atta*; sometimes also used for the fem., e. g. *lu aššati atta* 'thou art not my wife' (V R 25, 10 b). The form *at-tam* (IV R 20 No. 3, 18) must be explained as *atta* with *ma* (*m*) added for emphasis.—2. f. On the form *at-ti-e* (IV R 57, 45—54 b) see top of p. 78. Plur. 1, c. § 55.

Notice the personal name *Ištu-Rammân-a-ni-nu* (Var. *ni-ni*) C[b] 233; *ni-i-ni* (IV R 53 No. 1, 40). 2. m. *at-tu-nu*, e. g. IV R 56, 47 a.—For the rare cases where *anâku* and *attunu* are used in place of the verbal suffix to express the dative (without special emphasis), see syntax § 135.

For *šû*, *šî*, *šunu* used as adjectives *v.* § 57, a.—*û* (no gender) 'he, it', with emphatic *ma* 'that very man or thing', e. g. *ina šatti û-ma* 'in that very year' (Senhb. Bav. 34) is very frequently used to indicate the repetition of one or more preceding words (note Neb. III 50 where *um-ma* is written). This meaning—corresponding to our 'ditto'—we also find in *šû*, *šûma*, especially in the vocabularies. Perhaps, too, in the oft recurring phrase *ina ûmê-šu-ma* 'on that very day', the *šu* is not the pronominal suff. but the expression should rather be read *ina ûmê šûma*, analogous to the above-mentioned *ina šatti ûma*. For the ideogram of *û* (*û-ma*), see the table of characters No. 268; for further details, see Dicty. No. 108.

b) To express the genitive and accusative. Sing. 1. c. On the reading of *ia-a-ši*, *a-a-ši* etc. as *âši*, *âti* (from *ịâši*, *ịâti* § 41, b) *v.* §§ 13 and 14; *ia-a-tu* written *ia-a-pi* (*v.* table of characters No 69) Assurb. Sm. 37, 9.—2. m. and f. are completely identical: *kâti*, *kâši*; in the 3 m. and f., also, no distinction of gender is implied in the final *ša*, *ši* of *šâša* and *šâši*, in contrast to *šâšu*—the masculine forms *kâša* and *âši* alone forbidding such a supposition. The fact is, as we learn from the forms of 1. c. plur. occurring in Bertin's list (*v.* p. 70), viz: *ni-ia-ti*, *ni-ia-šim*, *a-na ni-*

a-šim, that all these pronouns *âši*, *kâši* etc. are made up of the nominal suffixes and *ati*, *aši* (or *atu*, *ašu*) and *ata*, *âta* (*ăti*, *ăši* etc. or *âti*, *âši*? cf. *šu-a-tu* § 57, a). In the case of the 1. c. sing. this is another reason for putting aside *aiši* as an altogether impossible reading; in the 2 f. we have contraction from *ki-aši*, and in the 3 m. and f. contraction from *šu-aši* (*šu-ašu*) or *ša-aši*. The form *šu-a-šu* is still found e. g. Assurn. III 76 (*ana šu-a-šú* 'to him'). In the 2. and 3. pers. plur. the plural termination is appended to the singular forms.—To say that the pronouns above given serve to express the genitive and accusative is in general correct. As a matter of fact, in connexion with prepositions governing the genitive only these pronouns are used: cf. *ana âši* 'upon me' (lift up thine eyes, IV R 68, 29 b), *ana kâši* 'to thee' (fem., will he draw near), *ana šâšu*, *ana šâši* 'to him, to her' (he spake), *ana kâšunu* 'to you' (IV R 56, 46 a), *kîma ia-ti-ma* 'as I' (Tig. VIII 60), *kîma šâšunu* 'like them' (Khors. 96), *šanamma eli âši* 'another than I', *ela kâti* 'besides thee' (O goddess, there is no deity). In the same way, in such a connexion as: 'him (himself), his wife, etc. he carried off', or: 'her (herself) I took captive alive', we never find, in the accusative other than *šâšu*, *šâša*. Still we also find: *anâku u kâši* 'I and thou' (will do so and so, K. 3437 rev. 3), and when one of these pronouns is, for the sake of emphasis, placed before the verbal or nominal suffix, it naturally stands in the nominative, e. g. *šâšu êsiršu* 'him I shut in', prop. as for him, (nom. absol.) I shut him in (Senhb. III 20); *šâšu mašakšu aḳûṣ* 'as for him, I flayed him' (Khors. 35), *kâtu amâtka* 'thy command'. Other examples of this use of the pronouns in question will be found in the syntax §§ 119 and 135. For the rare cases—apart from *šulmu âši* 'my greeting'—in which these pronouns are used as a circumlocution for the nominal suffixes *v.* syntax § 119, and for the equally rare cases in which they are used in the same way for the verbal suffixes, where no sort of emphasis can be intended, *ibid.* § 135.

For the rare use of *šâšu* as adj. 'selfsame' (usually *šu'atu*) *v.* § 57, a.

c) In still another way do we find the nominal suffixes transformed into independent pronouns. *α*) Joined to *râmânu* (*râmênu*, *râmnu*) i. e. 'fear-compelling might' (st. $רא_1ם$), the nominal suffixes express the idea of 'self': *râmânî* 'I myself', *râmânka* 'thou thyself' etc. Cf. Khors. 77: *ina ḳât râmânišu napištašu uḳatti* 'with his own hand he took his life (committed suicide)'; in Beh. 17 we read: 'Cambyses *mîtûtu ra-man-ni-šu mîti* died by suicide'; *râmânkunu* 'you yourselves' (IV R 52, 23 a);—*šaknu ša râmêni'a* 'my own viceroy'

(Assurn. I 89);—*râmnu* e. g. Khors. 125. β) Joined to a t t u in the forms *attû'a* (1. sing.) *attûni* or *attûnu* (1. plur.; not to be confused with *attunu* 'ye'!) and *attûkunu* (2. m. plur.) they serve to emphasize the nominal suffixes, cf. *at-tu-ni ašâbani* 'o u r remaining' (V R 1, 122); for *at-tu-ku-nu v.* K. 312 l. 24. In the Achæmenian inscriptions, however, they are used simply as another way of expressing the nominal suffixes, the latter being even expressed, in some cases, over and above, see syntax § 119. In Beh. 18 we find *attûnu* with the signification of a possessive pronoun: 'from the days of our fathers the supreme power has been *at-tu-nu u ša zer-û-ni* ours and our family's'. γ) As a possessive pron.='thine' in expressions like 'heaven and earth are thine', e. g. IV R 29, 26 ff., we find *k u - u m - m u*, made up of the nominal suffix *ku* (a bye-form of *ka*, *v.* § 56) and the particle *ma* which appears in the case inflexion (cf. *kalâmu* gen. *kalâmi* and *mimmu, mimmû* § 58 end); for *mm* see § 53, d.

2. Suffixed personal pronouns. *a*) Nominal suffixes. For the way in which they are appended to the three cases of the sing. and to the various forms of the plural, and for the choice between the two forms *î* and *a* (=*ịa*, § 41 b) of the 1. c, sing., see § 74. For orthographical varieties like **§ 56.**

mu-te 'my husband' (*mu-ti-ma* var. *mu-te-ma* Nimr. Ep. 42, 9), see p. 78.—For *ka* of the 2 m. we also find *ku*; for which note especially the text IV R 46: *âl-ku* 'thy city' (l. 30 a), *bît-ku* 'thy house' (31 a), *bêlût-ku* 'thy glory' (28 a) and many others. For the change of *š* of the suffixes of the 3. pers. singular and plural into *s*, see § 51.—Plur. 1. c. Besides *ni* we also find *nu*, as in *attûnu* § 55, c, β and in proper names like *Šadûnu* (also *Šadûni*), *A-ḫu-nu* (also *A-ḫu-ni*). This suffix seems also to occur in the name of the Old Babylonian king *Samsu-i-lu-na*.—3. masc. The *m* of *bu-šá-šú-num* 'their (acc.) property' (Neb. VII 20) must be explained like that of *at-tam* (§ 55, a). An alternative form of *šunu* is *šunûti*; cf. *libba-šu-nu*(*-ti*) 'their heart' (V R 1, 120), [*eli-šu-*]*nu-u-te* 'over them' (Assurb. Sm. 35, 14), *balṭûsunûti*.—3. fem. Once we find *šinu*, viz: V R 66 col. II 19: *mandatti-ši-nu* 'their tribute' (countries are spoken of).

b) Verbal suffixes. For the way in which these are appended to the verbal forms—both to those ending in a consonant and those ending in a vowel—when the third radical of the verb is strong, as well as when it is weak, see § 118. The forms *iškulaššu*, *iptaššu* etc., which are found alongside of *iškulšu*, *iptišu* etc., call for a word of comment. *Iškulaššu*, for example, is not to be explained as if the simple pro-

nominal suffix *šu*,—and the same applies to *ši*, *ka* etc.
—were appended to the verbal form *išḳula*, which ends
in short *a*; for the verbal suffix does not draw the
tone to the last syllable: *tu-na-'-a-šu-uu* (V R 45
Col. II 52) might pass for such a form but never
išḳulaššu, *išḳulaššunu*. We should rather assume, in
the case of verbs tertiæ infirmæ, that forms like
iptašši are to be read *iptâ-ši* (=*ipti-a* + *ši*) according
to § 11. The analogy of verbs with a strong consonant as third radical, however, renders it practically certain that here also we have to do with the
stronger suffixes *aššu*, *ašši*, *akka*, which run parallel
with *šu*, *ši*, *ka*: *al-ḳa-šu-nu-'i-ti* 'I removed them' (Tig.
I 87) may be formed directly from *alḳâ*, but *iptašši*,
iptaššunûti certainly stand for *ipti-ašši*, *ipti-aššunûti*
(like *našanni* 'he drove me' perm. for *naši-anni* Neb.
III 19): we even find such forms as: *us-si-ṣi-aš-šu*
'I brought it out' (III R 4 No. 2, 7). What we have
just said does not exclude the possibility that in certain cases—as, for example, in verbal forms in a
relative clause — the *a* of *aššu*, *aššinâtu*, *annâši* may
at the same time represent the final *a* of the verb.
The verbal suffix of the 1. pers. plur. occurs only in
this stronger form: *annâši*; in the same way the suffix
of the 1. sing. is, without exception, *anni* after verbal
forms in the singular. Exceptions are found only

with verbal forms in the plur. (in *û*), e. g. Tig. VIII 30: *šalmiš littarrûni* 'may they lead me in safety'; V R 7, 105: 'the rule over whom the gods *iddinûni* had conferred on me'; Assurb. Sm. 11, 12: 'mighty forces *ušatlimûni* have they granted unto me'; Esarh. IV 41 (*ušâzizûni*). In passages like Assurb. Sm. 11 (cf. also 217, k) to refuse to recognize the suffix of the 1. pers. would result in a construction extremely harsh and forced, while to do so in the other cases is absolutely precluded by the context. *U-ṣal-la-a-ni* 'he implored me' (Esarh. III 7) stands for *uṣallânni*. The question as to the origin of the stronger suffixes *aššu*, *ašši*, *akka* (in certain cases *ikka*), *anni* (in certain cases *inni*), *aššunu*(*tu* or *ti*), *aššinâtu* (or *ti*) and *aššinîti*, *annâši* is to all appearance intimately connected with that as to the origin of the Hebrew suffixes ֶךָּ, ֶנִּי etc. Examples of the 3. and 2. pers. are: *ušêbilaššu* 'he made him bring', (V R 7, 44), *rîmûtu aš-ku-na-šu* (for *aškunaššu*) 'mercy he showed unto him' (end of sentence, Assurn. III 76), *lâ tanâšašši* 'break it not' (O Istar! Descent obv. 23), *iptašši* 'he opened to her' (ibid. l. 39), *a-da-na(k)-ka* 'I shall give to thee' (end of sentence IV R 68, 21 a. 58 c), *ši tu-ša-an-nak-ka* 'she gives thee to know' (Assurb. Sm. 125, 63); *rîmûtu aš-ku-na-(aš-)šu-nu* (end of a section, Assurn. III 56), *in-da-na-aš-šu-nu-tú* 'he gave them' (Beh. 96), 'what

I *a-ḳab-ba-aš-ši-na-a-tú* command them' (NR 24), *id-dan-na-aš-ši-ni-ti* 'he surrendered them, (viz: the countries) to me' (NR 21). No distinction can be detected, to all appearance, in the use of the weaker and stronger forms of the suffixes.

Addenda: Sing. 1. c. *Ašûr-še-zib-a-ni* (C[a] 28). *i-ki-pa-an-nim* 'he gave me up' (Neb. I 42), cf. *at-tam* § 55, a. After the 3. pers. fem. plur. we find *-inni*: *i-še-im-ma-'-in-ni* 'they obey me' (Beh. 7), 'the countries *ša ik-ki-ra-'-in-ni* which rebelled against me' (Beh. 40).—2. m. Contracted to *k*: *aḳ-ṭi-ba-ak* 'I have said to thee' (IV R 68, 39 c); *ku*: *liḳ-bi-ku* 'may he announce to thee' (IV R 66, 7. 8 a).—2. f. *li-bil-lak-ki* 'let him bring to thee' (IV R 65, 38 b).—3. m. On the change of the *š* of all the verbal suffixes of the 3. pers. into *s*, see § 51; for the long *û* of *šû* in forms like *liskipû-šu-u-ma*, § 53, d. The follg. are examples of the verbal suffix contracted to *š*: *u-šak-ni-šu-uš* 'they subdued him', *aḳ-bi-iš* (Neb. I 54), *u-še-ri-ba-aš* 'he made him enter' (V R 35, 17); *uš-mal-liš=ušmallišî*, viz. the palace (Senhb. Const. 86). *šu* is found strengthened by *m* (*ma*) in IV R 21, 30 b: *liḳ-ḳa-bi-šum* 'let it be told him'.—Plur. 1. c. *ikarrabannâši* 'he blesseth us' (Nimr. Ep. XI, 181), 'who *il-li-kan-na-ši* hath come to us' (Nimr. Ep. 60, 14); *iš-pur-an-na-a-šu* 'he hath sent to us' (K. 647 obv. 7).—2. m. *aḳ-bak-ku-nu-šu* 'I spake to you' (IV R 52, 27 b).—3. m. *du-ú-ku-šú-nu-ú-tu* 'kill them' (Beh. 48). *at-ta-nab-bal-šu-nu-ši* 'I offer to them' (V R 63, 22 a); note also II R 11, 25—28 b: *id-din-šú-nu-šim*, *i-na-din-šú-nu-ši* etc.—3 f. *ultêšib-ši-na-a-tú* NR 23. *iš-te-ni-'-e-ši-na-a-tim* 'he provided for them' (V R 35, 14). *aškun-ši-na-ši-im* (Hammur. Louvre II 6). The form *-ši-na* has as yet been found only with the particle *ni* appended enclitically: 'the countries *ša a-pi-lu-ši-na-ni* which I had conquered' (I R 27 No. 2, 23. Assurn. III 125. 133).

§ 57. Demonstrative Pronouns. *a*) *šu-a-tu* (*šu'atu*, *šu'âtu*, *šû'atu*?), a contracted form of which is *šâtu* cf. § 38, a. It occurs only in connexion with a substantive, after which it always stands, never before. A sufficient number of passages might be quoted in support of all the forms given in the paradigms. For the fem. of the sing. cf. Shalm. Obel. 50. III R 4 No. 1, 1. 2 and oft.: *ina šatti-ma ši-a-ti* 'in that same year'.—Plur. m. *âlâni šu-a-tum* also *šú-a-tum* or, as I would propose to read, *šu-a-tun* (*v.* § 49, b, p. 117) V R 56, 9. 11. In the same sense as *šu'atu* fem. *ši'ati*, plur. *šu'atunu* fem. *šâtina* we find *šû* fem. *šî*, plur. *šûnu*, and more frequently *šunûti*, fem. *šinâti*: cf. *âlu šú-u* and *šu-ú* 'said city' (Assurn. III 133), *âlu šú-ú* (var. *âlu* alone) 'this city' (V R 69, 21)—this explains the supposed suffix *šú* in Sarg. Bull Inscr. 91—, *ekallum ši-i* 'that palace' (Assurn. II 5); *mûrâni šu-nu* (*šú-nu*) 'said young lions' (Lay. 44, 16), *ṣâbê šu-nu-ti* 'those people' (Shalm. Ob. 154), *âlâni šu-nu-ti* 'those cities' (Assurb. Sm. 82, 7); as regards the fem., note how *eḳlê ša-ti-na* and *eḳlê ši-na-a-ti* change places in the two parallel passages III R 15 col. III 25 and Esarh. II 49. Very rarely, it would appear, was *šâšu* used for *šu'atu* (although they are at bottom identical, the one being = *šu* + *ašu*, the other *šu* + *atu*, see § 55, b), e. g. V R 64, 11 a: *eli âli u bîti ša-a-šú* 'against that city and that house'.

b) *annû*, from *an-ni-u*, cf. for example *an-ni-ú a-ḫi-ú* 'this other' (III R 54, 43 b), *ûmu an-ni-ú* (V R 54, 39 a), genly. *ina ûmi an-ni-i* 'to-day', cf. ܝܘܡܢܐ. It is always placed after its substantive, except in *an-na-a ḳa-bi-e* 'this speech' Nimr. Ep. 48, 178, III *an-nu-tú ṣâbê* 'these three people' (V R 54, 51 a). In *an-ni-a-am* (IV R 66, 30 a) we again meet with *ma*; so too in *šá-ma-mi an-nim* (*annêm*) 'of these heavens' (Neb. Bab. II 2). For the fem. sing. note *ištu ušmâni an-ni-te-ma* 'from that camping-ground' (Assurn. II 39 and oft.).—Plur. m. *an-nu-te* . . . *an-nu-te*, also *a-nu-te* 'some . . . others (. . . a third party)', *v.* Assurn. I 117. 90 f.

c) *ullû*, e. g. D, 20: 'what I have done and what my father did, *ul-lu-ú-um-ma* that may Auramazda protect'; D, 15: *tabbanûtu ullûtu* 'those buildings, works' (acc.). — Another contrast to *annû* 'this' is *ammu* in the phrase *ina padan* (? § 9 No. 261) or simply *padan*, also *padan*^{pl} *am-ma-(a-)te* 'on the other side' of a river (Tig. II 4. Assurn. III 1), opposed to *padan an-na-te* (var. *ti*) Assurn. III 49 f. (*padan am-ma-te*, var. *ti*).

d) *agâ* (in Assurbanipal and especially in the Achæmenian texts) is placed both before and after its substantive: e. g. *bît a-ga-a* 'this house', *a-ga-a šadu* 'this mountain', *ûmu a-ga-a* 'to-day', *šamê a-ga-a* 'this heaven' (acc.), *irṣitim a-ga-a-ta* 'this earth' (the fem. is always placed after). Plural forms (always put after the subst.): *ṣalmânu agannûtu* 'these portraits' (Beh. 106); *mâtâti a-ga-ni-e-tú* 'these countries' (Beh. 8. 9). In these forms of the plural *agâ* is clearly strengthened by *annû*, as in *agâšû* by *šû*. *agâšû* is always placed after a subst. or a proper name, e. g. *nikrûtu a-ga-šu-nu* 'these rebels' (Beh. 46. 65).

§ 58. The relative pronoun *ša* (originally *ša-a*, acc. of *šû*, *v.* II R 31 No. 2, 14 c. d, and oft., cf. Hebr. ־שֶׁ, ־שַׁ, origly. שָׁ) may also be used to express the genitive relation, e. g. *ina ṣilli ša Uramazda*. The original demonstrative signification still appears in such expressions as *ša bît ṣibitti* 'that (man) of the prison, the prisoner' (IV R 58, 32 a, and cf. V R 13, 8—10b), in which *ša* is used like the Arabic ذو.

The so-called pronomen relativum generale 'whosoever, whatsoever, all that, as much as, as many as' is expressed sometimes by the interrogative pronoun with or without *ša*, sometimes by the substantives *ma-la*, *mal* (doubtless=*mâla*) and *ammar* (always without *ša*, for which *v.* Syntax § 147), both of which originally signified 'fulness'. Cf. *man-nu ša itábalu* 'whoever shall take away' (*v.* Dict. p. 214), *man-nu atta šarru* 'thou, whoever thou art, that shalt be king' (Beh. 105), *ma-nu arkû* 'whosoever shall be in the future' (I R 35 No. 2, 12); *bêl mi-na-a ba-ši-ma* 'lord of all that exists' (said of Merodach, Neb. I 35);—*ilâni ma-la šum nabû* 'the gods as many as there be', 'the living beings *ma-la ina mâti bašâ*', often in the phrase *ma-la* (*mal*) *bašû* 'as many as there are (or were) of them', *gab-bi ma-la êpuššu* 'all whatsoever I have done' (E, 9); *ṣâbê am-mar ipparšidû* 'the men, as many as there were of them, had fled' (Assurn. I 66 and oft.). A third expression, by means of the indefinite pronoun with or without *ša*, is found only for the neuter: *man-ma* (doubtless to be read *min-ma* or *mim-ma*. *v.* § 60) *ša etépuša* 'all whatsoever I had done' (Shalm. Ob. 72); *mi-im-ma* or *-ma*—i. e. *mim-ma* (*v.* § 9 No. 212)—or *mimma* (apparently the sign. *nin*, *v.* ibid.)

šumšu 'whatsoever is named i. e. exists', *mimma išû* 'whatsoever I possessed' (Nimr. Ep. XI, 77 ff.), *mimma ša šuma nabû* 'all creation'. Note also *-mu-u* i. e. *mimmû eppušu* 'whatsoever I do' (V R 63, 11 a, cf. 41 b), *-mu-šu(-nu)* 'his (or their) property' (often in the contract-tablets) and cf. *man* (i. e. *mim*)*-mu-šu* 'all his goods' (K. 245 col. II 68).

§ 59. Interrogative Pronouns. For *mannu* and *minû* (e. g. *ina eli mi-ni-e* 'on whose account?' V R 9, 70) references are unnecessary. With *mannu* there is used interchangeably the pron. *a-a-u* i. e. *â-u* (*v.* §§ 13 and 31), e. g. *a-a-ú ilámad* 'who learns?' (IV R 67, 58 a) *a-a-ú ilu* 'which god?' (IV R 9, 52 a), which goes back, directly or indirectly, to the interrogative stem *â*, which, again, may be regarded either as contracted from *ai* (cf. Stade, Hebr. Gramm. § 99, 3), or better, as an interrogative existing independently alongside of *ai*.—The same applies, of course, to Hebr. אָן alongside of אַיִן; cf. *bâtîm* 'houses' alongside of *bait*.

§ 60. The indefinite pronoun is formed partly by the reduplication of the interrogative stem *man* (personal indef. pron.), partly by appending enclitically the generalizing particle *ma* to the interrogative stems *man* (for persons) and *min* (for things). Illustrations are to be found everywhere (cf. *ma-ma ša-na-a* 'any man'

IV R 45, 25; *mi-im-ma* or *mi-ma lim-na* 'anything wicked' Tig. VIII 70). *Mu-um-ma* 'any one whatever' (Shalm. Mon. rev. 71) stands quite alone. For *man-man* etc. employed as adjectives cf. *ilu ma-nu-man ul* . . . 'no god' (IV R 6, 14 c). *Manman* is usually, as here, followed by the negative. When the latter stands at the head of the clause, *la mammana* etc. also signifies 'nobody'.—Both *manma* (*mamma*) and *mimma* are very frequently represented ideographically by  with the phonetic complt. *ma*, and this when closely written looks very like the sign. *nin* (*v.* § 58 above). For -*ma* (*nin*) = *mamma* see, e. g., V R 6, 66 (*mamma aḫû* 'some stranger') and Dict. p. 293 f., for *nin*=*mimma v.* V R 63, 23 a (a variant of *mi-im-ma* Neb. II 32. VIII 11) and many other passages (always so in *mimma šumšu* 'all sorts of').—The neuter indefinite pronoun is also sometimes written *man-ma*; see § 58 above, and also cf. *man-ma amât limutti* 'anything wicked' (I R 27 No. 2, 80, for which in l. 42: *mimma amât limutte*). Since it is highly improbable that *manma* is also used as a neuter, we ought certainly to read *min-ma* or (*v.* § 49, b, p. 117) *mim-ma*, especially as there is express testimony V R 37, 34 d that the sign *man* has also the value *min* (cf. also *man-di-e-ma* IV R 53 No. 3, 37 corresponding to *mi-in-di-e-ma* Nimr. Ep. 65, 13).—For *â'umma*—as regards the reading and writing of which §§ 12—14 are to be compared—see e. g. Shal. Bal. V 3: *a-(i)a-um-ma ul ėzib* 'not one did I spare', *šarru ia-um-ma* 'some king or other' (Tig. I 67 and oft.), *la te-zi-ba a-a-am-ma* 'leave not one alive' (M 55 col. I 21).

Most of the pronominal stems mentioned in §§ 55—60 we shall meet again among the particles (*û*, *šû* in the adverb *umma* and the conjunction *šumma*, *agâ* in the adverb *aganna*, and so on); for details see under §§ 78—82.

Transition to the Noun and the Verb.

§ 61. In Assyrian as in all Semitic languages roots in which an idea or meaning is inherent are of two kinds. Either they originally consist of three or more consonants, or originally of two, which have been subsequently increased to three.

1) Roots composed of two consonants are still found: *a*) in those nouns that show complete reduplication—no verbs have yet been found.—Such nouns are: *laḳalaḳa* 'stork' syn. *raḳraḳḳu*, *ṣarṣaru* 'cricket', *barbaru* 'jackal', *panpanu* 'chamber for gods'; *dandannu* 'all-powerful', *kaškaš(š)u* 'very strong'; *ḳalḳaltu* 'panting, pining', *kamkammatu* 'ring';—*birbirru* 'brightness of the rising stars', *zirzirru* name of a tiny insect, *diḳdiḳḳu*, name of a very small bird;—*zunzunu* and *duḳduḳḳu* synonyms of the two last-mentioned words, *mulmul(l)u* 'javelin, lance'. *b*) in

those nouns and verbs that show imperfect reduplication of the root. Verbs are rare: *babâlu* 'bring'; *ḳaḳâru* II 1 'root out', *ṭaṭâpu* 'shut in' (part. II 1: *mu-ṭe-ṭip-tum*, to which add *ṭi-ṭip-pu*, a synonym of *daltum* II R 23, 2. 3c). As regards the nouns, the question sometimes suggests itself, whether it is not the case that the second radical of the biconsonantal root has been assimilated to the first radical, when the latter is repeated: as, for example, in *ka(k)kabu* 'star', *ḳaḳḳadu* 'head', cf. קָדְקֹד, *ḳaḳḳaru* 'ground', the masc. prop. noun. *Ḫaḫḫûru* Hebr. חַרְחוּר, *sissinnu* 'palm-branch' cf. סַנְסִנִּים, *ḳuḳubânu* 'stomach' (of animals), cf. Arab. قَبْقَب, Aram. קוּרְקְבָנָא. We must not, however, from these and a few other similar contractions (cf. *li-il-li-du* 'child' II R 30, 47 c) formulate any laws for the assimilation of Assyrian consonants of universal application, or even as applied to the derivatives from triconsonantal roots (cf. above § 50). Note further *papaḫu* 'chamber for the gods', *dadmu* 'dwelling-place', *mamlu* 'strong', *lallaru* 'crier', fem. *lallartu* 'wailing, loud crying' (also name of a bird and an insect), *sis(s)iktu* 'dress, robe', *dudittu* (=*dudîntu*) 'ornament for the breast', *pitpânu* (?) 'bow'. *c*) Possibly in some of the so-called primitive nouns to be discussed in § 62. — These biconsonantal roots may also be inferred from some of the so-called 'weak' stems or verbs, notably from the verbs tertiæ י and ו (*v.* § 62), verbs mediæ geminatæ, which probably go back to a biconsonantal root with a strongly accented *a* vowel (*v.* § 63), and verbs mediæ ו and י, which seem to be developed out of a biconsonantal root with *â* for the medial vowel (*v.* § 64).

2) As examples of roots composed of three consonants we have first of all the verbs with three strong radicals. Whether the *n* of verbs primæ נ, and the *u̯*, *i̯* of verbs primæ ו, י be of secondary origin, and if so, in what cases—are questions which will be difficult to decide. The gutturals, however, were without doubt as inseparably part and parcel of the root in verbs mediæ and tertiæ א, ע, ח, as in the case of verbs primæ א, ע, ח.

3) Roots composed of four consonants, employed as verbs, are but sparingly represented in Assyrian; the two principal examples are בלכת IV 1 'free one's self, be torn to pieces; cross over', and פרשׁד IV 1 'flee', cf. also שׁרבט, חרמט II 1. III 1 'destroy', פלסח, פרזח. Of the nouns we may mention: *aḳrabu* 'scorpion', *ḫarbašu* 'fright' (?), *paltigu* 'travelling-chair' (II R 23, 6 a), *parzillu* 'iron', *ḫab(b)aṣillatu* 'stalk (of grain and of a flower)', *paršumu* and *puršumu* 'old, venerable', *šuršummu*, *ḫurḫummatu*, *pur(par)-šú-'u-ú* 'flea', *šumêlu* 'left' ($שמא_1ל$), and many others.

From these examples we see the extent to which the liquids *l* and *r* have contributed to the formation of roots of four consonants.—For roots like פלכה and שחרר, which have four consonants in appearance only, *v.* § 117, 1 and 2.—I know of no roots composed of more than four consonants.

B. The Noun.

On the difficult question as to the existence of so-called primitive nouns, the following remarks may be made from the stand-point of Assyrian. § 62.

1) Primitive nouns alongside of roots tertiæ י. We have already, in § 39, referred to the extreme shortening which takes place in the forms of the part. of the Qal (and Shafel) in verbs tertiæ א and י, in the perm. of the Qal in verbs tertiæ י, and in the constr. state of the nominal stem فَعِل. This shortening, we found, resulted in the complete suppression not only of the final vowel, whether short or long, but also of the last consonant of the root. Among the derivatives of verbs tertiæ י, nominal stems formed like *têrtu* 'law' or *tûdtu* 'decision' (from ורה and ודה *v.* § 65 No. 32, a) deserve, in this respect, to be singled out. The same disappearance of the *auslaut* may also be observed in a series of nouns which, after what has just been said, must not, from

the mere fact that they contain but two radicals, be set down as primitive nouns, in the sense that the corresponding verbs tertiæ י never existed or, at least, had never reached the triconsonantal stage. Impossible as it is to derive forms like *šurb-at*, *têr-tu* from other than triconsonantal stems, it is equally unnecessary, to say the least, to regard as primitive nouns, *Anu* 'god of heaven', fem. *An-tu* [st. cstr. *Anat*], *šat-tu* 'year',=*šantu* [*šana*], *ķaš-tu* 'bow', plur. *ķašâti*, *am-tu* 'maid', *dal-tu* 'door', *šap-tu* 'lip', *bar-tu* 'rising, revolt'; *enu* 'lord' fem. *entu*, *enu* 'time', fem. *en-tu, ettu*, *ittu*; *binu* 'son' fem. *bin-tu*, *ilu* 'god' fem. *il-tu* [*ilat*], *iṣu* 'wood', *ir-tu* 'breast' [*irat*], *it-tu* 'side' pl. *itâti*, *šinu* (*šinâ*) 'two'; *šuķ-tu* 'drinking-trough', *ul-tu* originally 'direction', then prep. 'from', and others, especially as for the most of these nouns there exists a triconsonantal stem. In the latter as in the former case, we may have to do with examples of the extreme shortening of verbs tertiæ י,—a fact which no one questions in regard to *el*=*eli*, *elî*, *elai̯*; *mat*=*matai̯*, *le'-at* fem. st. cstr. of *le'û* 'strong', and many others (cf. also Hebr. צַד, קַו, רֵעַ).

While, therefore, *daltu*, *binu*, *bin-tu* etc. are not, any by means, necessarily primitive nouns, it is still, from another point of view, very remarkable that nominal formations like the above are not found from stems (verbs) tertiæ א (nominal stems like *mi-lu* 'flood' and *ze-ru* 'seed' are proved by the variants *mi-i-lu* and *ze-e-ru* to be of the same form as *zîmu*, *bûnu*, *v.* § 65 Nos. 1—3). It is evident that the third radical of stems tertiæ י (also ו?) was much less distinctly felt to be part of the root, and treated as such, than was final א; and it was for this reason that in § 61, 1 the stems tertiæ י (and ו) appeared to me to warrant, more than did any others, the assumption of biconsonantal roots.

The problem becomes more complicated when we take the case of those biconsonantal nouns, to which we cannot assign a definite and known stem, as, for example, *aḫu* 'brother' and 'side', and *emu* 'father-in-law'. Are these, by reason of their feminines *aḫâtu* 'sister' and 'side', and *emêtu* 'mother-in-law', to be set down as shortened forms from triconsonantal stems tertiæ י, or must they be recognized as biconsonantal primitive nouns, that are on the point of rising beyond the biconsonantal stage and appearing henceforth as triconsonantal (note the instructive *atḫû* 'companion')? For *aḫâtu* in the signification of 'sister' as well as for *emêtu*, the latter alternative seems to me to deserve the preference, because only in very rare cases do we find the form فَعَال with a concrete personal signification. The *â* seems to owe its existence to an effort at strengthening, or, so to say, expanding the short word of two consonants. In this respect it resembles the *â* in permansive forms like *dannâta* etc.—*Abû* 'father' (*û* is thoroughly well attested) cannot, from an Assyrian standpoint, be regarded as other than a derivative from a triconsonantal stem אבה (prob. 'decide').

2) Other primitive nouns. *Ummu* 'mother', originally 'womb', we may easily recognize in Assyrian as derived from the stem אמם 'be wide, spacious'; it may be allowed to pass for a primitive noun only in so far as all stems mediæ geminatæ are at bottom of biconsonantal origin. To set down words like *sâsu* 'moth' and *šûmu* 'garlic' as primitive nouns in the sense in which the term is usually understood (cf. Stade's 'isolated nouns') is very hazardous, to say the least, since it is perhaps a mere chance that the corresponding verbal stems with medial vowel are no longer to be, or have not yet been, met with in our texts. In the case of *dâmu* 'blood' and *âmu* 'sea', we might, looking at דָּם, דַּם, דְּמֵי, دَمٌ; יָם, יַם, יַמִּים, regard them as primitive nouns for the reason that the various Semitic languages—to a certain extent, each separate language—have adopted various plans in order to give to these words a greater stability; but who will guarantee that the Hebrew and Arabic forms,

let us say, represent only a comparatively late stage of development under the influence of continuous shortening, analogy etc., and that *dâmu* and *i̯âmu* must, nevertheless, be assumed as the ground-forms in primitive Semitic, from some unknown stem which has long ago disappeared? The same applies to *išâtu* 'fire' and others. We should be most inclined to see examples of primitive nouns in *mutu* 'husband', *idu* 'hand, side', and *immu*, connected with *ûmu* 'day' (cf. יְמֵי, יָמִים, acc. to Praetorius from an old word *i̯im*), whereas, on the other hand, *mâtu* 'country', *šumu* 'name', *mû* 'water', *pû* 'mouth' are altogether uncertain.

§ 63. An intermediate position between the so-called primitive nouns and the forms of nominal stems discussed in § 65 is occupied by the derivatives of verbs mediæ geminatæ and mediæ י and ו, inasmuch as these present unmistakeable traces of their descent from biconsonantal roots (*v.* § 61, 1). For this reason we shall treat both classes apart from the derivatives of the other stems, and shall begin with the formation of nouns from stems mediæ geminatæ. While the verbal forms from these stems follow in all respects the analogy of the strong stems (the only exception is the permansive of the Qal, *v.* § 87 and cf. § 89, also § 37, b), this cannot be said, to anything like the same extent, of the nominal forms. Nouns like *dannu* 'powerful', *šarru* 'king', *šallu* 'captured' are formed directly from the root, there being no proof—as is the case in the feminine forms of the nominal stems فَعّل (§ 65 No. 6) and فَعِل (No. 7)—of an intermediate stage with a vowel between the second and third radicals. Between *šarru* and *dannu, ellu, emmu* ('hot')—the three last mentioned, being adjectives, cannot by any possibility represent the form فَعّل—and between *šarratu* 'queen' and *dannatu* 'powerful', *dannat* 'she was powerful' (the permansive form is فَعِل), *šullatu* 'booty' (cf. the Hebr. masc. שָׁלָל) no difference can be detected: in other words, stems mediæ geminatæ, in place of all the forms of nominal stems enumerated in § 65 Nos. 1—10, are content with three: with فَعّل, which combines the meanings of substantive and adjective, and with فِعّل and فُعّل, which form only substantives. Of فَعّل examples have already been given. For فِعّل cf. *ṣillu* 'shadow', *sippu* 'threshold', *libbu* 'heart', *ḫissatu* 'perception'; *illatu* 'might', although found written *ellatu*, must also belong here on account of its feminine ending *atu* (*ellatu* would give *ellitu*), while *ṣirritu* § 34, δ, on the other hand, must be put alongside of the Hebr. צָרָה. For فُعّل cf. *gubbu* 'cistern', *zumbu* 'fly', *uzzu* and *uzzatu* 'anger', *kullatu* 'totality, whole'.

Corresponding to these forms we have *šarrûtu*, *šallûtu* (§ 65 No. 34); *ḫarrânu* 'street', *Rammânu*, *zillânu* (No. 35). Only when a long vowel appears between the second and third radicals, or when the doubling of the second or third radical is characteristic of the nominal stem, are the stems med. geminatæ compelled to follow the example of the strong stems. Hence *šalâlu*, *narâru* (*nerâru*) 'helper' (No. 11); *dumâmu* 'wild cat' (13); *ḫasîsu* 'intelligence' (14); *kililu* 'setting (of gem), garland', *ziḳîḳu* and *zaḳîḳu* 'wind' (15); *šarûru* 'brilliance', *abûbu* 'deluge', *ašûštu* 'sorrow' (17); *šibûbu* 'brilliance', *sinûndu* 'swallow' (18); *ṣulûlu* 'shadow, shade, covering' (19); *Dan-na-(a-)nu* prop. n. m., *al-lal-lu* 'strong' (25, or is it stem No. 23?); *nambûbtu* (28) name of a bird; *imbûbu* 'flute' (נבב, 30, e). For the nominal stem No. 31, a, cf. *maṣallu* 'herdsman's tent', *namaddu* 'measure', on the one hand, and on the other (like strong stems) *manzazu* 'stand, place' fem. *manzaltu*.—The stems *ḳunnunu*, *šuklulu* (also *namurratu*) see under § 88.

Stems mediæ ו and י agree with stems med. geminatæ in not belying their descent from biconsonantal roots. This descent is most distinctly visible in the permansive form of the Qal: *dâr*, *kân*, *târat* etc. (*v.* § 87 and cf. § 89). Impossible as it is to fit these forms into the scheme of the ordinary permansive § 64.

فَعِل, it is equally unnecessary to make nominal stems like *ṭâbu* 'good' contracted from an hypothetical original *ṭaịabu* (stem فَعَل); they are further examples, rather, of the oldest form of the root, which is still free from internal vowel change. Also for the semi-nominal infinitive of the Qal: *târu* (with feminine ending *târtu*), *ṭâbu* we must be content to give up the theory of intermediate forms, such as *tauâru*, *ṭaịâbu*. When once the characteristic of the infinitive, the vowel *â*, had appeared before the last radical (فَعَال), *târu* was the natural root-stem of the infinitive.

In connexion with the permansive forms above referred to, which will be thoroughly discussed in § 89, such as *da-(a-)ri*, *ka-ia-an* and *ka-a-a-an*, *ṭa-ab*, *ta-a-u-rat* etc., which must undoubtedly be read *dâri*, *kân*, *ṭâb*, *târat* (*v.* § 13), we would call attention, in the first place, to the most difficult forms of stems med. ו and י, that is to the nouns written *da-ia-nu*, *da-a-a-nu* 'judge', *a-a-bu*, *ia-a-bu*, *a-ia-a-bu* 'enemy', *ḫa-a-a-ru* 'consort' and many others. Looking at the Hebr. דַּיָּן, we naturally feel inclined to read the Assyrian word for 'judge' also *daịanu*; but apart from the fact, that such a form is at variance with the treatment of the intervocalic *ị* elsewhere (§ 41, b), in accordance with which *da'anu* is all that would be phonetically admissible, it is shown to be altogether out of the question by the orthographical variation *da-a-a-nu*. For this form, whether read *dâ'anu* or *da'ânu*—*dainu* is excluded for reasons both graphical (*v.* § 13) and grammatical — can never be classed under the form فَعَّل (§ 65 No. 24). The only way out of the difficulty would be to read *da'ânu*, which we might regard as a form فَعَّال; for this we might appeal to *za-ia-a-re* 'the adversary' (Assurn. I 8), to *a-ia-a-bu* and *ta-ia-a-ru* (*v.* § 14). Moreover, the form فَعَّال (No. 25), which, in any case, is scarcely found in Assyrian for names of professions, such as 'judge', appears quite unsuitable for words like *za-ia-a-ru, a-ia-a-bu*, while for a word like *ḫa-a-a-ru* 'bridegroom, husband', which can hardly be assigned to a different category from *a-a-bu* and *da-a-a-nu*, it is utterly impossible to assume a form with the second radical sharpened. A vastly more suitable explanation, however, appears to be suggested by the word *ḫa-a-a-ru*, just mentioned, which in II R 36, 39—42 d, appears alongside of the part. *ḫa-i-ru*; it is that these supposed nouns are nothing but participles with syncopated *i*, that *ḫâru* accordingly stands in the same relation to *ḫâ'iru* as do *âšbu* to *âšibu*, *râmu* 'loving' to *râ'imu* (§ 37, a). If this explanation is correct, it of course disposes finally of the theory that *a-a=ai*; and further, whoever believes in the possibility of *ḫairu* and *aibu* being contracted from *ḫâ'iru* and *â'ibu*, will be obliged henceforth to relinquish this theory in face of the construct *a-a-ab* (§ 14). There is, moreover, another important consideration which tells against this view of *âbu*, *dânu* etc., viz. the fact that it is precisely the participles of verbs med. ו and י, formed after the model of the strong stems, that, in contrast to the فَاعِل of all other verbs, are wont, for a reason that is easily intelligible, to preserve in its purity the *i*-vowel before the last radical: cf. out of a great number of such participles only *za-'-i-re*, *za-i-re*, *za-e-re*, *za-e-ru-ut* (IV R 44, 25. Tig. VIII 32. 41. Assurn. I 28. Shalm. Ob. 20. Senhb. V 57. Neb. II 25 etc.), *da-i-nu-te* 'judging' pl. (Sarg. Cyl. 53), *ṣâ'idu*, *dâ'iku* fem. *dâ'iktu* (*v.* § 13). There is, consequently, no other course open to us but to read all these nominal forms as *dânu*, *âbu*, *zâru* (זָר), *târu*, *ḫâru* in connection with the permansive forms mentioned at the commencement of this paragraph, and in agreement with the two-fold employment of the Hebrew קָם as 3. m. perf. and as participle.—That these nouns have frequently *ût* in the plur. is entirely in harmony with their character as participles.—In the same way *ka-a-a-nam-ma* adv. 'continually'=*kânâma*, *ka-a-a-ma-nu* (st. § 65 No. 35) adj. 'everlasting; Saturn'=*kâmânu* etc.

It has already been shown in §§ 12—14 that there is no impediment from the side of the orthography: the permansive forms and the varieties in the way of writing a word like *târtu* (§ 13) corroborate anew the statements there laid down.

A-a-lu 'ram', in accordance with the laws of Assyrian writing and phonetics, can hardly be read otherwise than as *âlu*. In the case of words like *a-a-lu* 'stag', and the name of the mouth *A-a-ru*, we may on principle assume the form فَعَل as ground-form, but there can be no doubt, all the same, that they were respectively pronounced merely as *âlu* and *Âru*. Even if we were to read *A'aru* or quite falsely *Airu*, the Hebr. אִיָּר (same form as אַבָּר) would have to be set down, in any case, as a free Hebrew transformation of the Babylonian name (as in מַרְחֶשְׁוָן). *A'alu* 'stag' (Hebr. אַיָּל), we may be sure, was forthwith contracted to *âlu* (*v.* § 47), which affords the only satisfactory explanation of 'ram' and 'stag' being written identically: viz: *a-a-lu.*—The י in the first syllable of the name for Saturn כִּיּוּן, كَيْوان contrasted with the Assyro-Babylonian *kâmân*, *kâvân* (cf. p. 104 f.) goes back perhaps to a bye-form *kêvân*, with the first *â* modified to *ê*, which may have been current in every-day speech (cf. שִׁנְעָר in its relation to *Šumêr*, § 49, a note).

As examples of the remaining forms of nominal stems we would mention: *mûtu* 'death', *šûru* 'ox', *urru* (= *ûru*) 'light', *înu* 'eye', *îmtu* 'fright' (stem § 65 No. 1); *nîru* 'yoke', *dînu* 'judgment', *šîḫtu* syn. *pirḫu* 'shoot' (No. 2); *šûḳu* 'street', *nûnu* 'fish', *rû'tu* 'breath' (3); *mîtu*, *mêtu* 'dead' (abstr. noun *mêtûtu*), *kênu*, *kînu* fem. *kêttu*, *kîttu* 'true, just' (7); *târtu* 'return' (11); *ḳi-a-šu* 'surname' (? קיש 12); *šîmu* '(purchase) price', fem. *šîmtu* 'fate' (prop. that which is fixed), *dîktu* 'fallen host', *ḳîštu* 'present', *ḫîr(a)tu* 'bride, wife' (14); *makânu* 'place', *maḳâṣu* 'rack', *maḫâzu* 'town', *mâlu* (אוּל) 'front', *manâḫtu* 'resting-place', also 'care for one' (31, a); *mûtânu* 'plague, pest', *ṣi-da-nu* 'hunting-net' (35). For the stem *kunnu*, fem. *ṭubtu*=*ṭubbatu* (and the form *kut-tin-nu* derived therefrom) see § 88.

There yet remain many difficulties to solve: for example, does *pûru* 'young wild-ox' stand to *pîru* 'elephant (st. פיר 'be strong, powerful'), and *pûlu* 'dressed stone' to the more common *pîlu* (*pêlu*) with the same meaning, in the same relation as فُعَل to فِعِل? For the nominal stems *tidûku* 'killing', *titûru* 'bridge', *tinûru* 'stove' cf. § 83 note.

§ 65. Summary of the Nominal Stems in Assyrian.*)

I. Internal Vowel Change only (Nos. 1—19).

1. Short vowels only (Nos. 1—10).

a) A short accented vowel after the first radical and a short, unessential, vowel after the second

---

*) That is of those corresponding to verbal stems composed of three strong consonants. Weak stems will also be included, with the exception of stems med. gemin. and med. ו, י. For nominal stems of four consonants, in so far as they present internal vowel change only, see § 61, 1 a and 3; note also § 65 No. 35 (at end) and especially § 117, 1 and 2.—Arrangement observed in discussing Nos. 1—33: the derivatives of the strong triconsonantal stems, which include those of stems primæ נ, are taken first, and are separated by a period and a dash from the derivatives of the

(Nos. 1—5): confined most probably to substantives. The vowel heard after the second radical serves merely to prevent the stem from terminating in two consonants, and is syncopated, almost without exception, when inflexional endings are appended. There is entire uniformity among the stems in this division, except as regards the addition of the feminine ending *atu*: before the latter, Nos. 1—3 syncopate the second vowel, while Nos. 4—5 retain it (in the abs. state).

1. فَعْل (فَعْلُ st. cstr. فَعَلْ) fem. فَعْلَتُ. *kalbu* [*kalab*] 'dog' fem. *kalbatu*, *šamšu* [*šamaš*] 'sun', *mašku* [*mašak*] 'skin', *šaknu* [*šakan*] 'viceroy'.—*abnu* [*aban*] 'stone', *anbatu*, but also *erṣitu*; *eḳlu* [*e-ki-el*] 'field'; *enzu*, *erpu* fem. *erpitu* (*v.* §§ 34, γ. 35); — *rêšu* 'head' fem. *rêštu*; *ṣêru* 'back'; *rêmu, šêru*; *bêlu* fem. *bêltu*, but also *râdu* (*v.* § 32, γ);—*mâlu* 'abundance', *labbu* 'lion'; *zêru*, *di-mu* 'tear'=*dêmu*, *dâmu* (*v.* §§ 33. 47); —*bêru* 'glance' (IV R 45, 43), *bêru* 'middle' fem. *bêrit*; perhaps also *mênu*, *mînu* (=*mânu*) 'number' (*v.* §§ 33. 41);—*arḫu* [*araḫ*] 'month'.

2. فِعْل (فِعْلُ st. cstr. فِعِلْ) fem. فِعْلَتُ. *zikru*

weak stems; the latter, separated from each other by a semicolon and a dash, are taken in the following order: primæ, mediæ and tertiæ א, tertiæ י and ו, primæ ו and י. The forms of the construct state are always placed in square brackets, as in § 62.

[*zikir*] 'name', *šibṭu* 'staff', *kirbu* [*kiṛib*] 'interior', *kibratu* 'point of the compass, direction, region', *zibbatu* 'tail'.—*igru* 'pay';—*rîmu* 'wild ox', *šîru* 'flesh' (*v.* § 47); — *ḫiṭṭu*, *ḫiṭu* 'sin', *mîlu* 'flood, overflow' (*v.* § 47); — *simmu* 'blindness' (סמה, whence *samû* 'blind'), *limmu* and *lîmu* 'archonate', prop. 'period' (*v.* § 41).

Whenever the corresponding feminine is wanting in nouns of this form, derived from strong verbs, we cannot, of course, distinguish accurately between stems 2 and 4. The same applies to Nos. 3 and 5.

3. فُعْل (فُعُلٌ st. cstr. فُعُلٌ) fem. فُعْلَةٌ. *šulmu* [*šulum*] 'happiness, peace', *murṣu* 'sickness', *puḫru* 'totality, whole', *lubšu* 'dress, garment', *dumḳu* 'favour', *lumnu* 'evil'. — *urḫu* [*uruḫ*] 'road, street', *umṣu* fem. *umṣatu* 'want';—*mu'du* 'abundance' (מְאֹד), *bûru*, *bûrtu* 'well, ditch'; *nûru* 'light', *mûru*; *rûbatu* 'hunger' (*v.* § 47); — *tultu* 'worm'; — *ṣu-(um-)mu* 'thirst'; *bûnu* 'child'; 'countenance', *mûšu* 'night' (مُسْى, note *mušîtu*).

4. فِعْل (فِعْلٌ st. cstr. فِعِل) fem. فِعِلَةٌ. *riḫṣu* [*riḫis*] 'inundation' fem. *riḫiṣtu* (*riḫiltu*), *gimru* [*gimir*] 'totality, whole' fem. *gimirtu* [*gimrat*], *ṣimdu* and *ṣimittu* plur. *ṣimdâti* 'yoke (of oxen), team', *šipru* and *šipirtu* 'epistle', *sidirtu* 'battle-array', *sikiptu* 'defeat', *sipittu* (ספד) 'mourning', *niṣirtu* 'treasure', *piristu* 'decision', *širiḳtu* 'present', *libittu* [*libnat*] 'brick' plur.

libnâti. — *nîbu* 'number' fem. st. cstr. *nibit* 'name'; — here belong also *ilittu* 'shoot, child' (also *littu*), *biltu* [*bilat*] 'offering, tribute', *šiptu* 'exorcism', *ṣîtu* 'issue, end'?

Where no masculine form occurs, nor the plur. fem. nor yet the construct state of the fem. sing., the form No. 15 is also possible. And however improbable it may seem to me, I should like to call attention to the fact that the *i* of the first syllable, in forms like the above, might also be regarded as having arisen from *e* (*a*), from which it would follow that the *i* of the second syllable might be viewed according to § 35: consequently there would be no need for reading *ḫi-šiḫ-tu* in place of *ḫi-šaḫ-tu*, a variant of *ḫi-ši-iḫ-tu* 'need': *ḫešaḫtu* and *ḫešiḫtu* (*ḫišiḫtu*) might both represent the nominal stem فَعَلْتٌ (No. 6). For unmistakable examples of this origin of the *i* of the first syllable, see what is said in connexion with *ṣiḫru* i. e. *ṣeḫru* 'small' in the note to No. 7.

5. فُعْل (فُعُلٌ st. cstr. فُعُلٌ) fem. فُعُلْتٌ. *pulḫu* [*puluḫ*] and *puluḫtu* [*pulḫat*] 'fear', *tubḳu* [*tubuḳ*] and *tubuḳtu* [*tubḳat*] 'region', plur. *tubḳâti* and *tubuḳâti*, *tukultu* [*tuklat*] 'assistance', plur. *tuklâti* 'helpers, soldiers', *bukru* and *bukurtu* 'first-born', *nukurtu* 'enmity'. — Here belong also *šubtu* [*šubat*] 'dwelling', *šuttu* 'dream' plur. *šunâti*?

The remark made in the note to No. 4 also applies here: whether, e. g., *ukultu* 'food' has a long or a short *u* in the second syllable can only be decided by finding the construct state of the sing.—The intimate connexion between stems Nos. 2 and 4, 3 and 5 is well shown by masc. forms like *miṣiru* 'territory' (V R 8, 72), elsewhere always *miṣru* [*miṣir*]; *uzunu* 'intelligence' (Bors. I 5), elsewhere always *uznu* [*uzun*]; *udrê* and *udurê* 'dromedaries'; also by *tuḳuntu* [*tuḳmat*] 'fight' exchanging with *tuḳmatu* (to be taken as sing., in my opinion, in passages like Assurn. I 35. Sarg. Cyl. 25), plur. *tuḳmâti* and *tuḳumâti*, and by other cases. For the stem فِعْل fem. فِعَلَت, which corresponds in the same way to stem No. 1, *v.* note to No. 6.

b) A short accented vowel after the first radical and a short vowel after the second radical (Nos. 6—10): forms substantives and adjectives. The vowel of the second radical is much less frequently syncopated, and, in particular, is always retained—a few forms due to analogy excepted—before *atu* (the abs. state of the feminine).

6. فَعَل (فَعَلُ or فَعْلُ st. cstr. فَعَلْ) fem. فَعَلْتُ. *ḫatanu* [*ḫatan*] 'related by marriage, son-in-law', *nakaru* 'enemy', *rapšu* 'wide' fem. *rapaštu* [*rapšat*] plur. *rapšâti*.—*aḫru* fem. *aḫartu* 'the future'; *agalu* 'calf', but also *elamu* 'high' fem. *elamtu* (*v.* § 34, γ), *eširtu* 'ten' fem. (= *ešartu*, acc. to § 35), whence (*v.* § 36) *ešertu* [*ešerit*];—*ma'adu*, *mâdu* 'much' fem. *ma'attu*; *la'abu* 'flame';—*ḳanû* 'reed', *manû* 'mina', *šamû* 'heaven', *kalû* [*kal*] 'totality', *matê* (cf. p. 99) 'when?', *erû* 'chest, box', *adî* 'unto' (cf. עֲדֵי), *elî* (*eli*, *el*, *ela*) 'upon' (cf. עֲלֵי), *abîtu* and *abûtu* 'answer, wish' (st. אבי and אבו), *nagû* and *nagîtu* (also *na-gi-a-tu*) 'district, place';—*aḳru* 'precious' (יָקָר) fem. *aḳartu* plur. *aḳrâti*.

A few nouns of the form *fa'al*, fem. *fa'altu* stand in the same intimate relation to stem No. 1, as do Nos. 4 and 5 to 2 and 3 (*v.* No. 5 note); cf. e. g. *nakmu* and *nakamtu* 'treasure' plur. *nakamâti*, *si-ba* (doubtless = *sêba*) 'seven' fem. *sibittu* (*sebittu* = *sebattu*, *seba'tu*), also *karašu* 'interior' (Assurb. Sm. 11, 8), *rakabu* 'ambassador', *palagu* 'canal' (plur. *pa-la-ga-šú*, Neb. VIII 39), which stand apparently in the same relation to *karšu*, *rakbu*, *palgu* as *uzunu* to *uznu*. In view of the difficulties in the way of an exact classification, we do not attempt to set up a stem with the vowel *a*, analogous to Nos. 4 and 5. The surest sign by which to know if a noun belongs to stems Nos. 6—12 or to Nos. 1—5, is an observation, the accuracy of which appears to me beyond question, that adjectives are not found under any of the forms 1—5.—When the second vowel is syncopated and no feminine or constr. state is known, it is very difficult, if not impossible, to decide between Nos. 6 and 1, and between 6 and 7: with regard to *admu* 'something created, child, young (of animals)', Hebr. אָדָם might perhaps justify us in thinking of No. 6; but we shall never perhaps be able to say with certainty whether *šadû* 'mountain' and *ṣabîtu* 'gazelle' belong to No. 6 or to No. 7.—In the case of words like *epiru*, *epru* [*epir*] 'dust', we must not forget the possibility of explaining the *i* acc. to § 35, which would place *epru* on a par with the Hebr. עָפָר. For feminines like *ḫišiḫtu*, *si-ḫar-tu*, *si-ḫir-tu* 'circuit, city wall', *v.* remarks on No. 4 above. Again, of the nouns assigned to No. 7, having *e* in the first, and *i* in the second syllable, one or two may belong to No. 6: *erištu* 'desire' e. g. may be = *araštu* אֲרֶשֶׁת. Also *mi-ḫi-ir-tu*, st. cstr. *mi-iḫ-rit* (*miḫ-ri-it* Tig. jun. rev. 16, *miḫ* sign § 9 No. 109) alongside of *mi-iḫ-ra-at* (Neb. VII 61), and *mi-ḫi-ra-at* (Neb. Bab. II 18, same form as *siḫ-ḫi-rat*, II R 21, 16 d), might be looked upon as the fem. of *maḫru* [*maḫar*] when pronounced *meḫru* and *miḫru*. With what has now been said compare my remarks p. 48 f.—Finally, we may hesitate at times between Nos. 6 and 11; *ga-ra-bu* 'leprosy', however, is shown by the Hebr. גָּרָב to belong to No. 6.

7. فَعِل (فَعِلٌ or فَعُلٌ st. cstr. فَعِل) fem. فَعِلْتٌ. *nakiru* 'strange, hostile' fem. *nakirtu*, *kabtu* 'heavy'

fem. *kabittu* [*kabtat*] plur. *kabtâti*, *kabittu* 'disposition', *napištu* [*napšat*] 'soul, life' plur. *napšâti*, *namru* 'brilliant' fem. *namirtu* (and *na-mi-ra-tu* 'brilliancy' K. 40), *labiru* 'old' fem. *labirtu*, *damḳu* 'gracious' fem. *damiḳtu* [*damḳat*], *gamru* [*gamir*] 'complete' fem. *gamirtu*, *ḫamšu* 'five' fem. *ḫamiltu*. The fem. of *maliku*, *malku* [*malik*] 'prince' (and of a few other nouns) follows the analogy of stem No. 1: *malkatu* [*malkat* and *malikat*].— *eširtu* [*ešrit*] 'temple' plur. *ešrêti*, *er*(*i*)*nu* 'cedar', *egitur* 'letter'; *erîtu*; *ebru* [*ebir*], *eklu* 'dark' fem. *ekiltu*; *edlu* fem. *ediltu*, *epištu* [*epšit*] (*v.* § 34, γ and observe No. 6 note); — *na'idu*, *nâdu* 'exalted'; — *malû* 'full' fem. *malîtu*; *petû* [*pet*, *pit*] 'opened, open' fem. *petîtu*; *nisû* 'distant'; — *rabû* 'great' fem. *rabîtu*; *šaḳû* 'high' fem. *šaḳîtu* (Lay. 51 No. 1, 2).

Just as *nakaru* 'hostile' is another form of *nakiru*, syncopated *nakru*, so there was, to all appearance, alongside of *aplu* [*apil*] 'son' a bye-form *aplu* [*apal*]. — Regarding *ṣiḫru* [*ṣiḫir*] 'small' we may have some hesitation, at first, in deciding between Nos. 2, 4 and 7; but even if it should prove not to be the case that the stems 1—5 are confined to substantives, the form *ṣi-iḫ-ri-tu* (II R 36, 57 a. 37, 51 h), which occurs alongside of *ṣiḫirtu* as the fem. of *ṣiḫru*, points through the *i* of its second syllable to the existence of *e* in its first (*v.* § 35), so that *ṣiḫru* may certainly be taken as *ṣeḫru*, and this again, with its fem. *ṣeḫirtu* as stem No. 6 (the original *ṣaḫru* is still found alongside of the other, like *râšu* alongside of *rêšu*). The same applies to *gišru*, alongside of *gašru* 'strong': for although *gi-šar-tu* (sign *šar*, *šir* § 9 No. 141), the fem. of *gišru*, suggests the possibility of stem No. 9, the reading *giširtu* (=*geširtu*) is also possible. On the circumstance of the forms *ṣaḫru* and *ṣiḫru*, *gašru* and *gišru* etc. being placed side by side, cf. the interesting list II R 32, 31—36 c: *šamkatu* and *šamuktu*, *ḫarmatu* and *ḫarimtu* (the first [and last] members of each couple clearly representing the same nominal stems); finally, *kazratu* and *kizritu* (=*kezratu*), plur. *kiz(i)rêti*. See also the note to No. 8.

8. فَعُل (فَعُلٌ or فَعْلٌ st. cstr. فَعُلْ) fem. فَعُلْتٌ. *šamuḫu* 'growing luxuriantly' fem. *šamuḫtu*, *maruštu* (*marultu*) fem. 'bad, mischievous'. — *rûmtu* syn. of *kabittu* (masc. *ra'umu*, ראם?); *rûḳu* 'far, distant' (also perm. of the form فَعُل) fem. *rûḳtu* [*rûḳat*]; — *šaḳû* 'high' (=*šaḳuį*) fem. *šaḳûtu* (alongside of *šaḳû*, st. فَعِل. No. 7). Note also § 76.

A parallel to *ṣiḫru*=*ṣeḫru* is afforded by *limnu* 'wicked' fem. *limuttu*, but also *lim-ni-tu* (V R 6, 114): here too, the latter form, *limnitu*, proves that *i* of the first syllable is really an *e*, that is, a modified *a* (§ 35); *limnu* therefore=*lemnu* (*lemunu*). In this way are also explained the permansive forms *li-mun* (*le-mun*) 'he is wicked' (IV R 6 Col. VI), fem. *limnit*=*lemnat*, *limnêtunu* 'ye are wicked' (*v.* Pinches in PSBA, Nov. 7, 1882, p. 28).

For the stems Nos. 6—8 cf. also § 87.

9. فِعَل (فِعَلٌ st. cstr. فِعَلْ) fem. فِعَلْتٌ. *šikaru* 'wine' (שֵׁכָר), *zikaru* 'male, man' fem. *zi-ka-rat* (III R 53, 31 b). — *niḳû* 'offering', *binûtu* 'creature', *ḫidûtu* 'joy', *minûtu* 'number', *nigûtu* (also *ningûtu*) 'joy, rejoicings' (plur. *nigâti*), *ḳilûtu* 'burning'; *i-ti-a-tu* 'side, enclosure' (II R 30 No. 4 rev.), *šiḳîtu* 'watering', *bikîtu* 'weeping', *bišîtu* 'being, possession', *šisîtu* 'speech',

also with *ê*: *limêtu* (and *li-mi-tu*) 'enclosure, territory, period', *ki-ri-e-tu* 'feast' (Esarh. VI 35; כֵּרָה).

In the case of a few of these nouns with *ê* in the second syllable, the possibility of the origin of *ê* from *â* must be left an open question.—*zikru*, which occurs alongside of *zikaru*, is not a syncopated form of the latter, but, as we see from the const. st. *zikir*, an independent variant, and is perhaps to be explained in the same way as *gišru*, *nikru* 'hostile' (Beh.). *Bi-'-šu* 'wicked' and *ṣîru* 'exalted' will also be found to admit of an explanation which renders it unnecessary to assume that فِعْل also forms adjectives.

Note on Nos. 6—9. I am also unable, for the present, to determine with certainty the nominal stem of *imnu* 'right (hand)' fem. *e-mit-tu*, *i-mit-tu*, and *i-ša-ru* 'right, straight' fem. *išartu* and *iširtu*. It almost seems as if both *emittu* and the *i* in the second syllable of *iširtu* point to an *i* = *e* (= *a*) in the first syllable.

10. فُعْل fem. فُعْلَةٌ. Perhaps *ugaru* 'fields';—*urû* 'shame, nakedness', *unûtu* 'vessel', *utûtu* (also *itûtu*) 'appointment'; *mušîtu* 'night', *bušû*, *bušîtu* 'goods, property'.

2. A short vowel after the first radical and a long vowel after the second (Nos. 11—19).

11. فَعَال *taḫâzu* 'battle', *karâšu* 'camp', *ḳarâbu* 'fight'. It is the form of the Inf. Qal, e. g. *pa-ḳa-a-du* 'to house' (Senhb. VI 29), *ka-na-(a-)šu* 'submit one's self' (Tig. III 74. IV 51); for the forms with modified vowel, such as *amêru*, *ṣeḫêru* 'be small' (written *ṣi-*

ḫi-ru opp. *rabû* K. 2867 obv.) *v.* §§ 32, γ. 34 β. — *atânu* 'she-ass'. — *ḳi-be-tu*, *ḳibîtu* 'order' (V R 51, 50 b: *ki-ba-a-tu*); — *amâtu* 'speech, affair', *kamâtu* 'enclosure, city wall' (cf. p. 99).

With these feminine infs. of the Qal employed as nouns, such as *amâtu*, *ḳibêtu*, *rêštu* 'shouting' plur. *rêšâti*, *târtu* (*v.* § 64), cf. the analogous forms discussed after Nos. 24, 33 and 40, and also § 88, b, note.

12. فِعَال. *lišânu* 'tongue', *pisânu* 'reservoir, granary'. — *igâru* 'wall' pl. *igârâti*, *imêru* 'ass'; — *ri'âšu* 'creeping thing'; *ti'âmtu* 'sea'; — *ḫimêtu* 'cream'; *šipâtu* 'garment', *piḫâtu* 'vice-royalty', *kinâtu* 'servants, menials' (cf. p. 99).

Haupt also places here *pi-ti-e-ḳu* 'child' (II R 36, 51 c).

13. فُعَال. *ḫurâṣu* 'gold', *turâḫu* 'wild goat', *ḫušа(ḫ)-ḫu* 'famine'; *ḳurâdu* 'brave'. — *ubânu* 'peak, finger'; — *tu'âmu* 'twin' plur. f. *tu'âmâti* 'folding-doors' (cf. תְּאוֹמִים); — *rubû* 'great, noble' fem. *rubâtu*, *šupâtu* 'garment', *usâtu* 'assistance' (cf. p. 99).

14. فَعِيل. *ḫarîṣu* 'city moat', *zaḳîpu* 'post, stake', *maḫîru* '(purchase)price', *salîmu* 'inclination, compassion, treaty', *talîmu* 'full brother' fem. *talîmtu* [*talimat*]. — *alîbu* 'sweet milk'; — *rîmtu* 'beloved' (V R 9, 75).

15. فِعِيل. *ziḳîpu* 'post, stake' (esp. in Assurn. and Shalm.); or is the occurrence of both *ziḳîpu* and

zaḳîpu (cf. *ziḳîḳu* and *zaḳîḳu* § 63) to be explained by § 34, δ?

16. فَعِيل. *u-di-i-nu* 'eagle or vulture'; also, we think *šú-pi-lu*, *šú-pil-tu* 'mulieris pudenda', *butiḳtu* (more frequently *butuḳtu*) 'eruption (of water), flooding'.

17. فَعُول. *batûlu* 'young man' fem. *batûltu* 'maiden', *ka-ru-bu* syn. of *rubû* 'great, noble', *gašûru* 'beam'.— *Ašur* 'the god Ashur' (as the 'bringer of good'), the plant *a-du-ma-tu*, *ebûru* 'fruits of the field' (coll.), *emûḳu* 'might';—*ba'ûlâti* plur. 'subjects'.

18. فِعُول. Cf. the examples in § 63 (p. 153).

19. فُعُول. *rukûbu* 'vehicle', *rukûšu* 'possession', *lubûšu* 'garment, clothing', doubtless also *gušûru* 'beam'; fem. *šubûltu* 'ear (of corn)', *uzûbu* 'an understanding', *uṣûrtu* 'ban', 'end'. — *usûmu* 'ornament, distinction'.

Note on Nos. 11—19. The only example of a long vowel after the first radical and a short vowel after the second, is فَاعِل, which is confined to the participle of the Qal.

II. Internal Vowel Change with sharpening of one of the Consonants of the Root (Nos. 20—29).

1. Sharpening of the third radical (Nos. 20—23).

a) with the same vowel after each of the two first radicals (Nos 20—22).

20. فَعَلّ. *parakku* 'chamber of the gods, holy of holies, throne-room; monarch', *kalakku* 'lath-work', *kaparru* (V R 12, 36 b). — *adannu* 'strong', *agammu* 'marsh, pool', also *agappu* 'wing', *agannâti* plur. 'basins'.

21. فِعِلّ. *kisimmu* 'a destructive insect' (grasshopper ?), *gimillu* 'good deed, presentation', *nigiṣṣu* 'fissure', *sipirru* (to be preferred to *siparru*) 'bronze'. *ki-bi(r)-ru* 'burial', *šibirru* 'staff, rod' — *isinnu* 'feast, festival'.

22. فُعُلّ. *suluppu* 'date', *kurunnu* a kind of wine, *ḫubul(l)u* 'interest', *duruššu* [*duruš*] 'foundation', *sugullatu* 'possessions (in herds)'. — *uruḫḫu* 'way', — *uḫummu* 'rocky precipice', the demon *Utukku*. See also stem 38.

b) with a different vowel after each of the two first radicals (No. 23).

23. فُعَلّ and other forms: *šaḳummu* 'sorrowful' fem. *šaḳummatu* 'sorrow, suffering'.— *abullu* 'city gate',

agurru 'enclosure', coll. 'burnt bricks'; — *da'ummatu* 'darkness, lamentation'.—*ekimmu* 'robber' (a demon). —*pilaḳḳu* 'axe', *pilakku* 'spindle'.

Note on Nos. 20—23. It is difficult to decide whether the sharpening of the third radical of stems 20—23 is a result of accenting the second syllable or is to be explained, in certain cases, as compensation for an original long vowel in the second syllable. The latter explanation must by no means be accepted without question in those cases where we find the last radical doubled, alongside of variants with it written but once, for, as is well known, we also meet with the reverse process, where the sharpening of a consonant is compensated for by lengthening the vowel (*v.* § 53, d). What has now been said applies to nouns like *lamassu*, for example, for which we find *la-ma-su* (Neb. Grot. II 55), *ḫazannu* 'overseer' (cf. חַזָּן), but plur. *ḫa-za-na-a-ti*, *ku-nu-(uk)-ku* 'seal' etc.

2. Sharpening of the second radical (Nos. 24—29).

24. فَعَّل (forms names of occupations and intensive adjectives). *gallabu* 'one that flogs', *kallabu* 'pioneer' (who makes a path with axes), *kaššapu* 'magician, enchanter' fem. *kaššaptu*, *makkasu* 'publican (as in N. T.)', *maṣṣaru* 'watchman'; *ḳarradu* 'brave', *nakkaru* 'hostile', *gammalu* 'camel', *bakkaru* 'young camel', *šapparu* fem. *šappartu* a species of antelope. Cf. also *šallaru* 'wall'.—*allaku* 'messenger', *aḫḫazu* 'Siezer' (a demon), *annabu* 'hare' (prop. 'springer'), *ammaru* 'plenty', *apparu* 'marsh, jungle of reeds'; *irrišu* 'gardener' (= *arrašu*), cf. *ippišu* (V R

13, 39 b); — *tap-pi-u*, *tappû* 'companion' (doubtless = *tappai̯-u*).

im-me-ru 'lamb' might also come under this form, if we explain its *e* acc. to § 36, and assume *immiru* to have arisen from *emmiru* and *emmaru* (§ 36). Such questions are included among those discussed under Nos. 4, 7 and 8. And for this reason we abstain, at present, from indicating the stem of such nouns as *in-di-ru* 'threshing-floor' (doubtless=*iddiru*)—cf. *diggiru*, *dingiru* as they appear in *di-gi-ru-ú* 'god' — *ṣi-iḫ-ḫi-ru* 'small, young' (also written *ṣi-ḫi-ru*) *zinništu*, [*zinnišat*] 'female, woman' (also written *zi-ni-eš-tum*) and others.

The form فُعَّل appears as the inf. of Piel, or as the inf. used as a noun; also as adjective (always with pass. signification), e. g. *bussurtu* [*bussurat*] 'glad tidings', *nukkusu* 'cut off', *burrumu* 'particoloured' fem. *burrumtu*, *uḫḫuzu* 'enclosed, enchased'; *ullû* 'moved up, distant, eternal', *v.* § 88, b and note.

25. فَعَّال (cf. § 63 No. 25) varies with فَعَّل (like Hebr. קַנּוֹא with קַנָּא) but is much rarer. *za-am-me-ru* 'singer, musician' fem. *zammêrtu*.

26. فُعَّال. *ummânu* 'artist'.

27. فَعِّيل. *ḫab-bi-lu* 'wicked', *ša-ag-gi-šu* 'criminal' (Neb. Grot. II 2).

28. فَعُّول. *Aššûr* 'city and land of Assur', *ma-ak-ku-ru* 'possession', *paššûru* 'dish, bowl', *šak-ku-ru* 'intoxicated'.—*ak-ku-lu* 'gluttonous' (II R 56, 23 c).

29. فِعُّول. *sik-ku-ru* 'bolt', *bi-iṣ-ṣu-ru* 'shame'.

Notes on Nos. 20—29. *a*) As regards the quantity of the vowel of the second syllable, and, to some extent, the doubling or not doubling of the second radical, not a few nominal forms present all sorts of difficulties in the way of correctly determining their stem. Thus, e. g. *uḫḫaztu* name of a creeping plant, *ṣu-(um)-me-rat libbi* 'the hidden thoughts of the heart'; *ḫa-ṣi-in-nu* and (st. cstr.) *ḫa-aṣ-ṣi-in* 'axe', etc. Nouns like *aggullu* 'pick-axe', *sattuk(k)u* 'daily sacrifice', *akkullu* 'tribulation, darkness (metaph.)', *ikkillu* 'lamentation', *ziḳḳurratu* 'temple-tower, pinnacle' (*zi-ku-ra-at* in Neb.) seem to present the sharpening of the second and third radicals.

b) Following the forms with sharpening of the second or third radical, those may here be mentioned which repeat the second or third radical: *zu-ḳa-ḳi-pu* 'scorpion', *adudîlu*, *a-mu-meš-tu*, *a-gu-gi-il-tu* (*v.* Dict., No. 61), *a-ṣu-ṣi-im-tu* name of a plant (cf. Hebr. חֲצִצָה), etc.—*a-dam-mu-mu* name of a bird, *alka-kâti*, *ilkakâti* 'ways, events, issues', *nam-ri-(ir-)ru* 'brilliancy', *ir-nintu* (*irnittu*) and *urnintu* (*urnittu*) 'strength, victory', *ren-nin-tu* fem. 'luxuriant' (of growth of plants, cf. רַעֲנָן), etc. *Šaḫrartu* (and *šqḫarratu*) 'straits, difficulties' comes from שחרר; for this kind of quadriliteral verbs, *v.* § 117, 2.

III. Internal Vowel Change with external formative Additions (Nos. 30—40).

1. Preformatives (Nos. 30—33).

30. א: أَفْعَل etc.

a) أَفْعَل. *arba'u* 'four' fem. *erbitti* (= *erbatti*), *irbitti*. To these we may add *azkaru* 'crescent of the new moon', *ašgagu*, *ašlaku*. See also *b*.

b) إِفْعَل. *ismaru* 'lance', also *asmaru* (or *û*?), *in-ṣabtu* 'ear-drops', also *anṣabtu*. Doubtless also *iš-ka-ru* 'fetters, chains', *išparu* fem. *išpartu*. Or do these belong to *c*?

c) إِفْعَال. *ip-te-en-nu* i. e. *iptênu* 'meal', also, we think, *ip-ṭi-ru* 'ransom', *ik-ri-bu* 'prayer', *iš-di-ḫu* 'way', *iš-kip-pu* an animal, the same as *ipṭêru* etc. Note *iš-ri-i-ru* II R 32, 10c.

d) أَفْعُول. Perh. *askuppu*, *askuppatu* 'threshold'.

e) إِفْعُول (cf. § 63 *imbûbu*). *iš-ru-ub-bu* (V R 32, 35 b), whence *iš-ru-bu-u*.

Forms with prosthetic א do not, of course, belong here.— I am not aware of any certain example of י as preformative; the names of two of Merodach's dogs *Ikšuda* and *Il-te-bu* (II R 56, 24, 25 c) are certainly pure verbal forms, like the name of the deity *Iš-me ka-ra-bu* (III R 66 obv. 2 e).

31. מ and נ: مَفْعَل, نَفْعَل, and similar forms.

a) مَفْعَل (forms nomina loci and nom. instrumenti, serving also to express that wherein the idea implied in the verb is realized): *magšaru* 'might, strength', *maškanu* 'locality, pledge' (or was 'pledge' *maškânu*?), *ma(n)dat(t)u* 'tribute', *maṣṣartu* 'watch'.— *mêsiru* 'siege, cover, case'; *mâlaku* 'way'; *mêtiḳu* (=*mêtaḳu*, *v*. §§ 32, γ and 35) 'way, course of events' (the orthographical variation *mi-te-ki* III R 55, 59 b is a parallel to *ne-mi-ḳu* and *ni-me-ḳu* p. 78) fem. *mêtaḳtu* 'procession, march (of events)' (Shams. IV 27), *mêdilu* 'bar, bolt'; — *ma-a-a-lu*, *ma-a-a-al-tu*, i. e., on the analogy of *narâmu* from ר‎א₃ם, *ma'âlu*, *ma'âltu* 'couch, bed'; — *messû* (*me-is-su-u*) and *messêtu* (*me-si-e-tum* II R 20) 'street', hence perhaps *mil-ki-tum* 'possession' is to be taken as representing *melḳêtu* (=*malḳâtu*); — *mašḳû* 'drink' fem. *mašḳîtu* 'drinking, drink', *maltû* 'vessel for drinking' fem. *maštîtu* 'beverage', *maršîtu* 'possession', cf. *markîtu* 'refuge'; *maḳlûtu* 'burning'. — *mûšabu* 'dwelling', *mûṣû* 'starting-point'; *mêšaru* 'righteousness, justice', *mêkaltu* 'streamlet' (II R 38, 19 b, cf. Hebr. מִיכַל מַיִם).

Instead of the above, نَفْعَل appears when the stems contain a labial (Barth): *naḳbaru* 'grave', *narbaṣu* 'couch, hiding place', *nadbaku* 'incline, wall' (נִדְבָּךְ), *nappašu* 'dormer-window', *napraku* 'bolt, bar', *nalbašu* 'dress', *našramu* 'sharp-edged tool', *narpasu* 'threshing-roller or sledge', *napsamu* 'bit and bridle', *naglabu* 'scourge', *narkabtu* 'chariot', *naḫlabtu* 'dress', *nakpartu* 'lid', *napḫaru* 'totality', *našpartu* 'mission', *nabšaltu* (sic) 'boiled food' (IV R 64, 7 b), *namraṣu* 'grievance', *našpatu* (also *nišpatu*, C[a] 96) 'court, justice'. — *nabbaḫu* 'rack', *nannabu* 'shoot'; *nâbaru*, *nâbartu* 'cage' (st. א₃בר); *ni-bi-ru* i. e. *nêbiru* (=*nâbaru*, *v*. §§ 32, γ and 35) 'ferry' fem. *nîbartu*, *nîbirtu* (*î*=*ê*=*â*) 'crossing, the other side', *nêribu* (*nîribu*, *nirbu*) 'entrance, pass', *nîpištu* (= *nêpištu*, *nâpaštu*) 'work, production' (cf. מַעֲשֶׂה); for *ni-me-ḳu* a variant of *ne-mi-ḳu* *v*. § 30

p. 78, acc. to which *ni-me-du* 'room' would also come under this form; — *narâmu* 'love, darling' fem. *narâmtu* (formed after the analogy of verbs med. ו, י); —*naḫbû*, *naḫbâtu* 'quiver' (חבא, חבן); *naptêtu* 'key'; *namba'u* 'fountain', *našmû* and *nišmû* (doubtless = *nešmû*) 'hearing', *nišbû* 'satiety'; *namšu* 'washing-green'; *narbû* (*narbûtu*) and *nirbû* 'greatness, size'; *nabnîtu* 'production'.

For words like *nirbû* 'size', *nirmû* foundation', *niptû* 'key', *nirdamu* (also *nardamu*, K. 4378 col. VI 57), *nirmaku* 'pitcher', *nir'amtu* a weapon (I R 28, 12 a), *nibrêtu* 'hunger' we may assume a special form مِفْعَل. — *mêtuḳu* 'way' (Assurn. III 110) stands alone. — The following are exception to Barth's law: *mâmîtu* 'word, oath' (though from אמה), *mûšabu* (*v.* above), *mušpalu* and *mudbaru* (*v.* below).

b) مُفْعَل. *muš-pa-lu* 'depth', *mûlû* 'height' (II R 29, 66 f. b), *mudbaru* 'wilderness' (Tig. V 45, also *madbaru*). — *mu-nu-u* (and *ma-nu-u*) 'couch' (II R 23, 57 f. c). In its place نُفْعَل: *nunṣabtu* (Nimr. Ep. 51, 14).

The form نَفْعَل occurs as inf. of the Nifal or as infin. used as a noun, and also as an adjective e. g. *namkuru* 'property', *na'duru* 'dark', *v.* § 88, b and note.

32. ת: تَفْعَل etc.

a) تَفْعَل. *tarbaṣu* 'court, womb', *tapšaḫu* 'resting-place', *tamḫaru* 'hostile meeting, fight'. — *tâmartu* 'being seen, appearance, sight'; *tallaktu* 'way'; *takkaltu* 'weeping', *tênû* 'couch, bedchamber'; — *tanâttu* 'majesty' (formed after the analogy of verbs med. ו, י); —*tarbû* fem. *tarbîtu* 'shoot, offspring', *tabrû* fem. *tabrîtu* 'gazing, view' plur. *tabrâti*, *târîtu* 'woman with child'; —*tûšaru* 'throwing down'. Cf. the short forms: *têltu*, *têrtu* (also *tûrtu*) 'law', *tûdtu* 'decision' (*v.* § 62, 1).

b) تَفْعِل. *tak-ti-mu* 'covering, envelope', *taškirtu* 'lie', *tazzimtu* 'lamentation', *tazmertu* do. (cf. § 36).—*tâniḫu* 'sighing', *tâdirtu* 'fear', *tâmirtu* 'horizon', *têriktu* 'length', *têniḫu* 'couch', *têništu* 'human being'; — *ta-nit-tu* 'majesty';—*têniḳu* 'suckling, tender shoot'.

A few of the forms with *ê* in the first syllable and *i* in the second may belong to *a*. Others, such as *têdištu* 'renewal', *ta-am-ši-lu* 'likeness, similarity' suggest *d.*—*ta-lit-tu* 'posterity' (st. ולד) is evidently formed by analogy.

c) تَفْعَال. *tašmêtu* 'hearing, granting', cf. *taḫ-ra-aḫ-ḫu* (V R 48 Col. IV 28. V 28).—*tal-la-ak-ku* 'way' (V R 65, 26 b)?

d) تَفْعِيل. *tašrîtu* 'consecration', cf. *šurrû* 'consecrate, begin' (also *tišrîtu* from *tešrîtu*, cf. תִּשְׁרִי), *taṣlîtu* and *teṣlîtu* 'prayer' cf. *ṣullû* 'ask', *teṣbîtu* 'wish, request' cf. *ṣubbû* 'to request'; — *tamlû* (also written *tam-li-a*) 'terrace (cf. *mullû* 'fill up'), setting (of gems)' plur. *tamlêti*.

Cf. also *te-di-(iḳ-)ḳu* 'dress': *c* or *d*? *te-me-ḳu* 'fervour', 'fervent entreaty': *c* or *a* (*b*)?

e) تَفْعُول or تَفْعُل. *taḫlubu* and *taḫlubtu* 'covering, cover, roofing', *tapšuḫtu* 'rest, resting-place', *taḳrubtu* 'attack, fight', *tamgurtu* (II R 40 No. 4), *tam-ḫu-uṣ kakki* (IV R 13, 10b); cf. *targûm-ânu*, *turgûm-ânu* 'interpreter'. — *ta-ḫu-za-tu* a creeping plant, *ta-lu-ku* 'procession, course (of events)'.

f) تُفْعُول. *tur-bu-'u* fem. *tur-bu-u'-tu* 'tumult'.

Note, finally, the peculiar *tabbanû* 'building' plur. *tabbanûtu* (D, 13. 15).

33. ש: شَفْعَل and similar forms, very rare.

a) شَفْعَل. *šapšaḳu* 'necessity' also 'steep path'.

b) شَفْعُل (شَفْعُول?). *šaḫluḳtu* 'destruction', *šal-pû-tu* (doubtless = *šalputtu*) 'fall, devastation, ruin'.

The form شُفْعُل fem. شُفْعُلْتُ occurs as inf. of the Shafel, or as an inf. used as a noun, and also as an adjective, e. g. *šulputtum* 'fall, ruin' (III R 62, 31 a), *šûšurtu* 'a throwing down' (II R 43, 4 a), *šú-ru-ub-tum* 'produce (of fields)' — prop. what they bring in, return — *šûluku* 'current, suitable', *šurbû* 'large', *šušḳû* 'high' *v.* § 88, and note.

2. Afformatives (Nos. 34—39).

These are confined to the formation of nouns from the nominal stems already given, and from their masculine forms almost exclusively.

34. *ûtu* forms abstract nouns. *aplûtu* 'sonship', *abûtu* 'fatherhood', *ilûtu*, *bêlûtu*. Sometimes with col-

lective signification (cf. § 67, a, 6), e. g. *amêlûtù* 'humanity', *littûtu* 'posterity'.

35. *ân*, also modified to *ên*, forms substantives and adjectives. *admânu* 'place of abode'; *râmânu* and *râmênu* (§ 55, c). — *šil-ṭan-nu* 'potentate, ruler' (II R 31, 27a); *ištânu* and *ištênu* 'one, single'; *mi-ra-nu* 'cub'; *lidânu* 'child, young (of animals)' — *dulḫânu* 'disturbance, unrest', *Šulmânu* name of a deity, *ḳur-ba-an-nu* and *ḳir-ba-an-nu* 'offering, alms'; *Uznânu* (n. pr.), *uš-ma-nu* and *uš-man-nu* 'camp'; *bu'šânu*, *bûšânu* 'noisome disease'; *bu-un-na-nu* 'edifice', *bu-(un-)na-(an-)ni(-e)* plur. 'outward appearance, likeness, image'; *šurmênu* 'cypress'. — *adannu* 'tent', *da-la-ba-na-a-ti* plur. fem. (Neb. III 52); *e-ri-in-nu* 'chest, box', doubtless = *erînu*, *erênu*. Compare also the two bird-names *kakkabânu* (from *kakkabu* 'star') and *ḫurâṣânîtu* ('the golden yellow'), *targûmannu* and *turgûmannu* 'interpreter' (*v.* No. 32, e), *nabalkuttânu* 'rebel' (from *nabalkuttu* 'rebellion', (*v.* § 117, 1 under IV 1).

For quadriliterals cf. *argamannu* 'red purple', *kurkizannu* 'rhinoceros', *ḫarbaḳânu* name of a bird (II R 37, 7f). Some of these forms in *anu*, *annu* (*innu*) are doubtless to be regarded as stems with short *ăn*, e. g. *ḳurbannu*, *bit-tan-nu* 'palace' (Esarh. V 32) Hebr. בִּיתָן; it is however no easy matter to separate these from the others, for which reason we did not, for the present, attempt to do so.

36. *ăm* and *âm*, very rare. *êlamu* 'front'. — *ṣu-ma-mu* 'thirst', *si-ri-ia-a-am* 'coat of mail', *pa-li-ia-a-mu* (VR 28, 7a). And with *pu-ri-mu* 'wild ass' cf. Hebr. פֶּרֶא?

37. *â*, origly. *âi̯*, forms adjectives of relation, esp. nomina gentilicia. (For the reading of *a-ia*, *a-a* as *â*, *v.* §§ 13 and 14). *Ar-ma-da-a-ia* 'of Arwad' (I R 28, 2a), *Ṣur-ra-a-a* 'Tyrian'. With the *u* of the nom. sing. *E-la-mu-u* 'Elamite', *U-ru-u* 'of Ur'; also with *û* of the plur.; *amêlu*-*Aššûr-û* 'Assyrian' (Khors. 32), *ṣâbê Nip-pur-û Bâbil-û* (V R 56, 3). Fem. sing. sometimes *â-i-tu* sometimes *îtu* (*v.* § 41, b, p. 99); *ar-ka-a-a-i-tu* 'those of Erech', *Dûr-Šarru-kên-a-a-i-ti* (1 Mich. I 14); *aššû-rîtu*, *akkadîtu*.—Of adjectives with other significations we find e. g. *aḫrû* and *arkû* 'future' (plur. fem. *aḫrâtu*, *arkâtu* 'the future', *dârû* 'lasting', *maḫrû* 'former', *elû*, *šaplû* 'upper, lower' fem. *elîtu*, *šaplîtu*, *ḳaḳ-ḳar*, *ṣu-ma-ma-i-tum* 'wilderness' (Desct. 11 and often). Cf. also § 117, 1.

This *âi̯* is also found appended to the ending *ân* (No. 36): besides *ḫurâṣânîtu* mentioned in No. 35, cf. *rêmênû* (*rêmnû* fem. *rêmnîtu*) 'compassionate', *barânû* 'rebellious' (st. ברה). With participial forms it indicates the continual or professional exercise, so to say, of the particular action: cf. IV R 57, 3. 4. 49a etc. and the common word *mutnennû* 'the pleader' from *utnen* 'I pled for mercy' (*Haupt*).

38. *ai*, which with *u* of the nom. sing. is always contracted to *û*: *eribû* (and *aribu*) 'locust' st. ארב₁ 'lay

waste' (cf. אֲרְבָּה). The same form is apparently found in *egirrû* 'dreams', *igisû* 'present'. This ending may also be recognized in nouns that go back, in the first place, to فُعُّل, such as *nudunnû* 'dowry', *purussû* 'decision', *sulummû* 'favour', *duluḫḫû* 'excitement', *ḫuluḳḳû* 'destruction' (*v.* Pinches' *Texts* p. 18) etc. (*nušurrû*, *pugurrû*, *rugummû*). In many nouns ending in *û*, the origin of the latter is as yet obscure.

As a note to the foregoing, we may also mention *si-ḫi-pu-u* (V R 36, 39 f.), *di-gi-ru-u* and *ḫi-li-bu-u* 'god', *id-di(š)-šu-u* (*v.* Dicty. s. v. אדש₃), *si-su-u* 'horse', *ki-ru-bu-u* 'piece of ground', *šalḫû* 'rampart', *du-ḳa-ḳu-u* 'youth'.

39. *ak* (*âk?* with *u* of the nom. *akku*, *aku*) has the same meaning as *âi̯* (No. 38): note, in the same prop. name, the two varieties *Za-za-a*(-*a*) and *Za-za-ku* i. e. prob. 'endowed with a vast body' (C[a] 220). For *ud-da-ak-ku* ,matutinus' *v.* § 80, *a*.

Cf. also such names and words, belonging to or taken from the artificial language of the grammarians, as *gešpu-tukullâku* (S[c] 25), same formation as *mušên-dûgû* (l. 51); *ša-na-ba-ku* 'possessor of the No. 40' (said of Ea, II R 55, 51 c. d), *ḫe-nun-na-ku* (IV R 61, 45 a), synonymous with *za-za-ku*.—For adjectives in *i-šu* (*i-šam-mu*) *v.* § 80, *α* and *β*.

3. Informatives (No. 40).

40. ת after the first radical: فِتْعَال and similar forms.

a) فِتْعَال. *it-ba-a-ru* 'friendly, friend', *ri-it-pa-šu* 'wide', *git-ma-lu* 'perfect', *mit-ḫa-ru* 'one' (prop. 'meeting, harmonizing', a form with Ifteal signification) fem. *mitḫârtu* (adv. *mitḫâriš* 'in the same way'), *Ištârtu* (prob. = *Itšârtu;* or does עַשְׁתֹּרֶת point to a groundform with *a* in the first syllable, like *atḫû* 'companion, brother', *atmû* 'word, speech'? cf. V R 20, 17 b); *itpêšu* 'careful, prudent'. *Tiz-ḳa-ru* 'exalted' = *zitḳâru*? (cf. § 83 note).

b) فُتْعَال. *šutmâšu* and *šutmêšu* (IV R 52, 43 b). Also *kuštâru* 'tent' (with the same transposition of consonants as in *Ištârtu*)?

The form فِتْعُل fem. فِتْعُلَت appears as the ordinary inf. of the Ifteal, as the infin. used as a noun, and as an adjective, e. g. *ḳitrubu* 'attack' also 'offering', 'gift', *mit-ḫur-tu* 'agreement' (III R 52, 39 b), *šitḳultu* (ibid. 52 a), *mitluktu* 'consultation, decision', *šitultu* (= *šit'ultu*, שׁאל) 'decision', *šitmuru* 'anger; angry', *pitḳudu* 'heedful', *šitluṭu* 'victorious' (Khors. 74), *ḫitmuṭu* 'hasty', *v.* § 88, b and note.

Case-inflexion of nouns in the singular. Apart § 66. from the names of the gods, which, in many cases, have not developed case distinctions, (cf. *Šamaš*, *Sin*, *Marduk*, *Ištâr*), and names of persons, the nominal parts of which very often dispense with the case-endings, (cf. *Adar-malik*, *Šamaš-šum-ukîn*, *Ašûr-aḫ-iddina*), the Assyrian noun, when not standing in the construct state, appears but rarely without a final vowel: cf. *muruṣ ḳaḳ-ḳad* (IV R 3, 43 b), *ku-dur u-kin-nu* 'the boundary they fixed' (II R 65 rev. col. III 21), *mâla šú-um nabû* (IV R 26, 59 a), *unammer kîma ù-um* (V R 34 col. I 52), *simma lâ âṣ* (for *lâ âṣâ*) 'unyielding blindness' (III R 43 col. IV 17). As a rule, all masculine nouns, as well as those with the feminine ending *at*, end in one of the three vowels *u*, *i* or *a*, which, in nominal stems already ending in a short or a long vowel (as is the case with most of the stems derived from verbs tertiæ infirmæ and with the stem § 65 No. 37, cf. 38), unites with the latter to form a long vowel: *û*, *î* (*ê*), *â*. Moreover, it must be laid down as a general rule that *u* is the sign of the nominative (so always in the Assyrian vocabularies), *i* of the genitive, and *a* of the accusative — despite the number and variety of the exceptions that are everywhere found: cf. e. g. *nûru ul immarû* 'light they see not' (Desct. obv. 9), *ṭêmu ut-têrûni* 'they brought the news' (Assurn. I 101), *tar-pa-šú-ú* 'the expanse', acc. (Lay. 38, 17); *ana nâru inad-dûšu* 'they throw them into the river' (V R 25, 6 b); *iplaḫ libbašunu* 'their heart was afraid', Nebuchadnezzar *mu-da-a e-im-ga* 'the prudent, the wise' (Neb. Bors. I 4), *ru-ba-a-am na-a-dam* (nom.); *pîšu imsi* 'he washed his mouth', *rubbiši zêrim* 'increase the offspring', *ma-a-ti u ni-ši* 'land and people' (acc., Neb. Senk. I 9), etc. In Babylonian vocabularies the vowel *i* is often found in the nominative. To the short case-endings (*u*, *i*, *a*) an *m* may be appended, identical in origin with the emphatic particle *ma*, which here and elsewhere is frequently shortened to *m* (*v.* § 79): *um*, *im*, *am*, fem. *atum*, *atim*, *atam*. With long vowels, however, the mimation is found only in isolated cases, e. g. *re-e-um* 'shepherd' i. e. *rê'ûm*, *ra-bi-im* gen. of *rabû* (I R 52 No. 4 rev. 8), *ru-ba-a-am* 'the great'. The mimation has no reference to the definite or indefinite signification of the noun: *ilum* and *ilu* both denote *the* god and *a* god.

For the contraction of the final vowels of the stem (*a*, *â*, *i*, *î*, *u*, *û*, *ê*) with *u* of the nom. and *a* of the acc. to *û* and *â* see § 38, a. With *i* of the genitive, one might suppose that final *i*, *î*, *u*, *û* and *ê* would be contracted to *î*, *a* and *â*, on the other hand, to *ê*, but as a matter of fact we find as frequently *ê* in the former case as *î* in the latter: *šakû* (فَعِل) gen. *ša-ki-e* and *ša-ki-i*, *ina ra-mi-e-ka* 'when thou openest', but also *a-ṣi-i* gen. of *aṣû*, *nam-si-e* 'washingplace' gen. of *namsû* (= *namsî-u*) etc. Cf. § 30 p. 78.

Formation of the plural of nouns (excluding those with the feminine ending *atu*). § 67.

a) The following terminations occur in the plural of substantives:

1) *ê*, *passim*. The frequent cases in which the plural is written so as expressly to emphasize the *e*

of the *auslaut* (examples p. 75) seem to justify us in also reading plural forms like *mal-ki*, *ar-ḫi*, *gi(r)-ri* 'ways' (Assurn. I 43. 45) as *malkê*, *arḫê*, *girrê;* also *laḳ-ti* 'fingers', *ḳa-ti* 'hands' as *laḳtê*, *ḳâtê*. In any case, notwithstanding the interchange of *ê* and *î* in pronunciation, we must regard *ê* as the original plural ending, and must admit that *ê* was also the original pronunciation. *ê* is found construed as feminine e. g. in *emûḳê ṣîrâti* 'surpassing strength', *emûḳê rabâte* (Senhb. VI 59). From stems tertiæ י (ו) cf. *abê* 'fathers' (*abû*^{pl}*-e-a* 'my fathers' I R 7 No. E, 5), *ru-bi-e* 'the magnates', *šamê* 'the heavens', *mi-e*, *me-e* 'the waters'. The two last-named substs. have also *šamâmi* and *mâmi*. An *m* is found appended to *ê* in Neb. II 14. 34: *ša-di-im* i. e. in my opinion *šadê-m* 'mountains', IV R 61, 19. 32 b: *še-rim* (*šêrê-m*) *u lîlâti* 'morning and evening'. Cf. § 57, b.

2) *âni* (*ânu*), *passim*. *ilâni* 'gods', *ziḳîpê* and *zaḳîpâni* 'stakes' (Lay. 72 No. 2, 8), *ḫuršâni* and *ḫur-ša-a-nu* (I R 28, 12 a), *ḫarbânu* and *tilânu* (III R 66 rev. 36. 37 d), *ṣal-ma-a-nu* 'images' (Beh. 106). From stems tertiæ י cf. *šadâni*, adverbially *šá-da-ni-iš* 'like mountains' (e. g. Neb. VI 34).

3) *ân*, always construed as feminine: *e-mu-ḳa-an*, *e-mu-ḳan ṣîrâte* (e. g. Lay. 33, 6), *i-da-an paḳlâte* 'powerful forces' (Sarg. Cyl. 24), *ur-maḫ-ḫe pi-tan*

bir-ke (Senhb. Kuj. 4, 21). *ên* (with *â* modified to *ê*) is also found; observe the interesting form *e-mu-ki-in* i. e. *emûḳên gašrâtim* 'the powerful forces' (Hamm. Louvre II 15). This ending is found as the plur. of a masculine substantive in *ar-di-en* (1 Mich. II 4).

4) *â*, very frequently construed as feminine. *VI ur-ra* (elsewhere also *ur-re*) '6 days' (Nimr. Ep. XI, 121), *ru-bi-e u šak-kan-nak-ka* (V R 35, 18), *ni-ri-ba-ši-in* 'their entrances' (Neb. V 63), *ar-na-a-šu* 'his misdeeds', *nam-ra-ṣa* 'difficulties' (Neb. II 21, elsewhere *namraṣê*), *puggulû e-mu-ga-a-šû* 'powerful are his forces' (V R 64 col. I 25), *nidbâšu ellûtim* (Neb. Grot. I 13), *ši-in-na-a-šu* 'his teeth', *si-ba ḳaḳ-ḳa-da-šu* 'his (its) heads are seven' (II R 19, 14 b), *rêšâšu* 'its top', *išdâšu* 'its foundation', *sittâtim ma-ḫa-za* 'the other cities' (V R 35, 5), *il-la-ka di-ma-a-a* 'my tears do flow', *kat-ma šap-ta-šu-nu* (Nimr. Ep. XI, 120). This form in *â* is the favorite form for the plural of the names of those parts of the body that occur in pairs, e. g. *bir-ka-a-a* 'my knees', *še-pa-a-a* 'my feet', *u-zu-na-a-šu* 'his ears' (mind); the plur. in *ê*, however, is also of frequent occurrence. For the formation of the numerals 20, 30, 40 and 50 by means of the plur. in *â*, see § 75.

We cannot enter here into a further discussion of the question as to the possible relationship existing between these four terminations. A very instructive form in this connexion, however, which is deserving of special mention, is *i-na-an*, which according to the ideograms, and therefore according to the Assyrians' own teaching, denotes 'the two eyes' and 'the two words *înu*' (viz. eye and fountain); see the Zurich vocab. rev. 17—19, and cf. V R 36, 39 c.

5) *û*. *pa-ar-ṣu rêštûtu* 'the laws in force from the beginning' (Nerigl. I 20), *ù-mu rab-bu-tum* (IV R 1, 19 a), *še-e-du* (IV R 5, 4 a), 470 *pil-ḫal-lu-šu* (III R 5 No. 6, 12), cf. III R 66 rev. 38—40 d. In *annû'a ma'idâ* 'my sins are many' (IV R 10, 37 a) it is construed as feminine (*v.* also § 70, b). An *m* is appended to *û* in IV R 20 No. 1 obv. 25: *be-el be-lum* 'the lord of lords'.

6) *ûtu* (*ûti*, *ûta*, *ûtum*); very rare, without question identical with the afformative *ûtu* of the nominal stem § 65 No. 34, to some extent, therefore, a so-called 'broken plural'. *tab-ba-nu-ú-tu* 'buildings' (D, 13. 15: *mâdûtu* 'many', *ullûtu* 'these'), *a-me-lu-ú-tú* (e. g. D, 3), *a-me-lu-ta* (I R 27 No. 2, 69), *a-me-lu-ti* (IV R 68, 27 b) etc. 'human beings', *ša-mu-tum* 'the heavens' (verb: *ušazninâ*, Senhb. IV 76).

b) Adjectives and participles, in so far as they preserve their signification as such, always form their plural by means of the termination just given, viz:

ûtu (*ûti*, *ûte*, *ûtum*). *ilâni šur-bu-tú* (IV R 59, 49 b), *ḫuršâni šaḳûti* (*šaḳûtu*, *šaḳûte*) 'lofty mountain ranges', *ûmê ru-ḳu-ti*, *arḫê* or *girrê paškûtc* (Assurn. I 43. 45), *ma-ru git-ma-lu-tum* (IV R 1, 6 c), *limnûti* 'the bad ones' (Assurn. I 8), *balṭûti* 'the living ones'; *(i)a-a-bu-ut* 'enemies' (cf. § 64 p. 154); *âlikût(u)* 'current, living' plur., *mu-ut-tab-bi-lu-ut* 'governing' (Tig. I 15), etc.

Since adjectives and participles, however, very readily assume, or at least tend to assume, the significations of substantives, we find in addition to *ûtu ê. ru-bi-e* 'the great ones, magnates' (V R 35, 18, cf. § 67, a, 4), *lâ ma-gi-re* 'the unsubmissive' (Senhb. I 8), *multaḫṭê* 'the rebels', *mun-nab-ti* 'the fugitives', *mundaḫ(i)ṣê* 'the warriors', etc.

The ending *û* occurs IV R 2, 40 b: *ul zik(a)rû šú-nu*; or is *zi-ka-ru* to be taken as sing. notwithstanding the parallel *zinnišâti?*

Formation of the Feminine. The Assyrian § 68. noun distinguishes but two genders, the masculine and the feminine, the latter having also in the case of adjectives a neuter signification, e. g. *ṭâbtu* 'good' (*das Gute*), *limuttu* 'evil', *šîmtu* 'what is appointed, fate' (cf. § 9 No. 212). The feminine ending is *at* (*atu*, *ati*, *ata; atum* etc., *v.* § 66), which attaches itself to the nominal stem stripped of the case endings (in certain cases with syncope of the vowel of the second syllable, *v.* § 65 before Nos. 1 and 6): *kalbu* fem. *kalb-atu*, *rapšu* fem. *rapaštu*. When *ê* or *ė* precedes, the feminine ending is *it*, hence *bêlitu*, *ellitu* (*v.* § 35). Very frequently the *a* of the ending *atu* is syncopated, which produces the appearance of *tu* alone being appended to the stem of the masculine: cf. *šattu* 'year' (= *šan-tu* = *šan-atu*, st. cstr. *šanat*), *ti'âmtu* (= *ti'âm-atu*), *ṣi-ḫirtu* (= *ṣiḫir-atu*) etc., and *v.* § 37, a, where we have already remarked that forms like *bikîtu*, *rabîtu*, *šaḳûtu* (Ishtar *ša-ḳu-ut ilâni*), *šurbûtu* (Ishtar *šur-bu-ut ilâni*, II R 66 No. 1, 4) etc. are to be considered as syncopated forms of *bikî-atu* (*bikai̯-atu*), *rabî-atu* etc.; cf. the interesting singulars *na-gi-a-tu*, *i-ti-a-tu* (*v.* § 65 Nos. 6 and 9), *ta-mi-a-tu* (*v.* § 108 end). A large number of illustrations of what has now been said is contained in § 65. A few of the participles formed from verbs tertiæ infirmæ are peculiar in this respect, that they suppress their final vowel and with it their last radical in the st. cstr. before the feminine ending: cf. *še-ma-at ik-ri-bi le-ḳa-at un-nin-ni* (II R 66 No. 1, 7), *mušalḳat*, *mušamṣat* (ibid. l. 6). The same phenomenon appears to a still greater extent, in the derivatives of stems tertiæ י where, besides the regular feminine participles like *ka-mi-tum*, *lâ pa-di-tum* (IV R 57, 50. 53 a), *bânîtu* (*ba-ni-ti-ia*, cf. *Zêr-bânîtu*), we find the contracted forms *bântu* (*ba-an-tum* V R 29, 66 h), and where, besides the usual constr. form *ba-nit ilâni*, we also find *ba-na-at ilâni*. In the same way the nominal form فَعِل, in addition to the regular feminine forms like *rabîtu*, for example, admits a formation like *le'atu*, whence *lêtu* ('might, power, victory' and 'wild cow'), st. cstr. *le-'a-at*, from the masculine *le'û*. See § 39 above, and for *le'at* § 62, 1.

Note 1). On the femin. forms in *utu*: ***mut-tal-ku-tu ša sûḳê*** 'that roams the streets' (IV R 57, 1 a), ***ru-uḳ-ḳu-ti*** (E, 12, elsewhere, even in the Achæmenian inscriptions, ***rûḳti***, fem. of ***rûḳu*** 'far') I do not venture to pronounce an opinion. For ***šanûtu*** 'secunda' *v.* § 76. ***Ina ummânišu i-ṣu-tu*** 'with his scanty army (V R 64 col. I 30) must be understood in the light of Nabon. II 42. 51, compared with § 70 b, end (*ummânêšu*!). Quite unique is the fem. in *âtu* in Desct. 5: ***ina ḳaḳ-ḳar a-ga-a rap-ša-a-tum. tap-'pat-tum*** 'companion, concubine' (V R 39, 62 d) is also difficult; the form reminds one of ***a-ḫat-tum*** 'sister', but for the fem. of ***tappû*** 'companion' (*v.* § 65 No. 24) we should expect ***tappîtu***.

2) Not a few Assyr. substantives have a fem. termination in the sing. where Hebrew (in most cases like the other Semitic languages) has none: thus e. g. ***erṣitu, ti'âmtu, napištu, rû'tu, rûtu*** 'breath, spirit', ***kabittu*** 'liver, disposition', ***zibbatu*** 'tail', cf. also ***Elamtu*** 'Elam', ***Idiḳlat, Diḳlat*** 'Tigris'.

Plural of Feminines in *atu*. Substantives and adjectives having *atu* in the sing. take the plural in *âti* (*âte*, *âtim*, also *âtum*, *âtu*, *âta*): *šar-ra-a-ti* 'queens', *ta-ma-a-ti* 'seas', *kibrâti* 'regions', *pulḫâti* 'fear' (for forms like *nakamâti*, *tubuḳâti* *v.* § 65 Nos. 5 and 6 note), *um-mânâte'a gab-ša-a-te* (Senhb. III 43), *mâtâti ru-ga-a-ti* 'distant lands' (Neb. II 13). When the stem of the singular, to which the fem. termination is to be attached, ends in *î* or *û*, e. g. *rabî^a^tu*, *ḫidû^a^tu*, this ending unites with *â* of *âti* to form *â* (*v.* § 38 a): *nišê ra-* **§ 69.**

ba-a-ti 'the mighty nations' (IV R 32), *tabrâti* plur. of *tabrîtu*, *ḫidâti*, *minâti*. *unâti* plur. of *unûtu*, *ugnâtum* plur. of *ugnîtu*, *ruššâtu* (sing. masc. *ruššû*). The cases are rare where the vowel is retained: *mâtâti ša-ni-a-ti* 'other lands' (Shalm. Mo. rev. 33), *nam-zi-a-te* (Assurn. II 67), *e-ri-a-tum* 'women with child' (III R 62, 26 a) alongside of *e-ra-a-ti*. For feminine forms in *êti* (with change of *â* to *ê*) like *girrêti*, *ešrêti*, *bêlêti*, *kudurrêti*, and even *mâdêtu* (note also *mâtâti ša-ni-ti-ma* Desct., 7) *v.* § 32, *α* and *γ*.

For the feminine plurals with suff. of 1. pers. sing. like *ḫa-blâtû'a v.* § 74, 2, e. Cases are rare in which the plural termination *âti* is appended to a feminine in *atu* with retention of the *t* of the sing. The best attested examples are: *le-ta-at ḳur-di-ia* 'the victories of my courage' (Tig. VIII 39), *lêtât* plur. of *lêtu*, 'might, victory' (st. לאה), and *i-si-ta-a-te* (Assurn. I 109) or *a-si-ta-a-te* (Shalm. Mo. rev. 53), plur. of *isîtu*, *asîtu* 'pillar', alongside of which we also find (Tig. VI 27) the regular plur. *a-sa-ia-te*, pron. *asâte* (§ 12). Cf. also *ṣalmatâte* 'defences' (Assurn. Mo. rev. 40) in the second syllable of which the reading is uncertain. Does *mâtâti* 'countries' belong to this category? The Hebr. קְשָׁתוֹת is in Assyr. *ḳašâti*. The plural ending *ê* (*ân*) is taken by a couple of substantives, which have forgotten the origin of their *t*, viz. *daltu* 'door', plur. *daltê* (Hebr. דְּלָתוֹת), and *šaptu* 'lip', cf. *šap-te-e-šu* 'his lips' (V R 3, 80), *šap-tan* (construed as fem., IV R 16, 61 b), also *šaptâ* (*v.* p. 185).

§ 70. *a*) A number of Assyr. nouns have the feminine plural in *âti*, although the sing. lacks the feminine termination; thus *nâru* 'stream' plur. *na-ra-a-ti* (IV R 22, 11b), *înu* 'fountain' plur. *înâti*, *gurunnu* 'heap' *gu-*

runâti (*guruneti*, Shams. IV 30), *ḳanû* 'reed' *ḳanâti*. *miṣru* 'territory' *miṣrêti*, *kudurru* 'boundary, boundary stone' *kudurrêti*, *pîru* 'elephant' *pîrâti*, *atânu* 'she-ass' *atânâti*, *ekallu* 'palace' *ekallâti*, *papaḫu* 'chamber' *papaḫâti*, *pit*(?)*pânu* 'bow' *pitpânâti*, *pilaḳḳu* 'axe' *pilaḳḳâti*, *riksu* 'bond, league' *riksâti*, *ḫarrânu* 'street, procession' *ḫarrânâti*; *ḫazzanu* 'ruler of the city' *ḫazzanâti*, etc.

Mu-ša-a-ti 'nights' may be plur. of *mûšu* or *mušîtu*. The sings. of *ba-ma-a-ti* 'high places' and *par-ṣa-a-tú* 'lies' (Beh. 100) are unknown to me. *lîlâtu* 'evening', *re-ša-a-tum* 'shouting' (e. g. S[b] 352) and *ši-na-a-tu* 'urine' (S[b] 229) are probably used only in the plur.; cf. the masc. plur. tantum *uššê*, *uššû* 'bottom, foundation'. *Ṣâtu* 'eternity' plur. of *ṣîtu* 'exit'?—A number of adjectives unite seemingly with the plur. in *âti* the meaning of substantives, by leaving a subst. of the fem. gender to be understood; cf. *aḫrâtu* 'the future', prop. future (times), *ana dârâti* 'for ever', *ana ru-ḳa-ti* 'to distant ages' (IV R 44, 31), *ana ru-ki-e-ti* 'afar, to a distance' (he fled, Senhb. II 10, IV 14 and oft). *Ṣalmat* (*ṣalmât?*) *ḳaḳḳadi* Babyl. *gagada(m)* also 'the black-headed' men (supply *šiknât* or *ni-šim?*) possibly comes under this head.

b) Many nouns, which lack the feminine termination *atu* in the sing., have in the plural the (exclusively feminine) ending *âti* and also one of the (mainly masculine but occasionally feminine) endings given in § 67 *a*, 1—5. Examples: *ep*(*i*)*ru* 'sand, earth, dust' plur. *epirê* (construed as masc.) and *eprâti*, *girru* 'way' *girrê* and *girrêti*, *ṭûdu* 'way' *ṭu-ud-de* (Tig. IV 53) and *ṭu-da-at* (Sarg. Cyl. 11), *šûḳu* 'street' *sûḳâni* and *sûkâti*, *nîribu* 'entrance, pass' *nîribê*, *nîribâ*, *nîribêti*, *mâtu* 'country' *mâtâti* and *ma-tan* (V R 62 No. 1, 3), *ubânu* 'point of finger, peak' *ubânê* and *ubânâti*, *bâbu* 'gate' *bâbâni* (*ba-bi* Senhb. Const. 71) and *bâbâti*, *bîtu* 'house' *bîtâni* and *bîtâti*, *igâru* 'wand' *igârû*, *igarê* and *igârâti*, *lišânu* 'tongue, speech' *li-ša-(a-)nu* (IV R 20 No. 1 obv. 24, construed as fem. B, 3) and *li-ša-na-a-ta* (O, 16), *kursinnu* 'ankle-bone' *kursinnâ*, *kursinnû* and *kursin(n)âti*, *šinnu* 'tooth' *šinnâ* and *šinnâti*, *ḳarnu* 'horn' *ḳar-ni* (also V R 6, 29 var.!) and *ḳarnâti*, *ṣumbu* 'cart' *ṣumbê* and *ṣumbâti*, *ûmu* 'day' *ûmê* and *ûmât* (I R 28, 14 a), *kuppu* 'jet of water, spring' plur. *kuppê* and *kuppâti*, *ud(u)rê* and *udrâti* 'dromedaries', *tuppu* 'tablet' (S^c 38) *tuppê*, *tuppâni* and *tuppâti*, *kultârê* and *kultârâti* 'tents', *ummânu* (rarely *ummâtu*, *v.* p. 116) 'army, troops' *ummânâte*, but also *ummânê* (*um-ma-ni* V R 35, 24. 64 col. I 39. 43 must be so understood, *v.* § 74, 1, b); *nasîku* 'prince' *nasîkâni* and *nasîkâti*, etc.

§ 71. Gender. Many substantives even without the fem. ending *atu* are of the feminine gender. *a*) The names of parts of the body that occur in pairs, such as *uznu*, *ênu*, *šaptu*, *ḳâtu*, *birku*, *šêpu*. But also *šinnu*, *lišânu*, *kursinnu*. *b*) Other words of the fem. gender are: *abullu* 'city gate', *bâbu*, *ḫalṣu* 'fortification' (*ḫalṣi rabîtim* acc., Neb. Bab. II 16), *ḫarrânu*, *ušmannu* 'camp', *ummânu*, *elippu* 'ship', *ḫaṭṭu* 'staff, sceptre' (*nâš ḫaṭṭi ṣirti, elliti*), *pitpânu* (but *pitpânu šu'atu* III R 16 No. 4, 51), *birḳu* 'lightening' (Tig. VIII 84), *zuḳtu* 'point, top', *emûḳu*. Also *mâtu* 'country'. *c*) The names of rivers, cf. at least the common *Purât ina mîliša êbir* (Shalm. Ob.).

The following are of the common gender: *abnu* 'stone', *eḳlu* 'field' (masc. III R 43, fem. Esarh. VI 49), *girru* 'campaign' (fem. Senhb. V 26), *urḫu* 'way', *kussû* 'chair, throne', *bîtu* 'house', *ekallu* 'palace', *ummânu* 'army' (masc. Senhb. Const. 30. Nabon. II 42. 51), etc.

The Construct State. *a*) Singular. When, § 72. with a noun in the singular, there is joined a substantive in the genitive (the so-called nexus of the construct state), the first member of the nexus drops the mimation and also, in the nom. and acc., the vowel of the case ending. For the re-appearance (in words without the feminine ending *atu*) of the short vowels of the stem, that had suffered syncope before the case ending, and for their continuance in that state before the permanent *a* (*i*) of the feminine ending *at* (*it*), in the nominal stems given in § 65 Nos. 1—8, see there. The *i* of the genitive of the first member is retained; even in the nom. and acc. the vowel *i* may take the place of the constr. state. Examples: *ba-ab bîti, bêl ilâni, miṣir Aššûr, muruṣ kaḳḳadi, erêb Šamši, napḫar mâtâti; bêlût mâtâti, gimrat ilâni rabûti*

(Shalm. Ob. 1). — *ana nîri bêlûti'a, ša-ak-ni Bêl* 'of Bel's vicegerent' (IV R 44, 14), *ina tukulti ilâni rabûti, ṣi-ir zuḳti Nipur* 'on the top of the mountains of Nipur' (Senhb. III 69). — *bi-ši-ti šá-di-im ḫi-iṣ-bi tâmâtim* (Neb. II 35), 'I love *puluḫti ilûtišunu*' (Neb. I 38). This use of the genitive in place of the constr. state is especially frequent in nominal stems ending in the nom. sing. in long *û*, and derived from verbs with a weak letter as their third radical: cf. *ša-ni-e ṭêmi* 'madness' (nom., Assurb. Sm. 135, 54), *mu-pi-(it-)ti durug šadâni* (Tig. II 86), *mu-di-e tuḳunti* 'experienced in fight' (acc., Shams. II 18), *ḫi-ri-e nâri* (acc., Sarg. Cyl. 46. 55). But we find also e. g. *rab šaḳê*. — If the first member retains the case-endings *u* and *a*, the construct nexus is broken, and *ša* must appear before the genitive which follows as the second member e. g. *erêbu ša Šamši.*

To these rules, as to the rules regarding the case endings (§ 66), there are a great number and variety of exceptions. It is an extremely common thing to find the first member retaining the case endings *u* and *a*, without *ša* appearing before the second member; e. g. *šalâmu Šamši* 'the west' (Tig. VI 44), *ḫarbašu taḫâzi'a* (III R 4 No. 4, 48), *ṣubâtu bêlûtišu* 'his royal robe' (acc., III R 4 No. 4, 45), *mandattu bêlûti'a* (Senhb. Const. 15), *šušḳû tamlî* 'the heightening of the terrace' (Senhb. Bell. 54); *mâla libbi*, *kullata ilâni* 'the totality of the gods' (V R 35, 34). The same is the case with participles as the first member, see § 131. Even the mimation is sometimes retained: *kîma pûrim ṣêri* 'like the wild-ox' (IV R 63, 49 b), *ḫarânam namrasâ* (Neb. II 22). On the other hand expressions like *ṭêm ša Arabi* 'news of the Arabs' (K. 562, 10) are extremely rare.

b) Plural. The plural terminations *ûti* and *âti*, when standing in the constr. state, also, in most cases, drop the final vowel: *âbût Ašûr* (Assurn. I 28); *idât ilâni* (Tig. I 81), *šanât nuḫše* 'years of plenty' (Tig. VIII 29), *ba'ûlât Bêl* (Tig. I 33. Lay. 33, 5 and oft.), *šinnât imêri* 'asses' teeth'. But cf. also *šalmâta ḳurâdêšunu* 'the corpses of their warriors' (Shams. IV 29). For the plural ending *ê* cf. *mê nâri* 'the waters of a stream', but also *kâpê ša šadê* 'the rocks of the mountains' (Assurn. I 65); for the other plural endings; cf. *ilâni ša šamê* (IV R 28, 20 b), *gubbâni ša mê* 'water cisterns', but also *ma-ši-ḫa-an eḳli* 'land surveyor' (III R 41 col. I 14); *gi-me-ir ma-al-ku šadî u ḫuršâni* 'all the princes of the high lands and the mountains' (IV R 44, 18).

Composition of words or the fusion of two nouns to one word as the expression of a single idea is found *a*) with two nouns standing in the construct relation (including the cases in which the first member is a participle): *apil šarrûtu*, 'princely dignity, right of succession to the throne' (V R 1, 20), *âlik pânûtu*, 'headship' (K. 312, 11), *nâš paṭrûtu* 'right of carrying a dagger' (V R 61 col. V 25); — *bît nakantu* 'treasure-house' plur. *bît nakamâti* (V R 5, 132 ff. con- § 73.

strued as masc. plur.), *murnisku*, i. e. doubtless *mûr nisku* 'horse' (so called as being the 'noble' animal), cf. *aban nisiḳti* 'precious (*i. e.* 'noble') stone', plur. *mur(mu-ur)-ni-is-ḳe* (Esarh. IV 26 and oft.), *mu-ur-ni-is-ke-ia* 'my steeds' (III R 38 No. 2 rev. 62). Expressions like *bin binim* 'grandson', (as is shown by *lillidu*, doubtless = *lid lidu*, cf. p. 145) are also to be regarded as single words. *b*) Adjectives, preceded by a substantive which stands virtually in the accusative. A peculiarity of Assyrian syntax consists in placing the object before the finite verb on which it is dependent (*v.* § 142), a construction which we also find in rare cases with the participle of the Qal (cf. *Zêr-bânîtum*, *Sammu-râmat*, i. e. 'incense-loving'? see § 131 note), frequently with infinitives (e. g. *mîta bulluṭu* 'raising of the dead', see § 132) and not less seldom with the adjectives (§ 88) corresponding to the perm. and inf. of the derived verbal stems (cf. *ḫurâṣu uḫḫuzu* 'set in gold'). An extension of this construction, apparently, led to other classes of adjectives having placed before them accusatives that had been added for more precise definition. We usually find, it is true, *ṭâbat rigma* (Nimr. Ep. XI, 111), *rapša uzni* 'of a far-reaching mind', *pit uzni* 'of an open mind', 'Sin *bêlu nam-ra ṣi-it* the lord, glorious in (his) rising' (IV R 2, 22 b, elsewhere: *ša ṣêsu namrat*), but we also find *še-ip u-rik* 'longfoot' (a bird II R 37, 46 b), *ilu ḳa-at ra-bu-tú* (III R 66 rev. 23 d), *libbu rapšu*, *libbu ritpâšu* 'magnanimous' (V R 4, 37. 35, 23), *libbu rûḳu* do., *libba palḫu* 'of a god-fearing heart' (V R 63, 4 a), *šumu ṭâbu* 'fair-named' (of Nebo), *a-ša-ri-du* 'the first, noblest' properly *ašar edu* 'the first in place, he that occupies the foremost place', whence the plur. *a-ša-rid-du-ti* (Khors. 31), an abstr. noun *ašaridûtu* 'foremost place, precedence, majesty'.

We would here add in a note a word or two regarding the numerous and still somewhat puzzling Assyro-Babylonian substantives like *gù-maḫ-ḫu* 'great bull', *paramaḫ(ḫ)u* 'holy sanctuary', *kisalluḫ(ḫ)u* 'floor-polisher' (V R 13, 1—4 b, fem. *kisalluḫatu*), *tupšarru* 'tablet-writer'. That words like these, which are commonly regarded as 'Sumerian' compounds and loan-words, really served as *words*, did not, that is, possess merely ideographic value, is as little open to question as is the fact that many of them can only be explained as compounds. Now whoever cannot bring himself to see in the Assyr. *parakku* (and with it the Hebr. פָּרֹכֶת, cf. also Syr. ܦܪܟܐ), with its etymon of the best Assyro-Semitic, a loan-word from an hypothetical Sumerian *bara(g)*, but finds in *bara(para)*, which accompanies the ideogram for *parakku* as a gloss and is also used as a syllabic value, only a contraction of *parakku* (*ba-rak-ku* Senhb. Kuj. 4, 6. 8 and oft.), must recognize in the whole word *pa-ra-ma-ḫu*, *para-maḫ(ḫ)u* (Sarg. Cyl. 49. Bull Inscr. 47) a coin from the Semitic mint. This conclusion is all the more unavoidable from the fact that we do not first require to cast about for a plausible derivation of *maḫḫu*. The Assyr. *paramaḫu* bears the stamp of a word coined for a purpose by Semites. There is a host of such artificially formed words in Assyrian, although but a comparatively small minority has been adopted into the language of every-day life. As examples of words whose artificial character has never been denied, and whose Semitic origin has been universally admitted, we would cite the names of the Assyrian characters and groups of characters: the sign *ar* compounded of *ši (igi)* and *tal* has the name *igitallu* (S[a] 1, 2); the ideogram for *ṣupru* 'nail, claw' etc., made up of *gad, tak* and *ûr*, bears the name *gadatakkurû* (S[c] 298). The collections of ideograms, therefore, made by the Babylono-Assyrian scholars, which now serve us as vocabularies, merit our serious attention. They show us the tolerably extensive use of words which have been artificially developed from the ideographic method of writing. Accustomed as they were to express every idea, every object, not only by a phonetic reproduction of the word but also by a variety of ideograms, and to regard these groups of ideograms as having precisely the same meaning as the words themselves, the masters of the art of writing in Babylonia, the priests and the scholars, in learning and using these ideograms, must have felt the boundary between the latter with their conventional readings, the ideogram-words, so to say, and the proper words corresponding thereto being gradually and imperceptibly effaced. Most of these artificially formed words, of course, as we find them again and again in the 'vocabularies' (cf. e. g. V R 32 No. 1 obv. 7—17), never got beyond the stage of *termini technici*, never, that is, came into general use. For all that, the number of words of this stamp which one meets in cuneiform texts of the most diverse contents is by no means small. They will all have to be questioned one by one as to the manner of their composition and properly arranged; we may perhaps be able to discover a certain class of ideas, to which all the conceptions and things represented by such words belong. To two points only would I here call attention. The Babylonians and Assyrians call a written document, destined in particular to hand down the name of its author, *šiṭir šumi* or *šumu šaṭru* (also *šumu zakru*, v. II R 40, 46 f. c. d. IV R 45, 12. 14) and this they express ideographically, following closely the Semitic term just given, as *mu-sar-(a)*, from which was derived a new word that afterwards became the usual term for 'document, inscription', viz. *mu-sa-ru-û*

(Khors. 159 *musarrû*, Esarh. VI 64 *mu-ša-ru-ú*). Now when we find appended to this *musarû* in Senhb. VI 68. Esarh. VI 64 ff. V R 64 col. III 45. 47 (cf. II 43) and other passages the appositional expression *šiṭir šumi*, do we not feel inclined to suspect that *musarû*, notwithstanding its frequent use, must have continued to give the impression of a rare word that needed to be explained? We must also call attention once more (*v.* the beginning of this note and cf. § 25 p. 68) to the fact that many words belong only in appearance to this class of artificial neologisms, their ideograms being based on the reverse process, the artificial breaking up of a genuine Semitic substantive with three or four consonants. Such is certainly the case, for example, with *ki-sur-ru* (Khors. 82. 136, cf. V R 31, 3 e. f) i. e. *kisurru* (or *kisurrû*? cf. *kusurrû*) 'boundary, district' from כסר 'hem in, mark off' (not a compound, therefore, from *ki-sur-ra*) and apparently with *ki-maḫ-ḫu* 'coffin', which, in spite of its being written ideographically *ki-maḫ*, must be derived from the triliteral stem קמח, as is proved by *gi-ma-ḫi* a variant of *ki-ma-ḫi* Sm. 50 l. 14. Do *ekallu* 'palace' (ideogr. *e-gal*), *ḫu-ḫa-ru* 'bird-trap' Tig. jun. obv. 15. 32) and others also belong to this category?

I give here in conclusion a short list of additional words which in my opinion are to be understood, or at least deserve to be examined, from the point of view here laid down: *ab-kal-lu* 'chief ruler' (*kal* sign § 9 Nos. 162 and 169, *v.* Dicty., No. 23), *gû-gal*(169)-*lum* 'large bull' (IV R 23, 10 a) — same formation as *gu-uk-kal-lum*, *gu-uk-ka-al-lam* (S[b] 1 obv. col. III 12. Neb. Grot. III 12)? —, *dim*(?)-*gal*(169)-*le-e* plur. 'architect' (Senhb. VI 45; for the sign *dim* = *banû* *v.* S[c] 279), *ki-ši-ib-gal*(169)-*lum* 'chief overseer' (V R 13, 34 b; cf. with *kišib* 'oversight' Hebr. כבשׁ?), *šú-uš-kal-lu* a species of snare or such like (ideogr. *šú-uš-gal* and *šú-uš-kal*), *ú-šum-gal-lu*; *amêlu*-*sur-maḫ-ḫu* the name of a class of priests (Khors. 157), *iṣu*-*sar-maḫ* 'large park' (Esarh. VI 14), *ur-maḫ-ḫe* plur. 'lions' (Kuj. 4, 21); *zag-mu-ku* 'beginning of the year' Neb. II 56 with the explanatory addition *rêš šatti* (without the latter Neb. IV 1 and oft., *zag-muk-ki* Esarh. VI 46, *zag-muk* III R 52, 37. 51 b, cf. IV R 18, 23/24 a), *im-ḫul-lu* 'ill wind', repeatedly with the explanatory addition *šâru limnu* e. g. IV R 5, 39 a, *egi-zaggû* (*v.* Dicty. No. 58), *agargarû* (*v. ibid.* No. 74), *šà-gurrû* 'compassion', prop. 'turning of the heart to one' (V R 21, 55 a), *kiḫullû* 'weeping, lamentation' (Khors. 78. V R 7, 15. 47, 44 b), *ḫegallu*, also *ḫengallu* (IV R 20 No. 1 obv. 22), 'overabundance' cf. *ḫe-nun* (*ḫe* sign § 9 No. 138) = *nuḫšu*, whence the adj. *ḫenunnâku* (cf. § 65 No. 39 note).

For the fusion of the noun with the independent pronouns of the first and second persons to form the seeming permansives *ṣîrât*, *šarrâku* etc. *v.* § 91.

§ 74. Union of the Substantive (and the participle) with the pronominal Suffixes (cf. § 56, a).

1) The substantive (and participle) in the singular. *a*) The suffixes except the first pers. sing. These suffixes may be appended either to the construct form of the substantive or to the forms with case endings. The former method is the favourite one when the subst. stands in the nominative; it is also frequently found with the accusative; the genitive, however, regularly retains its *i* even before suffixes. Examples: Nom.: *šumšu* 'his name', *kabtatsu* 'his disposition', *aššatka* (Nimr. Ep. 42, 9), *Bi-li-it-ni* 'our lady'; but cf. *mêlammušu* 'his glory' (Tig. I 41), *šuškallaka* or *-šu*, *kabittaša* (and *kabtatsa*), *zêr-ú-ni* 'our race' (Beh. 3), *tu-kul-ta-ni* 'our helper' (Senhb. V 25). Acc.: *šumšu* 'his name', *ša-pat-su* 'his lip', *ummânka* (Senhb. V 23), *bâbka*, *admânšun* (V R 35, 9), *malikšunu* (Lay. 33, 8),

mašakšun, *bilatsunu*, *ḫubussunu*, *bêlûtsun*, *ašaršin* (Shams. II 49), *kullatsin*, *pu-ud-ni* 'our side' (Nimr. Ep. XI, 181); but cf. *bukrašu* 'his first-born', *ta-martuš*, 'the king *lâ pâliḫišu*' (V R 35, 17), *libbakunu*. Gen.: *ṣi-ir bîti-šú* 'upon his house' (I R 7 No. F, 26), *ina ḳibîtišu* or *-ka*, *ki*, *ina idiša*, *ina ašrišina* (NR 23), *lib-bi-ku-nu* (Tig. I 19. 20); but cf. 'to the king *pâliḫšu*' (V R 62 No. 1, 20. 35, 27). *b*) The suffix of the 1 pers. sing. If the subst. is in the nom., *î* is appended, almost without exception, to the construct state: *li-ib-bi* 'my heart', *ḳa-ti* (Tig. VI 45), *mu-ti*, *áš-šá-ti* (V R 25, 4. 10 a), *ma-a-ri* 'my son' (also vocative). It was for this reason that in § 70, b *um-ma-ni-ia rapšâtim* (nom., V R 35, 24) was taken as *ummânê'a* (plur.). When forms like *bêli'a*, *bêlti'a* are found in Babyl. letters even for the nom., we may apply to them the remark made at the bottom of p. 180. The suffix also appears as *î*, for the most part, in the accusative: *a-ma-ti* 'my order', *bi-in-ti* (Khors. 30), *ḳa-a-ti* or *ga-ti* (Tig. I 51. IV R 10, 59 a), *ma-a-ti* (Senhb. II 29), but cf. *arda-a* 'my servant' (K. 312, 10). For *um-ma-ni-ia rapšâti* (acc., V R 64 col. I 39. 43) see below. The genitive, on the other hand, again retains its *i*, to which *a* is added for the suffix *ia*: *âl bêlûti'a* (*be-lu-ti-ia*), *ana šarri bêli'a* or *eni'a*, *ina ta-a-a-ar-ti-a* (Shams. III 37), *ana ma-ti-ia* (NR 33). — What has been said under *a*) and *b*) applies, as the student will have observed, only to such substantives (and participles) as end in a consonant when the case endings are removed; for nominal stems (and participles) ending in the nom. sing in *û* I should like, instead of giving rules, to confine myself to a few examples (it appears that, with the partial exception of the 1 pers. sing., the pronominal suffix is appended to the substantive with the case ending): thus we find not only *a-bi-ia* gen. 'of my father', but also *a-bu-šu, a-ba-šu, a-ba-ka*, cf. also *a-gu-ku* 'thy crown' (IV R 46, 16 a), *bu-šá-šú-num* (from *bušû* 'property'), *i-ta-šin* 'their boundary' (V R 6, 67), *Šadûnu* and *Šadûni, Aḫûnu* and *Aḫûni* (prop. names). For the 1 pers. sing. joined to a substantive in the nom. or acc. cf. on the one hand *kussû'a* 'my throne' (V R 66 col. II 13), *dimmi-ir-ú-a* 'my god' (Neb. I 23), *abû'a* 'my father' (Beh. 1), and on the other *a-bi*, 'my father' (nom., voc. and acc.). For the part. of the Qal of verbs tertiae י cf. *abû bânû'a, malku ba-nu-šu-un* 'the prince, their builder' (Khors. 191), but we also find *ilu ba-ni-ia* (nom., IV R 17, 24 b), *abû ba-ni-ia* (nom., *v.* Dicty., No. 13); in the gen. of course *ili ba-ni-ia* (Neb. I 30), *a-bi ba-ni-šun(u)*.

The whole of the examples given under *a*) and *b*) show that the nominal suffixes do not draw the tone to the last syllable of the substantive, containing the case ending. That we must not infer the contrary from forms like *ṣîruššu, pânukka, šaptukka,* we learn from § 80, e; the accentuation, however, may be the reason of the exceptional position of the tone in cases like *ḳinnaššu gabbi* or *Nu-ur-an-ni-ilu* 'our light is God' (n. pr. m. II R 63, 37 c, cf. however *nu-ur-a-ni Nabû* III R 16 Nr. 3, 39), and *Nabû-re-ṣu-u-a* 'Nebo is my helper' (n. pr. m. II R 64, 51 c), *Nûrû'a* etc.; cf. § 53, d, note and for *rêṣû'a* = *rêṣú'a* see the analogous cases pp. 125 ff. The comparatively few cases in which the substantive retains the mimation before the suffix are still unexplained, cf. *za-ku-tum-šu-nu* 'their freedom' (V R 55, 50), *ana šûzub napiš-tim-šu(-nu)* (V R 8, 38. 43), *aššu balâṭ napiš-tim-šu* (V R 3, 17). There is also much that is obscure in prop. names, consisting of a subst. with suffix of the 1 pers. sing. There would be no great difficulty with the acc. in names like *Šu-ma-a(-a)*, *Ap-la-a(-a)* (have we perhaps an exclamation, as e. g. 'alas for my child!'?), but how shall we explain *Nûr-e-a* 'my light' (a variant of *Nu-úr-ú-a* as a name of the same individual) *Aḫe-e-a* 'my brother', *Ardê'a* (written *Ar-di-ia, Ardi-ia*, just as *Nu-ur-ia* is to be pronounced *Nûrê'a*), *Zêrê'a*? Has *Aplê'a* arisen, by change of *â* to *ê*, from *Aplâ'a*, which was usually pronounced *Aplâ* (cf. § 13 end) and which is nothing more than the accus. with the accent on the case ending = *Aplá'a* (cf. *Nûrû'a*)?

2) Substantives in the Plural. *a*) The plural termination *ê*: *ḳu-ra-di-e-šu* 'his warriors' (R R 5, 109), *laḳ-te-e-šu* or *laḳ-ti-šu* (doubtless also read *laḳtêšu*) 'his fingers' (V R 2, 12), *kul-ta-ri-e-ša* 'her tents' (Assurb. Sm. 291, n), *aš-ri-e-ki* 'thy temples' (Assurb. Sm. 121, 33), *abê'a* 'my fathers' (written *abu*^{pl}*-i*, var. *e,-a* I R 7 No. E, 5, *ab-bi-e-a* V R 34 col. II 46), *ilu*^{pl}*-e-a* 'my gods' (K. 647 obv. 8), *sîsê-ši-na* (Senhb. VI 10). *b*) *âni*: *ilâ-ni-ia* 'my gods' (III R 38 No. 1 obv. 38), the only passage that occurs to me. *c*) *â*: *ḳar-na-a-ša* 'its

horns' (Nimr. Ep. 42, 11), *še-pa-a-a* 'my feet'; other examples *v.* § 67, a, 4. *d)* *û*: *še-pu-uš-šu* 'his feet' (V R 35, 18), *ga-tu-ú-a* (Neb. I 46. Bors. I 14), *ar-nu-ú-a* 'my misdeeds' (IV R 66, 45 a), *pa-nu-uš-šu-un* 'their countenance' (V R 35, 18). *e)* *âti* (*âte, âtu*), the only plural termination that presents any difficulty as regards the addition of the suffixes. Looking at orthographical forms like *ep-še-ti-e-šu* (III R 38 No. 1 rev. 22), *ep-še-te-e-šu* (III R 15 col. II 12), *i-ta-te-e-šu* (V R 10, 105), *si-ma-te-e-ša* (var. *si-ma-ti-ša* V R 6, 109) and again *e-ep-še-tu-ú-a* (Neb. Bors. II 18 etc.), *šá-na-tu-ú-a* 'my years' (V R 34 col. III 43), *ḫi-ṭa-tu-u-a*, *ḫab-la-tu-u-a* (IV R 10, 37 a. 44 b) we cannot help reading plural forms, written *um-ma-na-te-šunu* (Tig. III 98 and o.), *um-ma-na-te-ia* (Tig. II 43), *um-ma-na-ti-ia* (I R 7 No. F, 9), *ba-ú-la-a-tu-šú* (Neb. VII 29) as *ummânâtê-šunu, ummânâtê'a, ba'ûlâtûšu.* Still, in this lengthening of the final vowel of the plural termination I am inclined to trace not so much the influence of the suffix, which might be credited with having drawn the tone to the immediately preceding syllable, as a certain influence on the part of the other plural terminations in *ê*, *â* and *û*. By means of the plural forms ending in these three vowels the Assyrians would seem to have become so accustomed to pronounce the last syllable of a substantive in the plural before the pronominal suffix with a long and therefore accented vowel, that they transferred this pronunciation to the feminine plural form in *âti*. Consequently *âtê-šu*, *âtû-a* etc. now appear like a combination of two plural terminations. This, of course, is merely thrown out as a conjecture.

Appendix to the Pronoun and Noun.

Numerals and Particles.

1) *Numerals.*

The following represents the present state of our knowledge regarding the cardinal numbers in Assyrian: **§ 75.**

1 *ištên* (from *ištân*, § 65 No. 35): *iš-tin* (e. g. Khors. 126), always pronounced without an inflexional ending when a real numeral, and generally written with the cypher I and the phon. complt. *ên* (e. g. D, 5. F, 11). The feminine form, which acc. to Assurn. I 118 ended in *it* must have been pronounced (in the constr. state) *ištênit*: cf. *iš-ti-en-i-ti* (sic! V R 34 col. I 28). We also find, however, *ištâttu*, from which is derived *iš-ta-at* 'in the first place' and other forms, *v.* § 77. For *edu* and *aḫadu* *v. ibid.* **2** *šinâ* (§ 62, 1): *ši-na* (IV R 22, 53 a. V R 12, 33 f). **3** [*šalâšu*, *šelâšu*, § 65

No. 11]. Fem. *šalâltu* u. ä.: *šá-la-aš-ti* (V R 12, 34 f), *ša-lal-ti* (e. g. S^c 124), *še-lal-tu* (IV R 5, 64 a). **4** *arba'u* (§ 65 No. 30, a), also *erba'u* (*irba'u*): *ar-ba-'(-i)* (II R 38, 44 a. Sarg. Cyl. 2. 9), *ša ir-ba šêpâšu* (V R 50, 16 a). fem. *erbitti* (*irbitti*, from *erba'ti*, *v.* § 35): *ir-bit-ti* (II R 35, 40 b), *irbit-tim*, *ir-bit* (V R 37, 5 c). **5** [*ḫamšu*, § 65 No. 7]. fem. *ḫa-mil-ti* (K. 4378 col. VI 22). **6** as is proved by the equation VI = *su-du* . . . . (ABK 237), certainly began with *s* (doubtless in order to be dissimilar to the third radical *š*), and brought it about that 'seven' and, in part, 'eight' followed its example and also began with *s*. **7** *si-ba* (form discussed in § 65 No. 6 note): *si-bi*, *si-ba* (II R 19, 14 b). fem. *sibitti* (e. g. IV R 2, 31 b), *si-bit* (IV R 66, 47 a). **8** also began with *s*, as is proved by the equation VIII = *su-ma-nu* [*-u*?] (ABK l. c.): [*samânû*?]. **9** [*ti-šu*, § 65 No. 4]. Fem. *ti-šit* (Sm. 699, acc. to Pinches). **10** [*ešru*, § 65 No. 6 and *v.* note]. Fem. *eširtu,* also pronounced *ešertu* (*v.* § 36): *ešir-te* (II R 31, 45 c. III R 51 No. 5, 3), *e-še-rit* (K. 4378 l. c. 21) and *ešrit,* see below.

11 *iš-ten-eš-rit* (K. 3437 rev. 32). — **15** *ḫa-miš-še-rit* (K. 4378 l. c. 20).

20 *eš-ra-a*. **30** *ša-la-ša-a* (V R 37, 45. 50 f), *še-la-ša-a* (also *ša-la-še-e*, IV R 23, 5 a, ?). **40** *ir-ba-'-ia* (var. *a*), pronounce *irba'â* (*erba'â*), phonetic modification of *arba'â,* cf. *ar-ba-a* (V R 37, 7. 14 c). **50** *ḫa-*

an-ša-a (see for these numbers K. 4378 l. c. 16—19; for *â* § 67, a, 4).

60 (*ištên*) *šú-(uš-)šu* or *-ši*, *še*, σῶσσος; II *šú-ši* 120, III *šú-ši* 180, etc. **600** *ne-e-ru* (AL³ 130, 138), *ni-e-ir* (V R 18, 23 b), νῆρος. **3600** *ša-ar* (S^c 79), σάρος. cf. also *šú-uš-ša-ar* (II R 45, 29 f.).

100 doubtless *mê* (*v.* § 9 Appendix 1).

The ordinal numbers as yet met with are: **§ 76.**

1. *maḫrû* (*maḫrê*, *maḫrâ*), fem. *maḫrîtu* (prop. 'situated at or in the front, *maḫru*). *rêštû* (prop. 'situated at the top, *rêštu*) which is akin to the Hebr. רִאשׁוֹן, denotes merely 'first in order, or in time' (hence also 'in the beginning'). **2.** *šanû* (*šanê*), written *ša-nu* (IV R 5, 15 a), *šá-ni-e* (IV R 66, 3 b), fem. *ša-nu-tu* (*v.* § 77). **3.** *šal-šú* (IV R 5, 18 a, var. *-ši*), fem. *šaluľtu* (*ina šá-lu-ul-ti šatti* 'in the third year', V R 64 col. I 28). **4.** *re-bu-ú* (IV R 5, 20 a). **5.** *ḫa-aš-šu* (l. 22 a) and *ḫanšu*. **6.** *seš(siš)-šu* (l. 24 a). **7.** *si-bu-u* (= *sebû*), fem. *si-bu-tum* (*v.* § 77). **8.** The ordinal number appears in the name of the month *araḫ-šamnu*, *araḫ-samnu* as *ša-am-nu*, and as *sa-am-nu*, *sam-na*, but there was also another form, as we learn from the phon. compl. *e* after the cypher VIII (Senhb. V 5. V R 5, 63), which, according to Nimr. Ep. 55, 24 (*ḫa-an-ša siš-ša u si-ba-a sa-ma-na-a*, sc. *ûma*), was pronounced *samânû*. **9.** [*tešû*]. **10.** *ešru*. With these ordinals compare the fractional numbers in § 77. The common view that the Assyrian ordinals from 3 to 10 are of the same formation as the Arabic ثَالِث and خَامِس must be entirely given up in the face of the feminine forms for the 'second', 'third', and 'seventh'. In any case *seššu* (§ 48 less accurately *šeššu*), if it were really =*šêššu* = *sâdišu*, would be the only example of the change of *â* to *ê* in the participle of the strong verb; we should also expect to find a stray example, at least, of *ḫâmišu* without syncope. The formation of the Assyr. ordinals is *faʿul*!

[*Umu*] *XIV-tu* 'on the 14th day' *v.* K. 3567 l. 18.

§ 77. Other numerals. Fractions. $^1/_2$ *mišlu* (V R 37, 44 f), plur. *mišlânu, mišlâni* 'the halves' (V R 40, 51 d. K. 56 col. I 25). $^1/_3$ *šú-uš-ša-nu* (var. *-an*, S^b 50); the feminine form with phon. complt. appears in Tig. III 101 ('a third of a day'). $^2/_3$ *ši-(i-)ni-pu* (e. g. S^b 52), plur. *ši-ni-pa-(a-)tum* (V R 37, 13 c. 40, 57 d), cf. *ši-ni-pat* (st. cstr. sing., K. 56 col. III 45. Nimr. Ep. XI, 73). $^5/_6$ *pa-rab* (S^b 54). The last two fractions remind one of Hebrew expressions like פִּי שְׁנַיִם (e. g. Deut. 21, 17). All the other fractional parts were expressed in Assyrian as in Hebrew by the fem. of the ordinal. As in the latter, $^1/_3$ or the third part was rendered by שְׁלִישִׁית (sc. חֶלְקָה), so in the former the 'thirds' were expressed by *šalšâtu* (*šal-šá-a-tu*, *šal-šá-ti* etc.), the 'fourths' by *rebâtu* (*re-ba-a-tum*, *re-ba-a-ti*), the 'fifths' by *ḫaš-ša-a-tum* or *ḫa-an-šá-tu*(*ti*), the 'tenths' or the tithes by *ešrêtu* (*eš-re-tum*, *eš-re-ti*). For these numbers see V R 40, 52—56 d, where we find *uš*-[*ri*??]-*a-tum* given as a synonym of *ešrêtu*, also K. 56 col. II 16. 22—33 and III 4—8. To these feminine plural forms is to be added *înâ*, according to K. 56 col. II 16. It is to be noted, also, that in the contract tablets we occasionally find the masc. *šalšu* used for 'one third'; *šalšâi̯* in *aḫu šal-ša-a*(*-a*) (V R 3, 48. Assurb. Sm. 130, 1) formed from *šalšu* by the addition of *âi̯*, seems to denote a brother who (probably as the third in age) can claim only one third of the rank of the firstborn. — The feminine of the ordinals is further employed in two other numerical categories: in the first place to express 'secondly' 'thirdly' and so on—for that II-*tum*, III-*tum* etc. up to VI-*tum* (Nimr. Ep. XI, 205 f.) are to be read *šanû-tum*, *šalul-tum* (cf. l. 215!) etc., we learn from *si-bu-tum* 'seventhly, in the seventh place' (*ibid.* l. 207). What subst. we are to supply is still uncertain. 'Firstly' is expressed by the fem. of the cardinal number: *iš-ta-at* (*ibid.* l. 204); *ištât*(*u*) = *ištântu* (cf. § 49, b on p. 116). In the second place, the feminine of the ordinals serves in conjunction with *šanîtu* 'repetition, time' (ideogr. § 9 No. 88) to denote 'for the second, third, ... time': cf. *ša-nu-te šanîtu* 'for the second time' (Shalm. Ob. 77. 174), Hebr. שֵׁנִית; in place of which we find in lines 85. 87 etc. the cyphers *VIII*, *IX* (etc.) *šanitu* (which must also of course be read as ordinals). To express 'for the second time' and 'for the third time' and for these only, special adverbs were formed, viz. *šani'ânu* (*šanî* gen. + *ânu* § 80, c?), written *ša-ni-ia* (var. *'a*)-*a-nu* (V R 4, 18), *ša-ni-*(*ia-*) *a-nu* (V R 8, 41), *ša-ni-a-nu* (Assurb. Sm. 215, d), and *šal-ši-a-nu* (Assurb. Sm. 217, k). — Numeral Adjectives. *ištânu* 'one, only' (*ilu iš-ta-a-nu* 'one God', IV R 16, 8 a), *edu* (*idu*) 'one (with negative, 'none, nobody'), only, of one kind'; *šunnû* 'double'. The etymological relationship of *edu* to *aḫadu* (cf. Assurn. I 81: *a-ḫa-da-a-ta* . . . *a-ḫa-da-at* . . . *a-ḫa-de* 'one party . . . another party . . . a third party') is still obscure, see Dicty., No. 139. The fem. of *edu* is *ettu* (= *edtu*, *idtu*), cf. *ašarittu* (ASKT 126 l. 21). 'One' in the sense of 'in harmony, agreed' is *mitḫâru*. For the indefinite 'one' both *edu* and *ištên* (e. g. V R 3, 118) are used. The corresponding adverbs are *ištêniš*, written *iš-te-niš* or *I-niš*, 'each for himself, mutually' (e. g. Khors. 118. II R 65 rev. col. IV 21. 22), also 'in one, together' (e. g. to mix); *ediš* 'alone, single'; *mitḫâriš* 'in the same way, in harmony'.

2) *Particles.* *

Adverbs.

1) Adverbs without a special termination. § 78.
a) Those that can stand alone (independent adverbs).

Adverbs of manner: †*ki-a-am* 'so, thus' (Beh. 1. 2 and oft.), to be read *kî'am* (cf. § 10). †*ma-a* and †*um-ma* (prop. *û-ma* 'this', cf. § 55 note) 'thus, as follows', both introduce direct speech (Assurn. I 102. III R 16 No. 2, 34; Assurb. Sm. 123, 52 and oft.); the former is also frequently used in communications extending to some length to remind the reader that the exact words of the speaker are being continued (*um-ma* is much less frequently used in this way). *ki-(i-)ki-i* perh. 'in some way', with the negative 'not at all' (Nimr. Ep. XI, 169).

Adverbs of place: †*a-gan-nu* (Beh. 12), †*a-gan-na* (Assurb. Sm. 125, 63. E, 8) 'here' (cf. § 57, d), *a-na-gan-nu* 'hither'. Cf. the adverbial expressions: *ina libbi* (written *lìb-bi* or *libbi* § 9 No. 259) 'there', also 'thereon' (e. g. I wrote), *ana libbi* 'thither' (e. g. Tig. VI 92), *ultu libbi* 'from thence' (Beh. 15). *aḫannâ*, *aḫen(n)â* 'on this side' (*v.* Dicty. p. 279 f.); with *ana*: 'to this side, to the hither bank', also *a-ḫa-na-a-a*

* Particles accompanied by † are of pronominal origin; the rest are or may be derived from nouns, or present a union of parts derived from both noun and pronoun.

a-ga-a (H, 9 f. 16 f.); *aḫul(l)â* 'on that side' (*v.* Dicty. p. 280 f.), also *a-ḫu-ul-lu-a-a ul-li-i* (H, 11, 19).

Interrogative adverbs: †*ia-ú* (V R 23, 57 d), usually †*a-a-nu*, *a-a-na* (e. g. K. 823 obv. 5) and †*ia-nu* 'where?' (V R 23, 57 d; *ia-nu-uk-ka*, *ia-nu-uš-šú*, *ia-nu-ú-a* 'where art thou?' etc. II R 42, 12—14 g), also *ia-'-nu* (cf. § 20 note) written (*ia-'-nu atta*, *anâku* etc., V R 40, 3 ff. a. b); *ištu ia-nu* 'whence?' (II R 42, 15 g); for the reading *â'u*, *ânu*=אָן *v.* §§ 12. 13. †*e-ka-a* 'where?' (cf. אֵיכָה, e. g. IV R 15, 20 a: *e-ka-a-ma*), †*a-a-ka-ni* and †*a-a-kan* 'where? whither?' (Nimr. Ep. XI, 220. IV R 68, 34 b), †*e-ki-(a-)am* 'where? whither?' (e. g. IV R 57, 34 a. V R 23, 56 d). †*a-li* 'where?' (e. g. V R 23, 56 d. 40, 12 ff. b: *a-li at-ta*, *anâku* etc.), originally perhaps like *ia-ú*, אֵי, an interrogative of very general signification (cf. V R 36, 33 a. c). An ideographic equivalent of all these interrogatives is *me-a*, which reminds one of *ilî me-e-eš at-ta* 'my God, where art thou?' (K. 143 rev. 7).—†*ak-ka-a-a-i* (K. 828, 18), *ak-ka-a-'i* (K. 312, 5) 'how?' (also *a-ki-i*, perhaps used as an interrog. adverb in Senhb. Bav. 24), originally *â-kâi* (*â* interrog. particle as in *ânu*, *kâi*, of which *kî* is a contracted form, origly. 'as, so' then 'how'). †*ak-ka-'-i-ki* 'how manifold?' (NR 25, cf. אֵיכָכָה). †*me-i-nu*, *mi-i-nu* (V R 1, 122), *me-e-nu* 'how?' (in an indirect question *me-nu ša*, *mi-i-nu ša*), *ana mêni* (*me-i-ni*), *am-*

mêni (*am-me-ni*, *am-mi-ni*) 'why? wherefore?' (e. g. Desct. obv. 43 etc.).—*mi-in-di-e-ma* 'why?' (Nimr. Ep. 65, 13), also written *man-di-e-ma* (*v.* p. 143), cf. Hebr. מַדּוּעַ.—*matê*, *mati*, *mat* 'when?', *a-di ma-ti*(*m*), *a-di mat* 'how long?' (for the 'synonyms' *aḫulâ*, *aḫulâpi* *v.* Dicty. No. 144).

Adverbs of time: *adû* 'now'. *u-ma-a* 'now'. *i-nu-šu* 'at that time, then'. *e-nin-na*(*-ma*), *e-ne-na* 'now'. *an-nu-šim* 'just now'(?). (*i-*)*ti-ma-li* 'yesterday'. *ina am-šat* 'the previous evening' opp. *ud-di-eš* 'early in the morning' (IV R 67, 61a). *ul-tu ul-la*(*-a*) 'from of old'. *ina maḫ-ra* 'formerly' (Tig. IV 54), *ina pa-na*, *ina pa-an* (also *pa-na-ma*) do., *ar-ki* (Beh. passim), *ar-ka* (Esarh. III 19) 'thereon, thereafter, afterwards'. *ap-pit-ti* (and *ap-pit-tim-ma*, *v.* § 79, α) 'in future', e. g. K. 95, 9 (cf. Proll. p. 151 f.). *matêma* (*ma-ti-ma*, *ma-ti-e-ma*) and *immatêma* (*im-ma-ti-ma*, 1 Mich. II 1) i. e. *in*(*a*) *matêma*, 'whensoever'; with negative 'never'. *immu u mûša*, *urra* (*u*) *mûša*, *urru u mûšu*, *mûša u urra*, *mûši u urri*, *mûšam u urri* and similar forms (*v.* Dicty. 236 f.) 'by day and by night'. *ina pit-ti*, *ina pi-it-ti* 'suddenly, at once' (also *pi-te-ma* K. 486, 10, *ina pi-it-tim-ma* Nimr. Ep. XI, 207). Other adverbs of time in § 80, a, b (and c).

Demonstrative adverbs: †*en-na*(*-a*) 'behold!'.

Adverbs of degree: *ma-a-du* 'very' (Beh. 20).

ap-pu-na-ma = *ma'adiš* V R 47, 54. 55a (cf. Proll. p. 135 ff.).

Adverbs of emphasis: *lu*(-*u*) 'verily'; placed before the 3. m. and 1. c. sing. and plur. preterite, it calls attention to the actual occurrence of what is predicated by the verb, but its force in this connexion was gradually weakened: *lû allik* 'I went', *lû ašti*, *luptéḫir*. More rarely we find this *lû* with the perm., e. g. *lû šaknâ šêpâka* (*v.* § 89).

Adverbs of exhortation and desire: *lû* (identical with the *lû* just mentioned, *v.* my Proll. p. 134 f.) serves as optative and cohortative particle. It unites with the preterite—the 3. pers. f. sing. excepted—to form a single word. See details in §§ 93 and 145. *ê*, *î* 'go to!', e. g. *ê rid* 'go to! go thou down' (to the wood, Nimr. Ep. 69, 41); for *i* (*î*) as cohortative particle before the 1. plur. pret. see § 145. The imper. *al-ka* 'go!, go to!' may also find a place here.

Adverbs of negation: *la*, *la-a*; *ul* (*ul*—*ul* 'neither—nor'); *a-a* (for the pronunciation see § 31), *ê* 'not'. For the various uses and constructions of these negatives see §§ 143. 144.

§ 79. *b*) Adverbs appended enclitically.

α) †*ma* (identical with *mâ* § 78; cf. Ethiop. መ:, Pognon), the particle of emphasis appended enclitically to the independent pronouns, to nouns and verbs, with and without the pronominal suffix, to adverbs, whether derived from nouns or pronouns, and to adverbial expressions. For the position of the tone *v.* § 53, d. Examples: *at-ta-ma* 'thou' (in opposition to others IV R 17, 14b. 19, 53a. 29, 2. 4. 6. 8b); *kîma ia-ti-ma* 'like me' (Tig. VIII 60); for *û-ma* (same origin as *um-ma* § 78), *šû-ma* (same origin as the conj. *šum-ma* § 82) *v.* § 55, a, note; *ištu uš-ma-ni an-ni-te-ma* 'from this camp' (I set out, Assurn. II 65).—*šar Aššûr-ma* (Tig. VII 67), *Ilu-ma-damiḳ* (prop. name m.); cf. *e-nu-ma* § 82; *ina šatti-ma ši-a-ti* (*v.* above p. 138) as *ina ta-lu-uk gir-ri-ma šû-a-tu* (Tig. V 33); *ana uš-ma-ni-ia-ma* (I returned, Assurn. II 75); for *ina ûmê-šu-ma v.* § 55, a, note.—'on his throne *u-šib-ma* he took his seat' (Senhb. V 4), *u-pa-ḫir-ma* 'I gathered together' (Esarh. I 27), *lû ašibma* 'let him, may he dwell' (Nimr. Ep. XI, 184); *iḳ-bi-šu-ma* 'he spake to him' (also, *um-ma*). Other examples *v.* § 53, d.—*a-a-ma* 'not' (Nimr. Ep. XI, 116), *êkâma* 'where?', *min-dêma* 'why?', cf. also *kî-ma* § 81, c, etc.; *kîma labirimma*, *ištu* or *ultu ullânumma*, *appittimma* (IV R 52 No. 1, 19), etc. Adverbs with enclitic *ma*, which have been derived from nouns, as e. g. *kânamma*, *ûmišamma*, are specially discussed in § 80, a and b, β.—Added to words of a very general signification, *ma* lends emphasis to the indefiniteness, so that *ma* seems to have the function of a particle of generalization: *ša-nu-um-ma*, *ša-nam-ma* 'any other (whoever it may be), something else', *ka-la-ma* (pron. *kalâma*) 'everything possible, everything' (Senhb. Kuj. 4, 20)—note *ka-la-mu* (V R 6, 8 etc.), *ka-la-a-mi* (gen., var. *ka-la-ma*, Nimr. Ep. 1, 4), *ka-la-me* (gen., K. 4931 obv. 10) and cf. § 55, c, end—; *matêma* 'whensoever' may also belong here. Another enclitic *ma* see in § 82.

A really indefinite signification attaches to *ma* in the indefinite pronouns discussed in § 60 (cf. § 58), viz. *manamma*, *manma* and similar forms *mimma* (*mimmu*, *mimmû*, the latter also IV R 56, 38—40 a) and *â'umma*. Cf. also *man-de-ma* 'for some reason or other' Senhb. Bav. 40? The *m* which is frequently found attached to independent pronouns and pronominal suffixes, e. g. *at-tam* (§ 55, a), *bu-šá-šú-num* (§ 56, a), *i-ki-pa-an-nim* and others (§ 56, b), was correctly explained in the §§ cited as a contraction from *ma*. It has been already remarked (§ 66) that the enclitic *ma* is the ultimate source of the so called mimation in the masc. and fem. sing. of the noun (*v.* § 66) and in the fem. plurals in *âti* and *âtu* (§ 69), more rarely with the other terminations of the plur. (§ 67, a, 1 and 5). This *m* is also pretty common with verbal forms, both in the sing. and in the plur.: cf. *ab-nim* 'I built' (Neb.); *ušamgatim* 'he will cast down' (IV R 55, 13 a), *lu u-bil-lam* 'I brought' (Neb. Grot. II 37), *i-ta-ma-am libbam* 'the heart thinketh' (Neb. Bab. I 23); *i-bar-rum* 'they march forth', *iš-ta-(na-)'-a-lum* 'they ask'. See further § 147. I am also inclined to see a contracted *ma* in the *m* of adverbs like *kânam*, *šattišam*, analogous to the *m* of the prep. *aššum* (alongside of *aššu*, *v.* § 81, c) and to the *m* of *ki-a-am* § 78?; see § 80, a, note.

β) †*ni*, rarely *nu*, especially common with verbal forms in a relative clause, to which it is enclitically appended whether they have or have not a pronominal suffix. Like *ma*, it draws the tone to the immediately preceding syllable. Examples: 'he that *na-šu-ni* brings the head of the king of Chidali' (K. 2674, 7), *ak-kar-u-ni* (rel., IV R 68, 15 a), *tadanûni* (rel., V R 53, 56 d), 'may the king *kî ša i-la-u-ni lêpuš* do as it pleaseth him' (V R 54, 61 a), *ḳâlâkûni* 'I speak' (IV R 68, 36 b): *šá aḳ-ḳa-ba-kan-ni* 'what I say to thee' (IV R 68, 17 a, cf. 48 a), 'Achiababa, whom they from Bit-Adin *ub-lu-ni-šu-nu* (var. *ublûni-šú-ni*) had fetched' (Assurn. I 82), *i-sa-si-ú-šú-ni* (rel., Tig. II 26), *i-ḳab-bu-šu-u-ni* 'they call it' (rel., Tig. jun. obv. 10), 'the Persian sea, which they *nâru* *Marratu i-ḳa-bu-ši-ni* (Shalm. Co. 83), *ušaṣbitu-šu-nu-ni* (rel., Assurn. I 103), 'the lands *ša a-pi-lu-ši-na-ni*' (*v.* § 56 end). *ni* is less frequently found after nominal suffixes: cf. Assurb. Sm. 228, 76: *Šûšinak ša manman lâ immaru epšiṯ ilu-ti-šu(-ni)*.

γ) †*ú*, interrogative particle. *an-ni-tu-u bêlitsa ša* 'is this the lady of . . .?' (III R 16 No. 2, 34), *ul a-na-ku-ú* 'am I not' (the daughter of Bel? etc., ASKT p. 126), *i-nak-ki-su-u ḳaḳḳad šarri Elamti* 'do they behead a king of Elam?' (V R 4, 16), *uznê'a tu-pat-tu-u* 'wilt thou inform me?' (K. 95, 17), *a-mat-ú ša-lim-tu ši-i* 'is such really the case?' (Assurb. Sm. 187, j); see further § 146.

§ 80. 2) Adverbs with special termination (in some cases, however, the termination is only apparent).

a) We would, first of all, again call attention to the nominal adverbs in *ma* and *m*, which we were able to discuss along with *ma* in § 79, *a*, but which we would here place in a group by themselves. Cf. *an-na-ma* (written like *ma-na-ma* = *manamma*) prob. 'of one's own accord' (II R 65 col. I 4. 7), *mu-šam-ma* 'yesterday'; *ka-a-a-nam-ma* (V R 65 col. II 20) and *ka-a-a-nam* (Neb. I 17 etc.) 'continually' alongside of *ka-a-a-na* (IV R 16, 4 b), *ka-ia* (var. *a-a*)-*na* (var. *nu*) (Assurn. I 24) and *ka-a-a-an* (V R 10, 68), *sa-at-ta-kam* do. (Nerigl. II 12) alongside of *sa-at-ta-ak-ka* (V R 34 col. III 52), *ud-da-kam* or *kan* (Neb. III 34. IV R 64, 36 a) 'very early' alongside of *ud-da-ak-ku* (Neb. Bab. I 22), origly. an adj. 'matutinus' (*v.* § 65 No. 39).

With regard to adverbs in *m* one might think it an open question whether perhaps we have not simply the mimation of the accus. of the corresponding adjective; but the co-existence of the forms *kânamma* and *kânam* (cf. under *b*, β *ûmišamma* and *ûmišam*) and especially the analogous and unquestionable cases of the contraction of *ma* to *m* which were discussed in § 79, *a*, note, render contraction in the case of adverbs very probable.— We would in passing hazard the conjecture that the familiar orthography of the adv. *rabiš* as *ma-gal* (sign § 9 No. 169) owes its origin to the adverbs in *ma*: *ma* may have been prefixed to *gal*, a freak like those we meet with in the ideogr. for *apsû* (*zu-ab*) and others.

b) The adverbial ending *iš*, *eš*, indicates in what manner, in what degree, in what place, at what time, or in what direction an action takes place or a condition or state exists; it corresponds, accordingly, to prepositional phrases containing *kîma*, *ina* or *ana*. *α*) Examples of *iš* (*eš*): *ediš* 'only', *ad*(*d*)*anniš*, also repeated, 'very', *mâlmâliš* 'in two (equal) parts' (*v.* Dicty. p. 223 f.), *abûbiš* and *abûbâniš* 'like a flood', *iṣ-ṣu-riš* 'like a bird' (he fled, Senhb. III 57), *še-la-biš* 'like a fox'; *ma'adiš* 'much, very'; *e-liš* 'above', *šapliš* 'below'; *mûšiš* 'during the night'; *rûḳiš* 'afar' (Khors. 102), *ša-ma-meš* 'to heaven, heavenwards' (they mounted up, I R 49 col. II 8), *na-ba-liš ušêlûšinâti* 'they brought them (the ships) on dry land' (Senhb. Kuj. 2, 16), 'the temple *la-ba-ri-iš il-lik* 'had become old' (I R 68 No. 1 col. I 20), *šallatiš* (or *ana šallati*) *amnu* 'the city *ḳaḳ-ḳariš amnu*'. After long *û* the termination *iš* or *eš* has in most cases maintained its independence, cf. *da-bu-u-eš* 'like a bear' (? Senhb. Const. 36), *gû'iš* 'like a rope' (Senhb. V 77), *ušâlika na-mu-iš* 'he brought to ruin, destroyed' (IV R 20 No. 1 obv. 4); we also find, however, contracted forms like *ud-di-eš* (from *uddû*), *v.* § 78 on p. 213. Cf. *a-ḫa-iš* (see Dicty. p. 269 f.) alongside of *a-ḫi-iš* ('on both sides', e. g. K. 481, 13). Adverbs in *iš* may also take prepositions, e. g. *ana ma'-adiš* 'in great abundance' (III R 5 No. 6 l. 5), *dâriš* and *ana dâriš* 'ever, for ever' (preferably from *dâru* 'lastingness', not from *dârû* 'lasting').

The origin of the adverbial termination *iš*, *eš* is still very obscure. The adverbs *dabû'eš*, *namû'iš* show us that the termination is really *iš*, *eš*, and not simply *š*, which one might have been tempted to regard as the worn-down pronominal suffix of the 3. pers. sing. (comparing it with *edišišu* or *-ka*, *-ia*, 'he, thou, I alone'). The Assyrians, it is true, in expressing their adverbs in *iš* by ideograms, have often treated the *š* as if it were identical with the pronominal suffix, but such orthographical methods, in many cases quite superficial, ought not to lead us astray, especially as in this case we know that the Assyrians were well aware of the true explanation, as we may infer from their explaining the 'postposition *eš*' by *ina*, *ana*, and *kîma* (see above p. 70). The adv. in *aš* is well worthy of notice, as e. g. *aḫrâtaš*, *v.* § 130, as are also the syntactical peculiarities of the adverbs discussed in the same section. It must also remain an open question, whether adjectives in *išu* and *ešu* like *šat-ti-šu* 'yearly' (II R 33. 18 f), *u-me-šu* 'daily' (*e-diš-šu* alongside of *e-di-šu* 'only, singly' S^b 171. S^c 17 suggests *îšu*) are secondary formations from the corresponding adverbs, or whether, on the contrary, the adjects. represent the original formation; cf. *mar-ṣa-ku i-[bak-]ki-ka* 'sorely he wept before thee' (IV R 61, 10 a)—where *mar-ṣa-ku*, here used quite like *marṣiš*, is also without doubt an adj. (*v.* § 65 No. 39)—also *kâna*, *kânu*, *kân*, and *šaplânu*, *šaplân*, and similar forms. Pognon (*Inscription de Bavian*, p. 38 *note*) regards *iš*, which he identifies with the Syriac ܐܝܬ, as '*une véritable postposition signifiant comme*'.

β) In adverbs in *iš*, with temporal signification, we find the termination strengthened by *ma* or *m*, the result being the forms *išamma*, and *išam*, e. g. *ù-mi-šam-ma* and *ù-mi-ša-am*, *ù-me-šam* 'daily', *ár-ḫi-šam-ma* (V R 64 col. II 34) and *ar-ḫi-šam* (III R 52, 40 b) 'monthly', *dà-ri-šam* 'for ever' (Senhb. I 62), *šat-ti-šam-ma* and *šá-at-ti-šam* sometimes 'yearly', sometimes (cf. *ana šatti* 'for ever' Nabon. III 36. II R 66 No. 2, 7) 'for ever, eternally'.

The two elements *ma* and *iš* are found in the reverse order in the very common adv. *a-ḫa-miš*, *a-ḫa-mi-iš*, *ana aḫamiš* 'mutually', *itti aḫamiš* 'with each other', derived from *a-ḫa-ma* (cf. above *a-ḫa-iš*, *a-ḫi-iš* derived from *aḫu*). *ù-mi-šam-mu* 'daily' (Nabon. I 16) is an adject. which has been formed with *-išamma* as a basis. In this note we would also mention in a word the two adverbs *ù-mu-us-su* 'daily' and *arḫu-us-su* 'monthly': the former is found with extraordinary frequency in the beginning of Assyro-Babylonian letters, for the latter, see K. 700, 7. A conjecture as to the origin of these adverbs will be found in § 136 note.

c) The adverbial termination *ânu*, *ân* (also *ăn?*). *ar-ka-(a-)nu*, *ár-ka-nu*, *arkâ-nu* 'after, afterwards, thereafter' (often), *šap-la-(a-)nu* 'under, underwards' (Senhb. Rass. 81. Lay. 38, 15 opp. *e-la-niš*). Cf. the numeral adverbs in § 77, and *šaplân(u)* 'beneath', *elânu*, *ellân* 'above' § 81, b which are used as prepositions. Adverbs like *ar-ka-niš* 'thereafter' (Senhb. Const. 30) and *elâniš* should make it clear that the apparent adverbial ending *ân* originally formed nouns (cf. also *ana elâni* Senhb. VI 40) and was, in consequence, originally identical with *ân* in § 65 No. 35. Cf. also *ki-lal-la-an* and *ki-lal-li-en* (Hamm. Louvre I 23) 'round about' (? formed in the first instance from the noun *kilallû*), *ultu ṣitan* (*ṣi-tan*—*tan* another value of No. 82 § 9—, *ṣi-ta-an*)*adi šillan* (*ši-la-an*, *šil-la-an*) 'from beginning to end, from top to bottom' or such like (V R 42, 43. 44 c. d. Khors. 166. I R 7 No. F, 9 etc.), also the common *e-bir-tan* 'on the other side', *ištu e-bir-ta-an* (Assurn. II 127) 'from the other side'. The termination *ân* (*ăn?*) seems also to be appended to a feminine noun in *ki-la-*(*at-*)*ta-an* 'on both sides' (Esarh. V 54. Neb. V 59, cf. Hebr. כִּלְאַיִם).

d) The adverbial termination *tan* (probably *tân*) appears to have a collective signification, which explains its being used to represent plural forms (cf. V R 35, 19: *mi-tu-ta-an* 'the dead', *kul-la-ta-an* 'all'). The principal example is *mâti-tan: dadmê ma-ti-tan* 'the inhabitants of all lands' (Khors. 165), *ḫiṣib šadî u ma-ṭi-ta-an* (V R 63, 48 b), *malkê ma-ti-tan* 'the princes of all lands' (Khors. 177), *ma-ti-tan* 'through the whole land' (I had it brought for inspection, Assurb. Sm. 138, 83), *ki-ir-bi ma-ti-ta-an* 'in all lands' (Neb. VIII 26). Cf. also *u-ma-tan* (from *ûmu* 'day' V R 25, 20 b).

e) A substantive with a pronominal suffix, depending on *ina*, *ana* or *ištu*, may be changed into an adverb by having a long *û* inserted between the noun and the suffix and dropping the preposition. Hence *libbû'a* is equivalent to *ina libbi'a* 'in my heart' (Neb. VIII 32), *ki-bi-tu-uk-ka* to *ina ḳibîtika* 'at thy command' (often), *mu-šá-bu-ú-ka* to *ana mûšabika* 'to thee for a dwellingplace' (Desct. rev. 27), *kir-bu-uš-šu* to *ina kirbišu* 'in it, into it' (often), *âlu-uš-šu* to *ištu âlišu* 'from his city' (Khors. 41. 114). Cf. also *el-la-mu-u-a* 'before me, opposite me' (Senhb. II 9. 77 of space, Sarg. Cyl. 45 of time), *ul-la-nu-u-a* 'before me' (of time, prop. 'in the time before me' Senhb. IV 5. Senhb. Rass. 64), *ki-(e-)mu-u-a* 'in my stead' (V R 1, 38), *imnûšu ḳa-tu-ú-a* (Assurb. Sm. 217, i), 'the spear I grasped *laḳ-tu-u-a* in my fingers' (Senhb. V 60), *šê-pu-ú-a* 'to me' prop. 'to my foot' (I subdued, they submitted), *pânukka* 'before thee', *šaptukki* 'upon thy lip', (O goddess), *ṣîruššu* 'upon it (I wrote)', *edânuššu*, *edênuššu* 'he alone', *ma-tu-uš-šu-un* 'into their land' (Senhb. Bav. 39). The key to the origin of these, at first sight, strange formations is afforded by the cases where we find this 'postposition' *û* with a following genitive in place of a pronominal suffix: cf. *lib-bu-ú šamê* 'in heaven' (K. 81, 11); *lib-bu-ú ša anâku ṭême aškunnuššunu* 'in accordance with the command which I commanded them' (Desct. 20), 'what I command them, they do', *lib-bu-u ša anâku ṣi-ba-a-ka* 'in accordance with my will' (NR 24).

Prepositions.

§ 81. The prepositions, whose origin in substantives may still be clearly recognized, we would arrange in the following groups:

a) Those that do not unite with another preposition (which then forms the first member of a compound expression), or at least that have not yet been found so united. *i-na*, *ina* (§ 9 No. 91), and *in* (Senhb., Neb.), 'in' (of time and space), in signification = Hebr. בְּ. *e-ma* 'in' (in such a context as: 'doors, thresholds etc. I set up *e-ma bâbâniša* in the palace gates', e. g. Neb. VI 14 and oft). *a-na*, *ana* (§ 9 No. 204), rarely *an* (e. g. Nabon. I 23: *a-a iršâ an ḫiṭêti;* cf. also p. 116 above) 'after, for', etymologically identical with the Arab. عَنْ, and in meaning = Hebr. לְ, which is preserved only in *lapân* (see under *b*). *mâla* 'for', see Dicty. p. 222 f. and observe a fresh confirmation of what is there laid down in *ma-la*, K 56, col. II 17, signifying 'over against, in comparison with'. *iš-tu* and *ul-tu*(*tû*) — to be kept apart etymologically (see my Proll. p. 132 f. 141 note)—ideogr. *ištu*, *ultu* (§ 9 No. 95), 'out of, from, since'. *a-du*, usually *a-di*, *adi* (§ 9 No. 62) 'during; till, with', *ga-du* 'along with' (e. g. Khors. 28). *it-ti*, *itti* (§ 9 No. 40) 'with' (as friend and foe), e. g. *it-ti-šu* (also *it-te-šu*) 'with him'. *is-si*, *i-si* 'with', peculiar to the language of every day life, therefore often in Assurn.; cf. *anâku is-si-šu-nu* 'I with them' (K. 538, 16), *is-si-ka adabubu* 'I talk with thee' (IV R 68, 17 b), *is-si-ia* 'with me' (*ibid.* 22 b), 'the chariots etc. *i-si-ia a-si-kin* (*asêkin=asêkan=aštâkan*) I took with me' (Assurn. III 58. 63); observe Haupt's acute remark on page 102 f. *ku-um* 'in place of, instead' (e. g. Assurb. Sm. 264, 43. III R 47 No. 11, 1 and oft.), also *ke-mu* (III R 41 col. II 33). To swear 'by' some person or thing is expressed by *niš* (constr. st. of *ni-šu* 'name'); details at the end of § 138.

b) Those that are used not only by themselves but also united with another preposition which forms the first member of a compound expression. *ki-rib*, *ki-ri-ib* (before substs. and suffixes), quite rarely *ki-ir-ba* (V R 35, 30, *ki-er-ba-šú* Neb. Grot. III 22), and *ina ki-rib* (before substs.), *ina kir-bi*, *ki-ir-bi*, *ki-er-bi* (before suffixes) 'in'; *ana ki-rib* (*ana ki-ir-bi* V R 35, 34) 'after'; *ištu* or *ultu ki-rib* 'from, out of'. *libbi* (written *libbi* § 9 No. 259 with or without the phon. complt. *bi*), usually *ina libbi* 'in, after; among (the number of), of; through, with the help of'; *ana libbi* 'in, after', also 'on account of' (Beh. 2: *ana libbi agâ* 'on that account'); *ištu* or *ultu libbi* 'from, out of, of the number of' (e. g. Esarh. V 7. V R 2, 107); *adi libbi ûme annê* 'unto this day'. *ḳabal* (§ 9 No. 254) and *ina ḳabal tâmtim* 'in the sea', *ḳa-bal-ti*, *ḳabal-ti* and *ina ḳa-bal-ti mâti'a* 'in my land' etc. (Assurb. Sm. 275, 32. V R 9, 48. I R 27 No. 2, 40). *e-li*, *eli* (§ 9 No. 189), *muḫ-ḫi* and *ina eli*, *ina muḫḫi* 'upon, over against, in behalf of', also 'to' (go to some one etc.); e. g. *elišunu*, *ina elišunu* and *ina muḫḫišunu* 'upon them', *eli* and *ina eli nâri* 'on the bank of the river'; *ana eli* and *ana muḫḫi* 'to' (to bring something to some one etc., Assurn. I 58. II 81); *ištu eli nâri* 'from the bank of the river'; *a-di eli tâmtim* 'unto the sea'. Less frequent forms and orthographical varieties are: *i-li* (K. 4931 obv. 16: *ša i-li-ša ṭâbu* 'what is well pleasing unto her'), *el* (e. g. IV R 12 obv. 16: *ša epšêtušu el Bêli ṭâbâ*), *e-la* (K. 101 rev. 2), *e-lat Parsû* 'in addition to Persia' (NR 8). We would also mention here *e-la-nu*, *el-la-an*, *e-le-nu*, *e-le-na*, *e-li-en* 'above' (e. g. a town) and its opposite *šap-la-nu* (Senhb. Const. 82) *šap-la-an* 'below'. For 'beneath' (one's feet), e. g. to trample under one, to fall at anyone's feet, *šapal* is used (e. g. V R 2, 119). *Šú-ut*, *šu-ut* (dental uncertain) 'concerning, regarding' (e. g. V R 7, 16. 25). *ṣi-ir* (also written ideographically with the sign § 9 No. 240 in the texts of Assurbanipal) 'upon, against', e. g. *ṣi-ir zuḳti Nipur* (Senhb. III 69), *ṣi-ir bîtišu* 'upon his house', (I R 7 No. F, 26), *ṣi-ir* 'against' (Senhb. IV 3); its original signification is particularly well brought out in III R 4 No. 4, 49:

ul-tu ṣi-ir sisê ḳakḳariš imḳut. pa-an, pân (§ 9 No. 86) and *ina pân* 'at the head of, before', also *pa-na-at* (Shalm. Ob. 176) and *ina pa-na-at* (ibid. l. 142. 149; *ina pa-na-tu-u-ka* 'in front of, before thee' IV R 68, 23 a, *ina pa-na-tu-u-a* 'before me' in time, Beh. 3); fear, flee etc. 'before' any one: *pa-ni, i-na pa-an, iš-tu* or *ul-tu pa-an, ištu pa-na* etc., and *la-pa-an* (= Hebr. לִפְנֵי, e. g. III R 15 col. IV 26, a variant of *ul-tu la-pa-an* Esarh. III 41), *la-pa-ni* 'from'; defend 'from' something, NR 33; rebel 'against' some one (Beh. 16). *ma-ḫar,* e. g. *ma-ḫar-šu-un* (Senhb. Bav. 55), *ma-ḫar-ka* (also *maḫ-ra-ka* IV R 61, 41 a) and *ina ma-ḫar* (Tig. V 13) 'before, in the presence of'; *a-di maḫ-ri-ia* and *ana maḫ-ri-ia* 'into my presence' (they brought, etc.); *ina maḫ-ri-ia* V R 1, 71, before a subst. *ana maḫar.* To these we would add *mi-iḫ-rit* (e. g. Khors. 162. V R 9, 89), *miḫ-ri-it* (Tig. jun. rev. 16, *v.* § 65 No. 6 note), *mi-iḫ-ra-at* (Neb. VII 61), 'in view of, over against, before'. Cf. also *ina tar-ṣi* and *ina tir-ṣi* (e. g. V R 3, 23) 'in the days of', *ina tar-ṣi* 'opposite' (a town II R 65 obv. col. II 16), *a-na tar-ṣi* 'opposed to, against' (e. g. Beh. 50), *iš-tu tar-ṣi* 'from over against'; applied to time: 'since the days of' (*abê'a* 'my fathers' Tig. VI 97). *pu-ut* and *ina pu-ut* (dental not quite certain) 'at the entrance (e. g. of a town), in front of' (Assurn. I 62. III 84. III R 5 No.

6, 46). *ar-ki*, *arki* (§ 9 No. 245) 'behind, after' (in space and time), e. g. Tig. III 21. Senhb. VI 22; note also *ar-ki-e-šu* 'close behind him' Lay. 67 No. 1, 9; 68 No. 2, 7 and *ana arki-ia* 'behind me' (I left so and so, Esarh. III 32). *ina bêri*, *ina bîri* (*ina bi-e-ri-šû-nu* 'between them' Neb. VIII 52, *ina bi-ri-šu-nu* V R 9, 58, *ina bi-ri-(in-)ni* V R 1, 125 f., cf. § 53, d, note); *bi-rit* (Assurb. Sm. 130, 6) and *ina bi-rit* (Khors. 129), *ina bir-ti* (Assurn. II 66) 'between, among' (*ina bi-rit* 'in' Beh. 8. 9. 95); *ana bi-rit* 'between' (Assurn. II 66); *ultu bi-ri-šu-nu* 'from their midst' (V R 2, 8). *bat-tu-bat-te* (Assurn. I 91) and *ina ba-tu-* [*ba-ti*] (Shalm. Mo. rev. 54), *ina* (sic) *bat-ti-bat-ti* (IV R 68, 25 b) 'round about', *ištu ba-ta-ba-ti-ia* 'from about me' (K. 513, 7). *ṭi-iḫ* (Tig. jun. obv. 24), *ṭi-ḫi* (Esarh. II 12) and *ina ṭi-iḫ*, *ina ṭi-ḫi* (IV R 27, 48 b. Esarh. II 3) 'near to, close to, at, beside'. Cf. also *idâ* 'at the side of', e. g. *i-da-a-ni iziz* 'stand at our side' (Senhb. V 24), *i-da-a-ka nittallak* 'we go at thy side' (III R 15 col. I 9), *i-da-a-a ul illik* 'she went not at my side' (IV R 67, 58 b). *ba-lu* (*ba-lu ilâni* 'without the gods', *ba-lum ṭe-me-ia* 'without my order' Khors. 84), also *ba-la* and *ina ba-lu* (Assurn. I 3) 'without'.

c) Unter this heading, finally, a place may be found for the prepositions of pronominal origin: †*ki-i* 'as, according to', e. g. *ki-i ṭêm râmânišu* 'of his own accord' (Esarh. III 57), *ki-i mê* 'like water' (1 Mich. IV 8), *ki-i li-ṭu-te* 'as hostages' (I took them, Assurn. I 108 and oft.), *ki-i pi-i* 'in harmony with, corresponding to'; also †*a-ki*(-*i*) 'like'. In cases like *Mannu-ki-ilu-rabû*, *Man-nu-ki-Rammân* (nn. prr.) the line between preposition and adverb vanishes. With the negative *lâ* cf. *ki-i lâ libbi ilâni* 'against the will of the gods' (Khors. 124), 'whoever shall do anything *ki-i lâmâri u lâ šasê* to prevent men from seeing and reading' (I R 27 No. 2, 65). †*ki-ma*, *kîma* (§ 9 No. 197) 'as, like' (passim); cf. for *ma* § 79, *a*; the following are less frequent orthographical varieties: *kim-ma* (IV R 9, 44 b) and *ki-i-ma* (III R 43 col. IV 18; *ki-i-ma mê* 'like water', for which 41, col II 31 *ki-ma mê*). †*aš-šu*, *áš-šum* 'concerning, for the sake of, on account of', e. g. *aš-šu epêš ardûti'a* (he came to Nineveh, Esarh. II 36), *aš-šu danân Ašûr nišê kul-lu*(*m*)-*mi* (var. *me*) -*imma* 'in order to show the people the might of Ashur'. (I 47), *aš-šu nadân ilânišu uṣallâni* (III 7).

Conjunctions.

The conjunctions most frequently in use are: †*u* § 82.
(signs § 9 Nos. 5 and 267, No. 4 is extremely rare) 'and' — doubtless originally *û*, see Dicty. p. 212 note 7 — the most usual copula; it is used e. g. in joining together sentences that have otherwise no in-

timate connexion, in transitions, like our 'and now', and, in particular, between nouns. †*ma* 'and' is the copula joining verbs together, and is appended enclitically to the first of the two verbs or to its suffix, if it has one (cf. Amharic ም::, Haupt); for examples see § 53, d, where the place of the tone is also discussed. *ma* as copula is never reduced to *m*. †*ki-i* 'as, if, when', e. g. *ki-i tam-ma-ri* 'when thou shalt see' (Beh. 106), *ki-i* 'when' (so and so happened, Senhb. V 15); *ki-i ša* and †*a-ki-i ša*, *a-ki ša* 'as': *ki-i ša aḳbû* 'as I have spoken' (V R 3, 7), *ki-i ša ilâ'û*, *a-ki-i ša ilê'û* 'as he will'. †*šum-ma* 'if', hypothetically (prop. *šû-ma* 'in case that', cf. § 79, *a*). †*aš-šu* 'because, since', e. g. *aš-šu lâ iṣṣuru* 'because he had not kept'; also *aš-ša-a* (V R 52, 27 a), *aš-šu ša* and simply †*ša* signify 'because' (*v.* for the latter V R 2, 51. 112). †*am-ma-ku*, *am-ma-ki* 'instead of' with verbs (? Nimr. Ep. XI, 172—175). *u-la-a* 'perhaps that' (? III R 16 No. 2, 33; *v.* Dicty., No. 112). — *û* (signs § 9 Nos. 5 and 267, more rarely No. 4), *lû* (*lu*, *lu-u*, *lu-ú*), *û lû* 'or' (*v.* Dicty., No. 104), *lû* . . . *û*, *lû* . . . *lû*, *lû* . . . *û lû* 'whether . . . or', 'either . . . or' (e. g. IV R 16, 16—22 a. 1 Mich. col. II 5 f. 10 ff. V R 56, 34), with a following negative 'neither . . . nor'. *ultu* and *ištu* 'since, when, as soon as', *ultu eli ša* do., *iš-tu* or *ul-tu ul-la-nu-um-ma* 'from the moment that (?), after'

(Desct. obv. 63. rev. 6). *a-di* 'while, so long as' (V R 56, 60. 3, 93 etc.) *a-du*, *a-di* 'till, until' (Assurb. Sm. 125, 67), *a-di eli ša*, *a-di muḫḫi ša* 'while, so long as; until' (Beh. 84. 109. Beh. 10. 27. 47). *ár-ki ša* 'after' (Béh. 11. 66). *i-nu* 'at the time that, when' (e. g. *i-nu imbû* 'when they called' Nabon. III 24), *i-nu* and *i-nu-um* (*i* sign *ni* § 9 No. 57) do. (whether *m* is the mimation or is = *ma*, is hard to say), e. g. *i-nu(-um) Marduk . . . iddina* 'at the time when Marduk committed to me the rule over land and people' (Neb. Senk. I 7; the follg. words are: *i-na* var. *i-nu ûmišu* 'in those days' there came to pass so and so; in Nerigl. II 15. V R 34 col. III 5 we should accordingly read *i-nu-mi-šú*), *i-nu-um Marduk ibnanni* 'when M. created me' (Neb. Bors. I 10); with *ma* (*v.* § 79, *a*): *e-nu-ma* 'at the time when, when'.

C. The Verb.

The triliteral verb* in Assyrian forms ten principal stems or voices, often, but less appropriately, called conjugations, viz: § 83.

---

* Up to § 116 we shall treat only of the triliteral verbs, i. e. verbs having three consonants in the root.

I 1. Qal.	I 2. Ifteal.	I 3. Iftaneal.
II 1. Piel.	II 2. Iftaal.	
III 1. Shafel.	III 2. Ishtafal.	
IV 1. Nifal.	IV 2. Ittafal. (= Intafal),	IV 3. Ittanafal. (= Intanafal).

There is no Afel or Hifil in Assyrian, and no passive stems or voices formed by internal vowel change. Of the stems II 3 and III 3, which are wanting in the above scheme, the only instances known to me are, of the former: *um-da-na-al-lu-ú* (Assurb. Sm. 285, 8) and *u-ṣa-na-al-la-a* (=*uṣṣanallâ, uṣtanallâ*) 'he besought' (ibid. 290, 54); of the latter: the presential form *ul-ta-nap-ša-ḳa* (Shalm. Mo. obv. 8); we may also, perhaps, include *uš-ta-na-al-ḫab* (IV R 65, 42 d, akin to *alluḫabbu*?).

The *t* of stems I 2—IV 2 was originally prefixed, not infixed. It is still found in Assyrian at least once in its original position, namely in the permansive form *tiṣmur* Neb. I 12: 'the untiring ruler who the restoration of the temples daily *ti-iṣ-mu-ru-ma* planned and . .'; cf. Neb. Bab. I 8: *ti-iṣ-mu-ru-ú-ma*. Here *tiṣmur* evidently stands for *ṣitmur*. Note also the close connexion in sense between *tidûḳu* and *mitḫuṣu* (they are often used together e. g. Assurn. I 115. II 55) which suggests an affinity of grammatical form (cf. § 64 end). Does the adject. *tizḳâru*, briefly mentioned when we were treating of the noun § 65 No. 40 a, present an analogous case (= *zitḳâru*? st. זקר 'to project upwards')? — A few forms of stems I 2—III 2 are found with *ta* (*te*) doubled, e. g. *e-te-te-bi-ra* 'I have crossed' (Nimr. Ep. 71, 27); *uḳ-ta-ta-ṣar* (var. *uḳtaṣṣar*) 'he collects himself' (V R 5, 76), *tu-uḫ-ta-tab-bil* (V R

45 col. I 39); *uš-te-te-eš-še-ir* 'I erect' (Nerigl. I 19), *uš-te-te-ši-ir* 'I set up' (*ibid.* II 5). — For verbs, apparently denominatives, like פרכת and פלכת, see the quadriliteral verbs § 117, 1; in the same section (§ 117, 2) are treated quadriliterals like שקלל and שחרר, which are derived from triliteral verbs by repeating the last radical.

The signification of these ten principal stems (putting aside, meanwhile, the permansive and infinitive) coincides in the main with that of the corresponding stems in the other Semitic languages: § 84.

The Qal (I 1) is sometimes transitive, sometimes intransitive and sometimes the same verb is both transitive and intransive: *šaḳâlu* 'weigh, count', *rapâšu* 'be wide'; *na'âdu* 'be exalted' and 'exalt'.

The Piel (II 1) has intensive signification: *nabû* 'announce' *nubbû* (*numbû*) 'cry aloud, howl', *kibû* 'speak', *ḳubbû* 'scream loudly', *šarâṭu* 'tear', *šurruṭu* 'tear to pieces'; and makes intransitive verbs transitive: *ruppušu* 'widen, extend', *ṣaḫâru*, *arâku*, 'be small, long', *ṣuḫḫuru*, *urruku* 'diminish, lengthen'.

The Shafel (III 1) has both a transitive and a causative signification: *pazâru* 'be hidden', *šupzuru* 'hide', *našû* 'bear', *šuššû* 'make to bear', *barû* 'behold', *šubrû* 'cause to behold, show', *šumruṣu* 'strike with disease', *šûduru* 'annoy, frighten', *šurdû* 'let flow, let go', *šûšubu* 'cause to sit, make to dwell', 'whoever *ušaḳḳaru inaḳḳaru* shall cause to lay waste or shall himself lay waste this field' (IV R 41, 16. 17 c); not unfrequently it has an inchoative signification e. g. *šul-buru* 'grow old', *bâ'u* III 1 'bring' but also 'to fall foul of one', *šušmuru* 'become angry, be angry with' (also *šamâru* and *šitmuru*). The Shafel sometimes serves as the causative of the Nifal, e. g. *ippariš* 'he flew', *ušaprašû* 'they caused to fly' (IV R 27, 19 b).

The Nifal (IV 1) has always a passive signification: *mašû* 'forget', IV 1 'be forgotten': *iššakin* 'it came to pass'. An active meaning appears to attach to *nâbutu* (IV 1 cf. אבת₁) 'flee'. How is the Nifal in *ippalis* 'he saw', *ippariš* 'he, it flew' to be explained?

Stems I 2—III 2 have strictly speaking reflexive signification, but it is only in the rarest cases (as e. g. in *maḫâṣu* 'strike', I 2 'fight') that a clearly marked distinction is recognizable between them and the corresponding simple stems I 1—III 1. On the other hand, a passive signification attaches to all these reflexive stems, especially to II 2 and III 2.

The Ifteal (I 2) has pretty much the same meaning as I 1. It would be difficult to state the precise distinction in meaning between *ibtáni* 'he built', *ittanbiṭ* 'he shone', *itámar* 'he saw', *itépuš*, *itérub* and *ibni*, *ibbiṭ*, *êmur* etc. A passive meaning appears in *lim-te-is-si* 'let him be washed' (IV R 19 No. 1 rev. 16).

The Iftaal (II 2) has sometimes the same meaning as II 1, and at other times serves as the passive of

II 1: *uptarriṣ* 'he lied' (Beh. 90 ff.), *uṣṣabbit* 'I took captive' (Beh. 90), *umdašir* 'he quitted, forsook' (Shalm. Ob. 37), but 'the palaces which *umdašerâ* were forsaken' (Tig. VI 98); *umdallû* 'they filled' (V R 9, 45), but *umdalli* 'he has been filled' (IV R 16, 28 b), *utanniš* 'he has weakened' and 'he has been weakened', *ša lâ ut-tak-ka-ru* 'unchangeable' (IV R 16, 6 a).

The Ishtafal (III 2) has sometimes pretty much the same meaning as III 1, and sometimes serves as its passive, thus: *uštasḫir* 'I caused to surround' (Neb. VI 52), *ultašpir* 'he ruled, reigned' (*išpur, iltanapar* do., what may the distinction be?), *ultakṣirû* 'they assembled' (Tig. IV 85); *lištaklil* 'may he become perfect' (IV R 19 No. 1 rev. 17), 'the divine command *ša lâ uštamsaku*' (V R 66, 11 b).

The Ittafal (IV 2), like IV 1, has always a passive signification: *ittaškan* 'it was done'. For *ittapraš* 'he flew' *v.* IV 1.

The Iftaneal (I 3) has always an active (transitive or intransitive) signification: *etanamdarû* 'they feared', *ištanatti* 'he drank', *ittananbiṭ* 'he shone', *attanâdu* 'I raise, praise' (cf. *itta'id* 'he raised, praised').

The Ittanafal (IV 3) without a doubt had originally only a passive signification; where it now has an active meaning, the course of its development has still to be ascertained: *ittananmarû* 'they are found', *ittanádar* 'he rageth' (prop. he has been made mad, cf. *innadir* 'he raged'), *attanasḫar* 'I turn', *ittanabrik* 'it has lightened'.

§ 85. Among the stems of the Assyrian verb a peculiar position is occupied by a Shafel and an Ishtafal formed from the Piel (which I denote by III^{II} 1, III^{II} 2). I shall give a number of examples to illustrate both form and meaning.

III^{II} 1. Preterite: 'his grave *uš-rap-piš* I caused to be made so many cubits wide' (I R 7 No. F, 18), *uš-nam-mir* 'I caused to shine' (I R 7 No. D, 6), *uš-malli* 'I had (= caused to be) filled up' (Esarh. V 10), *uš-ma-al-lam* 'I fitted up, had fitted up, handsomely' (Neb. VI 21), *ušrabbi* 'I enlarged, had enlarged', *uš-raddi*. Present. *u-ša-na-ma-ra* 'I will cause to shine' (IV R 68, 35 c), *tuš-nam-mar* 'thou shinest' (IV R 64, 35 a), *tu-uš-ka-at-ta-ma* (V R 41, 50 d), *tu-ša-bal-ṭa* (V R 45 col. VI 55). (Inf. *šuparrušu*).

III^{II}2. Present: 'with cries of pain *uš-ta-bar-ri* is he daily surfeited' (IV R 3, 1 b), *ḳašâti ul-ta-ma-la* (i. e. *uštamallâ*), 'the bows are furnished (prop. filled) with arrows' (II R 47, 59 d). Part. *muštabarrû* 'vain-glorious'.

For the forms of the stem III^{II} from verbs med. ו and י, such as *ušmît*, inf. *šuṭubbu*, imp. *šumît* v. § 115; for the corresponding forms of verbs med. א see § 106.

In the simple (Qal) and augmented verbal stems, with their transitive, intransitive and passive meanings, Assyrian originally, it would seem, distinguished two modes of existence*, according as the condition of doing, being or suffering expressed by the verb was one already existing (*eine seiende*), that is, completed and continuing, or one only about to exist (*eine werdende*), one commencing and therefore still uncompleted, regardless whether this continuance or this commencement, this completeness or incompleteness belonged to the present, past or future. These two modes of existence are clearly and sharply distinguished by the fact that the pronominal formative syllables which denote the person or thing concerned in the doing, being or suffering, are in the former case affixed (corresponding to forms like *šarrâku* 'I am king', *v*. § 91), in the latter prefixed to the theme of the verb. § 86.

To give expression in speech to these two modes of existence we have the verbal themes 1) of the Qal: their nature, their original significance and the gradual differentiation in their meanings shall now be discussed. *a*) In the Qal the root, with its original § 87.

* I cannot at this moment find a better name; it is justified in so far, at least, that *existere* unites the two meanings of entering into existence and existence.

and primitive vocalisation, served from the very first as the primary theme for both modes of existence. *dân* 'he is or was judge', *i-nâr* 'he subdues' and 'he subdued', *târ-at* 'it (the road) turns back', *ta-târ* 'she turns back'; *râm* 'he is or was a lover', *i-râm* 'he falls or fell in love' (further examples of this species of permansive forms see in § 89 compared with §§ 63 and 64). But just as Hebrew and the other Semitic languages employ, in addition to the form *fa'al*, the forms *fa'il* and *fa'ul* to express states and qualities, so in Assyrian we find *kabit* 'he is or was heavy', *mêt* (*mît*) 'he is or was dead', *maruṣ* 'he is or was sick'. In fact these two forms, or more precisely, since *kašud* is comparatively very rare, the form ***kašid*** exceeded in frequency the principal and primary theme *kašad*, although the latter also served to express states and qualities (*v.* § 65 No. 6). The form *kašid*, in short, gradually took the place of *kašad* as the theme to express the continuance or completion of an action or of a state of being or suffering, that is, as it is usually put, as the permansive theme in all verbs with the exception of those med ו, י, א and med. geminatae. The form ***kašad***, on the other hand, came to be used as the theme to express the commencement or incompletion of an action, or of a state of being and suffering, that is as the present-preterite theme:

i-kašad 'he is becoming or has become a conqueror'. From it was developed by syncope at a very early period *ikšad* (or *ikšud*, *ikšid*); this form then continued in use alongside of the older *ikašad*.

A somewhat analogous case of syncope is found in the permansive theme of the Ifteal, where *kitšud* is syncopated in the same way from *kitašud* (*kitâšud*), the two forms continuing in use side by side (*v.* § 88, b). The reason of the change of vowel which so often accompanies the syncope is still unexplained: verbs tertiae infirmae without exception, we may say, retained the vowel *a* even in the shortened form, and the same is the case, to a certain extent, in verbs med. א, but why they said *êmur* 'he saw' and *ikšud* 'he conquered' but *êsir* 'he shut up' and *ipḳid* 'he entrusted' remains a mystery. No law of general application can be deduced from the nature of the third radical (see especially the numerous examples in § 96). Great freedom in this respect seems to have been the rule from the outset, a freedom which was only gradually curtailed to some extent by the pressure of analogy.

b) The theme *kašid* (*kašud*) is identical, of course, with the nominal stem discussed in § 65 Nr. 7 (8). Like the nominal stem *fâʿil*, the permansive theme embodies in the first place the idea of state or condition (*labir* 'old', *labir* 'he is or was old') and afterwards, in connexion with the intransitive signification, the idea of passivity or suffering (*peti* 'being opened, open', *peti* 'it is or was opened', *šakin* 'laid, deposited' — observe *mak-kûri šak-na šukutta ša-kin-ta* IV R 23, 24 b —, *šakin* 'it is laid, it lies', 'the city *ṣabit* is or was in a state of capture, is or was captured'). The permansive theme in Assyrian serves in addition to express continuous action, e. g. *paḳid* 'he superintends', prop. is continuously in the condition of superintending, is superintendent. Further details will be given with the examples in § 89. That the principal and primary theme *kašad*, which may probably be taken as the oldest pronunciation of the root, likewise embodied all these ideas of condition, passivity and, above all, of action, goes without saying; the corresponding nominal stem § 65 No. 6 embodies, in particular, the ideas of condition and quality.

c) In the permansive, as we have seen, no account is taken of any relation of time, and as little can there have been originally in the theme inflected by means of prefixed pronominal elements, viz. *i-kašad*, syncopated *ikšad* (*ikšud*), any distinction of time, any indication, that is to say, as to whether the action etc. began in the past, the present or the future. At a later, though still comparatively early, period, however, such a distinction was made by making the difference between *ikašad* and its syncopated parallel *ikšad* (*ikšud*) one of time. Such a distinction, however, could not have existed from the first, as is evidenced by a consideration of the following points. It is noteworthy, to begin with, that the forms *inâr* and *ibâ'* are still used indiscriminately for present and preterite; it is also a fact worthy of special attention that all imperatives and the participles of the augmented stems are formed from the preterite, not from the present; further, the prohibitive particle *a-a* is joined to the preterite, *lâ* to the present, while the optative particle *lû*, again, is joined to the preterite (*v.* § 93). The only conclusion to be drawn from these phenomena is that the subsequent clearly marked distinction between present and preterite did not exist in the earliest stage of the language. At a very early period, however, as we have already remarked, *ikašad* was set apart as exclusively the form of the present, as distinguished from *ikšad* (*ikšud*), which was stamped as exclusively the form of the preterite (the accenting of the *a* in *ikâšad* is possibly another result of this effort at differentiation). This form of differentiation was extremely natural and was the readiest means of accomplishing the end in view, since the permansive in Assyrian continued to retain its original signification and was not, as in the other Semitic languages, transformed into a perfect.*

---

* These conjectures as to the origin and development of the tenses of the verb in Assyrian and in Semitic generally are of course given with all reserve. I feel myself justified in hazarding them, in the first place, because the Hebr. יִקְטֹל still presents unmistakeable traces of the original indifference regarding the commencement of an event etc., whether in the present, past or future; this is evident from the fact that the present-future theme

§ 88. The two themes 2) of the augmented (derived) stems. While the verbal themes of the Qal discussed in § 87 clearly display their identity with the noun (the intimate connexion between noun and verb being otherwise proved by the two numbers, by the similarity in the termination of the feminine etc.), the points of contact become fewer and fewer as we study the augmented stems. Even permansive themes like *nukkus*, *šuklul*, *mitḫuṣ*, for example, although they are

---

(יִקְטֹל) in connexion with וַ conversive, with אָז and otherwise suddenly assumes an aorist signification. In the second place, because the Hebrew perfect is intimately connected, not only as regards form but also as regards signification, with the Assyrian permansive, and that not only in cases like צָדַקְתִּי ,I am just' (Job 34, 5) גָּדַלְתָּ 'thou art great' (Ps. 104, 1), קָטֹנְתִּי 'I am little' (Gen. 32, 11). Moreover the transition from the permansive to the perfect signification would admit of easy explanation, since the completion of an action must have been preceded by the occurrence of that action in the past, just as states or conditions are very often the result of a preceding course of development. From *ḳatal* 'he is a murderer', *labaš* 'he is clothed', *nakar* 'he is hostile', *ma'ad* 'it is much' there is but a short step to 'he has murdered, put on, rebelled', 'it has increased'. The Assyrian permansive even, on occasion, assumes involuntarily a perfect or pluperfect signification; cf. Beh. 17: 'thereafter Cambyses died (*mîti*) by his own hand'; Senhb. V 48 f.: 'in such and such a place *šitkunû sidirta pân maški'a ṣabtû* they had put the battle in array, had taken their position over against me', and in other passages. The theme יִקְטֹל, which originally was able to denote the commencement of an action etc. in all the three spheres of time, and which, moreover, never ceased to denote, under certain conditions, the commencement of an action etc. in the past (like the Assyr. *ikšud*) would seem to have been more employed with reference exclusively to the present and the future, from the time when the theme קָטַל assumed with increasing frequency, and developed in various ways, its signification as a perfect.

also used as adjectives, cannot be regarded as strictly speaking nominal stems; in contrast to other formations with the second radical sharpened, with a prefixed *š*, or with an inserted *t*, they rather appear, to judge by their signification if by nothing else, as inseparably connected with the corresponding verbal stems. Compare, for example, with *mitḫuṣu* 'fight' *amdaḫiṣ* 'I fought', with *ḳitrub taḫâzi* the common *aḳṭérib*. *šêzuzu* 'raised', moreover, seems formed directly from *ušêziz*. The relation of the *š* and *t* as formative elements in nominal stems to the *š* and *t* in verbal stems is still very obscure.

a) The present-preterite themes, the meanings of which have been given in § 84, may be represented in a tabular form as follows:

	I 2. *kᵃtašad*	I 3. *kᵃtanašad*
II 1. *kaššad*	II 2. *kᵃtaššad*	
III 1. *šakᵃšad*	III 2. *šᵃtakšad*	
IV 1. *nᵃkašad*	IV 2. *nᵃtakšad*	IV 3. *nᵃtanakšad*

In the preterite the *a* of the last syllable is mostly thinned to *i*. In stems I 2, I 3, IV 2 and IV 3 of the strong verb, however, we find in many cases for pres. and pret. but one form with *a* in the last syllable; in the strong verb a present with *i* after the second radical in the augmented stems is extremely rare: cf. *i-ta-na-ar-ḫi-iṣ*. For details see § 97.

b) The permansive themes, the meanings of which may be learned from § 89 are as follows:

	I 2. *kitášud, kitšud*	I 3. *wanting*
II 1. *kuššud*	II 2. *kutaššud*	
III 1. *šukšud*	III 2. *šutakšud*	
IV 1. *nakášud, nakšud*	IV 2. *wanting*	IV 3. *wanting.*

All these permansive themes serve at the same time as infinitives of the corresponding stems, and the greater part, especially those of stems II 1, III 1 and I 2, we also find employed as adjectives. Thus *uḫḫuz,* for example, signifies 'it (the stone) is or was set', *uḫḫuzzu* 'to set' and 'set' (e. g. in gold); *šuklul* 'it is completed', *šuklulu* 'complete' and 'completed, perfect'; *šitmur* 'he is or was full of anger', *šitmuru* 'to be angry, anger' (also *šušmuru*) and 'angry'. It is moreover the recognition of the identity of these permansive themes and the respective infinitives which proves that *kitšud,* the permansive theme of the Ifteal is syncopated from *kitášud:* just as in the inf. I 2 *gitpulu* changes with *šitálulu* (*v.* § 98), *itḫuzu* with *itétuḳu* (§ 104), *bitrû* with *bitákû* (§ 110), so in the perm. there must have existed alongside of *kitšud* the more primitive form *kitášud* (the form *mi-taḫ-ḫu-ru* cited in § 98 is a fresh proof of what has just been said!). The same holds good of the permansive theme IV 1 as is shown by the two infinitives *našlulu* and *našalulu* (§ 98). For a parallel case of the syncope of an accented *a*, *v.* § 94. We would further remark in passing that, having regard to this existence side by side of two infinitive forms of I 2, having regard, also, to *italluku* (§104 note) and *itanbuṭu* (§ 101), we cannot for a moment doubt that *itappuṣu* and *itakkulu,* which are placed in the vocabularies alongside of *itpuṣu* and *itkulu* (*v.* §§ 101. 104) are merely bye-forms of the latter. A point in favour of the Semitic origin, and at the same characteristic of the frequently meaningless and deluding freaks of the Assyrian ideograms is the circumstance, that although there was not the least shade of difference of meaning between *itkulu* and *itákulu,* the longer or fuller forms were rendered by fuller ideograms; this, as is well known, is also the case with *italluku* and with the present of the Qal.

In our treatment of § 88, b we have taken for granted that the three forms with respectively permansive, infinitive and adjective significations are really identical. This, however, is open to doubt and it may be objected that their identity may be only apparent and that the vowel *u* may not be short in all three. For the permansive forms, it is true, no one will seek to maintain that the vowel (*u*) of the second radical is long: a glance at the examples adduced in § 89 and afterwards among the 'noteworthy miscellaneous forms' of §§ 98. 101 etc. is sufficient to place beyond a doubt the accuracy of the readings *kuššud, šukšud, nakšud, kitšud.* The only instance known to me where the third radical is written double, viz.: *kabtassu na-an-kul-lat-ma* 'his spirit is darkened and' (IV R 61, 11 a—read *nankulátma*) is powerless, for reasons that are sufficiently evident, to alter this conclusion. Besides this, the transition of *na'kul*, *na'ḫuz* (IV R 61, 12 a) to *nankul*, *nanḫuz* points conclusively to the accentuation of the first syllable, and therefore to the fact that the *u* of the second is short. But the forms used as adjectives, corresponding to these permansive forms, are certainly identical with them; for even as regards signification the permansive and the adjective are intimately related (*nalbušâku* 'I am clothed' like *kabtâku* 'I am respected' might, *per se*, be equally well regarded as a permansive as classed with the formations mentioned in § 91, such as *ḳarradâku*, for example), so intimately related, in fact, that in certain cases it is difficult to decide whether we have before us a perm. or an adj.; cf. e. g. I R 7 No. E, 5: 'the asnan-stone which in the days of my fathers *šûḳuru* (var. *aḳru*) was found valuable as an amulet'. Moreover what we learn from the signification is confirmed by the orthography: thus the forms *uḫḫuzu*, *šuklulu*, etc. when employed as adjectives are found in the overwhelming majority of cases with the third radical written but once: cf. the variety of examples given in § 65 in connexion with Nos. 24. 33. 31. 40, also *kuššudu* 'captured' (Senhb. VI 19), *šuklulu* 'complete', *šupšuḳu* 'hard, steep, laborious', *šûnuḫu* 'lamentable' (Assurb. Sm. 123, 46) and many others. A few rare cases like *ša ašaršina šug-lud-du* (Sarg. Cyl. 11), *šú-zu-uz-zu* (K. 246 col. I 6) are to be explained acc. to § 53 c. For the orthographical form *nam-kur-ri-šu-nu* from *namkuru* 'property' prop. 'something earned, earnings', see § 53, d, note. The *ŭ* of the infinitives II 1. 2. III 1. 2. IV 1 is also confirmed by a number of examples; a series of references will be found under the head of 'noteworthy miscellaneous forms'. In these circumstances there is little to favour the giving of the inf. I 2 as *kitšûdu*, all the less that the ground-form *kitašudu* had without a doubt the accent on the *ta*, thereby excluding a long *û*, and that all these infinitives I 2, with the single exception of *mitḫuṣu* 'to fight, a fight' for which Assurb. Sm. 89, 27. 175, 45. V R 8, 16 (= Assurb. Sm. 261, 20) gives *mit-ḫu-uṣ-ṣi* in addition to *mit-ḫu-ṣi*, are written in every case with the third radical single. In fact the suspicion forces itself upon one that *mitḫuṣṣi* is owing to a faulty edition of the text (so Haupt); or was it that the writer meant us to lay special stress on the word? Whatever may be the true explanation of the anomaly I am at present of Haupt's opinion that formations like *mitḫuṣu* are to be read with short *u*. The question as to what was the original signification of the permansive themes adduced under b), whether they had originally an adjective-permansive or an infinitive signification had better not be raised at present—the transition from the adjective or participle to the abstract infinitive signification is at all events noteworthy (cf. גּוֹלָה). In the cases where the above-mentioned permansive themes appear as feminines with nominal signification we may, with equal justice, regard them as feminines (neuters) of an adjective or participle or as feminine infinitives. To the examples of these fem. permansive themes already given in § 65 above (cf. § 65 No. 11 note) we would here add: *suḫḫurtu* 'to put to flight' (Senhb. V 66), *ṭubtu* 'friendship' (*ṭu-ub-ta* II R 65 obv. col. II, addition), fem. of *ṭubbu* (= *ṭubbatu*, St. טוב), as is shown by the plur. *ṭu-ub-ba-a-ti* 'what is friendly, friendliness' (V R 3, 80), (*kuttênu* acc. to this, is a formation in *ênu*, *ânu* from *kuttu* = *kuntu* = *kunnatu* fem. of *kunnu* 'true, genuine'), *šûšubtu* 'little seat'. Sometimes with masculine forms, however, both explanations are admissible, e. g. in the case of *nûdušu* 'fresh, green herbage' (*v*. Dicty. p. 202) and *šutâbšu* (III 2) 'turban, head-dress' (*v*. Dicty. No. 45). In this category I would also place *namurru* st. cstr. *namur*, *namurratu* st. cstr. *namurrat* and *namrurat* 'anger, terror, horror'.—The most of what has been laid down in this note applies to the quadriliterals as well, and in fact receives from them additional confirmation; cf. for the identity of the forms used as adjectives and infinitives *lâ naparkû* 'not to cease' and 'unceasing'; for the quantity of the vowel *ŭ*, *šuḫárruru* and *šupárruru* (likewise infins. and adjs.); of feminine forms cf. *napalsuḫtu* (alongside of *napalsuḫu*). For full details see § 117, 1 and 2.

Considering the importance of the permansive for **§ 89.**

Assyrian grammar we feel justified, before passing to the meaning of the permansive in the augmented stems, in illustrating the meaning of the permansive of the Qal by a few additional examples—by way of supplementing the short remarks of § 87.

I 1. Verbs med. gemin. (cf. §§ 87 and 63): 'the town *da-an* (written *dan-an,* phon. compl.) *dan-niš* was exceedingly strong' (Assurn. I 114. III 51, variant of *marṣi danniš* II 104), 'who *ḫa-as-su* remembered not', *ellâ, ebbâ* 'they are bright, pure' (3. f. plur., V R 51, 36 b). Verbs med. ו, י (cf. §§ 87 and 64): *Šarru-lû-dâr(i)* 'may the king endure for ever', *lû kân* 'let him, it be' (written *ka-ia-an* IV R 45, 42, *ka-a-a-an* K. 246 col. IV 45), 'the road *ša alaktaša lâ ta-a-a-rat* goes not back' (Desct. obv. 6), *Ašûr-da-a-an* 'Ashur is judge' (Tig. VII 49. 66), 'my greeting *lû ṭa-ab-ka* (or—*ku-nu-ši*) do thee (you) good' (often), *ânu* 'it is or was not' (written *ia-a-nu* Beh. 19 etc.); 'thy command *ki-na-at* stands fast' (e. g. *kênat,* K. 3258), *dîktu ina libbišunu ma-'a-da di-e-ka-at* 'many of them were killed' (IV R 54 No. 3, 25 f.), *mi-i-ti* 'he died' (Beh. 17). —*kašid*: *a*) Condition. *ša-lim* 'he is safe and sound', *na'id* 'he is or was exalted', 'Auramazda *ra-bi* is great' (H, 1), *ša 'a-ad-ru* 'who is in trouble, is troubled' (IV R 5, 60 b), 'the city which *šak-nu* lies in such and such a place' (Nimr. Ep. XI, 11), plur. *šaknû* (Tig.

III 57), *ša-ak-nu-ú-ni* (Assurn. III 98), *bal-ṭu-'* 'they live' (H, 3), *lab-šú* 'they are clothed (Desct. obv. 10), *lû šak-na šêpâka* 'may thy feet rest' (IV R 17, 10 b), *aš-ba-ak* 'I tarried' (Assurb. Sm. 119, 18), 'the palace *ša eli maḫrîti ma'adiš šú-tu-rat ra-ba-ta u nak-lat*' (Senhb. VI 44 f.), *annû'a ma'idâ rabâ ḫîṭâtû'a* (IV R 10, 37 a), *ma-la ba-šu-u.* *b*) Passivity. *'-a-bit* 'it was destroyed', 'the city *ṣab-ta-at* was taken' (C[b] rev. 31), (')*-al-du* 'they were or are born' (IV R 15, 22 a. 2 b), *kat-ma-ku* 'I am overpowered' (IV R 10, 4 b). *c*) Action continuing or already completed. 'The god *ša kippât šamê irṣitim ḳâtûšu paḳdu* who holds the ends of the heavens and of the earth in his hand' (Assurn. I 6), *Adar-pa-ḳi-da-at* (name of a king, V R 44, 37 d), *tarṣât* 'thou stretchest out', 'Ishtar entered, right and left *tu-ul-la-a-ta išpâti tam-ḫa-at pitpânu ina idiša šalpat namṣaru* .... she had quivers hanging (*v.* under II 1), a bow she held by her side, from the sheath she drew the sharp sword of battle' (Assurb. Sm. 124, 53 ff.), *aḫzû* 'they have', *našûni* 'they bring', 'which *na-šú-u* carry' (NR. 18. 27), *šiknât napišti mâla šuma na-ba-a ina mâti ba-ša-a* (IV R 29, 38 a). — *kašud.* *ma-ru-uṣ* 'he is ill' (K. 524 l. 13), 'over door and bolts *ša-pu-uḫ epru* dust is spread' (Desct. obv. 11), 'whose face *ta-ru-ṣu* was directed' (Assurn. III 26), '*man-nu-um-ma ba-ni man-nu-um-ma ša-ru-uḫ* among men' (Nimr. Ep.

49, 201), *epuš* 'it is made' K. 63, i. e. IV R 25, col. II 25), *ša ašaršu rûḳu* 'whose place is afar off'; *rûḳu* might, *per se*, be considered as an adj. (cf. § 147), but the feminine form *ša ḳibîtsu ru-ḳa-at* (K. 3258) suggests the permansive as the better explanation (cf. *ibid.*).

II 1 *kuššud* has an active and a passive (or intransitive) signification. *a*) 'Fear etc. *ḳud-du-šum-ma* have humbled him' (= *ḳuddudû*, IV R 61, 9 a), *tu-ul-la-a-ta išpâti* 'she had hung quivers, had quivers hanging' (around her) (*v*. under I 1, c; for the termination *âta* cf. § 53 p. 125). *b*) 'how long, O lady, *su-uḫ-ḫu-ru pa-nu-ki* has thy countenance been turned away?', 'in which treasures *nu-uk-ku-mu* were heaped up' (Assurb. Sm. 225, 51), 'on rain *turruṣâ înêšun* were their eyes directed' (Senhb. Bav. 7), *uššušâku* 'I am vexed' (IV R 10, 4 b).

III 1 *šukšud* has as an active and a passive (or intransitive) signification. *a*) 'Sargon, who for the subjection of his foes *šutbû kakkûšu* sent forth his arms (weapons)' (Lay. 33, 3. Sarg. Cyl. 7), '[who?] more than his fathers *arna šú-tu-ru šur-bu-u ḫiṭṭušu kabtu* let evil gain the upper hand, multiplied sore transgression' (III R 38 No. 2 obv. 61). *b*) 'lofty slopes, on which *ur-ḳi-tu lâ šú-ṣa-at* no green thing had been produced, had sprung up' (Sarg. Cyl. 35), 'on firm ground *ul šuršudâ išdâšu* its foundation had not been laid' (Lay. 33, 14), 'a flood, which by night *šur-da-at* is made to flow, breaks forth' (IV R 26, 20 a), 'that which *šuk-lu-lu* is completed' (IV R 9, 20 a), *šú-tu-ga-ta* 'thou art magnificent' (IV R 30, 7 a).

IV 1 *nakšud* has a passive signification. *na-al-bu-ša-ku* 'I am clothed' (K. 3456), 'cedars which *na-an-zu-zu* stood (prop. were placed) concealed on the mountains of Sirâra' (Senhb. Kuy. 4, 11).

I 2 *kitšud* has an active and an intransitive (occasionally passive) signification. *a*) 'who *šit-pu-ru* had sent troops', 'who like a fish *šit-ku-nu šubtu* had set up a dwelling-place' (Esarh. III 55. Assurb. Sm. 76, 28), 'they put their trust in the mountains and *lâ pit-lu-ḫu bêlût Aššûr* (Assurb. Sm. 81, 7). *b*) 'who *pit-ḳu-du* gives heed to' (*ana,* Assurn. I 24), 'who *kit-nu-šu* submitted not to my yoke' (this and similar expressions are very common), 'whose dwelling *šit-ku-na-at* was situated like the nest of an eagle' (Senhb. III 70), 'Ishtar *išâtu lit-bu-šat* was clothed with fire' (V R 9, 80), *ḫi-it-pu-ṣu-nik-ka* 'then have asked for thee' (IV R 17, 11 b).

III 2 *šutákšud* has a passive signification. 'Nineveh, whither every kind of artistic work *šú-ta-bu-la* was brought' (Senhb. Rass. 63), *mi-lam-me šú-ta-as-ḫur* 'with glory is he surrounded' (K. 63, i. e. IV R 25, col. III 11, cf. *šú-tas-ḫur* IV R 18, 51 a).

Further examples of the permansive will be given when we come to treat of the precative (§ 93, 2); also among the 'noteworthy miscellaneous forms' of §§ 98. 101 etc.

I have not yet met with permansive forms of stems II 2. IV 2. I 3. and IV 3.

The fact of the permansive themes II 1 and III 1 possessing both an active and a passive meaning reminds one of the employment of the infinitives, see § 95 end.

§ 90. Conjugation (inflexion for person and number) of the two verbal themes: 1) the present-preterite theme *a*) in the Qal

	Sing.	Plur.
3. m.	*i-ṣ(a)bat*	*i-ṣ(a)bat-û(ni, nu)*
3. f.	*ta-ṣ(a)bat*	*i-ṣ(a)bat-â(ni)*
2. m.	*ta-ṣ(a)bat*	*ta-ṣ(a)bat-û*
2. f.	*ta-ṣ(a)bat-î*	*ta-ṣ(a)bat-â*
1. c.	*a-ṣ(a)bat*	*ni-ṣ(a)bat*

i̯a is to be assumed as the original preformative in the preterite of verbs primæ א (except *alâku*) and primæ ו, י: *êkul*=*i̯êkul*=*i̯âkul* (*i̯a'kul*); *ûšib*=*i̯ûšib* =*i̯au̯šib*, *îši*=*i̯îši*=*i̯ai̯ši* (for the loss of the initial *i̯* see § 41, b; for other details see the sections devoted to these weak verbs); but in all the other present and preterite forms both of the strong and of the weak verb, as well as in the corresponding forms of the

Nifal, Ifteal and Ittafal the original preformative is *i*, which in § 41, b was assumed—possibly incorrectly—to have arisen from *ịa*.

The uniformity of the scheme given above is of course destroyed by parts of the verb formed by analogy, which are very frequent in the present of the Qal. In the strong verb the vocalisation of the second radical is greatly influenced by the pret., the original *a* of the present in many cases, and *i*, it would appear, in all cases, being displaced by the corresponding vowel of the preterite, cf. in § 96 *ibáluṭ*, *išágum*, *itárur*; *ilábin*, *inádin*, *isákip*, *išábir* (these younger forms are occasionally found alongside of the older forms in *a*, cf. *izánan* and *izánun*, *idâbab* and *idábub*, like *ima'ad* and *imá'id*, *iḫḫaz* and *iḫḫuz*). In the weak verb, in the same way, the whole of the present, preformatives included, is not unfrequently formed from the preterite, the older forms, in this case also, being sometimes found side by side with the younger. I refer to such presents as *izzaz*, *iddan* (*v.* verbs primæ נ, § 100); *ennaḫ* (from pret. *ênaḫ*) alongside of *innaḫ* = *i'ánaḫ*, *eppuš*, *errub*, 2 m. *terrub* (*v.* verbs primæ א, § 103); *urrad* (from pret. *ûrid*, *v.* verbs primæ ו, § 112); *iturrû* 'they become' (from pret. *itûr*) alongside of *itârû* (*v.* verbs med. ו, י, § 115). Verbs med. א present formations by analogy in pres. and pret., e. g. in *râmu* and *bêlu*; for these see § 106.

b) The present-preterite themes in the augmented stems. The afformatives do not call for special remark, they are the same as in the inflexion of the Qal; for the preformatives it is sufficient to adduce the form *ikkašid*, *takkašid*, *akkašid*, *nikkašid*; *iktášad*, *taktášad*, *aktášad*, *niktášad*; *ukaššid*, *tukaššid*, *ukaššid* (1. sing.), *nukaššid* (1. plur.). It is worth noting that the preformatives take *u* if the permansive has *u* in the first syllable, but *i*, if the permansive has *a* or *i* in the first syllable.

Here too, as a matter of course, the formations due to analogy take their own way: for *etêli* and *etêpuš* see § 34, *a*, note, and also verbs primæ א, § 103; for *ittúbil*, *ittúṣi* (alongside cf. *ittáṣi*) *v.* verbs primæ ו, § 112; for presents like *iṣṣanundu v.* verbs mediæ ו, § 115.—For the vocalisation of the 2. radical, first adverted to in § 88, *a*, see § 97.

c) Additional remarks on the preceding scheme. The 3. m. sing. is very often used promiscuously for the 3. fem.; e. g. *i-ra-an-ni* 'she conceived me', *ul i-ri-man-ni Iš-ta-ri* (IV R 67, 58 b), *šîmtu ûbilšu* 'fate carried him off' (Esarh. III 19), *kabittaki lipšaḫ*, *rêbitu litbal* 'may the road take away', *Ištâr ušarḫiṣanni libbu*, etc. etc.—The plural forms of the 3. masc. in *nu* are much less frequent than those in *ni*, but cf. *ul-te-bir-ú-nu* (K. 823 obv. 11), *iḳ-ta-bu-nu* 'they said' (K. 82, 16), *iṣbatûnu*, *i-tab-šú-nu*, *i-ḳab-bu-nu* etc. (K. 831), *lu-ú-ter-ru-nu* 'let them bring back', *i-na-aš-šú-nu* 'they bring' (NR 10).—It is by no means rare to find the 3. and 2. m. plur. ending in *â* instead of *û*; cf. side by side V R 64 col. III 49 ff.: 'the gods *li-im-gu-ra*, *lil-li-ku*, *li-ša-am-ki-ta*'; *tu-kin-na* 'ye have ordered' (Tig. I 22), 'which ye *tu-up-pi-ra-šú* have covered' (Tig. I 21). The same remark applies to the imperative, *v.* § 94. Plural forms in *i* (=*ê*=*â*?), on the other hand, such as: 'may the great gods *libbika li-ṭi-ib-bi* rejoice thy heart' (V R 65 col. II 19), are very rare exceptions (cf.—for the perm.—§ 91).

For the adverb *lu*, very frequently prefixed, for emphasis, to the 3. m. and 1. c. sing. and plur. of the pret., see § 78.

Conjugation 2) of the permansive theme. § 91.
The following scheme will serve to show the conjugation of the permansive in Qal and the augmented stems.

	Sing.	Plur.
3. m.	*kašid*	*kašd-û(ni)*
3. f.	*kašd-at*	*kašd-â(ni)*
2. m.	*kašd-â-t(a)*	*kašd-â-tunu* (?)
2. f.	*kašd-â-ti*	vacat
1. c.	*kašd-â-k(u)*	*kašd-â-ni*, *-nu*

The 3. m. sing., like the 3. m. sing. of the perf. in the other Semitic languages, is not expressly distinguished by any pronominal element. The formation of the 2. m. and f. sing. and 1. c. sing. and plur. is in all respects the same as we find in the case of substantives and adjectives, that unite with a pronoun serving them as subject to form a single word; cf. *atta ṣi-rat* 'thou art exalted' (IV R 9, 54 a), *šarrâku bêlâku na'idâku . . . ašaredâku ḳarradâku* etc. (Assurn. I 32 f.), *ṣi-iḫ-re-ku* 'I am small' (K. 4931 obv. 18). The *â* inserted between the last radical of the permansive theme and the afformatives (*kašd-â-ta*,

dann-â-ta, *ban-â-ku*) recalls the Hebrew perfects סַבּוֹתָ, נְקוּמוֹתָ. For the 2. f. sing. cf. *šak-na-a-ti* (IV R 63, 54 b), for the 1. plur. *na-i-da-â-ni* 'we are exalted' (IV R 68, 39 b). The form of the 2. m. plur. of the permansive, as usually given and as inserted in the paradigms at the beginning of the book, seems to be very suspicious: the passage generally adduced in support of *kašdâtunu*, viz. IV R 34, 61 (*ba-na-tu-nu*), the context of which is still obscure, is at variance with *ku-uṣ-ṣu-pa-ku-nu* (IV R 52 No. 1, 26, cf. 1. sing. *ku-uṣ-ṣu-pa-ku* l. 10). *â* is also found in the 3. m. plur. of the permansive (*v.* § 90, c end), cf. *aš-ba* 'they sit, dwell' (Desct. obv. 9), while *i* (*î*) is extremely rare, cf. Nimr. Ep. XI, 119: 'the gods *aš-bi ina bikîti* sat there in tears'. — For the syncope of the vowel *i* in *kašdat*, *kašdâku* etc. *v.* § 37, b.

§ 92. The Modus relativus and the supernumerary final vowels of the Assyrian present-preterite and permansive. Every form of the present and preterite that ends in a consonant, and in verbs tertiæ infirmæ every form that ends in a short vowel (the plural terminations *ûni*, *ûnu*, *âni* of course excepted) may, when standing in the principal clause, assume one of the three short vowels, without any change of meaning being associated with the change of form. *a* occurs most frequently, more rarely *i*, and still more rarely *u*. For *a* cf. *illika uruḫ mûti* (Khors. 118), *ûbil* or *ub-la* 'he brought', 'his army *idḳa* he summoned', *isdira miḫrit ummâni'a* (Assurb. Sm. 39, 16), *taššuka* 'she bit', *šîmta tašâma* 'thou determinest the fate', *uṣabbita* 'I caused to seize', *upaṭṭira* 'he opened', *aš-takkana* 'I made' (V R 3, 133), *at(t)arda* 'I went down' (esp. frequent in Assurn.), *ušêbira* 'I poured out' (Senhb. IV 32), *nindagara* (V R 1, 125), etc. This final *a* is very common with verbs tertiæ ו and י, e. g. *aḳḳa* 'I poured out', *iršâ* 'he laid hold', *ušellâ* 'I brought hither', *uṣallâ* 'he besought'. It is also found in many cases with forms of the precative, e. g. *lu-uš-ba-a* 'I will take my fill' (Neb. X 8 etc.); also with the imperative (*v.* § 94). For the employment of this *a* in copulative sentences *v.* Syntax § 150. I do not recollect any permansives with a final *a* outside of relative clauses. — For *i* cf. *êṣidi* 'I reaped, harvested', *akšiṭi* 'I cut down' (Sams. IV 18), *uzaḳip* and *uzaḳipi* 'I impaled' (Assurn.), 'his heart *ir-ti-ši* rejoiced', *ušêribi* 'I brought in' (V R 35, 34), *ušatriṣi* (V R 62 No. 1, 15), *ušâlidi* (Lay. 44, 14. 17). Also in precative forms: *liḫnubi* (III R 41 col. II 33); and in permansive forms: *ma-ši-ḫi ka-ni-ki* (III R 43 col. III 16. 17), 'the city *marṣi danniš*' (Assurn. II 104), *mîti* 'he died', *bi-e-di* 'he was struck down' (Epon. Canon), *na-(a-)di* 'he was high', *ašbâti* 'thou (O Merodach) dwellest' (K. 3426).—For *u* cf. *arâmu* 'I love' (Neb. I 38), *unakkilu* 'I formed artistically' (V R 64 col. II 8). Also in precative forms: *lušbû* 'I will take my fill' (I R 67 col. II 34).

Every form of the present, preterite and permansive, however, must assume a vowel when standing in a clause introduced by a relative or a conjunction. This vowel is mostly *u*, though many examples of *a* are also found; to find neither the one nor the other is extremely rare. See full details regarding relative clauses § 147, and for clauses with a conjunction § 148.

Cases are by no means rare where there is the further addition of an *m* to the final vowel now discussed; such cases are found both in principal and in subordinate sentences. Examples in § 79, *a*, note, and in § 147.

§ 93. From both preterite and permansive Assyrian forms a precative by means of the adverb *lû* 'verily' (*v.* § 78). With the forms of the preterite that begin with a vowel *lû* unites to form a single word, but before the *t* of the feminine and before all forms of the permansive it preserves its independence.

1) From the preterite precatives are formed for the 3. m. and f. sing. and plur. and the 1. c. sing. *a*) 3. pers. m. sing., m. and f. plur. With *i* of the preformative in stems I 1. 2. IV 1. 2, *lû* unites to form *li*: *likšud*, *likšudû*, *likšudâ*, *limmir*, *liṣṣur*, *illikûni* 'may they

come', *limsi* 'may he wash', *limsû*, *litûr* 'may he return'; *litabbib*, *lit-tal-lak* 'may he walk' (IV R 61, 41 a); *lippaḳid* 'let him, it be ordered', *littabik*, *lippaṭir*; *littapraš* 'let him flee, escape'; with *i* and *ê* of the Qal in verbs primæ א it becomes *lî* and *lê*: *li-kul* 'may he eat', *li-ru-ru* 'may they curse', *li-lil*. *li-bi-ib* (doubtless =*lêkul*, *lêrurû* etc.); cf. *lîšir* (ישר, IV R 64, 6 b); with *u* of the stems II 1 and III 1 it becomes *lû*, although *lî* is also found: *lu-*(*u-*) *ḫal-li-iḳ* 'may he annihilate' (Tig. VIII 88), *lu-šab-bi-ru* 'may they break in pieces' (Tig. VIII 80), *lubbibû*. *luddiš* 'let him renew', *lu-u-tir* 'let him bring back', and *li-ḫal-li-ḳu* (IV R 64, 64 b), *li-paṭ-ṭi-ru* 'may they release' (IV R 59, 52 b), *li-ma-'-i-da* (III R 41 col. II 23), *lu* (var. *li*)*-bal-lu-u* 'may they destroy' (Tig. VIII 79); *lûšeknišû* (Tig. VIII 33), and *li-ša-li-ṣa* 'may he cause to shout for joy' (Khors. 194), *li-še-ši-bu-šu* 'may they cause him to remain' (Sarg. Cyl. 77, but *lu-še-ši-bu-šu* Tig. VIII 83), *li-šam-'-i-da* 'may she increase'; with *û* of verbs primæ ו (Qal) it becomes *lî*, and sometimes *lû*: *li-rid*, *li-ri-du*, *li-bil* and *lu-bil* 'may he carry off' (IV R 66, 49 a. 14 b).

b) 1. pers. sing. With *u* of the preformative it becomes *lu*: *lubluṭ* 'would that I might live', 'whom *lu-uš-pur* shall I send?', *lu-zi-iz* 'I will take my stand', *lullik* 'I will go' (but *lillik* 'let him go'), *lu-um-id* 'would that I might increase' (K. 2455), *lu-uḳ-bi*, *lu-ub-ki* 'I will weep' (Desct. obv. 34. 35)—observe the orthography *lu-ú-up-te* 'I will open' (Nimr. Ep. XI, 252)—; *lu-ul-ta-ti* 'I will drink' (Desct. rev. 19). Likewise with *ê*: *lûbib* 'O, that I were pure', *lu-ru-ba* 'I will enter' (Desct. obv. 15); cf. *lûšir* 'would that I might prosper' (ישׁר). In the same way with *u* of stems II 1 etc: *lu-ša-an-ni* 'I will announce'. Cases in which *a* or *â* is retained are rare: cf., e. g., *la-šú-ṭa* 'I will draw' (V R 2, 125) and the masc. prop. name *Pân-Ašûr-la-mur* 'may I see the face of Ashur' (C^a 136. 153). A very difficult form is *la-ta-am* which occurs in an unpublished text in a clause of which the meaning is quite certain: *la-ta-am nar-bi-ka ana nišê rapšâti* 'I will announce thy greatness to the peoples that are afar off' (cf. the variants *Mar-la-ar-me* and *Mar-la-rim* C^a 244?). *c*) 3. pers. f. sing. 'Ishtar *kakkêšu lu-ú tu-ša-bir kussâšu lu te-kim-šu* break in pieces his weapons, take from him his throne' (Assurn. Balaw. rev. 20 f.).

Forms with *i* like *liḫallik*, *lišâliṣa* are no doubt occasioned by the effort to differentiate the 3. and 1. persons.—There are no precatives formed from the present: *linâr* is only an apparent exception (*v.* § 114), and the same is the case with the precatives IV R 7, 46, 48 a, which, of course, are to be read *likkalip*, *lippašir*.—For the 1. pers. plur. with cohortative signification *v.* Syntax § 145.

2) Precative forms from the permansive I have as yet found only for the 3. and 2. persons. 3. pers. *lû*

ašib 'may he dwell', *lû baliṭ lû ša-lim* (III R 66 rev. 23 c), 'may his rule *ina dumḳi lû bullul* be crowned (lit. poured over) with favour' (V R 33 col. VII 15), 'may hill and valley *lû na-šú-nik-ka biltu* bring thee tribute' (Nimr. Ep. 43, 17), *lû emû kîma ilâni* 'may they be like the gods' (Nimr. Ep. XI, 183). 2. pers. *atta aganna lû aš-ba-ta* (Assurb. Sm. 125, 64), *lû ta-mat* 'be cursed'; fem. *lû šak-na-a-ti, lû na-ša-a-ti* (IV R 63, 54 f. b). — Note finally the concurrence of the two sorts of precatives in V R 33 col. VII 12 f.: *ûmêšu lû ar-ku šanâtešu lêrikâ.*

The imperative is formed from the preterite by § 94. suppressing the preformative, the first radical, which has thus been rendered vowelless, being supplied with a helping vowel. The vowel of the second radical is preserved unchanged. This explains, in the augmented stems, the relation of the imper. II 1 *kaššid* to the pret. *ukaššid*, I 2 *kitášad* (and with syncope — cf. § 88. b — *kitšad*) to *iktášad*, III 2 *šutakšid* to *uštakšid*, likewise of IV 1 *nakšid* to *ikkašid* (i. e. *inkašid*). The form *kaššid* of the imper. of II 1 is at the bottom of all the impers. of verbs med. ו and י, hence *ka-in, kên*; elsewhere, however, this form has been gradually supplanted by the form *kuššid*, which is to be explained by the influence of the *u* of the preformative. In fact, in the case of the imper. III 1, so far as the strong verb is concerned, we no longer find a single instance of *šakšid*, which must be also assumed as the original form of this imper.; we always find instead the form *šukšid*, and only verbs primae א$_{4.5}$ and primae ו — the latter in this respect following the analogy of the former — take (as we might expect from the pret.) *šêzib* (pret. *ušêzib*) and *šêbil* (pret. *ušêbil*), sometimes *šûzib* and *šûbil*. The imperatives of the Qal in verbs primae ו reject the whole of the *û* of the pret., that is, the first radical as well as the preformative, hence *šib, bil*. The strong verbs and verbs tertiæ infirmæ take for their helping vowel the vowel of the second syllable: *kušud*, *piḳid*, *ṣabat*; *miṣi*, *piti*, *šiti*, *munu*. So too verbs primæ נ, which in addition allow their נ to disappear in the spiritus lenis: *uṣur*, *idin*. Only verbs primæ א — in order, perhaps, to differentiate them from verbs primæ נ — take *a*, sometimes modified to *e*, as the vowel of the first radical, hence *akul*, *amur*; *alik*; *etiḳ*, *epuš*; *erub*.

The imper. is inflected for gender and number in precisely the same way as the preterite. We also find in the imper. the 2. m. sing. used promiscuously for the 2. fem.: *kišâdki su-ḫi-ir-šum-ma* 'incline (O goddess) thy side to him' (K. 4623 obv. 19), *šullim* alongside of *ṭibbî*, *uṣur* alongside of *kinnî* (V R 34 col. III 46. 47); the 2. m. plur is also frequently found in *â*: *a-ku-la* 'eat ye', 'ye great gods, *di-ni di-na* grant me justice' (IV R 56, 14 a), *uṣ-ra-a-ma ṣu-ub-bi-ta-niš-šu-nu-tu* 'give heed and take them prisoners' (K. 82, 22), etc. The vowel *a* is the favorite ending of the 2. pers. m. sing.: *al-ka* 'go to!' *ir-ba* 'enter', *pi-ta-a* 'open' (Desct. obv. 14 f.), *šubšâ* 'leave alone' (Neb. I 71), *šuptâ* 'cause to open' (*E. M.* II 339), *šul-li-ma* 'let . . . succeed, success to! (*ibid.*), *šú-ṣa-a* 'bring out' (Desct. rev. 33); also strengthened with *m*: *šú-ur-ḳam*, *šú-ur-ka-am* 'present' (I R 52 No. 4 rev. 22. Bors. II 22 etc.).

For the formation of the participles the paradigms may be consulted; in the augmented stems, they are always formed from the pret. by means of the preformative *mu*, the second radical, however, being everywhere pronounced with *i* (cf. *muktašidu* notwithstanding *iktašad*). For the infinitives of these stems, see § 88 b and note. The infs. *šêburu* (primae א₄) and *šêbulu* (primae ו), alongside of *šûzubu*, *šûšubu*, are doubtless due to the influence of the corresponding forms of the pret. and imper. The part. of the Qal has the form *kâšidu*; the inf. is *kašâdu* (cf. § 65 No. 11 and the note appended to No. 19). All the infs. have both an active and a passive signification (cf. § 89); accordingly *šalâl ilâni*, for example, 'the gods' carrying off' may also denote their being carried off. § 95.

Strong Verbs*,

i. e. verbs with three strong radicals

including verbs mediæ geminatæ not beginning with א or נ**

(See Paradigm B, 1).

§ 96. Summary of the most common *** verbs with their pronunciation in the preterite and present Qal (I 1) and in the preterite of the Ifteal (I 2):

Pret. *u.* *a*) Pres. *a*: בקם 'cut off, tear', גמר* 'complete'† גצץ 'tear, rend in pieces', דגל 'gaze on', דלל 'be subject, submit one's self', זכר* 'name, announce, call', זנן 'fill, equip, furnish thoroughly', זקף 'erect', חסס* 'be mindful of, reflect', כבס 'tramp down, tread', כרב* 'bless (with *ana,* I 2 c. acc.), pray', כשׁר*

* The conjugation of the strong and weak triliteral verbs is to be learned from the paradigms B, 1—12; §§ 96—116 are simply intended to serve as remarks to supplement the paradigms.

** These are taken up with the verbs primae א and נ, to which they properly belong.

*** In §§ 96. ff. and in §§ 99. 102 etc. we have set down as 'the most common verbs' only such as are found in the Qal; the others find their place in the two sections respectively devoted to the various classes of verbs. 'Verbs' that appear only in nominal derivatives are excluded.

† The Assyrian verbs of which the first radical is marked by an asterisk have the vowel of the present in the preter. of the Ifteal as well; the same indication is given by the asterisk in §§ 99 and 102. In other cases, where the pret. I 2 is found to have a different vocalization from the pres. I 1, or where the latter is still unknown to me, the vowel of the pres. I 2 is added in parentheses.

'reach, capture, conquer', כתם 'cover, overcome', מדד
'measure', סחה 'overthrow', סלח 'sprinkle', ספן (also
written שׁפן) 'cover, overcome', פטר* 'cleave, tear in
pieces, release, etc.' פרס* 'break, keep back, hinder',
פשׁר 'release', שׁבם and סבם (very rarely סבשׂ) 'be angry
with', שׁחט 'flay, tear in pieces', שׁטר 'write', שׁכן* 'lay,
make', שׁלל* 'carry off, plunder', שׁלף 'tear out', שׁפר*
'send', שׁקל 'weigh, pay', שׂרק* 'burn' (act.), שׁרק 'present, lend', תמח 'sieze, hold', תרך 'escape', תרץ 'set
up, put or lay straight'.

b) Pres. *i*: לבר 'grow old', שׁחת* 'bow, fall, lie
down'.

c) Pres. *u*: בלט* 'live', כפד* (קפד?) 'reflect, plan',
מקת* 'fall, befall', פחר 'assemble', רחץ 'trust to', רמד*
'pour out', רמם 'roar, thunder', רפד* 'lie down', שׁגם
'howl, roar', תרר 'tremble'.

d) Pres. as yet unknown: בלל 'pour over', בתק
'cut through, cut off, separate', גרר 'run', חבת 'plunder,
boot' (pret. I 2: *a*), חטט 'cut into, dig', חשׁח 'desire,
covet', חשׁל 'break in pieces', טבח 'slaughter', טרד 'drive
away', כנשׁ 'submit (one's self)', לפת 'surround; turn,
touch, overturn' (pret. I 2: *a*), לקת 'take, take away',
מגר 'be agreeable, obedient, gracious' (pret. I 2: *a*), מחר
'accept; go to meet, make up to, etc.' (pret. I 2: *a*),
מרץ 'be sick', משׁח 'measure', מתח 'set up', סהל 'pierce',
סחר 'turn' (*vertere* and *se vertere*, pret. I 2: *u*? see

§ 98 under I 3), ספח 'lay low, throw down', סקר and שׂקר 'talk, command etc., swear', פרץ 'tell lies', פרץ 'break, break into', פרץ 'order', פשׁשׁ 'rub in', צרק 'colour, dye', קדד 'bend down, bow' (pret. I 2: *u*? see § 98 under I 3), קצר 'bind, unite firmly, collect', קרב 'offer', רדד 'persecute', רכס 'bind, unite firmly', שׁדד 'draw', שׁדר 'command', שׁפך 'pour out, heap up' (pret. I 2: *a*), שׁקק 'set up, plant', שׁרט 'make an incision, tear in pieces', תבך 'pour out' (pret. I 2: *a*).

e) With a twofold pronunciation in the present: דבב 'speak (secretly), talk, reflect' (*iddbab* and *iddbub*), זנן 'rain' (*iznan* and *iznun*). See also the 'Supplementary Remarks'.

The follg. are known to me in the present only: דמם *lament', צרר 'oppress, press upon, be straitened', תקן 'be firm, constant'; the vowel of the present in all these verbs is *u* and points with certainty, in my opinion, to *u* in the preterite as well.

Pret. *i*. *a*) Pres. *i*: בטל 'cease, hold holiday', גמל 'keep perfect, unhurt; do good, grant (life)', דנן 'be or become strong', כמס 'bow, prostrate one'sself', כסר 'fence round, divide off', לבן 'to fall on one's face; make bricks', מלך* 'advise, take counsel, resolve', סדר 'arrange, put in order, range in order of battle', סכק 'throw, cast down', סנק 'squeeze, press together', פקד* 'take care; commit, entrust; appoint', פשׁט 'destroy, blot out', קרב* 'draw near, approach (to battle)', שׂבר 'break in pieces', שׂלם 'be well, be uninjured', (applied to money:) 'be paid', also 'be carried to completion'.

b) Present as yet unknown: ברק 'lighten', בשׂל 'boil', בשׂם 'be good; beautify, set up', חלק 'perish; flee' (pret. I 2: *i*), חתן 'protect, help', כבר 'be or become large', כסם 'cut in pieces', כשׂט (כ, ג, ק?) 'cut down, fell', כשׂף 'employ charms, bewitch one', סכר 'close, stop', סלם 'turn towards, take pity on', פרך 'bar, bolt', פתק 'form, create, build', צמד 'harness, yoke', רבץ 'encamp, lie in wait', רחץ 'overflow, flood', רצף 'join, arrange, etc.', שׂקשׂ 'ruin, destroy, slay'.

The follg. are known to me in the present only: זבל 'bring, carry', חבל 'destroy', חכם 'understand', טמר 'cover, hide, bury', קבר 'bury', רסף 'strike, break in pieces', שׂבט 'strike, kill', שׂדח 'walk' (pret. I 2: *i*): the vowel of the present of these verbs is *i*, from which we may best infer that the preterite was also in *i*.

Pret. *a*. *a*) Pres. *a*: למד 'learn', מחץ 'strike, break in pieces' (pret. I 2: *i*, more rarely *a*; cf. *im-ta-ḫa-aṣ* III R 4 No. 1, 29 etc., *im-da-ḫa-*[*ṣu*] Assurb. Sm. 89, 28), פלח* 'be afraid', פשׂח 'calm one's self', צבת* 'take', רכב* 'mount, drive, ride', חבל* 'take away'.

b) Present as yet unknown: צלל 'lie down'.

The follg. are known to me in the present only: שׂנן 'compete with, be equal with one' (pret. I 2: *a*);

from *a* being the vowel of the present we may infer that the pret. had either *a* or *u*.

A twofold pronunciation is found in the pret. Qal of the follg. verbs: *u* and *i*, כנש 'submit one's self' (*iknuš, v. supra*, but V R 65 col. II 45: *ikniš*); *a* and *u*: צבת 'sieze' (*iṣbat, v. sup.* but, especially in Assurb. and Shalm., *iṣbut*); *i* and *a*: תכל 'trust' takes *at-kil* (e. g. V R 3, 127) and *at-kal* (e. g. I R 49 col. IV 2).

[Among those known to me in the pret. I 2 only are *ištámar* 'he kept', *ištápil* 'he was lowly'].

§ 97.   Pret.(Qal): For *imḳut* and *iḳḳut v.* § 49, a. For forms of the 1. pers. sing. like *eptiḳ* for *aptik v.* § 34, *a*. In the imper. an exception to the rule given in § 94 is found in *li-mad* 'learn' (IV R 17, 44 c, cf. *lim-di*, fem., and *lim-da*, plur., IV R 56 obv. 14); we should expect *lamad*: has *a* perhaps been modified to *i* as in the comparatively rare permansives *niksu ni-ki-si* = *nekisi, nakisi*, V R 53, 14 a, or as in *lemnit* 'she is wicked' (*v. sup.* p. 164 and cf. § 35)? For infins. with *um-laut* in the 2. or in the 1. and 2. syllables, like *naméru*, *sekéru v.* §§ 32, γ (p. 83) and 34, β. Presents with modification (*umlaut*) of the accented *á*, like *tekébir* mentioned in § 34, *a*, are rare; other two examples will be found in § 98 (cf. § 101). On the other hand the interchange of *a* and *e* is very common in the augmented stems: for *ukaššid* as a variant of *ukéšid* (*ukêšid*?), and for the forms II 2 *uštépil*, *luptéḫir* see § 33, for *ušakšid*, *ušekšid*, *mušaknišu*, *mušeknišu*, also for the forms III 2 *uštasḫir*, *ultesḫir* § 34, *a*. For the accenting of the syllable *ta* in I 2, and of *na* in I 3 see § 53, a, and for the accenting of the 2. syllable of the present in IV 1 *v. ibid.* For forms like *iptéḳid v.* § 34, *a*, for *aṣṣabat*, *aḳṭérib*, *agdámar*, *amdáḫar* § 48, for *attaḫar* § 49, a, for *asakan* = *aštakan* (also III 2 *ussîbila* = *uštêbila*) § 51, 2. For the vowel of the second radical in the pret. I 2, which is in most cases *a*, but which, like the *a* of the pres. Qal, is in many cases influenced by the vocalisation of the pret. Qal, § 96 (also §§ 99 and 102) must be consulted in each individual instance. As to the vowel of the corresponding syllable in the pres. I 2, I do not as yet venture to formulate a rule for those verbs which have a vowel other than *a* in the preterite, notwithstanding *ibtalaṭ*, V R 53 No. 4 rev. In the pres. I 3 the second radical has mostly *a*, while the vowel of the pret. I 3 seems to follow the pret. I 2; this vowel is then occasionally retained for the pres. which in this way becomes completely identical with the pret. Examples will be found in § 98 (cf. also § 101). The pret. II 2 takes *i* with the second radical, the pres. takes *a*: *uktaššid*, but *uktaššad*. I fail to see the reason why the tablet V R 45, which confines itself to 2. pers.

sing. masc. of presents, should place *tu-uḫ-ta-bal* alongside of *tu-uḫ-tan-ni-ib*, *tu-uḫ-tar-rib* etc. (col. I): in other texts I have not met with a single thoroughly attested present II 2 with *i* after the second radical. It is, however, worthy of note, that the form we should naturally expect, viz. *tuḫtabbal* begins the series of forms from the stem II 2: is it the case, perhaps, that a single slip in line 20 has caused all the subsequent forms to be written with *i* after the second radical? The vocalization of stem IV 1 calls for no remark: just as in II 1 and III 1 a preterite signification attaches, without exception, to *ukaššid*, *ušakšid* and a present signification to *ukaššad, ušakšad*, so we find it the case with *ikkašid* on the one hand and *ikkášad* on the other. The only exception is with the stem צרח 'rage, be in a passion', which has *iṣṣariḫ* and *iṣṣaruḫ* in the pret. IV 1 (III R 15 col. I 2. II 13: *iṣ-ṣa-ri-iḫ,* V R 1, 64: *iṣ-ṣa-ru-uḫ*). The pret. IV 2, has as a rule, an *a* after the second radical: *ittaškan* 'it was done, came to pass', *it-ta-ad-laḫ* 'was disturbed' (IV R 11, 2 a), *littapraš* 'let escape'. Forms like *it-taḫ-kim* (III R 51 No. 9, 25), and *it-taš-kin* (IV R 52, 19 b) appear to be less common; so with *i-ta-am-gur*, which is a present, it is true ('is graciously received, is courteous' IV R 67, 55 a), but points to a pret. *it-tamgur*. For infs. IV 2 like *itaktumu* = *nitaktumu* v.

§ 49, b, end. The vocalization of the pret. and pres. IV 3 may be learned, meanwhile, from the examples in § 98 (cf. also § 101): *a* appears to be the ordinary vowel in the pres., a form like *ittanarḫiṣ* being rather exceptional.

Verbs mediæ geminatæ are, in general, conjugated quite regularly, like the strong verbs (cf. § 63). Even in the permansive of the Qal, which otherwise has its peculiar inflexion (*v.* § 87 and cf. § 89), we find, after the analogy of the strong verbs, forms like *ṣa-lil* 'he lies' (IV R 23, 28 a; in the relative clause, however, we find immediately thereafter *ša ṣal-lum*, ibid.) It is to be expected that, in cases where the two identical radicals are separated merely by a short vowel, contraction should frequently take place, accompanied by the syncope of the intervening vowel. To the examples given in § 37, b, viz. *ša i-da-bu* 'who will speak' (III R 43 col. III 5) and *aštallum* add *a-sa-la* (= *aštâlala*, Shalm. Ob. 129), *i-za-an-nu* 'they fulfil' (= *izânanû*, Nerigl. I 27 etc.), *it-tar-ru* 'they trembled', *at-ta-ri* 'I trembled' (Nimr. Ep. XI, 87), *lit-tar-ri* 'let (him etc.) tremble' (V R 65 col. II 44), *ir-tam-ma-am-ma* 'he thundered' (= *irtamumamma*, Nimr. Ep. XI, 94), *ḳud-da-a-ta* (= *ḳuddudâta*, cf. *ḳuddû* § 89 under II 1), 'the eastern canal which with heaps of dust *iz-za-an-nu-ú-ma imlû* (= *izzaninú-ma*, I R 52 No. 4

obv. 17), *ip-pa-aš-šu* 'they were anointed' (= *ippašišû*, V R 6, 21), *uḫtaṣṣi* 'he is cut off' (= *uḫtaṣaṣi*, IV R 3, 6 a), etc.

§ 98. Noteworthy miscellaneous forms:*

I 1. Perm. *lû pa-aš-ša-a-ti* (IV R 63, 63 b), *ša-an-na* (3. plur. f., IV R 27, 17 a). Pret.-pres. *lil-ḳu-tum* 'may they snatch away' (IV R 41, 37 c), *ni-ip-ki-dak-ka*, *ta-pa-ḳid-da-na-ši* (Nimr. Ep. 20, 18 f.). *a-da-bu-bu* 'I am talking' (IV R 68, 18 b), *i-dib-bu-ba* (prop. *idébuba*) 'he speaks' (IV R 67, 69 a), *i-ḫi-ib-bil* 'he will bring to shame' (IV R 52 No. 1, 42). Imp. *ku-šû-ud* 'subdue' (V R 2, 99), *ma-ḫa-aṣ* 'break in pieces' (Desct. rev. 31), *pi-ḳid-su* 'command him' (IV R 4, 45 b), *pi-iḳ-dan-ni* 'command me' (Sm. 949 obv. 4), *pi-šiṭ* 'destroy' (IV R 12, 35), *ḫu-ub-ta-a-nu* 'spoil ye' (K. 10 obv. 11).

II 1. Imp. *lu-(ub-)bi*(V. *be*)-*ir* 'let ... become old' (V R 65 col. II 24), *ḳu-di-da-an-ni* 'incline me', *ru-ub-bi-ši* 'increase' (fem., *E. M.* II 296), *suḫ-ḫi-ra-ni pa-ni-ku-nu* 'turn (O ye gods) your face' (K. 143 obv.), but also *ra-am-me-ik* 'pour out' (Desct. rev. 48), *ra-si-pan-ni* 'strike, pierce me through' (V R 7, 35). Inf. *ruppušu* 'extend'.

III 1. Pret. *u-šim-ḳit* 'I threw down' (Tig. V 71 etc.;

---

* The forms of the permansive and preterite in this and the follg. §§ are to be compared throughout with § 89 and § 93 respectively.

ḳit sign § 9 No. 11), *ušazin* 'I caused to rain' (*u-ša-za-nin* do., Assurn. II 106. Shalm. Mo. rev. 68, must be III^{II}, cf. § 85), *lišaznin* 'may he fill up'; Imp. *šuk-lil* (IV R 16, 35 b), *šur-ši-di* 'establish firmly' (fem.). Inf. *šuknušu* 'to subdue', *šuklulu* 'to complete'.

IV 1. Pret. *v.* § 97 and note *it-ti-kil* 'he entrusted' (Assurn.) alongside of *ittakil*, *iḫ-ḫi-kim* (III R 51 No. 9, 20). Pres. 'the land *ik-kaš-šad* will be subdued' (III R 65, 22 a). Imp. *nag-mir* 'be carried out, completed' (IV R 13, 43 a), *natkil* 'entrust' (I R 35 No. 2, 12). Inf. *na-gar-ru-ru*, *na-šal-lu-lu* (II R 27, 1,3. 16 b; for *namurratu*, which presupposes an inf. form *namurru*, *v.* § 88, b, note), but more usually (cf. § 88, b) *nalbubu*, *naplusu* 'see', *napšuru* 'be released', *nasḫuru* 'inclination, favour'.

I 2. Pret. *in-da-ḳut* 'it fell' (IV R 53 No. 2, 20), *ik-tan-šu-uš* 'they fell down before him' (K. 133). For *asuḫra* 'I turned back' *v.* § 101 note (on I 2). Pres. *ap-tal-la-ḫu* 'I worship' (rel., Assurb. Sm. 103, 46). Is *iš-tam-da-ḫu* (i. e. *ištádaḫu*, Shalm. Mo. obv. 10) pres. or pret.? The latter elsewhere appears as *ištamdiḫ* (cf. e. g. Senhb. III 76). Imp. *šitakkanî* (Nimr. Ep. XI, 200) and *pit-laḫ* (Assurb. Sm. 74, 17); on the existence side by side of such forms cf. § 94. Part. *mug-da-áš-ru* 'strong' (IV R 21, 60 a), *mu-un-dag-ri* 'obedient' (IV R 20 No. 1 obv. 6). Inf. *ši-taḫ-ḫu-ṭu* (K. 4329), *ḫi-*

tan-nu-bu, *pi-taš-šú-lum* (V R 19, 37 d), *šitamduḫu* (i. e. *šitdduḫu*) 'go (on foot), go' (of chariots, Esarh. IV 59), *ši-tar-ru-ru* 'shine', *ši-ta-du-du* (V R 42, 48 d), *mi-tan-gu-gu* (II R 20, 53 d) and (cf. § 88, b) *git-pu-lu* (II R 38, 3 h), *šitnunu* 'rival'. Perm. 'which *mi-taḫ-ḫu-ru* he received as price' (III R 41 col. I 30). 'Nebuchadnezzar who, for the purpose of giving battle, *kit-pu-da emûḳâšu* collected his forces' (V R 55, 7).

II 2. Pret. *uptaṭṭir* 'was burst' (Neb. Bors. II 3), *uptarriṣ* 'he told lies' (Beh. 90 ff.), also *uptaššiṭu* (rel., V R 56, 33). Pres. *uḳtaṣṣar* 'he collected himself' (circumstantial clause, V R 5, 76), *uktannašu* 'I gather, collect' (rel., Neb. Grot. III 30). Inf. *pu-tal-lu-su* (Zurich. Voc. col. IV 35).

III 2. Pret. *uš-tam-ḫi-ir* 'he went to meet' (IV R 26, 12 b). Inf. *ši-tap-ru-šu* 'spread out (Assurn. III 26), the only occurrence known to me. The infs. *šutêšuru* etc. would lead us to expect *šutakšudu* as the form of the infinitive.

IV 2. Pret. *v.* § 97. Part. *muttaprišu* 'flying, that soars'. Inf. *itaktumu* (V R 41, 58. 61 d), *i-tap-lu-su* 'see' (Nimr. Ep. XI, 88), *i-ta-aṣ-bu-ru* (II R 20, 23 d), cf. *i-tag-ru-ur-rum* (II R 62, 17 d) with peculiar accentuation.

I 3. Pret. *iḫtanabbat* 'he plundered', *ištanappara* 'he had sent' (V R 2, 111), *im-da-na-aḫ-ḫa-ru* 'they received' (Senhb. Bell. 38); *i-ta-na-ḳu-tu-ni* 'they fell' (Shalm. Mo. rev. 73); from *iḳ-ta-na-ad-du-ud* 'he bowed down' (V R 31, 26 *h* or pres.?) may we conclude that *u* was the vowel of the pret. I 2 and also of the pres. I 1? Pres. *iš-ta-na-kan* (IV R 26, 63 b), *ip-ta-na-la-ḫu* 'they worship' (V R 6, 37); *i-ta-na-ar-ra-ru* 'they tremble' (IV R 28, 10 b), but also *is-sa-na-aḫ-ḫu-ru* (rel., IV R 16, 45 a, cf. III R 54, 30 c)—this surely points to pret. I 2 and to pres. I 1 in *u*? — *id-di-ni-ib-bu-ub* (i. e. *iddenêbub, iddanâbub*) 'he thought' (V R 35, 6).

IV 3. Pret. *idâ-a-a it-ta-na-as-ḫa-ru* (sic) 'they declared themselves on my side' (III R 15 col. I 26), but also *it-ta-nab-riḳ* 'it has lightened' (IV R 3, 4 a). Pres. *at-ta-na-as-ḫar* 'I turn' (IV R 10, 6 b), *it-ta-nap-raš* 'it flies', *it-ta-nag-ra-ra* 'he roams about' (IV R 3, 18 a), *it-ta-na-aš-ra-ṭu* (Assurb. Sm. 127, 81), *ittanaḫlal*; rarely *i-ta-na-ar-ḫi-iṣ* 'will inundate' (III R 61, 11 a).

Verbs primae נ.

(See Paradigm B, 2).

Summary of the most common verbs with the characteristic vowel of the preterite and present Qal (I 1) and of the preterite Ifteal (I 2): § 99.

Pret. *u. a)* Pres. *a*: נטל* 'behold, regard*), נסח

*) For the meaning of the asterisk with the first radical see note † to § 96 on p. 264.

'pull out, remove forcibly', נפץ 'overwhelm, destroy', נצר* 'keep, watch over, protect', נקר* 'demolish, lay waste'.

b) Pres. *u*: נסך 'set, lay, do', נפש 'widen, expand; breathe' (pret. I 2: *a*), נרט 'restrain one's self' (?, II 1 'restrain, hinder, impede, etc.').

c) Pres. as yet unknown: נבל 'destroy' (pret. I 2: *a*), נפח 'come up, come out', נפח 'kindle, fan' (pret. I 2: *a*), נשך 'bite'.

The follg. are known to me in the pres. only: נגג 'scream, call (*inágag*), נשר 'tear to pieces' (*indšar*) and נסס 'lament' (*indsus*, from which we may infer—especially as regards נסס—that the pret. was in *u*).

Pret. *i*. *a*) Pres. *i*: נדן* 'give', נשק* 'kiss' (I 2 'to arm for battle').

b) Pres. as yet unknown: נבט 'shine' (pret. I 2: *i*), נזם 'weep, lament', נכל 'be treacherous, cunning', נכס 'cut down', נכר 'be different, hostile, rebel' (pret. I 2: *i*), נמר 'be or become bright, shine' (pret. I 2: *i*), נתל 'lie' (pret. I 2: *i*). Cf. also נזז 'stand, rise, tread' (pret. I 2: *i*), for the pres. of which, *izzaz*, compare § 100.

The follg. verb is known to me in the pres. only: נכם 'heap up' (*inákim*).

Cf. also the follg. doubly weak verbs: נא₁ד 'be exalted, raise, praise'; נא₂ל 'lie down' (cf. § 105); נבא₁

'announce', נשׂא₁ 'take, bear'; נגא₂ 'shine, rejoice'; נסא₄ 'remove, take one's departure'; נדה 'throw, lay, do', נקה 'empty, pour out, offer (in sacrifice)' (cf. § 108). For the hollow verbs primæ נ see § 114.

The pres. (and the same applies to the perm., §100. part., and inf.) of the Qal, as likewise the stems II 1 and IV 1 present no peculiarity. For the assimilation of *n* in the forms *iṣṣur*, *ittáṣar*, *ušaḳḳar* (=*ušanḳar*) etc. *v.* § 49, b; orthographical varieties like *akis*, *abúl*, *aḳur*, *asuḫ*, *a-ḳi* (I R 27 No. 2, 10) instead and alongside of *akkis*, *abbul* etc. are to be explained according to § 22. For the loss of the *n* in the spiritus lenis in the imper. I 1 and in the inf. I 2 (II 2), *v.* § 49, b (p. 117). For a variety of other points see the quotations in § 97. A series of forms from stems נדן and נזז which are due to analogy deserves special notice. From נדן we find in the pres. Qal. the regular forms, *inádin*, *inamdin*, but alongside of these we often find the form *iddan*, formed directly from the pret.; in the case of נזז this metaplastic form is the only one in use (cf. § 90, a, note). Cf. *ta-ad-dan-na-ma* 'thou wilt give and' (Nimr. Ep. XI, 246), 'the goddess who *ta-da-nu-u-ni* bestows' (V R 53, 56 d), *a-da-an-na* 'I bestow', *a-da-na* 'I give up' (IV R 68, 22 c. 33 a), *a-dan-nak-ka* 'I will bestow on thee' (*ibid.* 58 c)—it is very striking that in Beh. and NR *iddan* is also used as pret.: *id-dan-nu* 'he has bestowed' (Beh. 4. 11, cf. NR 21), *in-da-na-aš-šu-nu-tú* 'he gave them' (Beh. 96)—; cf. also *izzaz* 'he stands, advances' (oft.), *i-za-zu-ú-ni* 'they stand' (Assurn. I 105). The pret. III 1 of נזז is *ušâziz* (Assurb. Sm. 224, 46) and *ušêziz*, from which we get *ušziz* (*v.* § 37 end) and *ulziz* (*v.* § 51, 3); *ušâziz* may be explained as a form due to the analogy of verbs primæ א, but the conjecture mentioned in § 52 seems to me preferable. Then from *ušêziz* there seems to have been formed an infinitive *u-zu-zu* 'stand' (e. g. S[c] 309, *u-zu-uz-zu* IV R 5, 67 a) and a participle *muzziz*, cf. *mu-uz-zi-iz maḫ-re-ku* 'who stands before thee' (V R 65 col. II 32). Very difficult to explain is the infinitive and permansive form *ušuzzu*, *ušuz*, which cannot, in my opinion, be separated from *nazâzu*: inf. *u-šú-uz-zu* 'be placed' (V R 66 col. I 27); perm. *u-šú-uz* 'he stood' (IV R 34, 44), *u-šú-uz-zu* 'they were set up' (Beh. 34), 'so long as they *u-šú-(uz-)zu* remained in Assyria' (V R 3, 94). The same is true of the following forms, resembling the Ittafal, which are derived from those just mentioned: *ittišu it-ta-ši-iz-zu* 'they have placed themselves on his side' (K. 10 rev. 20), *it-ta-ši-iz* (3. m. sing., V R 55, 42), *itti bêl dabâbi'a ta-ta-ši-iz-za* 'ye have placed yourselves on the side of my calumniator' (IV R 52, 32 a) etc.

Noteworthy miscellaneous forms: § 101.

I 1. Pret. *ni-id-din* 'we gave', *ta-zi-iz* 'she stood' (III R 15 col. I 23), *lu-uṭ-ṭul* 'would that I might see' (IV R 66, 55 a). Pres. *inamdin* 'he gives', *a-nam-ṣar* 'I keep watch' (IV R 53 No. 2, 22 f.), *ni-na-ṣar* (V R 54, 15. 16 b), *ul i-nir-ru-ṭa* (i. e. *inéruṭâ*) *šêpâka* 'shall not restrain thy feet' (Assurb. Sm. 125, 69). Imp. *usuḫ* 'be off!', *uṣ-ra-a-ma* 'keep ye watch and' (K. 82, 22), *i-zi-zi* 'halt!' (fem. Desct. obv. 23), *i-ziz-za-am-ma* 'Up! (O Shamash', IV R 17, 22 b), *i-zi-za-nim-ma* 'Go to! (O ye gods, IV R 56, 13 a).

II 1. Pret. *u-na-ḳip* 'she pushed, threw down' (with her horns V R 9, 78). Part. *munarriṭu* and *munirriṭu* 'impeding, opposing' (V R 6, 72; also in the name of the rampart of the city of Ashur: *Munirriṭi kibrâti*, Shalm. Throne Inscr. III 7).

III 1. Pret. *u-ša-as-si-ku* 'he put on' (rel., Fragm. 18 obv. 14). Pres. *u-ša-az-za-ḳa* 'they will bring to shame' (fem., III R 61, 52 a), *tu-ša-an-mar* (V R 45 col. VI 49). Inf. *šú-uḳ-ḳur dûrânišu* (III R 60, 84), *šumkuru* (*v.* § 49, b on p. 117).

IV 1. Pret. *li-in-na-pi-iš* 'let it be pulled to pieces' (IV R 7, 35 etc.). Pres. *in-na-ga-ru* 'they will be laid waste', *in-na-as-sa-aḫ* 'it is freed from chains' (IV R 4, 6 b), *innamdarû* 'they rage' (*v.* § 52). Inf. *nanduru* 'to rage'.

I 2. Pret. *lit-tan-biṭ* 'may he shine' (IV R 4, 41 b, cf. § 52), *lu-ut-ta-mir* 'may I shine' (IV R 64, 14 b), *ni-(it-)ta-ṣar*, *lit-ta-aṭ-ṭa-la* 'may they behold', *it-ta-kir* 'he rebelled', *it-te-ik-ru-'* (plur., Beh. 30), *ni-it-te-ki-ru-uš*. Part. *mut-ta-ad-di-na-at* (fem., II R 55, 6 d), *muttaḳpûtum* 'wandering, roaming' (plur.). Inf. *it-pu-ṣu* and (*v.* § 88, b) *i-tap-pu-ṣu* (K. 4386 col. III 43. 44), *itanbuṭu* 'to shine' (V R 42, 45 d), *itanpuḫu* (ibid. l. 47 d).

The form so often occurring in Assurn. and Shalm., *a(t)-tu-muš*, *a(t)-tú-muš*, *a(t)-tum-muš*, *at-tum-ša* 'I set out', 3. pers. *it-tu-muš*, is derived from the stem נמשׁ (II 1 pres. *u-nam-maš*, cf. V R 45 col. V 43) from which are also derived *nammaššû* 'worms' and *nammaštu* 'every living thing' (IV R 19, 4 b, where it is represented by the ideogram for human beings!): *attúmuš* stands for *attâmuš*, which is also found (Assurn. III 14); the vowel of the third syllable has found its way into the second. *Attumša* is= *attúmuša*; precisely the same Ifteal form is found from the stem סחר, viz: *a-su-uḫ-ra* 'I turned back'=*assúḫura*, and, like the preceding, occurs in Assurn. (III 31. 45). As we may infer from the pres. I 3: *issanáḫur*, the pret. I 2 of סחר was originally *issáḫur* (*issaḫra*, *issaḫrûni* therefore=*issaḫura*, *issaḫurûni*), which, in the language of every-day life became *issúḫur*.

II 2. Pret. *ut-ta-as-si-iḫ* 'he has torn off' (Nimr. Ep. 9, 10). Pres. *uttakkar* 'it is changed' (e. g. Assurn. I 5), *uttappaš* 'it will be wide, extended' (II R 47, 18 a). For the forms *utûl* (perm.), *utûlu* (inf.) *v.* § 104 on II 2.

I 3. Pret. 'his horns are like the rising of the sun, which *it-ta-na-an-bi-ṭu* has risen in glory' (IV R 27, 22 a, cf. § 52). Pres. *it-ta-na-za-zu*, *it-ta-nam-za-*

(*az*)-*zu* 'they advance' (IV R 2, 56. 17 b), *lâ ta-at-ta-nam-za-az* 'advance not' (IV R 30 No. 3).

IV 3. Pres. 'lions *it-ta-na-da-ru* will rage' (III R 60, 64), *it-ta-nam-da-ra-nin-ni* 'they are angered at me, rise up against me' (IV R 66, 54 b, cf. § 52), also written *i-ta-nam-dar* 'he rages' (II R 28, 11 a).

Verbs primæ gutturalis.*)

(See Paradigms B, 3 and 4; for *alâku* in particular No. 5.)

Of verbs primæ $א_2$ the most frequently occurring, § 102.
viz. *alâku* 'go', with its various peculiarities, is to be learned from paradigm B, 5, compared with §§ 47 (for forms like *illik*, *allik*, *ittâlak*), 38, b (for *illak*) and 42. For a few of the more important references see § 104 note. The other verb primæ $א_2$, *erû* 'be with child', as also the verbs primæ $א_3$ in regard to which, especially as to the nature of their א, there is still considerable uncertainty, are found so rarely, comparatively speaking, in the Qal, that we may deal with them here by anticipation: ארה$_2$, pret. *i-ra-an-ni* 'she conceived me' (prop. 'was pregnant with me') (III R 4, 57 a), inf. *erû*.—ארשׁ$_3$ 'be new', pret. *êdiš*, inf. *edêšu* (only Nimr. Ep. XI, 235 cf. 241); אצר$_3$? 'to

*) In the case of verbs primæ and mediæ א, primæ and mediæ ו and י, and those tertiæ infirmæ we have departed in the follg. §§, for good reasons, from the division carried out in the paradigms.

harvest', pret. *êṣidi* 'I harvested' (Assurn. II 117 etc.), inf. *eṣêdu*; אצן$_{3?}$ 'bring together', also 'to take in', esp. by means of the sense of smell, hence 'to smell', pret. *êṣin*, *îṣin*, also written *e-ṣi-en* (Nimr. Ep. XI, 77 ff.), inf. *eṣênu*; ארר$_3$ 'be hot, be dried up', pres. *irrur* (III R 64, 9 b etc.), אשׁר$_{3?}$ 'collect', pret. *e-šú-ra* 'he brought together' (Senhb. V 30), inf. *ašâru* (=*sanâḳu*, Frgm. 4 obv.); אשׁשׁ$_3$ 'be sorrowful, troubled, bring sorrow upon', pret. *i-šú-uš* (K. 3657 col. I 9), pres. 'the sickness which *i-aš-ša-šú* brings sorrow upon the land' (IV R 1, 42 c), inf. *ašâšu*. The Piel, Shafel etc. from these stems do not call for special notice since they are identical with those of the other primæ א verbs; a few other verbs primæ א$_3$, found almost exclusively in the Piel etc., will be mentioned in § 104, especially אכל$_3$ 'be troubled, sad'.

Summary of the most common verbs primæ א$_1$ and א$_{4.5}$, with the characteristic vowel of the pret. and pres. Qal (I 1) and of the preter. Ifteal (I 2):

א$_1$ (including a few verbs, of which it is not etymologically certain whether the א=א or ח or ח$_1$): **Pret.** *u*, pres. *a*,: אבת$_1$* 'to destroy'*), אדר$_?$ 'be afraid, fear; be oppressed; be darkened', אחז$_1$ 'sieze, take', אכל$_1$ 'eat', אלל$_1$ 'bind', אמר$_1$* 'see', אפל$_1$ 'answer, retort';

*) For the meaning of the asterisk with the first radical see note † to § 96 on p. 264.

of אבך$_?$ 'turn, reverse', אבר$_1$ 'be strong', אגג$_?$ 'be irritated, angry', אגר$_1$ 'hire', ארר$_1$ 'curse' (pret. I 2 *itdrar*) the present is unknown to me (presumably likewise pronounced with *a*).—**Pret.** ***i***, pres. *i*: אפר$_1$* 'clothe, cover over', ארש$_1$* 'ask, request'; of אבב$_?$ 'be bright, shine' (pret. I 2 *itdbib*), אלל$_?$ do., אנש$_1$ 'be or become weak', אסר$_1$ 'shut up; enclose, overlay', ארך$_1$ 'be long', the present is unknown to me (presumably likewise pronounced with *i*).—**Pret.** ***a***, pres. *a*: אנח$_1$ 'decay, fall off, become weary'.

א$_{4,5}$: **Pret.** ***u***, pres. *u*: אפש$_{4?}$* 'make' (pret. I 2 takes both *u* and *a*, just as we find here and there *epaš* in the pres. Qal, I R 27 No. 2, 46. 55); ארב$_5$* 'enter'. —**Pret.** ***i***, pres. *i*: אבר$_4$* 'cross, set across, pass', אזב$_4$* 'leave, leave behind', אטר$_4$ 'cover, protect, preserve in safety', אמד$_4$* 'stand; place, lay upon', אחק$_4$* 'march, derange, advance'; of אדל$_{4?}$ 'to bolt, bar' (pret. I 2 *e-te-dil*), אכם$_{4?}$ 'take, take away', אלץ$_4$ 'rejoice' (pret. I 2 *itêliṣ*), ארש$_?$ 'smell', ארש$_5$ 'plant', the present is unknown to me (presumably likewise pronounced with *i*).

A twofold pronunciation is found in the pret. Qal of אזז$_4$ 'be angry, irritated': pret. *êzuz* (*îzuz*) and *êziz* (*îziz*), pres. *izzuz*, I 2 pret. *itêziz*.

Cf. also the doubly weak verbs אטה$_5$ 'be clouded, dark' (inf. *eṭû*), אלה$_4$ (אלי$_4$) 'go up, mount', אמה$_4$ 'be, make equal', נוא$_4$ 'bend, oppress, do violence to' (cf. § 108). For the 'hollow' verbs primæ א see § 114.

In the case of verbs primae א it must be kept in mind that the vowel of the pret. and pres. I 1 (and I 2) may, acc. to § 35, have arisen by modification (*Umlaut*) from *a*.

§ 103. For the general treatment of the breath (*Hauchlaut*) in verbs primæ א see § 47; on the fact that verbs primæ א$_{4.5}$ are more inclined to the modification of *a* to *e*, and of *â* to *ê* than are those primæ א$_1$ (*tâkul*, *âkul*, but *têpuš*, *êpuš*; *akâlu*, *âkilu*, but *epêšu, êpišu*; imp. *akul*, but *erub*; perm. *abit*, but *epuš*, etc.) *v.* partly §§ 32, β and γ. 34, β and γ, partly § 42. That verbs primæ א$_1$ are not complete strangers to this phonetic change, and that, on the other hand, even verbs primæ א$_{4.5}$ on occasion preserve the *â* pure, we may learn from the paradigms and from the examples in § 104. Pret. Qal. For *êkul*=*i̯êkul*=*i̯âkul* (*i̯a'kul*) *v.* § 90, a and § 41, b. For the interchange of *e-gug* and *i-gu-ug* 'he was irritated' (V R 1, 64. I R 49 col. I 19), *e-bu-uk* 'he reversed' (Khors. 79) and *i-bu-uk* (Khors. 122), *e-zi-bu* and *i-zi-bu* 'they quitted', *i-mur*, *i-kul*, *i-ni-šu* 'he had become weak' (V R 62 No. 2, 55), *i-ru-bu* (V R 55, 48) etc. *v.* § 30; *ê* remains, however, in the majority of cases. Pres. For the interchange of *i-'a-ab-ba-tu* (I R 27 No. 2, 57, without *'a* V R 62, 28) and *ib-ba-tu* (V R 10, 116) *v.* § 38, b. The orthography *lâ te-zi-ba a-a-am-ma* 'leave none in life' (M. 55 col. I 21) points to *tezzib*, 3. m. *ezzib*; for this reason *eppuš* (*ippuš*), *errub* (*irrub*) etc. were adopted for the paradigm. They are all formed directly from the pret. (*v.* § 90, a, note), the vowel of the preformative being sharpened in consequence of the now suppressed but originally accented *a* after the first radical. We also find similar forms among verbs primæ $\aleph_1$; cf. *en-na-ḫu* (Senhb. VI 67), *e-na-ḫu* (IV R 45, 11. Tig. VIII 55) alongside of the regular and usual *innaḫ*; in addition to *iḫḫaz* 'he takes' we find once (K. 183 l. 18) *iḫḫuz* (*eḫḫuz*). Note also the curious form 'whoever *e-ma-ru* shall see the tablet' (Assurn. Balaw. rev. 18. 21). (For orthographical varieties like *ta-kal* 'thou wilt eat', IV R 68, 62 a, *v.* § 22). For the imper. see the examples § 104. For the infin., which is sometimes *amâru*, *abâku*, *agâgu*, *adâru* 'fear', *akâlu* ($\aleph_1$ and $\aleph_3$), *arâku* 'be long', *apâlu*, sometimes *erêšu* ($\aleph_1$), *esêru* 'shut up', *enêšu* ($\aleph_1$), *edêšu* ($\aleph_3$) and practically without exception *epêšu*, *erêbu* ($\aleph_{4.5}$) *v.* §§ 32, γ (p. 83). 34, β. Augmented stems. Pret. and pres. II 1: for the interchange of the forms *u'abbit* and *ubbit*, *u'abbat* and *ubbat v.* § 38, b. For *šêzib* (imp. III 1) alongside of *šûzib*, *šêburu* (inf. III 1) alongside of the more frequent *šûzubu* (cf. §§ 94. 95), see the references in § 104. For the forms of the infinitive and permansive IV 1 *nanduru* = *nâduru*, *nankullat* = *nâkulat* and related forms *v.* § 52 compared with § 11. For the *té* of the second syllable of the stem I 2: *itébir*, *itépuš*, *itérub*, *etétiḳ* 'I marched' alongside of *etápuš*, *etárub*, *etátiḳ* (Lay. 43, 1) and in contrast to *itámar*, alongside of which, however, we also find *etériš*, *v.* § 34, *a* and cf. § 42. For the third pers. pret. I 2 of verbs primæ $א_{4.5}$ there are two forms: one with *i* in the first syllable (cf. *iktášad*), e. g. *i-te-pu-uš* (Beh. 49), *i-tep-pu-šú* (III R 15 col. II 21), *i-te-ip-šu* 'they have exercised' (Beh. 3); *i-te-ru-ub* 'he went in' (IV R 28, 24 b), *i-ter-ba* (K. 562 l. 20), and one with *e* in the first syllable (a few examples of this form were given above, § 34, *a*, note), e. g. *e-te-zib* 'he left behind' (Nimr. Ep. XI, 281), *etéli* 'he ascended', plur. *etélû*, *e-tab-ru* 'they crossed', *e-te-it-ti-ḳu* 'they marched' (V R 8, 86), *etépuš* 'he made' (also *e-tap-pa-aš*, Shalm. Mo. rev. 63). The latter form appears to have been the only one in use in the first (and second, in my opinion, exx. § 104) person sing.: cf. *e-te-ti-iḳ* 'I marched' (Tig. II 77), *e-te-bir* 'I crossed', *e-te-el-la-a* 'I ascended' (Senhb. IV 11), *e-te-pu-uš*, *e*(var. *i*)*-te-ip-pu-šu* (rel.), also *etappaš* (Assurn. II 6, *e-tap-aš* III 29); the form *a-tap-pa-aš*, as already remarked § 34, *a*, note, is quite unique. These forms with *e* in the first syllable re-appear in the present of I 2 and in I 3 (*v.* § 104). In the third person one might be tempted to regard *e* as incorrect orthography for *i* (*v.* § 30), but the cases where it occurs are too numerous for such a supposition; in the 1. pers. sing., again, one might regard *e* as modified from *a* under the influence of the $א_{4.5}$. It seems better, however, to explain the *e* of the 3. and 1. persons by one and the same motive, namely a tendency on the part of the Ifteal to adopt the corresponding forms of the Qal (*v.* § 90 b, note). The *e* of the pret. and pres. I 2 would then have further influenced certain forms of the imperative and infinitive I 2 (*v.* § 104) with *e* in the first syllable. It is, moreover, remarkable that without exception, so far as my knowledge goes, the *t* in these reflexives is written but once, e. g.: *itámar*, *itébir*, *itéli*, *nitámar*, never *ittámar*, *ittébir* etc. No attempt was made to indicate whether the initial *e* was long or short.

Noteworthy miscellaneous forms: §104.

I 1. Perm. 'so many *ina muḫḫišu amrûni* are at his command' (V R 53, 7 a); *Ba-ú-el-lit* (prop. noun f., V R 44, 19 b); *ša lâ e-nu-ú mil-lik-šu* 'whose decision is unalterable' (Assurn. I 17), *en-de-ku* 'I stand' (Sm. 949 obv. 16). Other examples in § 89. Pret. and Pres. Exx. in § 103 above; note further: *ta-ru-ur* 'thou didst curse' (V R 2, 124), *a-bu-ut* 'I destroyed'

(III R 38 No. 1 obv. 53), *ni-mu-ur* 'we saw, found' (Nabon. II 56), *šá e-ri-šú-ka* 'for which I entreated thee' (IV R 65, 33 b); *ta-gu-gi* 'thou wast angry' (fem., K. 4623 obv. 21), *a-bu-uk* 'I forgave' (Khors. 51), *a-bu-ka* 'I carried off' (Esarh. I 26); *e-zi-ba*, also written *iz-zi-ba* (*ez-zi-ba*), 'I left over', *te-di-li* 'thou didst bar, shut' (fem., Nimr. Ep. 65, 21). Assurn. II 84 is quite unique: 'the city which so and so *i-'a-ab-ta* had destroyed'. Pres. 'whose knees *lâ in-na-ḫa* weary not' (IV R 9, 39 a); *lâ ta-ad-da-ra* 'fear not', *minâ tir-ri-ši-in-ni* 'what desirest thou of me?' (Nimr. Ep. 44, 71); *ib-bir* 'he will cross' (Nimr. Ep. 67, 23); *erruba* (*ir-ru-ba*) 'I shall enter' (Desct. obv. 16). Imp. *a-kul* 'eat', *a-ku-la* 'eat ye' (IV R 21, 53 a), *a-ḫu-uz* 'sieze', *am-ri* 'see' (fem., Nimr. Ep. XI, 192), *en-di-im-ma* 'stand' (fem., K. 3437 rev. 3); *ir-ba* 'enter', *ir-bi* (fem.). Inf. *v.* § 103.

II 1. Pret. *uššiš* 'I founded', *tu-ub-bi-ti-in-ni* 'thou (fem.) hast destroyed me' (IV R 57, 51 b); *ubbib* and *ullil* 'I purified'; *uddiš* 'I renewed'. Pres. *tu-ub-bab*, *ullalû*. Imp. *u-ri-ki* 'prolong' (fem., V R 34 col. III 43). Part. *mu-ab-bit* (Assurn. I 8), *mu-ur-rik* 'prolonging'; *mu-ub-bi-ib*. Inf. *uṣṣunu* 'smell' (Tig. jun. rev. 76), *ubburu* 'curse' (st. אבר$_3$).

III 1. Pret. *u-ša-kil* 'I caused to eat' (V R 4, 75); *u-ša-li-ṣa* 'I caused to rejoice' (Khors. 168), *ušêbira* 'I had (caused to be) sent across'; *ušêrib*. Pres. *u-še-ba-ar-ka* 'I will make thee cross' (IV R 68, 45 c); *u-še-rab-an-ni* 'he will bring me in' (V R 6, 115). Imp. *šûrik* 'prolong'; *šú-ti-ḳa-an-ni* (IV R 66, 54 a); *šú-ri-ba-an-ni* (IV R 66, 59 a), but *šêzib* (also *šûzib*) in nn. prr. like *Nabû-še-zib(-a-ni)*. Inf. *šú-pu-uš* 'make, build' (Lay. 38, 10), *šûzubu*, *šú-lu-u* 'take away', but also *šêburu* 'bring across'.

IV 1. Pret. *innamir*, *innabit; lu-un-ni-ṭir* 'may I be preserved' (K. 254 rev. 54), *in-nen-du* (= *innêmdû*) 'they stood (V R 63, 26 a); they took up a position' (Senhb. V 42 etc.), *li-in-ni-pu-uš* (V R 63, 1 b). Pres. *in-na(m)-mar* 'he is seen' (III R 51 No. 8, 52 etc.); 'as this onion is no more *in-ni-ri-šú*, *in-nim-me-du* planted, hidden' (IV R 7, 53. 54 a), 'till he *kaspa in-ni-ṭir-ru* (elsewhere *in-ni-iṭ-ṭi-ru*) is made secure as regards his money', *in-nin-ni* (rel. *in-nin-nu-u*) 'he is bowed down'. Part. *munnabtu* 'fugitive'. Inf. *na-a'-bu-tum* and *nâbutum* 'flee', *nâmuru* 'appearance'; *na'duru* and *nanduru* 'tribulation, distress; eclipse'. Perm. *na-an-kul-lat(-ma)* fem., *v.* § 88, b, note.

I 2. Pret. *i-ta-bat* 'he destroyed' (M. 55 col. IV 25), *a-ta-mar* 'I saw', *ni-ta-mar* 'we saw' (III R 51 Nr. 3, 11), *li-ta-am-mar* 'let him see'; *li-tab-bi-ib* 'let him become clean' (IV R 4, 39 b); for verbs primæ $א_{4.5}$ see § 103 above; cf. also *te-te-bir* (Nimr. Ep. 67, 26), *te-*

te-la-a 'thou didst march up' (K. 823 obv. 7), also (from ארשׁ$_1$) *te-tir-šá-an-ni* 'thou hast desired of me' (Desct. rev. 22); *ni-te-bi-ir* 'we crossed' (Beh. 35), *ni-te-pu-uš* (D, 16). Pres. *e-te-ri-iš* 'I entreat' (N R 34); *e-te-it-ti-iḳ* 'I come' (Neb. Grot. III 17). Imp. *e-tel-li-i* 'mount upwards' (fem.), *al-ki it-ru-bi a-na biti-ni* (Strassm. 3399, Ishtar is the person addressed), *itrubî* = *itérubî*. Part. *mu-tal-lu* (Assurn. I 5), *mut-tal-lu* (Shams. I 5) 'exalted'; *mu-ter-rib-tum ša bîtâti* (IV R 57, 2 a). Inf. *it-ḫu-zu* 'learn' (Khors. 158); *it-ku-lum* (א$_3$) 'be sorrowful' (K. 4386 col. III 40); *ina i-te-it-tu-ki* (IV R 17, 12 b), *e-te-ig-gu-gu* (st. *eḳêḳu*, K. 4309 obv. 16), *etélû* 'mount upwards'. Attention has already (§ 88, b) been called to *i-tak-ku-lum* which is named in K. 4386 col. III 41 alongside of *it-ku-lum*; it was then shown to be a bye-form of the latter and at the same time to be the older infinitive form, from which *itkulu* (so *itḫuzu*) has arisen by syncope. Cf. also *it-mu-šú* (II R 35, 51 c) on the one hand, *i-ta-aṣ-ṣu-lum* (st. *eṣêlu*, II R 27, 42 d) on the other.

II 2. Pret. *u-tan-ni-ša-an-ni* 'he made me weak' (K. 4386 col. II 31), and *u-te-en-niš* 'he weakened' (IV R 29, 22 c); *u-te-id-[di-iš]* 'it was renewed' (Nimr. Ep. XI, 239); *i-ni-šu u-ta-aṭ-ṭu-u* 'his eyes were darkened'. Pres. *ut-taḫ-ḫaz* (IV R 61, 12 a. III R 54, 14 b), *u-ta-sa-ar* 'he will be shut up'; *utabbabû* 'they make clean, wash' (their faces, V R 51, 40 b). Inf. *u-te-bu-bu*, *u-te-lu-lu* (S[c] 1 b, 14. 23); *u-te-ṭu-ú* 'darkness, faintness' (K. 246 col. I 19). It is as yet uncertain whether *u-tu-lu* 'rest, sleep' (S[b] 376) and its permansive *u-tu-ul* 'he slept' are Iftaal (II 2) of א$_1$א$_2$ל or (as now seems to me more probable) of נא$_2$ל.

As to the derivation of *ut-ni-en* 'I besought' (Neb. I 51), *ut-nen(-ni)-šum-ma* 'I besought him' (V R 62 col. I 26), inf. *ut-nen-nu* (K. 133 obv. 22)—for the part. cf. *mu-ut-ni-en-nu-ú* 'one who prays' (Neb. I 18 etc.) — from א$_3$נן, probable as it is (cf. § 65, No. 37 note), I should not like at present to pronounce decisively; nor is the equation *têníntu* 'sigh' (?prayer?) = תְּחִנָּה ܬܢܚܬܐ altogether above suspicion.

III 2. Pret. *uš-ta-ḫi-iz* 'I taught' (IV R 67 No. 2, 52 a), 'the fire *uš-ta-ak-ka-al-šu* consumed it' (the building, S. 11). Pres. 'the fire which I *uš-taḫ-ḫa-zu* apply' (K. 257 obv. 28), *uš-tan-na-aḫ* 'he sighs' (IV R 27, 35 a), *uštânaḫ* 'I sigh' (K. 101). Part. *mu-uš-ta-mu-ú* (from אמה 'speak'); *muštêmiḳu*. Inf. *šú-ta-nu-ḫu* 'a sigh' (V R 47, 31 a), *šú-ta-mu-ú*; *šú-te-mu-ḳu* 'implore'. Perm. *adrâku u šú-ta-du-ra-ku* 'I am in terror and am terrified' (K. 3927 rev. 9).

IV 2. Pret. *it-ta-bit* 'he fled', *e-ta-am-ru* (for *it-tamrû*) 'they were seen' (e. g. K. 481, 14). Pres. *it-tábat* 'he flees', *it-tan-mar* (= *ittámar*, III R 64, 1 a).

I 3. Pret. *e-ta-nam-da-ru* 'they were afraid' (Lay. 43, 2); *i-te-ni-ki-il* 'he was sad' (II R 28, 14 a); *e-te-*

ni-ip-pu-šu var. *e-ta-nap-pu-šu* 'they made, did' (V R 3, 111), *i-te-ni-ki-ik* (st. *eḳêḳu*, II R 28, 13 a).

IV 3. Pres. *it-ta-na-an-ma-ru* (= *ittanâmarû*, *v.* § 52) 'they are found' (IV R 66, 21 b).

For *alâku* **I 1** pret. cf.: *ni-il-li-ka* 'we went' (IV R 57 36 a); for **I 2** pret.: *at-ta-lak* 'I marched' (Senhb. Bav. 4), *at-tal-lak* (Esarh. III 36); pres.: *idâka ni-it-tal-lak* 'we go at thy side' (*v.* above p. 228); inf.: *i-tal-lu-ku* (S[c] 301); for **I 3** pret.: 'the chariots which *râmânuššin it-ta-na-al-la-ka* went about of their own accord (without charioteers)' (Senhb. VI 12); pres.: *i-ta-na-al-lak* 'he walks' (V R 31, 12 d).

Verbs mediæ gutturalis.

(See Paradigm B, 6 and 7).

§ 105. Summary of the most common verbs:

באר$_1$ 'fetch out, catch' (pret. and pres. *a*), מאד$_1$ 'be or become many' (pret. and pres. *i*), שאל$_1$ 'decide, demand, ask' (pret., pres. I 1, and pret. I 2: *a*). [באש$_1$ II 1 'make to stink', צאן$_1$ II 1 'adorn']. — ראב$_2$ 'rage, attack violently' (pret. *u*). [מאר$_2$ II 1 'send; rule']. — ראם$_3$ 'be gracious, love' (pret. and pres. originally *a*), שאח$_3$ 'flee' (pret. origly. *a*). — באל$_4$, very often, especially in Tig. and Assurn., written פאל$_4$, 'overcome, take possession of, rule' (pret. origly. *a*), ראש$_4$ 'shout' (pret. origly. *a*); זאק$_{4?}$ 'storm, press hard'.

Cf. also the doubly weak verbs נאד$_1$ (pres. *a*; pret.

I 2: *i*); נא₂ל (*v*. § 99); לא₁ה 'wish, will'; רא₄ה 'feed, herd, rule', שׁא₄ה 'gaze, look intently on something' (cf. § 108).

For the treatment of the breath (*Hauchlaut*) in verbs mediæ א see in general § 47; for the fact that verbs mediæ א₄ are more given to the modification of *a* to *e*, and of *â* to *ê* than are the other verbs mediæ א (inf. *ma'âdu* or *mâdu*, *bâru*, *râmu*, but *bêlu*; part. *nâ'idu* 'exalted', *lâ'iṭu* 'burning, consuming', st. לא₂ט, but *rê'û* 'shepherd') *v*. partly §§ 32, β and γ, 34, β, partly § 42. The conjugation of the pret. and pres. Qal follows, in some cases, the conjugation of the strong verb, e. g. *iš-al*, *iš-a-lu*, *iš-'-a-lu*, *ir'ub*; *ilu ta-na-'-ad* 'God shalt thou praise' (K. 2024); in others, in consequence of the weakness of the guttural breath, it follows the analogy of the 'hollow' verb. The latter mode of inflexion (cf. what was said in § 65, No. 31 regarding *ma'âlu* and *narâmu*) is that always adopted by verbs med. א₃ and א₄: *irâm*, with *umlaut irêm*, 'he loved', *irâm* 'he loves'; *ibêl* 'he ruled' (= *ibâl* for *ib'al*) and 'he rules' (= *ibâl*, *ibâ'al* or = *ibê'il*). That the pret. *irêm* is really derived from the older form *irâm* is shown by *li-ra-mu* 'may they love' (precative, Tig. VIII 25), *lû i-ra-man-ni* 'she became fond of, loved me' (III R 4 No. 7, 64). The derivation of *ibêl*, also, from *ibâl* still admits of demonstration: cf. Assurn. Stand. Inscr. 5: 'Assurnasirpal who *i-pe-lu* subdued all moun- § 106.

tains', var. *i-pa-lu*! The verb מ$א_1$ר takes sometimes *im'id*, sometimes *i-mi-id*; whether the latter form is to be understood as *immid*, as *îmid* or as *imîd*, is intentionally left undecided in the paradigms. The same remark applies to forms like *a-bar* 'I issued forth'. The perm. *bêl* also stands, without a doubt, for *bâl* and is on a par with the permansives of the 'hollow' verbs, *kân*, *dân* (a corresponding form of a verb med. $א_1$ would be found in *lû šâl* 'let him decide' AL[3] 96, 27, if the latter should really be derived from *ša'âlu*) while *ni-il* 'he lies' (IV R 17, 52 b) is perhaps to be placed alongside of the intransitive permansives *kên* and *mît* (§ 89). Of the augmented stems the causative calls for special notice. Like the 'hollow' verbs (*v.* § 115), a few verbs med. א form, in place of the stem III 1, a stem III^{II} 1 (§ 85). The forms of the verb נ$א_2$ל are particularly instructive in this respect: Pret. *uš-na-il* 'I, he threw, lay' (Tig. II 20), more frequently *uš-ni-il* (e. g. V R 7, 40), plur. 3. m. *uš-ni-il-lum* (V R 47, 50 a); pres. *uš-na-al-ka* 'I will give thee rest' (Nimr. Ep. 15, 36); imp. *šú-ni-'-il* (IV R 15, 17 a) and *šú-ni-il* (IV R 27, 48 b). From *pêlu*, *bêlu* 'overpower, offer violence to, etc.', observe the pres. *ušpêl* (alongside of *u-ša-pa-a-la*, V R 45 col. VI 52): 'her command *ša lâ uš-pi-e-lu* that they do not oppress' (III R 38 No. 1 rev. 10); part. *muš-pi-e-lu(m)* (Sarg. Cyl. 56), *muš-pe-lu*

(IV R 16, 8 a), *muš-pil* (Lay. 17, 3); inf. *šú-bi-e-lu* (Neb. Bab. II 30). A stem III[II] 2 is also found: cf. *uš-te-pe-lu* (V R 65 col. II 31), elsewhere *uš-te-pi-el-lu*, both presents in a relative clause. From ר$_3$אם we have a form III[II] 1 in Neb. I 69: *bêlûtka ṣîrti šú-ri-'-im-am-ma* 'make bright thine exalted rule and'; *šú-ri-'-im* precisely like *šú-ni-'-il.*

Noteworthy miscellaneous forms: § 107.

I 1. Perm. *re-šú-nik-ka mâtâti* 'the countries hail thee' (IV R 17, 11 b). Pret. (*v.* § 106 above). *i-mi-du* 'they multiplied, increased' (Beh. 14), *li-mi-da šanâti'a* 'let my years be multiplied, be many' (V R 66 col. II 12), *lu-um-id* 'let me increase' (K. 2455), *a-bar-šu* 'I brought him forth, took him away' (Esarh. I 18. 46); *ir-'u-ub* (fem., Desct. obv. 64); *irênšu* 'he presented to him' (*v.* p. 114), *išêtûni* 'they fled' (V R 4, 60); *i-be-el* 'he ruled', *li-bi-e-lu* 'let them rule' (often), so too *i-riš* 'he shouted, hailed', pronounced *irêš*; *a-zi-iḳ* 'I stormed'. Pres. *i-bar-rum* 'they bring out' (IV R 27, 15 b), *ilâ'i* and *ilê'i* 'he wishes'; *a-ni-el-lam-ma* (Nimr. Ep. 71, 22); *tarâm* 'thou lovest'; *i-sa-ar* 'he rages' (st. ס$_4$אר, V R 55, 32), 'Adar who *tuḳmatu i-pe-lu* overcomes opposition' (Assurn. I 6), *te-re-'i ulâla* 'thou rulest over the weak' (K. 3459); *izaḳḳa* (IV R 3, 2 a) and *i-ziḳ-ḳu* i. e. *izeḳḳu* (rel., IV R 16, 57 a). Imp. *ša-'-al* (K. 483, 9); *rîm* 'have pity', in prop. nouns like *Nabû-rîm-an-ni*,

Marduk-rîm-a-ni (C^a 133), *Rîm-an-ni-ilu* often written with the ideogram for *rîmu* (§ 9 No. 190). Inf. *ma-a-du* (S^c 69), *ma-du* (Beh. 14).

II 1. Perm. 'the daughter of Anu *nu-'-ú-rat* is like a lion' (IV R 65, 41 d). Pret. *uṣa'in* 'I adorned', *uma'ir* 'I, he sent'; *nu-ba-'-i* 'we sought' (st. בא$_5$ה, Nabon. II 56). Pres. *u-ma-'-a-ru* and *u-ma-a-ru* (cf. p. 127), *u-šal-lu* 'they called up' (III R 15 col. I 19), elsewhere *u-ša-'a-lu*, *lâ tu-ba-'-a-ša* 'does not render malodorous' (IV R 52, 22 a). Imp. *nu-'-id* 'praise'. Part. *muma'iru*, *mu-la-iṭ* 'burning up' (Assurn. I 19). Inf. *bu-'-u-rum*, *bu-'u-ru*, *bu-u-ru* (*v.* p. 112), *mu-'-ur* 'mission' (Tig. VI 57).

III 1. Pret. An example from מא$_1$ר *v.* § 93, 1, a, Cf. for III^{II} 1 § 106. Imp. *šú-mi-di* 'let (my years, O goddess) be many', V R 34 col. III 43.

I 2. Pret. *ittá'id*, *attá'id* 'he, I praised', *iš-ta-(na-)'-a-lum* 'they asked' (V R 9, 69); *ir-ti-ši* '(his heart) rejoiced', *ašté'i* (*ašte'êma*) 'I looked out, cared for, etc.'. Pres. *irté'i* 'he feeds, herds'. Imp. *ši-ta-al-šu* (IV R 61, 6. 8 b). Part. *mušté'û*. Inf. *ši-te-'u-u* (K. 4341 col. I 12).

II 2. For *utûl*, *utûlu* *v.* § 104 under II 2.

III 2. Cf. for III^{II} 2 § 106.

I 3. Pret. see under I 2. Pres. *a-ta-na-a-du* 'I raise on high' (Neb. I 32). Cf. *išteni'i*, *ašteni'i* (pret. and pres., st. שא$_4$ר).

Verbs tertiæ infirmæ.

(See Paradigm B, 8—10).

The most common verbs, all originally pro- §108. nounced with *a* in the pret. Qal (I 1), are the following:

חטֶ₁א 'sin', כלֶ₁א 'shut off, keep back, refuse', מלֶ₁א 'be full', מצֶ₁א 'find', קרֶ₁א 'call'.

לקֶ₃א 'take', פתֶ₃א 'open'.

דקֶ₄א 'collect, assemble', חפֶ₄א 'break in pieces', חרֶ₄א 'dig', טבֶ₄א 'dip, immerse', קבֶ₄א 'order, speak', רתֶ₄א 'strengthen, set up', שׂבֶ₄א 'be sated', שמֶ₄א 'hear', תבֶ₄א 'come'.

The only verb tertiæ א known to me, which is pronounced with *u* in the pret. Qal is פרֶא 'cut, cut off, cut through': *apru'* (V R 4, 135), imp. *puru'*, part. *pâri'*; II 1 pret. *uparri'*.

בכי 'weep' (*ibki*) *, ברי 'behold' (*ibri*), בשׂי 'be' (*ibši*), כסי 'bind, fetter, join firmly' (*iksi*), רמי 'throw, found, dwell' (*irmi*), רשׂי 'take hold of, receive, possess' (*irši*), שני (whence the numeral two) II 1 'relate, announce', שסי 'scream, call, read' (*ilsi*), שקי 'give to drink, water'

---

* I have expressly put down with ⁻ or ∵ as the last radical, and first in order, those stems which are proved to a certainty to be verbs tertiæ ⁻ or ⁱ by the form of the corresponding nominal stems (*v.* esply. § 65 Nos. 9. 10. 31, a) and which at the same time leave no doubt, in the majority of cases at least, as to the identity of their radical in the verbal forms as well, especially in pret. and imper. Qal. All the others are put down, as in Hebrew grammar, as verbs ל"ה with the addition of the preterite, wherever it is known to occur.

(*išḳi*) שׁתי 'drink' (*išti*).—דלו 'create' (pres. *idâlu*), חדו 'rejoice' (*iḫdu*), מנו 'number, count' (*imnu*), קלו 'burn' (pres. *iḳâlu*), קמו 'burn' (*iḳmu*).—בלה 'fade, be extinguished' (pres. *ibêli*), בנה 'build, beget' (*ibni*), בנה 'be bright, shine', גרה 'challenge to battle' (*igri*), זכה 'be pure, free', טחה 'approach' (*iṭḫi*), כמה 'bind, take captive' (pres. *ikâmi*), למה 'hem in, besiege' (*ilmi*), משׁה 'disregard, forget' (*imši*), סחה 'rebel' (also IV 1), סלה 'throw off' (a yoke), פחה 'shut' (*ipḫi*), צבה 'wish, be willing', קתה 'finish', רבה 'be or become great' (*irbi*), רדה 'flow, go' (*irdi*), doubtless identical with רדה 'lead, govern', רמה 'fall off, become loose' (*irmu*), שׁנה 'be different, change' (intrans.), II 1 'change' (trans.), שׁקה 'be high', תמה (see below).

Uncertainty still attaches to the last radical of *dakû* 'overturn, cast down' (*idki*, tertiæ א$_1$ or ה?), *zinû* 'be angry with', *misû* 'wash, cleanse' (*imsi*), *radû* (or *ridû*?) 'persecute' (pret. *irdi*, pres. *irêdi* IV R 67, 47 b), and also to the Qal of *ruddû* 'add'.

Cf. also the follg. doubly weak verbs: נבא$_1$, נשׂא$_1$; נגא$_2$ (inf. *nigû*); כסא$_4$; נדה (*iddi*), נקה (*iḳḳi*) (*v.* § 99); א$_5$טה, א$_4$לה (א$_4$לי), א$_4$מה (*êmi*), א$_4$נה (*êni*, *v.* § 102); לא$_1$ה (pres. *ilâ'i*); רא$_4$ה, שׁא$_4$ה (*v.* § 105); וצא$_1$; ודה, ורה; ושׁי (*v.* § 111). For ודא$_4$ (ידא$_4$) *v. ibid.*

Although it is now beyond all doubt that Assyrian originally distinguished verbs tertiæ י from those tertiæ ו, yet one class passes so frequently into the other—especially verbs tertiæ ו into the class tertiæ י—that we are quite justified in treating them together as (following the nomenclature of Hebrew) stems ל״ה. Even among the best attested verbs tertiæ ו and י occur instances of this uncertainty as to class, as e. g.: *am-ni-i-ma* 'I counted, allotted and' (Senhb. Bav. 47), *liḳ-mi-ki* 'I burn thee' (IV R 57, 28 a), *liḳ-mi* (IV R 7, 6. 16 etc.), and, on the other hand, *aš-ḳu-ma* 'I watered' (with emphatic *ma*, Senhb. Bav. 8). Cf. also *ridûtu*, but *ardi*; *abîtu* and *abûtu* 'decision, sentence', *nabnîtu* and *binûtu* (cf. the imperatives *bi-ni* and *bi-nu*, Nimr. Ep. XI, 20, ?). The verb תמה 'talk, speak, swear, conjure', for which *ta-mi-tu*, *ta-me-tu* (also *ta-mi-a-tu*) 'word, speech' probably points to י as the third radical, forms in the pret. *it-ma* (K. 4350 col. III 20), in the pres. *i-tam-ma* (*ibid.* l. 26), *i-ta-ma* (III R 54, 8 a), *i-ta-me* (*ibid.* l. 2 b) and *i-ta-mu* (K. 700 l. 3. IV R 61, 26 a).

While *itáma* (and *itma*) must be rėad as *itámâ* (and *itmâ*) — cf. *i-tam-ma-a* Assurb. Sm. 124, 57 — we find the same interchange of tertiæ י and ו forms in *i-ta-me* (also IV R 32, 33 a etc.) and *i-ta-mu*. The Hebr. terminology (verbs ל״ה) is particularly welcome in all those cases where no instance is found of the pret. or of the pres. Qal (not in a relative clause), and where there is no corresponding nominal formation to give us the clue to the last radical.

§ 109. For the contraction of the permansive stem in the Qal: *malî* fem. *mal-at*, *tebi*, *teb-at*, *bani*, *ban-at*, *banâta* etc. *v.* § 39; the permansives of the other verbal stems suffer the same contraction e. g. *šûṣat* (*v.* § 89). The third radical is preserved in a couple of forms in III R 4 No. 4, 37: 'where huge wild vines *še-ru-'-ú-ni* grow', and Tig. III 62: *ṣa-al-'u-ni* (sing. *ṣa-li*, Assurn. III 12. 15. 16); the first of the two is a permansive of the form فَعُل. For forms of the 3. sing. fem. like *našâta* for *naš-at(a)* *v.* § 53, c on p. 126 f. Permansives from verbs tertiæ י and ו with *umlaut* of the *a* of the first syllable *v.* § 110. In the Pret. Qal which was originally, in all cases, pronounced with *a* the various classes of verbs tertiæ infirmæ assume very different forms: for this short *a* with א becomes *â*, with י it becomes *aî* and then *ê*, with ו *au̯* and then *û*. Since, however, the *â* of verbs tertiæ א is without exception modified to *ê* and then shortened to *e* and *i*, like the *ê* which arises from *ai̯* being reduced to a monophthong, it results that the preterites of verbs tertiæ א and tertiæ י have one and the same form in the Qal: *imṣi, ipti, ibni.* For this and for the more thorough-going and less frequent contractions like *lu-uṣ=lûṣi* see § 39. For forms written with *e*, as e. g.

lu-up-te (Nimr. Ep. XI, 9) *v.* § 32, γ; we would also mention here *ir-me* 'he threw' (V R 62 No. 1, 9) alongside of *ir-mi* (No. 2, 48), *lu-ur-me, al-me* 'I besieged'. The original final *ê* maintains itself in all cases before the enclitic *ma* (*v.* §§ 32, γ. 39. 53, d above): *ad-ki-e-ma* 'I summoned' (Esarh. V 11), *aḫ-ri-e-ma* (Senhb. Bav. 52 etc.), *ir-me-ma* (IV R 5, 79 a); *êlâ* (*ilâ*) i. e. *îli-a* 'he went up' (*v.* § 38, a) with *ma* naturally forms *îlamma* (so *iḫ-ṭi-tam-ma* etc.). For uncontracted forms like *iḳ-bi-u-ni v.* § 38, a. All that has been said regarding the pret. Qal applies also to the present: thus *imaṣi* 'he will find', *iḳabbi* 'he speaks' like *i-bak-ki* 'he weeps'. For forms with final *e*, see § 32, γ; for *i-še-im* 'he will hear', § 39. For the *e* of the second syllable of *ipete* (*ipeti*), *iléḳi*, *išéme*, *išési* alongside of *išási v.* § 34, *a*; for the *e* of the first syllable in forms like *te-liḳ-ḳi-e* i. e. *teléḳî* (K. 101 obv. 6) *v.* § 34, β end. For the pret. and pres. of the augmented stems there is nothing to add, as regards the final vowel, to what has been said of these tenses in the Qal: the original long final vowel is shortened as in the Qal *ubannĭ*, *ušabnĭ*, *ibtánĭ* like *ibnĭ*; before *ma* it remains long (cf. *umaššîma* § 53, d). In the final *a* of many presents of the Piel and Shafel, such as *u-nam-ba* (variant of *u-nam-bi*) 'she calls aloud' (Nimr. Ep. XI, 111), *u-pat-ta* 'let him open', viz. *uznâ* (K. 95), *u-šam-*

ṣa-šu 'he will cause him to find' (Assurn. Balaw. rev. 26), *u-šab-la* 'he removed, put an end to' (Khors. 113) etc. — cf. the follg. from the list V R 45 which comprises only the 2. pers. sing. of the present of the augmented stems: *tu-mal-la* (Col. III 19), *tu-pat-ta* (I 1), *tu-šal-ḳa* (VII 27), *tu-šar-ša* (V 18) etc. — it is hardly likely that we have a mere shortening of the original final *â*; it is more probable that they include the *a* so often added to verbal forms (§ 91) like *tu-ba-an-na* (III 6), *tu-ṣal-la* (II 1) from verbs tertiæ ר. They therefore come under the same category as *lâ ta-kal-la* 'cease not' (K. 2674 l. 18), *iḳ-te-ra* 'he summoned to his presence' (Senhb. V 39; *iḳ-te-ram-ma* Khors. 127). We can easily understand how, in V R 45, this particular form receives the preference. The defective orthography of the *auslaut* in these forms (to which is to be added the perm. as in: 'since in Babylon a suitable site *lâ šú-um-ṣa* was not to be found' Neb. VIII 30) is to a certain extent an exception to the rule given in § 10; it is better to write, for example, *i-na-aš-ša-a* 'he will carry' (his weapons, III R 58, 42c). We should naturally expect the present to be in *i*, and examples of this form will be found in § 110. For the *e* of the second syllable in *mušemṣû* (*mušimṣû*) 'causing to find' (Tig. I 12) and in *iḳtérâ*, *iltéḳi*, *altéme* etc. *v.* § 34, *α*; for the same vowel in *uṭebbi* 'I sank, let down', alongside of *uṭab(b)i* see § 33. The imperatives Qal follow the pret. as regards the vowel of the second radical, which, however, is content with repeating the vowel of the first: hence *ši-mi, ši-me* 'hear', *bini* 'build', *munu* 'count' (*v.* § 94 above). With *ma* appended: *li-ki-e-ma* (masc. V R 64 col. III 19). For the orthography of the feminine forms *li-ki-e* 'accept' (K. 101 rev. 4), *pi-te-ma* (fem.) cf. p. 78 f. The infinitives and participles Qal, when furnished with case-vowels, are identical as regards their final vowel sound (*auslaut*) in all classes of verbs tertiæ infirmæ; for the first syllable of the inf., as in *malû, banû* on the one hand, and in *nigû, petû* (*pitû*), *leḳû, šemû, ḳebû* on the other, see § 34, β (and cf. § 42); for the older forms *patû* etc. see a few references in § 110. We find, also, in the inf. Qal of verbs tertiæ י and ו the change (*umlaut*) of *a* to *e*; see examples in § 110. For the first syllable of the participles, as in *nâši, bâni* on the one hand, *pêti, šêmi* (with the nominative termination *pêtû, šêmû*) on the other, *v.* § 32, β (and cf. § 42); for the loss of the last radical, which appears in *nâši, bâni* and makes itself distinctly felt in the construct state, e. g. *naš*, *bân*, and in feminines like *bântu*, cons. state *bânat*, (so also *mušamṣat v.* § 68) which are in use alongside of the longer forms *bânîtu* etc. — see § 39 (loss of the final vowel) and cf. §§ 47 and 41, a. b (loss of the last radical, א, י or ו).

§ 110. Noteworthy miscellaneous forms.

1. Perm. *ma-lat* 'she, it is full' (IV R 18, 57 b), *na-ša-ku* 'I carry' (II R 19, 54. 56 etc.), *našat* 'she carried', in pause *našâta* (*v.* p. 126); *ḫi-bi* (*ḫebi*) 'it is extinguished', 'kings *šá ni-is-sa-at šubatsun* whose dwelling was afar off' (Khors. 146), 'a maid whose hands (*ḳâtâša*) *lâ mi-sa-a* are unwashed' (IV R 26, 14 b); 'the city *ša .... na-da-ta* (var. *at*) *šubatsu* lies so and so' (V R 9, 116), *šanâta* 2. m. sing., *šanâ* 3. f. plur. (Nimr. Ep. XI, 4. 3), *ba-la-ak* 'I am mindful (Neb. I 47, cf. Targ. בלי); with *umlaut*: *si-ḫi* i. e. *seḫi* 'he revolted' (cf. *si-ḫu-šu-nu-tu* 'they revolted from them' IV R 52 No. 2, 22), 'whoever was not willing *ṣi-bu-ú*' (Sarg. Cyl. 52), *ṣi-ba-a-ka* (!) 'I am willing' (NR 24). For other examples see § 89 and cf. § 109. Preterite and present. Examples in § 109 above; note also: 'thine eyes *im-la-a dimtu* filled with tears' (Assurb. Sm. 123, 48); *liḳ-ba-nik-kim-ma* 'let them (fem.) say to thee' (IV R 56, 55 a); *im-nu* (I R 28, 22 a), *am-nu* (Senhb. IV 50 etc.), *aḳ-mu*, 'his heart *iḫ-du-ma* was glad and' (V R 61 col. IV 38), *ta-ḳab-bi* 'thou speakest', *a-ta-ab-bi* 'I come' (IV R 68, 28 a), *i-šeb-bi* 'he will take his fill' (K. 196 obv. col. I 3), *i-še-me* 'he will hear, grant (requests)' (IV R 45, 14), 'whatever

ta-šim-mu-ú thou shalt hear' (K. 562 l. 11); *ta-šat-ti* 2. m. 'thou wilt drink', *i-red-di*, 'he goes' (V R 55, 23), *lâ te-ṭi-iḫ-ḫi* 'approach not' (IV R 2, 25 b); *a-ḳal-lu* 'I burn' (IV R 56, 27 b). *i-kal-lu* 'it (the door) shuts out' (IV R 1, 30 a) is peculiar; have we transition of $כלא_1$ to כלה? Imperative: *i-ši* 'lift up', *i-bi* 'command' (*ki-bi* Neb. Bab. II 28); *pi-ti*, *li-ki-šu* 'take him' (Nimr. Ep. XI, 229); *ši-mi* 'hear' (Neb. Grot. III 46); *ši-ti* 'drink', *šiḳi* 'give to drink', *i-di* 'lay, put in', *ri-ši-šu rêmu* 'conceive love for him' (IV R 61, 31 c); *ḳu-mu* 'burn' (IV R 56, 8 b), *mu-nu-ma* (V R 50, 64 b). Part. 'Lands *na-(a-)aš bilti u madatte*' (Tig. I 65), *na-ši ḫatti ellite*; *ra-aš emûḳi* 'possessor of might' (Shams. I 21). Infinitive. Alongside of *pitû* etc. we still find *patû* 'open, consecrate'(Senhb. Bav. 27), *la-ḳu-u* 'take' (S^b 107), *ḳabû* 'speak, word' (e. g. K. 245 col. II 58 ff.), *ḫa-ri-e nâri* (Senhb. Bell. 40). But also, on the other hand, *ṭeḫû* (K. 2486 obv.) alongside of *ṭaḫû* (S^b 312), *piḫû* 'shut' (V R 36, 45 d).

II 1. Pret. *li-mi-li*, *li-mi-la-a* (III R 43 col. IV 4. 5) *li-mil-la-a* (V R 56, 42), 'may he fill up'; *u-ma-si* and *umes(si)i* 'I cleansed'; *li-še-en-ni* 'may he change' (III R 43 col. IV 2.) Pres. *râmânkunu lâ tu-ḫaṭ-ṭa-a* 'you shall not make yourselves sinners' (IV R 52, 24 a); *u-ṣal-li* 'I entreat', *ušanni* 'he will change' (III R 65, 61 a). Imp. *mul-li* 'fill thou'. Inf. *nubbû*, *numbû* 'call aloud'; *ḳubbû* 'cry aloud' (*ḳu-bi-e a-ḳab-bi* 'I cry aloud, scream' IV R 10, 2 b, *ina ḳu-ub-bi-e marṣûti* IV R 26, 55 b); *ḫud libbi nummur kabitti* (Esarh. VI 42, *ḫud* contracted form of *ḫuddû* like *tib* in *tib taḫâzi'a* from *tibû*?). Perm. 'whose entry *zu-um-mu-ú nûra* is cut off from the light' (Desct. obv. 7), 'the temple *ša su-uḫ-ḫa-a uṣ-ṣu-ra-tu-šu* whose walls were destroyed' (V R 65, 18 a).

III 1. Pret. *ušalḳû* 'they caused to take, delivered up' (Assurb. Sm. 108, e); *u-ša-as-ši* 'she has removed' (IV R 57, 16 a); *ušabri* and *ušebri* 'I caused to see', *u-sar-me*, *u-šal-me* 'I surrounded' (Senhb. I 59, note the *e* notwithstanding the ground-form *ušakšid*), *ša nu-šab-šu-ú* (*ša nibnû* IV R 65, 21 d). Pres. *ušellâ* 'I bring up' (Desct. obv. 19). Imp. *šu-us-si* 'remove' (IV R 61, 33 a); *šubra-an-ni* 'let me see' (IV R 66, 55 a). Part. *mušarbu* 'enlarging'. Inf. *šuššû* 'cause to carry'; *šú-ub-nu-u* 'cause to be built', *šušḳû* 'raise, heighten'. Perm. see § 89.

IV 1. Pret. 'let the gates *lip-pi-ta-*[*a*] be opened' (Desct. rev. 14); *innadi* 'he was thrown'; *is-si-ḫu* 'he has rebelled' (Senhb. V 5). Pres. 'whatever *iḳ-ḳab-ba-aš-šu-nu* is commanded you by me' (NR 10), 'a plant *ša la-la-šu lâ eš-še-bu-u* of whose abundance one is never satisfied' (IV R 9, 23 b); *in-naḳ-ḳu-u*, 'are spilt' (IV R 19, 49 b, cf. p. 123 above). Imp. *na-an-di*, 'be cast off' (IV R 13, 43 a).

I 2. Pret. *înâ ta-at-ta-ši-šum-ma* '(thine) eyes thou didst lift up to him and' (Nimr. Ep. 44, 67), *iḫtâṭi, iḫtaṭû* and *iḫtiṭṭû* 'they have sinned'; *al-te-me* 'I have heard', *it-te-bu-ú* 'they marched' (K. 82, 14), *im-ta-si* 'she washed'; *ar-ta-ši rêmu, ar-te-di, ar-ti-di* 'I marched', *li-ir-ta-du-šu* and *li-ir-te-id-du-šu* 'let them lead him' (I R 27 No. 2, 51. III R 41 col. II 37), *lu-ul-ta-ti* 'I will drink' (Desct. rev. 19), *lil-ta-si* 'let him read' (Sarg. Cyp. II 59). Imp. *Ši-tam-me ka-ra-bu* name of a deity (III R 66 obv. 7 e). Part. *mur-te-du-ú* 'leading, ruling' (Shams. I 28 etc.). Inf. *bitakkû* 'weep', *šitassû* 'read', (*ana ši-tas-si-šu* V R 37, 55), syncopated (*v.* § 88, b) *bitrû* 'gaze on'.

II 2. Pret. *umdallû* 'they filled up' (V R 9, 45), cf. *um-da-(na-)al-lu-u* (Assurb. Sm. 285, 8); *tuḫ-tap-pi* (Nimr. Ep. 69, 38); *uṭ-ṭe-iḫ-ḫa-a* 'he approached' (Nimr. Ep. XI, 248), 'whoever *uš-te-nu-ú* shall alter the words of my writing' (I R 27 No. 2, 47, 56, and cf. *šunnê* l. 74).

III 2. Pret. *uš-te-li, ul-te-la-an-ni*, 'he made me come up, brought me up'; 'its course *uš-te-eš-na-a* I changed' (Lay. 38, 15). Part. *multaḫṭê* 'rebels'. Perm. *šú-te-eš-na-a* (III R 65, 42. 43 b).

IV 2. Pret. *ittaḫsû* and *itteḫsû* 'they took refuge' (st. חסה, Nimr. Ep. XI, 108), *i-ta-ad-da-a* (i. e. *ittâddâ*) 3. fem. plur. of נדה (IV R 67, 50 b).

I 3. Pret. *im-ta-na-al-lu-ú* 'they filled' (IV R 56, 9 a); *balâṭu iš-te-ni-ib-bi* 'he was sated with life' (V R 31, 26 f.), *iš-te-nim-me* (Nimr. Ep. 8, 29), *it-te-ni-ib-bu-ú* 'they came, advanced' (K. 145 l. 12); *it-ta-nam-di* 'she uttered' (*ta-a-ša*, K. 3437 rev. 8), *iš-ta-na-at-ti* 'he drank', 2. fem. *tal-ta-na-at-ti* (IV R 63, 40. 44 b), *er-te-ni-id-di* 'I went' (Neb. I 29). Pres. *ta-at-ta-na-aš-ši lâ le-am-ma* 'thou (Merodach) sustainest him that has no strength' (K. 3459).

II 3. *v.* § 83.

IV 3. Pres. 'whoever *it-ta-nak-lu-ú* makes of himself a bar for the door' (IV R 16, 49 a).

Verbs primæ ו and י.

(See Paradigm B, 11.)

§ 111. Summary of the most common verbs with the characteristic vowel of the pret. and pres. Qal. (I 1) and pret. Ifteal (I 2):

ובל 'lead, bring, carry off' (pret. *i*, pres. *a*, pret. I 2: *i*), וכל 'can, be able' (pres. *a*), ולד 'bear, beget' (pret. *i*; pres. *a*), וסם 'be distinguished', II 1 'distinguish, make beautiful', ורד 'go down' (pret. *i*, pres. *a*, pret. I 2: *a*), ושׁב 'settle, sit, dwell' (pret. *i*, pres. *a*, pret. I 2: *i*), ושׁר 'lower, demean, humble one's self' (pres. *a*). וקר 'be dear, precious, respected' (pret. *i*) and ורק

'become yellow, pale' (pret. *i*, pres. *a*) are different from the other verbs of this class, *v.* § 112.

ינק 'suck' (pret. *i*), יצר 'form' (? pret. *i*), ירב 'increase' (pret. *i*), ישׁר 'be straight, succeed, etc.' (pret. *i*).

Cf. also the doubly weak verbs, which of course follow the corresponding weak verbs in the characteristic vowel of the tenses: וצא₁ 'go out'; ודא₄ (or ידא₄?) 'know'; ודה 'appoint, decide', ורה 'lead, bring'; — ישׁי 'have, be' (cf. § 108).

§ 112. For the conjugation of verbs primæ ו in general, for the inf., part., and perm. of the Qal in particular, as well as for the Shafel forms *ušâšib* (*ušêšib*) *v.* § 41, α; for the *ê* of III 1 (and III 2) *v.* § 32, β. For the pret. *ûrid* (= *i̯ûrid* = *i̯au̯rid*) see § 90, a, also §§ 41b and 31 (for *urdûni* from and alongside of *ûridûni v.* § 37). For the pres. *urrad* see § 90, note. The two verbs וקר and ורק follow in the pret. Qal the analogy of verbs primæ י: cf. *ê* (var. *i*)-*ḳir* 'it was precious' (V R 7, 32), fem. *te-ḳir* (V R 4, 57); *li-ri-ḳu pânûki* 'make pale thy face' (IV R 57, 44 b), pres. regularly *urraḳ*. Whether the verb for 'know' should receive ו or י for its first radical is hard to decide: much might be said even for ודא₄. First of all there is the derivative *mûdû* 'reasonable, sensible'; then it has been observed that the transition of verbs primae ו to primae י has its analogy in Assyrian, while the reverse process has not. Finally the conjugation of ודא₄ appears to me to have its exact parallel in ונא₄, if so be that the two forms about to be named, regarding whose meaning there is no doubt, are really to be combined with the Hebr. יגע. Looking at the inf. *egû* 'weary, be tired' (II R 20, 49 d, prop. *agû*, but *egû* on account of the א₄) and the pret. *êgi* 'I ceased, withdrew' (V R 64, col. I 38) we see no difficulty in deriving *idû* 'know' (prop. *edû*, cf. *e-du-tú* II R 39, 77 d), pret. *îdi* from a stem ודא₄. For the impers. *rid*, *šib* *v.* §§ 39 and 94. In regard to the Ifteal (pret. and pres.), on account of the double *tt* (*ittárad*, *ittáṣi*), I would not say that it follows the analogy of verbs primæ א (cf. § 103); the *u* in the second syllable of *ittúbil*, *ittúšib*, *ittúṣi* (alongside of *ittáṣi*) is occasioned by the *u* of the Qal *ûbil*, *ûšib* etc. (cf. § 90 b, note). For other instances of the same kind, where the impers. and infs. of the Shafel follow the analogy of the pret. (cf §§ 94. 95) see the reference in § 113. — For the conjugation of verbs primæ י it is as yet impossible to lay down precise rules applicable to all cases. The preterites *ênik* and *îšir* (interchange of *ê* and *î* as in *êgi* and *îdi*) present no difficulty; for *ê* = *i̯ê* = *i̯ai̯* *v.* §§ 90, a and 41, b and § 31. It is unfortunate that no inf. Qal has been found which throws light on the question as to whether the *i̯a*, which we must assume for the first syllable, became *a* or *i*. *i-ša-ru* S[c] 33 is probably an adj.; in the inf. *išû*, however, (although even this inf. is not altogether beyond doubt) the *i* may easily have arisen from an original *e* (= *a*) — cf. the infins. *piḫû* etc. § 110 — just as we find in the permansive now *iši* 'he has', now *eṣir* (see below). Cf. also the note to § 65 Nos. 6—9 on p. 166.

Noteworthy miscellaneous forms. § 113.

I 1. Perm. *ziḳnâšu a-ṣi-a* 'his beard is budding' (III R 65, 20 b); *e-ṣir* 'he is pictured' (K. 2674 l. 8), *i-ši* 'he is', *i-ša-a-ku* 'I possess' (Tig. I 58). Pret. *ûrid*, *ûbil* etc. (passim), *u-ra-a-šu, u-raš-šu* and similar forms, 'I brought him' (often); *e-ni-ḳu* 'they sucked' (V R 9, 66), *i-šir*, *i-ši-ra* 'it prospered, succeeded' (e. g. Senhb. Const. 79), *li-šir* (prec., IV R 64, 6 b), *êṣir* 'I formed' (Lay. 33, 18), *êrib* in *Sin-aḫê-er-ba*. Pres. *tuk-kal* 'thou canst', *ur-ra-da-ni* 'they (the women) descended' (IV R 57, 33 a), *nu-ur-rad* 'we shall go down' (K. 647 rev. 11), *imêru atâna ul u-ša-ra* (= *uššara*, Desct. rev, 7, cf. وثر ?). In the verbs *idû* 'know' and *išû* 'have, be' the pret. and the pres. are identical in pronunciation: *i-di* 'I, he knew', and *ti(-i)-di* 'thou knowest'; *i-ši* 'I, he had' and *ti-ši* 'thou art'.

II 1. Pret. *u-us-si-im*, *u-si-im* 'I adorned, made magnificent' (Neb.), *u(š)-še-ru* 'they tore down' (Assurn. II 113), *uttir* 'I made enormous' (ותר), *u-ad-di* 'he appointed', plur. *u-ad-du-ni*. Pres. *tu-at-tar* (V R 45 col. IV 13), *tur-ra-ki* 'thou makest pale' (fem., IV R 63, 3 b), *tu-us-sa-am* (V R 45 col. IV 32), *tu-ur-ra* (ibid. col. III 41). Part. *mu-al-li-da-at*, *mu-ad-du-ú šarrûti* 'who establishes the kingly power' (IV R 55 b 13 b). Perm. *lâ (u-)ud-da-a* 'they (the walls) were not recognizable' (Neb. Senk. I 16).

III 1. Pret. *u-šá-pa-a* (Neb. Bab. I 29) and *u-še-e-bi* (II 11) 'I caused to shine' (st. ופא₄), *li-še-pa-a* 'let them glorify' (IV R 66, 62 a), *tu-ša-id* (K. 828, 5) and *u-še-'-i-du-uš* (K. 13, 59), st. ואא₄ר; *u-še-ši-ru* 'they blessed' (Senhb. Bav. 30). Pres. *tu-ša-a-tar*, *tu-ša-a-ḳar* (V R 45 col. VI 31. 32), *tu-šeš-šab* (VII 17), *tu-še-e-ša* (VIII 38); *u-še-naḳ* 'she suckles' (IV R 65, 35 d), *u-šeš-še-ru* 'he leads' (rel., Senhb. Kuy. 2, 31). Imp. *šú-šib* (Desct. rev. 33), *šú-bi-la* 'cause to carry, have carried' (*E. M.* II, 339), but also *še-bi-la* 'deliver up' (K. 359, 8). Part. *mu-še-niḳ-tu* plur. *mu-še-ni-ḳa-a-te* (V R 9, 66). Inf. *šûšubu* 'plant a colony', *šûṣû* 'cause to go forth, announce', but also *šêbulu* 'to deliver up' (V R 7, 25 etc.).

I 2. Pret. *attarad*, *atarad*, *at(t)arda*, 'I went down', *it-ta-ṣu-ni* 'they are sprung from . . .' (IV R 15, 68 a), *littaṣi* 'let him drive off' (IV R 7, 7 etc.), *at-ti-ṣi* 'I came out' (Assurn.) and *ta-at-tu-ṣi* 'she (Ishtar) has gone forth' (IV R 68, 69 b), *ittarrû* 'they brought', *littarrû* 'let them bring' and *it-tu-ru-nu*, 'they brought' (tribute, Beh. 7: cf. in a similar connexion Tig. II 96: *littarrûni*), *it-tu-šib* 'he sat down' (C^b rev. 25^b), *it-tu-bil* 'he brought' (often); *li-taš-ši-ir* 'may it go well, change for the better' etc. (IV R 17, 2 b). Pres. *at-tašab* 'I sit down, seat myself' (Nimr. Ep. XI, 130), *it-ta-aṣ-ṣi* 'he goes out'. Part. *muttabbilu* 'bringing' also 'portable', *muttárû* 'bringing'. Inf. *ittarrû* 'lead, guide'. (Senhb. Bav. 2).

II 2. Pret. *tu-ta-at-tir* (2. m. sing., IV R 11, 40 b), 'his troops, whose number like the waters of a river *lâ u-ta-ad-du-ú* was unknown' (V R 35, 16). Do the preterite and infinitive forms *u-ta(-aḳ)-ḳu* (Neb. Grot. I 11. V R 34 col. I 15) and *u-taḳ-ḳu-ú* (V R 29 8 h) also belong here?

III 2. Pret. *uštâbil* 'he brought', *us-si-bil-ka* 'I have delivered up to thee' (K. 359, 8), *ultêšib* (*ina ašri-šina*) 'I restored (the countries) to order' (NR 23); *uš-te-(eš)-še-ra* 'I directed', *tu-uš-te-eš-še-ir* 'thou hast guided aright' (Neb. I 59). Pres. *tul-te-ši-ra* 'thou rulest' (IV R 67, 12 b). Imp. *šú-te-ši-ra* (IV R 17, 26 b). Inf. *šú-ta-bu-ul têrêti* 'to give laws' (Sm. 954 obv.); *šutêšuru*.

I 3. Pres. *at-ta-nab-bal-šu-nu-ši* 'I bring as an offering to you' (V R 63, 22 a), *it-ta-na-aš-ša-bu*, 'they dwell' (IV R 15, 26 a).

Verbs mediæ ו and י.

(See Paradigm B, 12).

§ 114. Summary of the most common verbs (including those that are also primæ א or נ, and a few other doubly weak verbs):

דוך 'kill', זוז 'divide, allot', כון 'be firm, stand fast', מות 'die', נוח 'rest', נוש 'quake, shake, tremble', סוק 'be narrow', צוד 'hunt', קול 'scream', קוף 'decay, be in ruins', קוץ 'flay', רוב 'sink, settle (of a foundation), etc.' (II 1 'get the better of, overcome'), שוט 'pull', שור 'wander about', תור 'turn (*se vertere*), turn back; become'. בוא‎₁ 'come, go' (pret. I 1 and I 2: *â*) is peculiar, *v.* § 115.

איר‎₁ 'go forth', דין 'judge', דיש 'tread down' זיר 'hate, resist', חיט 'see', חיל 'tremble, quake', חיר 'gaze, choose', חיש 'make haste', טיב 'be good', מיש 'despise, do away with', ניא 'hinder, oppose, make war upon', קיף 'hand over, grant full powers to', קיש 'present', שיא (more rarely שוא) 'fly', שיח 'sprout, grow', שים 'set, appoint, decide'. ניר 'overcome, subjugate' (pret. *â* and *i*) is peculiar, see § 115.

Of the verbs med. ו and י properly so-called a few appear in Assyrian as 'hollow' verbs, thus צית 'scream' (whence *ṣîḫtu*, 'cry of pain or grief', cf. צְוָחָה) and קוה (cf. *ḳû*, קַו 'string') II 1 'wait' (קִוָּה): *u-ḳi* (Tig. I 72), *uk-ki* (III R 15 col I 10) 'I waited', *uḳâ* 'he waits' plur. *uḳâ'û*, written *u-ḳa-a-a-u* and *u-ḳa-'û* (the latter Assurb. Sm. 134, 52; cf. § 13). Others appear as verbs med. *m* or *v* (see § 44), so especially *ṭamû* 'spin, weave' = טוה; there also seems to be some connexion between *lamû* 'shut in all round, surround' and לוה. The existence of *u̯* in Assyrian is of course not proved by the verbs just mentioned.

In § 61, 1 the conjecture was hazarded that verbs med. ו and י have their origin in a root consisting of two consonants with *â* for their medial vowel, and in § 64 an attempt was made to prove this theory from the permansive forms of the Qal. Another proof we are inclined to see in nominal formations like *makânu*, in so far as the explanation of such forms from *makuanu* etc. is as impossible as that of the adj. *ṭâbu* from *ṭaịabu*, or of the infs. *târu*, *ṭâbu* from *ṭau̯âru*, *ṭaịâbu* is unnecessary (*v.* § 64), not to mention *turru* = *tuu̯u̯uru*. Into these stems with medial *â*, internal vowel change must also have penetrated at a very early period (observe *kân* and *kên* in the perm. even), in consequence of which they gradually expanded to stems with medial *u̯* or *ị*, following a tendency to triliteralism; this explains how a noun like the Assyr. *šûru* can only be explained from a hypothetical *ṯau̯r*, and how verbal forms like *ka'in* (imp. II 1) § 115.

betray a formation on the model of the triliteral verb. All this, however, must not lead us to explain all the derived forms of these stems on one and the same plan. — The two verbs בוא and ניר occupy, as has been remarked, a position peculiar to themselves: the former takes the same form *ibâ'* in the pret. as in the pres. Qal, and in the pret. I 2 *ibtâ'*; the latter in the pret. Qal has sometimes *inâr*, *anâr* (e. g. III R 15 col. II 19. Esarh. II 31. Neb. II 25 etc.; in fact it is much the more common form of the two) sometimes *inîr*, *anîr* (I R 35 No. 3, 13, *a-nir* V R 9, 122); since elsewhere in Assurb. *inâr* is the favourite form (e. g. V R 4, 49), it is possible that we should give to the sign *nir* the phonetic value *nar*. For *ibâ'* and *inâr* as forms of the pret. and present, see § 87 above. Alongside of the regular forms of the present Qal, such as *imât*, *išâm*, we find an interesting series of presents which are formed from the preterite, retaining the vowel of the latter, but sharpening the final radical (cf. § 90 a, note). The following passages may be noted, in which there can be no doubt that the forms in question have a present signification: 'Sin without (?) whom city and country cannot be founded nor *i-tur-ru ašruššu* restored' (V R 64 col. II 27), *i-šur-ru* 'they wander about' (IV R 5, 39 a, also e. g. 1, 25 a), *ultu libbaša i-nu-uḫ-ḫu* 'as soon as her heart will calm itself' (Desct. rev. 16); *i-ṭîb libbašu* 'his heart is glad' (Nimr. Ep. 9, 41), 'Nebuchadnezzar who *di-in mi-ša-ri i-din-nu*' (V R 55, 6), 'Ishtar who, like Shamash, the ends of heaven and earth *ta-ḫi-ṭa* surveys' (II R 66 No. 1, 3 cf. 8), *i-ḫi-lu mâtâti išdâšina* 'the foundations of the countries shake' (Shalm. Mo. obv. 8). The same has been observed in the case of the Iftaneal (I 3) — no examples of I 2 occur — thus: *iṣ-ṣa-nun-du* 'he drives away' (IV R 5, 32 a), *it-ta-nu-ur-ru*, 'he returns' (rel. IV R 16, 42 a), *im-ta-nu-ut-tu* 'they will die' (K. 196 rev. III 7); cf. § 90, b, note. The place of the Shafel in these verbs is taken by the form III^{II} 1 (*v.* § 85), as was the case with the verbs med. א discussed in § 106. Cf. pret. *tuš-mit* 'thou didst kill' (IV R 30, 12 b), *uš-bi*(-') 'he, she broke out' (Desct. obv. 65. IV R 20 No. 1 obv. 4); *ušṭîb* 'I made good, beautiful, joyful'; pres. *tu-ša-za-a-za* (V R 45 col. VI 54); imp. *šú-mit* 'kill' (M. 55 col. I 20), *šú-bi-i'-ma*, 'bring and'; part. *mušmîtu* 'killing' (e. g. V R. 46, 41 b); inf. *šuṭubbu* 'make good, joyful' (Assurb. Sm. 121, 38. IV R. 12, 22).

Noteworthy miscellaneous forms. § 116.

I 1. Perm. see § 89. Cf. also 'the forest whose trees (*i-ṣu*) *ši-i-ḫu* are lofty' (IV R 18, 60 a). Pret. *idûk*, *i-ku-uš* 'he set snares' (IV R 16, 6 b, surely from קוש, though akin to *a-ḳa-šú* וקש II R 35, 52 e); *iṭîb*, *išiḫ*, written *i-ši-ḫu*, but also *i-ši-e-ḫu* (Sarg. Cyl. 38). In the same way from מיש, alongside of *i-mi-šú*, *a-mi-iš* we find *i-me-šu*, and even *e-me-iš* (Assurb. Sm. 37, 4) and I 2 *im-te-eš* (IV R 58, 35 a), all written with *e*. Cf. also *a-ir* 'I went forth' (III R 38 No. 2 rev. 63), *'i-ram-ma* 'he went and' (IV R 15, 14 a), *i-še-'*, *a-še-'* 'he, I fled', also *i-šú-'*. Pres. *i-dak* (III R 65, 59 b), *i-kan*, *i-ka-na* (III R 58, 10. 16 b), *a-ma-a-tu* 'I die' (K. 31, 48), 'Nergal who *i-na-ar-ru ga-ri-e-šu* subdues his foes' (III R 38 No. 1 obv. 4), *ni-na-a-ra* (III R 15 col. I 9); *ta-ša-ma*, *i'âr* and *'i-ir-ru* (rel.), *i-ša-'* 'he flees'. Imp. *nu-uḫ* 'rest', *ḳu-ti* 'present' (fem., V R 34 col. III 44), *du-ú-ku* 'kill ye'; *ši-i-mi ši-ma-tuš* 'appoint him as his portion' (*E. M.* II, 339), *ki-šim-ma* (II R 66 Nr. 2, 9). Part. *ṣa-i-du* 'a sporting dog' (II R 6, 28 b), 'hunter' (IV R 27, 23 b), *da-a-a-ik-tum* i. e. *dâ'iktum* (IV R 57, 52 a); *ḫa-a-iṭ*, *ḫa-'-iṭ* 'seeing', *da-(a-)iš*, *ḳa-iš* 'presenting' (Assurn. I 9). Cf. § 64 p. 156.

II 1. Pret. *u-si-iḳ*, *u-si-ḳa* 'I oppressed', *u-ḳa-a-a-iš* (*uḳâ'iš* = *uḳâ'iš*) 'I presented' (Senhb. Bav. 29), elsewhere *u-ḳa-i-ša*, *u-da-i-šu*. Pres. *u-ka-a-ṣa* 'I butchered' (IV R 68, 20 a), *tu-na-a-ḫa*, *tu-ta-a-ra*, *tu-na-'* etc. (V R 45). Imp. *ka-in* in the masc. prop. name *Ašur-bêl-ka-in* (C[a] 55), elsewhere contracted, as in *têr* 'bring back', fem. *ki-in-ni*; *ṭi-ib-bi šêrê'a* 'keep in health my body' (V R 34 col. III 46). Part. *munîru*, *mušîm*, *mu-ni-i' i-rat Kakmê* (Lay. 33, 9). Inf. *turru*, *nuḫḫu*, also *ṭubbu* st. cstr. *ṭub* 'being in health, to be kept in health', which, therefore, must not be taken as a noun from a st. טוב; cf. passages like Esarh. VI 42: *ṭu-ub šêrê ḫu-ud libbi nu-um-mur kabitti.*

III 1 or rather III^{II} *v.* § 115. Here cf. also *uš-id* 'he solemnly established' (st. $אוד_4$, V R 55, 49).

I 2. Pret. *im-tu-ut* 'he, she died'. Inf. *ki-ta-a-a-ú-lu* 'screaming' (V R 47, 32. 33 a). For *tidûku* cf. § 83 note.

II 2. Pret. *uk-tin* 'I laid, placed' (Khors. 67), *ut-te-ir-ši* 'he returned to her' (Desct. rev. 39 ff.).

I 3. Pres. see § 115.

Quadriliteral Verbs. In addition to the proper quadriliteral stems mentioned in § 61, 3, stems, that is, composed of four consonants such as בלכת (primitive signification: *rumpere*) and פרשד, we have here to consider certain quadriliteral stems which have been developed from roots of three consonants; such are the quadriliterals derived from nominal stems in *û* by the retention of *û* as the final radical, as, for example, פלכת III 1 'make wide' from *palkû* 'wide', פרכת IV 1 'cease' (cf. פרך 'shut, bolt') and a few others. In the case of פרדי IV 1 'be bright', כלבי (or כלפי, syn. it would appear of *ebêru*, Hebr. עבר) and others, it is possible that we may have proper quadriliteral stems with an א as the final radical. The § 117.

future must give us more light on this point. None of these proper, or primary, and secondary quadriliteral verbs is found in the Qal; the stems as yet met with are — to keep meanwhile for shortness' sake to the terminology employed in the triliteral verb — a Piel (II 1), a Shafel (III 1), an Ishtafal (III 2) and a Nifal with its *t* and *t-n*-stems (IV 1—3).

II 1. Pres. 'whoever shall deface and *uḫ-ḫa-ra-am-ma-ṭu* destroy the image' (I R 27 No. 2, 86).

III 1. Pret. *ušbalkit* 'he caused to revolt', *u-ša-bal-kit* do. (Assurb. Sm. 284, 97), *uš-ḫar-miṭ* (1. sing., V R 3, 69. Senhb. Bav. 54), *ušparziḫ* (Neb. Grot. II 38), 'Tiâmat *uš-pal-ki* opened wide (her mouth' K. 3437 rev. 17), *ušpardi* 'I caused to shine' (Senhb. Bell. 61), cf. also *u-še-kil-bu-ú* (3. plur., Senhb. Sm. 91, 62). Pres. *ušḫarmaṭ* 'he will destroy' (I R 27 No. 2, 39), *u-ša-bal-kat* 'I break open' (the doors, Desct. obv. 18); or should the sign *kat* (§ 9 No. 111), as in *tu-ša-bal-kat* (V R 45 col. VI 53), be here read *kut*, as is suggested by *u-ša-bal-ku-tú* 'they will break open' (V R 54, 19 c) and by the remark made below on the inf. IV 1? Part. *mušḫarmiṭ* (Assurn. I 35), *mušpardu* (Assurn. I 8). Inf. *šuparkû* 'cause to cease' (Tig. V 41), The same form occurs as an adjective (*v.* § 88, b, note), or perhaps better as a permansive, in *šú-pal-ka-a bâbânišu* (V R 65 col. II 15).

III 2. Pret. *uš-ta-bal-ki-tu* (3. plur., IV R 57 57 a).

IV 1. Pret. *ipparšid* 'he fled' plur. *ipparšidû(ni)*, *ibbalkit* 'he rebelled' plur. *ibbalkitû(ni)*, *abbalkit* 'I crossed'; *ippardi* (*ippirdi*) 'was merry, joyful', *ikkilmanni* 'he hath looked upon me' (IV R 10, 49 a), *lik-kil-mu(-šû)* 'may they look upon him' (e. g. Tig. VIII 75; *li-ki-el-mu-šú* IV R 45, 32), *i-kil-bu-ú* (3. plur., Senhb. Sm. 92, 69). Pres. *ip-pa-ra-aš-šid* 'he flees' (IV R 26, 45 a), *ibbalakkit* 'he penetrates' (IV R 16, 32 a); *ippiriddi* 'is merry, joyful' (Desct. rev. 16. III R 61, 10 b), *ap-pa-ra-ak-ka-a* 'I cease' (V R 63, 20 a). Part. *mup(p)-arkû* 'ceasing' (*lâ*— 'everlasting'). Inf. *naparšudu* 'flee', *nabalkutu* 'be rent asunder'; *naparkû* 'cease', whence *lâ naparkâ* 'unceasingly, perpetually' (Neb. Senk. II 25), *ni-kil-mu-u* (e. g. II R. 38, 10 f. h), *ni-kil-bu-ú* (K. 64 col. III 9—12). The same form, used as an adj. (*v.* § 88, b, note), occurs in *napardû*, *nepardû*, *nipirdû* 'bright, merry', *mê lâ na-pa-ar-ku-ti* 'perennial waters' (Nerigl. II 10), *napalsuḫu* and *napalsuḫtu* 'low seat' (S^c 270. II R 23, 8 a); we ought, accordingly, for the fem. *na-bal-kat-tum* (*kat* sign § 9 No. 111) to read *na-bal-kut-tum* 'rebellion' (V R. 20, 44 f); cf. under III 1 above and see § 65 No. 35 end.

IV 2. Pret. *it-ta-pal-si-iḫ* (Nimr. Ep. XII col. IV ll. 12), *ittapardi* (*ittapirdi*, V R 47, 29 b), *it(t)a-bal-kutû* 'they rebelled' (Assurn. I 103. III 27), so too *it-*

ta-bal-kat 'he rebelled' (Assurn. I 75, *kat* second sign § 9 No. 121) and *a(t)-ta-bal-kat* 'I crossed' (*kat* sometimes second sign § 9 No. 121, sometimes No. 111) are better read *ittabalkut*, *attabalkut*. Pres. *it-ta-pa-ar-ka* 'he ceases' (V R 25, 18 b). Part. *muttašrabiṭu* (IV R 2, 5. 42 b), Inf. *i-tab-lak-ku-tu* 'be rent asunder' (IV R 67, 49 b); *i-te-ik-lim-mu-ú* (V R 16, 45 d), *i-te-ik-lib-bu-u* (V R 41, 57. 60 d, placed along with *itaktumu*).

IV 3. Pret. *ašar it-ta-nap-raš-ši-du* 'whither he had fled' (V R 10, 14). Pres. *ittanablakkatû* 'they break through, march across' (V R 1, 27 etc.).

2) Following on these quadriliteral verbs, properly so called, those quadriliterals may most conveniently be discussed that are secondary developments from triliteral verbs by repetition of the last radical.

a) Assyrian stems such as שקלל, שחרר etc., which correspond to form IX of Arabic and the Piʿlel or Puʿlal of Hebrew. As is shown by the noun *šaḫarratu* compared with *šaḫrartu* (*v.* § 65 No 29 note b), there is a certain connexion between these verbal stems and nominal stems with the third radical sharpened *v.* § 65 (Nos. 20 ff.).

Simple Stem. Permansive: 'the city, like a cloud in (*ištu*) the sky *šú-ḳa-lu-la* hung suspended' (Assurn. III 51. Shams. II 48, identical with 3. f. plur.), 'a mountain peak which like a cloud in (*ištu*) the sky *šú-ḳal-lu-la-at* hung suspended' (Shalm. Mon. rev. 70; *ḳal* § 9 No. 107), cf. Assurn. I 62, where *šuḳalula* appears to be a variant of *šuḳululat*; 'he who *šuparruru* spread out' (Tig. VII 58). Preterite: 'the sea *ušḫarir* narrowed itself' (Nimr. Ep. XI, 125), *ušparir* 'he spread out' (e. g. K. 3437 rev. 12). Inf. *šú-gam-mu-mu* 'roar' (of lions, II R 21, 18 d), *šú-ḳa-lu-lu* 'hang suspended' (S^b, 145). *šú-ḫar-ru-ru* 'be narrow', or 'narrow, oppressed, hampered' (V R 19 11 b) and *šú-par-ru-ru* (S^b 237) may be taken as infinitives or (*v.* § 88, b, note) as adjectives.

t-stem. Pret. *uštaḫrirû pânûšu* 'his countenance was wistful, anxious' (Nimr. Ep. 9, 45).

n-stem. Inf. or adj. *na-zar-bu-bu* (Third Creation-tablet obv. 21).

b) We would also mention the altogether unique form *šú-ḳa-mu-mu* 'standing or to stand upright' (II R 44, 8 d), from which is derived *uš-ḳa-ma-am-mu* 'they take their stand' (IV R 30 No. 1 rev. 6).

As regards the union of the verb with the pronominal suffixes (cf. § 56, b), all needful information may be got from paradigm C. If the suffix is to be appended to a verbal form ending in a short vowel, it does not, as has been already more than once remarked, cause the tone to fall on this short § 118.

21*

vowel and, so falling, to lengthen it, but the Assyrians pronounced *iptīšu*, *ar-di-šu*, *li-ki-šu* 'take him', *ri-ši-šu* 'conceive for him' (love, and such like), etc. with the accent on the first syllable. Orthographical varieties like *a-šim-me-ši* (IV R 52, 14 a), *i-pi-te-šu*, *u-še-me-šu* can prove nothing to the contrary. For cases like *ab-bi-e-šú* 'I accosted, hailed him', however, see § 53, d, note.

Syntax.

A. The several parts of speech
in their simplest combinations.

1. The Substantive
in connexion with a pronominal suffix, an adjective or another substantive.

a) With a pronominal Suffix.

The place of the suffix to the noun is sometimes supplied by the independent personal pronoun with the force of a genitive or accusative (§ 55, b), as if, for 'my house', we should say '(this) house of mine'. It is always so in the royal greeting: *šulmu âši libbaka lû ṭâbka* (or *libbakunu lû ṭâbkunûši*, e. g. K. 312, 3 f.). *attû'a*, *attûnu* (§ 55, c, β), also, serve in the Achæmenian inscriptions as mere representatives of the suffix, e. g. *bîta at-tu-nu* 'our house' (Beh. 27); in fact the suffix may even be employed at the same time without receiving thereby any special emphasis, e. g. *abû'a attû'a* 'my father' (K III, 2), *attû'a abû'a Uštaspi* 'my father is Hystaspes' (Beh. 1). Such special emphasis is, however, bestowed upon the suffix by placing *kâši* etc., before it. With the illustrations § 119.

already given in § 55, b, compare further: *mannu ša ka-a-šu lâ idibbubu ḳurdiku* 'who should not proclaim thy strength?' (O Merodach, IV R 46, 27 a).

A phrase in apposition, referring to a person indicated by a pronominal suffix, is introduced by *ša*. Observe Assurb. Sm. 74, 18: *ša êpiš ardûti u nâdin mandatti lillikûš suppûka* 'as of one doing homage and paying tribute may thy request come before him'.

§ 120. Two substantives closely connected in sense may take the suffix only with the second of the two: *narkabâte u ummânate-ia* (Tig. I 71. II 43), *narkabâti sîsê-ia* 'my chariots and horses' (Senhb. VI 22); a third example will be found in § 122 end. But cf. also Shalm. Ob. 149. 176: *ina pa-na-at ummâni'a karâši'a* 'at the head of my army, of my camp'.

b) With an Adjective.

§ 121. Position of the adjective. The adjective is placed, in most cases, after the substantive, before it, however, wherever any stress is to be laid upon the adjective; hence *rabîtu(m) ḳâsu* or *ḳâtsu* 'his great (strong) hand' (Assurn. I 39. Sarg. Cyl. 26), *kabtu nîr bêlûti'a* 'the heavy yoke of my sovereignty' (Esarh. II 21), *rapšu nagû Ja'ûdi*, 'the wide Land of Judah' (Senh. Const. 15), *rapšâti mâtâti Na-i-ri* (Assurn. Balaw. 19), *šaḳûti Ištâr* (Assurb. Sm. 120, 27), *aḳrâte napšâ-*

têšunu 'their dear life' (Senhb. V 77), *ina emḳi libbišu* 'in his wise heart' (Desct. rev. 11), 'Ur and *sittâtim maḫâzâ* the other cities' (V R 35, 5), *utakkina daliḫtu mâtsu* 'I made secure his disordered country' (Khors. 52). The adj. is even placed before the preposition in Assurb. Sm. 76, 27: *rapašti ḳabal tâmtim* 'in the wide ocean'.

Agreement of Subst. and Adj. 1) in respect of case. Looking at § 66, we are inclined to think that *murṣu lâ ṭâbu, ta-ni-ḫa marṣam* (acc., IV 26, 63 b) was quite as good Assyrian as *šad-da-a mar-ṣu* 'the inaccessible mountain' (Senhb. Bav. 42), *malki išaru* 'a just king' (he sought, V R 35, 12). 2) In respect of state. Subst. and adj. stand in the absol. state; constructions like the following are less common: *ašar rûḳi* 'a distant place' (IV R 14 No. 1, 2), *iṣṣur mu-bar-šu* 'a feathered bird' (Shams. II 49), *lišân limuttu* 'an evil tongue' (K. 246 col. I 32), *Marduk mar* (sign § 9 No. 157) *rêštû ša apsî* (IV R 22, 30 b). For these the student is referred to the beginning of § 66. The follg. are striking: *ana ḳa-at dam-ḳa-a-ti* 'to the gracious hands' (IV R 8, 49 b), *pân limnûti* 'the evil contenance' (K. 246 col. I 31). 3) In respect of number and gender. The so-called *constructio ad sensum* is frequently found with *mâtu*, when the reference is not to the country but to its inhabitants. This is always the case with the name § 122.

of Media; observe Senhb. II 30 ff.: *ša*^{mât} *Ma-da-a-a rûḳûti ša ina šarrâni abê'a mamman lâ išmû zikir mâtišun mandatašunu kabitta amḫur*. Cf. also ^{mât} *Man-na-a-a dalḫûte* (Lay 33, 9), ^{mât} *Šubarî šapṣûte lâ magirê* (Tig. II 89, cf. III 88 f.). The two collective nouns *iṣṣuru* 'birds, the bird tribe' (*iṣṣur šamê muttapriša* Tig. VI 83, *iṣṣur* ^{pl} *šamê muttapriša* I R 28, 31 a, but also *iṣṣur šamê muttaprišûti* III R 9 No. 3, 56) and *ûḳu* 'people' (*v*. Dicty. p. 236) may be joined with the plural of the adj. We shall have to come back to this construction in § 141.

A single adj. referring to two substs. is found V R 35, 14: *ḳâta u libbašu išara* 'his just hand and heart'; for the suffix *v*. § 120.

c) *with another Substantive in Subordination.*

§ 123. The subordination of a subst. in the genitive to another substantive is expressed 1) by the so-called nexus of the construct state. For illustrations and also for the numerous exceptions see § 72 a and b. To the examples there given with *i* in the first member instead of the sing. of the construct, we would here add: *iš-di kussê šarrûtišu* (acc., Tig. VIII 78. IV R 18, 35 b), *alakti ilûtišunu* (acc., Neb. I 8). Note also the late and incorrect construction *malikûtim kullata nap-*

ḫar from a cylinder of Cyrus (V R 35, 12) instead of *malikût kullat napḫari.* 2) By *ša* before the substantive in the genitive (*v.* § 58). This periphrasis by means of *ša* is necessary when a suffix, adjective or other form comes between the *nomen regens* and the genitive. Examples: *ṣulullašunu ša šalâme* (V R 10, 64), *apil šipri-ia ša šulme* 'my messenger of peace' (accus., V R 3, 21); *šangû ṣîru ša Bêl* 'high-priest of Bel' (IV R 44, 13), *namṣaru zaḳtu ša epêš taḫâzi* 'the sharp battle-sword' (Assurb. Sm. 124, 55), *mûrê balṭûte ša rîmâni* 'the living young of a wild-bull' (I V 28, 6 a); *šarrâni kâli-šunu ša Na-i-ri* (Shams. II 3 f.). Cf. also *erêb šarrûti'a ša kirib Dûr-ilu* (Assurb. Sm. 127, 85). 3) By a pronominal suffix appended to the *nomen regens* and an explanatory *ša* before the genitive. Cf. the continually recurring phrase: X *aplu-šu ša* (son of) Y; also *âlânišu ša* 'the cities of such and such a one' (Shams. II 25 f.). In longer constructions, when the genitive has a certain emphasis laid upon it or when it receives further qualifying additions, it is very frequently placed at the head of the sentence with *ša*, the pronominal suffix then referring back to this anticipated genitive. Cf. *šá N. N. . . . aštakan abiktašu* (Senhb. I 19. III 45), *šá Lu-li-i . . . êkim šarrûsu* (Senhb. Const. 13), *ša* ^{mât} *Ma-da-a-a . . . mandat(t)ašunu amḫur* 'the tribute of the Medes I received' (Senhb. II 30), *šá Ašûrbânpal . . .*

šêpê rubûtišu ṣabat (Assurb. Sm. 73, 16), *ša šarri . . . ina imnišu* 'into the king's right hand' (IV R 18, 39 a).

d) With another Substantive in Apposition.

§ 124. The follg. are examples of the various kinds of apposition in Assyrian: *erinu zulûlu* 'the cedar roofing' (Neb. III 30. 43. 46, *erinum ṣulûlišu* 'its cedar roofing' Neb. Grot. II 19), *Rammân mušaznin zunnum nuḫšu* 'R. who sendeth rain overmuch' (Neb. IV 58), *ḫurâṣu iḫzu* 'gold that serves as a setting, a gold setting' (*v.* Dicty. under אחז₁); 'Astartarikku *ḫiratsu šarrat* his consort the queen' (V R 66 col. II 27) must be viewed acc. to the commencement of § 66. An apposition in Assyrian may often be rendered in English by an adjective or a participle, e. g. *ekallu šubat šarrûtišu* 'his royal palace', *âlânišu dannûti bît niṣirtišu* his strong, well guarded cities' (Senhb. Const. 37. Senhb. II 9 f.; cf. Neb. Bab. II 22: *Bâbilu ana niṣirtim aškun*). *aplê nabnît* and *âlâni bît*, just mentinoned, serve at the same time to illustrate one of the most important rules affecting apposition in Assyrian, according to which substantives, even when they stand in apposition to other substantives in the plural, remain themselves in the singular. Cf. also V R 64 col. II 40: '*Šamaš u Ištâr ṣi-it libbišu* his (Sin's) own children'. Hence also *âlâni dannûti bît dûrâni* 'strong, well-walled cities', literally, strong cities, dwelling-place with walls'. Participial expressions — to include these at this stage — are subject to the same law; cf. the frequent *šarrâni âlik maḫri'a* 'the kings, my predecessors', *šarrâni âlik maḫri abê'a* (Esarh. V 34 etc.), *ardâni dâgil pâni'a* (V R 3, 83 etc.), 'Asshur and Ishtar *ra'imu šangûti'a*' (Senhb. Kuy. 4, 10), *nišê âšib libbišu* 'the inhabitants of that place', *bêlê'a âlik idi'a* (Assurb. Sm. 39, 17). So also V R 33 col. VII 39 ff. But cf. 'the great gods', *râ'imût šarrûti'a* (Shalm. Mo. obv. 3).

Place of the word or phrase in apposition. § 125.
The word or phrase etc. in apposition usually stands after the substantive to which it belongs. Only when special emphasis is laid on the apposition — which is often the case in elevated style, in particular — do we find it preceding its substantive. Cf. *bêrit uzni ilâni Marduk* 'the wisdom of the gods, Merodach' (I R 52 No. 6, 6. Neb. II 3. III 3 etc.), *bêlu rabû Marduk* (V R 60 col. III 7), *nûr ilâni Šamaš* (V R 3, 113); see also Sm. 954 obv. 26. 28. rev. 12, 14 and many other passages. 'Merodach, the lord of deities' is always rendered *bêl ilâni Marduk*. We rarely meet with *šarru* placed first (V R 33 col. VI 42: *šarru Agum;* V R 61 col. VI 35 f.: *šarri Nabû-bal-iddina*).

The favourite mode of expressing the idea of § 126.

'all, the whole' is by placing *kalû* (gen. *ka-li-e* V R 34 col. III 44, elsewhere always *ka-li*, acc. always *ka-la*) or *gimru* 'totality, all' in apposition accompanied by a retrospective suffix: *mâtâti kališina* 'all lands' (Assurn. I 16. III 17), but also *eli kališina mâtâti* 'upon all lands' (Assurn. I 17. III 118), *mâtâte nakirê kališun* (Khors. 14); *ilâni gimrašun* 'all gods', *A-nun-na-ke gimiršunu* (IV R 19, 45 a). This does not, of course, exclude such constructions as *kal malkê* 'all princes', *kala tênešêti* 'all men' (Neb. Grot. III 52); *gimri mâtišu rapaštim* (Senhb. II 11). — *gi-mir ma-lik* 'all princes', in the text of Assurbanipal V R 62 No. 1, 3, is quite anomalous; strange, too, is the use of the adv. *kališ* in: *šá ka-li-iš kibrâta* 'from all regions' in Cyrus' cylinder V R 35, 29, though it is also found in Shamshi-Rammân: *mâḫir bilti u i-gi-si-i ša ka-liš kibrâti* (Shams. I 38), according to which Shams. I 28. Salm. Ob. 16 *murtêdû ka-liš mâtâte* is to be translated, 'who rules all lands'.

gabbu also serves to express the ideas of 'all' and 'whole', but in this case no retrospective suffix is employed; cf. *mâtâte gabbu* 'all lands' (IV R 52 No. 1, 21), *ûkû gabbi* 'the whole people' (Beh. 16 etc.), *ṣâbê bêl ḫiṭi gabbu* 'all debtors' (Assurn. I 82), *ina napḫar mât Ašûr gab-be* 'in the whole extent (lit. totality) of Assyria' (Tig. IV 101 f.), with the same piling up of words for 'all' that we find in *mâtâte ša napḫar(i) lišânû* (or *lišânâta*) *gabbi* 'the lands of each and every tongue' (B, 3. O, 16). Expressions like *mâtu gabbiša* (Assurn. II 47) are less frequent.

e) With another Substantive in Co-ordination.

The usual construction is the union of two substantives by the copula *u*, but very frequently the substantives are simply placed side by side without a conjunction (asyndeton): 'of heaven and earth' is almost uniformly expressed by *šamê u irṣiti(m)*, only in rare cases is the copula wanting (e. g. Assurn. II 135. II R 66 No. 1, 1); on the other hand *biltu mandattu*, for example, is quite as common as *biltu u mandattu* 'custom and tribute'; so, also, 'Nebo and Merodach' is now *Nabû u Marduk*, now only *Nabû Marduk*. The same applies to adjectives and infinitives. The following deserve notice on account of the construct form of the first noun: *gamâl u šûzubu tîdi* (IV R 67, 35 a), *ana šûzub u nirârûte Ḳummuḫi* (Tig. II 17); *ṣi-ḫir ra-bi* 'small and great' (IV R 19, 12 a), alongside of *ṣiḫru u rabû* (e. g. V R 5, 122). § 127.

Asyndeta like *ištên ûme šinâ ûmê ul uk-ki* (III R 15 col. I 10) we should render by: 'one or (much less) two days I waited not'. In Assurn. II 34: the mountain Niṣir *ša* *šadû* *Lullu* (*šadû*) *Kinipa iḳabûšûni*' and Esarh. II 25 'the inhabitants of Tilašurri, the name of which in the mouth of the common people is ^{âlu} *Meḫrânu* ^{âlu} *Pitânu* have we in each case two popular names?

Appendix: Numerals. Adverbs.

The Numerals.

§ 128. The oft recurring expression 'the four regions' (*kibratu*, also *tubḳatu*, *šâru*, rarely *sûḳu*) is particulary instructive with regard to the union of cardinal numbers with a substantive. We find *a*) *kib-rat irbitti(m)* (*ir-bit-ti*, *irbit-ti*, *irbit-ta* etc.), where *kib-rat*, to judge from *kib-ra-a-ti ir-bi-it-tim* (V R 35, 20) and *tu-bu-ḳa-tum ir-bit-ti* is certainly to be regarded as plural (*kibrât*); *b*) *kib-rat ar-ba-'(-i)* or *kibrâtim ar-ba-im* (gen., Hamm. Louvre I 5). Of these two constructions *kibrât(i) irbittim* and *arba'i* three explanations are possible, between which, in view of what has been stated in § 72, it is difficult to decide. First, the substantive may be regarded as in the constr. state ('the regions of the quartette', literally); or, secondly, the numeral — see under *d*) and cf. Hebr. בְּנוֹת שָׁלֹשׁ 'three daughters.' 1 Chr. 25, 5 — may be considered as in apposition to the substantive ('the regions, a quartette'); or finally, we may hold that both modes of expression were in use side by side. *c*) *ana ir-bit-ti ša-a-re* 'to the four winds' (Khors. 164). This construction — feminine of the numeral in the constr. state followed by a masculine substantive in the plural — is also found in *ir-bit naṣmadê* 'team of four' (K. 3437 obv. 16), *še-lal-ti ûmê* 'three days' (IV R 61, 32 b), *si-bit šârê* 'the seven winds' (IV R 66, 47 a); V *nirmak sipirri* (Tig. II 30) must accordingly be read *ḫamšat nirmak*. *d*) *ḫa-am-ma-mi ša ar-ba-'* (Sarg. Cyl. 9. Khors. 14). The numeral occurs without *ša* in *kursinnâšu* IV-*bi* or *ba* (III R 65, 39. 43 b), but here too it is to be understood as being in apposition. It stands in apposition at the head of the expression in *sibittišunu ilâni limnûti* 'the seven evil spirits' (IV R 5, 70 a). For the number 'two' cf. *šinâ û-me* (*v.* § 127).

The combination *a-na su-uḳ ir-bit-ti* (IV R 13, 52 b), *su-ki ir-bit-ti* (K. 2061 col. II 7) we would mention at least in a note. — Just as in Hebrew, when a numeral is joined to אַמָּה 'ell, cubit', the latter is very frequently introduced by בְּ, e. g. אַרְבַּע בָּאַמָּה so in Assyr. *ammatu* is introduced by *ina*; e. g. 'an edifice *ša 95 ina ištên ammat rabîtim arkat 31 ina ištên ammati rabîtim rapšat*' (Esarh. V 32 f.).

The Assyrian ordinal numbers are treated quite § 129.
like adjectives: in their original construction they follow the subst., hence *araḫ samnu* (for *araḫ* instead of *arḫu v.* § 122, 2), *ina ša-ni-ti šanûti*, *ina ša-ni-tum šaluštu* 'a second, a third time' (Beh. 55. 51); since, however, in longer sentences of reports of different expeditions or years, the ordinals stand in emphatic

contrast to each other, we find them in most cases placed before their substantives, thus: *ina maḫ-re-e gir-ri-ia* (but also *ina gir-ri-ia maḫ-re-e* Shams. I 53). *ina II-e, III* etc., *VIII-e girri'a* (Senhb.), *ina VIII-e, IX-e gir-ri-ia* (V R 5, 63. 7, 82), *ina šal-ši gir-ri-ia* (Senhb. Kuy. 1, 18), *ina maḫ-re-e palê-ia* (I R 49 col. III 9 f.), *a-di XV palê-ia* (Khors. 23); the orthographical varieties *ina maḫ-re-e palû* ^{pl}*-ia* (which must also be read *palê-ia*, Shalm. Mo. obv. 14), *a-di V palû* $^{(pl)}$*-ia* (Tig. VI 45) must not lead us so far astray as to wish to regard *girrê'a* as plural; it is much more likely that the plural determinative after *palê* is due to a mistake. Cf. in addition to the above, *ina ša-ni-e ta-lu-kt* 'on a second expedition' (Shalm. Balaw. IV 5), *ina šalulti šatti* (but *ina šatti šalulti* Khors. 144). Instead of the ordinal of 'one', when used in opposition to 'second, third etc.', we may have the cardinal; thus: IV R 5, 13 a: *ištên* 'the first' (followed by 'the second' up to 'the seventh'), Desct. obv. 42: *ištên bâbu* 'the first gate' (followed by: 'the second' up to 'the seventh' gate), Nimr. Ep. XI, 136: *ištên ûmu* 'the first day' (folld. by: *šanû ûmu, šalša ûmu* or *ûma, rebâ ûmu* or *ûma, ḫaššu, VI-ša, sebâ ûma* or *sebû ûmu*). Cf. the same usage in *iš-ta-at* 'firstly, in the first place' (followed by *šanûtum* up to *sebûtum*, 'secondly' up to 'seventhly') Nimr. Ep. XI 204 (*v.* § 77).

A distributive number occurs Nimr. Ep. XI, 149: *si-ba u si-ba adagur* 'seven incense vessels each' (see details in Dicty., No. 77). — For *a-di* (*a-de*) *VII-šu* (V R 6, 10), *a-di si-bi-šu* 'till seven times'; *a-di ištâ-tu*, *a-di šinâ*(*šu*) 'for the first, second time' and similar expressions *v*. Dicty. p. 127.

The Adverb.

'Of the adverbs those in *iš* and *eš* are worthy of notice from a syntactical point of view inasmuch as they are capable of taking a noun after them in the genitive: cf. *kakkabiš šamâmi* 'like the stars of heaven' (Neb. III 12), identical in meaning with *kîma kakkab šamâme* (IV R 3, 12 a), *la-ba-riš ûmê* 'in consequence of the becoming old of the days, in consequence of old age' (its foundation had become unstable, weak, Senhb. VI 32; Senhb. Const. 58), *aḫrâtaš* (*ûmê*) 'in the future (of the days), in future' (without *ûmê* e. g. Khors. 53. V R 34 col. II 48, with *ûmê* e. g. I R 7 F, 18). § 130.

2. The Verbal Nouns: Participle and Infinitive.

The Assyrian participle takes the object dependent on it in the genitive, the two together forming the members of a construct nexus. Hence *nâš ḫaṭṭi ṣîrti*, § 131.

nâš kašti elliti (V R 55, 8), *êmid šarrâni* 'the subduer of kings' (V R 55, 2), *lâ pâliḫ bêlûti'a*, 'Nebo *pâḳid kiššat šamê irṣitim*' (I R 35 No. 2, 3), *râkib abûbi* 'who rides upon the whirlwind', *tup-sar šâṭir narê annî* (V R 56, 25), *mu'abbit limnûti* (Assurn. I 8), *munakkir šiṭri'a* (Senhb. VI, 71), *namṣaru musaḫḫip namtâri* (IV R 21, 65 a); 'my war-chariot *sâpinat zâ'irê*' (Senhb. V 77), *pâtiḳat nabnîti* (V R 66 col. I 21. IV 63, 10 b), 'Šumalia *âšibat rêšêti kâbisat kuppâti* (V R 56, 47), *lû mulamminat egirrêšu* 'may she inspire them with evil thoughts' (IV R 12, 43); *lâ kânišût Ašûr* (Tig. IV 8; cf. with suffix: *lâ kânšûtešu* Assurn. I 14. 36). For *muštappi kika-ri-e* (IV R 14 No. 3, 14) with *i* in the end of the first member, and also for the periphrasis *ša* e. g. *utukku kâmû ša amêli* (K. 246 col. I 28), cf. § 123, 1 and 2, and also § 72, a there referred to. As exceptions of the same kind as those mentioned in § 72, a may be quoted *nâṣir kudurrêti mu-kin-nu ablê* (V R 55, 5), *šâlilu Kaššî* (alongside of *kâšid* ^{mât} *Aḫarrî*, ibid. l. 10); cf. also: *lâ pâliḫu ilišu* (IV R 3, 6 a), 'Ea *pâtiḳu kal gimri*' (*E. M.* II 339), *mupattû ṭûdâte* (Shalm. Mo. obv. 8), 'Asshur (or: the great gods) *mušarbû šarrûti'a*, *multašpiru tênišêt Bêl* (Tig. VII 50), etc. Details, also, regarding the place where and the time when the action denoted by the part. took place, are appended in the genitive to the constr. state of the participle, hence *âlik pâni* 'who goes at the head'; *âlik maḫri* do., fem. *âlikat maḫri* (II R. 66 No. 1, 4), *âlik maḫ-ri-ia* 'my predecessor', *šarrâni âlik maḫri abê'a*, cf. *âlik maḫ-ri-e-a* IV R 17, 43 b; *âlik idi* 'who goes at one's side', *âlik i-di-šu* or *-ia* 'his or my helper', also *a-li-kut i-di-e-šu* (V R 4, 24); *muttallik mûši* 'who walks, roams about in the night-time' (IV R 24, 42 a).

For the rare cases in which the participle of the Qal is preçeded by its object after the manner of the finite verb, see § 73 p. 196, and note also, for example, IV R 3, 6 a: *ša Ištâr pa-ki-da lâ i-šú-u* 'whoever doth not respect the goddess Ishtar'.

The infinitive in Assyrian is either treated as a substantive, in which case its object becomes the second member of a construct nexus, e. g. *ana epêš ardûti'a* 'to do me homage', *nadân ilâni* 'the giving back, restoration of the gods' (Esarh. III 7), *šumkut(u) nakirê*, *nasâḫ kudurri annî* 'to pull up this boundary-stone' (1 Mich. II 8), or it follows the construction of the finite verb, in which case, however, it is always preceded by its object (*v.* on this point § 73 b above). Cf. *mîta* or *mîti bulluṭu*, 'quickening of the dead' (IV R 29, 18 a. 19, 11 b), *šîmtum šâmu* 'to appoint (one's) fate, lot' (II R 7, 5 b), *šuttu pašâru* 'interpret a dream' (V R 30, 13 f), *kar-ṣi akâlu* 'calumniate', 'he assembled his army *ana mât nukurtim šalâli*' (K. 133 obv. 12), *ana mimma limnì ṭarâdi* 'to drive away all evil' (IV R §132.

21, 29 a), *rê'ùsina epêšu* 'to exercise his sway' (V R 7, 105), *aššu ṭâbu napišti ûmê rûḳûti nadânimma u kunnu palê'a* (I entreated, Khors. 174), *miṣir mâtišunu ruppuša iḳbiûni* (Tig. I 49), *aššu lipit ḳâti'a šullume* 'to prosper the work of my hands' (Senhb. Kuy. 4, 10), etc.

§ 133. For the sake of emphasis, the infin. is joined to the finite verb. in such cases as: 'lies in these lands *lû ma-du i-mi-du* are assuredly on the increase' (Beh. 14), *ḳâšu ḳišamma* 'give, I pray thee!' (Nimr. Ep. 37, 8), 'the city *ḫašâla iḫšul* he utterly destroyed' (*v.* Nimr. Ep. 51, 6); for II 1 cf. *adi zunnunu ina mâtišu iznunu* 'till there was heavy rain in his land' (Assurb. Sm. 101, 22).

For the meanings of the inf., active and passive, *v.* § 95 end. As an illustration of the passive use of the inf., which is often overlooked, I would here mention a single, but very important, passage, viz: Beh. 36 *ana Bâbilu lâ kašâdu* 'that Babylon may not be captured, to prevent the capture of Babylon'; that the words cannot by any possibility mean 'when Babylon was not yet reached' (Bezold) is self-evident.

3. The finite Verb.

a) Signification and Use of the Tenses and Moods.

§ 134. The signification of the various tenses in Assyrian has been already discussed at length in § 87 of the morphology, the permansive receiving, over and above, special treatment in § 89. For the use of the tenses in prohibitive sentences *v.* § 144, and cf. § 87, c; for the protasis of an hypothetical sentence, see § 149. The moods — the relative mood, the precative, formed both from the preterite and from the permansive, and the cohortative, from the preterite, — have also been discussed in §§ 92 and 93; see, in addition, for the relative mood §§ 147 and 148, and for the precative-cohortative § 145. We would here add the following brief remarks regarding the use of the tenses and moods. 1) The present assumes the meaning of 'shall' (i. e. of duty) even in other than prohibitive sentences: *tallak* means not only 'thou wilt go' but also 'thou oughtest to, thou shalt, go'. Cf. 'whoever shall do so and so, him *illalûšu* shalt thou bind, etc.' (I R 7 F, 27), *tušaṣbat* 'thou shalt cause to be siezed' (IV 54 33 a), 'soldiers *tašappar* thou oughtest to send' (IV R 54 No. 2, 34), *ikammisma kî'am iḳabbi* 'he shall fall down and speak thus' (IV R 61 No. 2), 'the king *ukân* shall place' (IV R 32. 33), 'what I know, *atta tîdi* oughtest thou to know (IV R 7, 31 a, Peiser). Accordingly we find with the negative *ul*: *pânûka ul urraḳ* 'thy countenance shall not grow pale' (Assurb. Sm. 125, 69), 'the king *ul išasi, ul ikkal* shall not speak, shall not eat' (IV R 32, 25. 30 a etc.). 2) The so-called relative mood (modus relativus) is also used in principal clauses incorrectly, as was explained in § 92, in place of the preterite (which does not, *per se*, end in a vowel); it is also used however in some cases — such a use is, at least, possible — to denote the pluperfect, which might be quite easily explained by the fact that such a pluperfect sentence from a logical point of view approaches very closely to a conjunctional sentence with the conjunction omitted (cf. the examples given in § 148, 3): 'he had done so and so, then came to pass'. An example beyond suspicion, however, is unknown to me. Neb. Senk. I 19 e. g. *(i)-ir-ta-šú salîmu* must be translated simply 'he (Merodach) took pity' (not: had taken); *irtášu*, for which in any case, were it in the relative mood, it would be better to write *ir-ta-šú-u*, is to be explained acc. to § 108 (i. e. as standing for *irtáši*).

b) Government of the Verb.

α) Pronouns governed by the Verb.

§ 135. The place of the verbal suffix is occasionally supplied by the independent personal pronoun with a genitive or accusative signification (§ 55 b), and in the examples about to be quoted the suffixes represented in this way have all the force of a dative: 'the powerful arms which Asshur had granted *ana a-ia-ši* (var.

ia-a-ši) me' (Assurn. II 26); without *ana*: *ušannâ ia-a-ti* 'he told it me' (V R 1, 63), *inbika ia-a-ši ḳâšu ḳišamma* 'give me thy *inbu*' (Nimr. Ep. 37, 8), *iṭiḫḫâ ana kâši* (ibid. 11, 11). These pronouns, however, must be employed, in the first place, when a word in apposition is added to the person denoted by the suffix, e. g. *ia-a-ti Nabû-kudurri-uṣur . . . uma'ir'anni* 'me, Nebuchadnezzar, he sent' (cf. V R 7, 94 etc.), he spoke 'to him, viz. to Nimrod' *ana šâšûma ana Namrûdu*; secondly, when more or less emphasis is to be laid on the suffix: in this case the pronominal suffix must never be dispensed with. Cf. *lû* (?) *anâku ana kâšunu ullalukunûši, at-tu-nu ia-a-ši ullilâ'inni* ('but ye do not enlighten me!' IV R 56, 46 f. a), 'the foundation-stone of Narâm-Sin *ukallim'anni ia-a-ši* he (Shamash) showed to me', (V R 64 col. II 60), *ana a-a-ši du-gul-an-ni* 'look upon, unto me' (IV R 68, 29 b), 'so and so *kâša luḳbika* will I announce to thee' (Nimr. Ep. XI, 10), *šâšu aḳbiš* 'I spoke to him' (Neb. I 54), cf. also Assurn. III 76: *ana šu-a-šú rêmûtu aškunašu* 'to him (himself) I showed mercy'.

The use of *anâku* and *attunu* for the verbal suffix is quite late and bad, all the more so that not the slightest emphasis is meant to be put upon the suffix (with dative force) thus represented. N R 9: *mandattum anâku inaššûnu* 'they bring me tribute'; NR 21: *anâku iddannaššinîti* 'he handed them (the countries) over to me'; Beh. 4: 'Auramazda *šarrûtu anâku iddannu*'. Cf. finally S. 15 f.: 'the gods *ana anâku liṣṣurû'inni*', where a slight emphasis is laid upon 'me' at least.

§ 136. When to a verbal suffix of the 3. pers. sing. or plur., or to the pron. *šâšu*, *šâša*, *šâšunu* (§ 55, b) a word is added to describe the state or condition of the person denoted by the pronoun at the time of the action in which he is concerned, this is done by means of the abstract noun in *ût* with the appropriate nominal suffix. The same method is adopted when a word is added to a preceding substantive or proper name. The verbal suffix (which in the latter case has a retrospective reference) may be present or wanting. Examples: *balṭûsu ina ḳâti aṣbatsu* (Senhb. IV 38); *šâšu bal-ṭu-us-su iṣbatûnimma* 'him (himself) they captured alive' (V R 8, 24 ff.), *šâša bal-ṭu-us-sa ina ḳâti aṣbat*; — 'the kings of the lands of Naïri *balṭûsunu ḳâti ikšud*' (Tig. V 9), 'who Hanno, the king of Gaza, *ka-mu-us-su ušêriba* *âlu* *Aššur*' (Sarg. Cyl. 19); *Sêni . . . šallûsu u kamûsu ana âli'a ubla(šu)* 'Seni I brought captive and bound to my city' (Tig. V 24).

The semi-adverbial use of the abstract noun in *ût*, joined to the suffix of the 3 pers. (*ussu*=*ûtsu*) has possibly brought about the formation of the two adverbs *ûmussu* and *arḫussu* mentioned in § 80, b, β note.

β) *Substantives governed by the Verb.*

The substantive, as the indirect object of the verb, is always introduced by *ana*; as the direct object, it generally stands in the accusative, which, however, does not necessarily end in *a* (*v.* § 66); in either case the substantive precedes the verb, although the converse arrangement is not unfrequent (details in § 142). Sometimes, however, the periphrasis with *ana* is also used for the accusative; cf. e. g. 'when Anu and Bel *ana ga-ti-ia umallû* entrusted to me such and such' (Hamm. Louvre I 14 ff.), *ana šalaṭ Ûri nîtu ilmêšu* (III R 15 col. II 4) — in both cases *ana* might be dispensed with, since the verbs quoted govern two accusatives (*v.* § 139). § 137.

Of Assyrian verbs which, contrary to our idiom, govern the accusative, the follg. may be here mentioned: *malû* 'be full of something' (e. g. I R 28, 7 b), *šebû* 'to take one's fill of something' (cf. II 1 with two accs.: *šizbu lâ ušabbû karašišunu*, var. *karassun*, 'with milk they could not satisfy their stomach', V R 9, 67), *šemû* 'hearken to, obey some one', *apâlu* 'answer some one' (e. g. *Êa mârašu Marduk ippal*), *nakâru* 'rebel against some one' (but only when the object is a verbal suffix, otherwise it is construed with *itti*, *la-pa-ni* or *ina ḳât*). *nâḫu* and *pašâḫu* 'to be quiet, com- § 138.

posed with regard to some person or thing' also take the accusative of reference, cf. Assurb. Sm. 105, 66: 'Asshur's angry heart *ul inûḫšunûti ul ipšaḫšunûti kabitti Ištâr*'; also *šalâmu* 'be freed from loss, be satisfied with regard to something' (money lent, for example), 'get back one's money', cf. the phrase so common in the contract tablets: *adi kaspa išallimmu* 'until he (the creditor) get back his money'. — No explanation is required of the accus. with verbs of motion to indicate the direction in which one goes or comes, e. g. *rêbitam ina bâ'išu* 'when he walks in the street' (IV R 26, 4 b), *šibûta lillik* 'may he reach old age'(Khors. 191). Special attention, on the other hand, is here called to the acc. with verbs of swearing to denote the person or thing by which one swears. Cf. for *saḳâru: niš* (ideogr. MU) *ilâni ana aḫameš isḳurû* 'by the name of the gods they swore mutually' (Esarh. I 42), 'never to do such and such *ni-iš ilâni rabûti ina narê šú-a-tum isḳur* hath he sworn by the name of the great gods upon this tablet' (1 Mich. I 22), *adê ni-iš* (var. MU) *ilâni ušašḳiršunûti* 'I made them swear (obedience to) the laws by the name of the gods' (V R 1, 21 f. etc.). So with *tamû: niš šamê lû tamât niš irṣitim lû tamât* 'by the name of heaven be thou exorcised, by the name of earth be thou exorcised'! It is evident that *ni-iš* has in these expressions, to a certain extent, the function of a preposition: to swear 'by' something; cf. § 81 a, end.

From the number of verbs that govern two accusatives we single out the follg.: *šaḳû* 'give some one something to drink' (*mê ellûti šiḳišu* IV R 26, 40 b), *salâḫu* 'sprinkle some one with something', *pašâšu* 'rub, anoint some person or thing with something, e. g. with oil', *ṣarâpu* 'dye something with something' (cf, the frequent *dâmêšunu kîma napâsi šadû lû aṣrup*, Assurn. I 53 etc.; but also *ina*), *ṣu'unu* 'decorate something with something, produce some beautiful object from something', *emêdu* 'lay something upon some one' (*annu kabtu êmidsu* 'a heavy punishment he laid upon him' V R 8, 10), *nadû* 'put something, (such as fetters) upon some one' (*Padî bi-ri-tu parzilli iddû* 'Padi they had put into iron fetters', Senhb. II 70 f.), *sanâḳu* 'press something into something else', and such like (e. g. 'the horses and oxen *isniḳa ṣindêšu* he put into harness, he harnessed, Senhb. V 30), *lamû* 'surround some one with something' (*nîtum al-me-šu* 'with war I surrounded him, I attacked him on all sides, Senhb. V 13, 'the city *nîti almê*' Senhb. Bav. 44), *zummû* 'to exclude some person or thing from something' (*ša êribušu zummû nûra*, Desct. obv. 7. V R 6, 103). *maḫâru* 'to take, receive something from some one': *madatušu amḫuršu* (Shalm. Ob. 177 etc.), *ḳâtêšun ḫarrê ḫurâṣi . . . ša laḳtêšunu amḫur* 'from their hands I took their golden rings' (Senhb. VI 2 f.).

B. The Sentence.

1. The simple Sentence.

a) Declaratory Sentences.

§ 140. The follg. are examples of simple nominal sentences with a noun or pronoun as subject and a noun (subst., adj., or part.) as predicate: *Ilu damḳu* 'God is gracious', *anâku Nabûna'id* 'I am Nabonidus'. The predicate is often found at the head of the sentence for the sake of emphasis, e. g. Beh. 100: *parṣâtum ši-na* 'they are lies', V R 2, 123: *šarru ša ilu idûšu atta* 'thou art the king whom God hath chosen'. In view of the preceding and following sections no additional examples are required either of complex nominal sentences with a finite verb as predicate, or of verbal sentences, consisting of or beginning with a finite verb; in the latter case the object or the adverbial adjuncts may take precedence.

§ 141. Gender and number of the predicate are determined, as a general rule, by the gender and number of the subject. Numerous exceptions, however, are found, the majority of which are due to the principle of constructio ad sensum. For gender cf. IV R 17, 11 b: *mâtâte rêšûnikka* 'the countries hail thee with joy'; for number cf. Tig. III 66 f.: *^mât Adauš tib taḫâzi'a danna lû êdurûma ašaršunu lûmaššerû* etc. Cf. § 122, 3. An exception due to the precedence of the predicate (unless it be simply a case of careless treatment of the gender, as explained in § 90, c) occurs perhaps in V R 35, 35: *littaskarû amâta dunḳi'a* 'let words be spoken in my favour'. The want of concord between subject and predicate Nimr Ep. 59, 4: *nissâtum* (plur.) *itérub ina karši'a* 'sadness has entered into my spirit', though admitting of explanation, still remains anomalous; the same remark applies to the passage quoted at the close of § 134, 1: *pânûka* (plur.) *ul urraḳ*.

For the union of one predicate with several subjects observe V R 6, 110 f.: *ina ûmê šu-ma šî u ilâni abêša tabbû šú-me ana bêlût mâtâti* 'at the time when she (Nanâ) and the gods, her parents, called my name to bear rule over the lands'; *tabbû* is 3 pers. fem. singular!

Place of the object dependent on the finite verb. In Assyrian the object dependent on the finite verb may be placed either before or after the verb, according as greater emphasis is to be laid on the object or on the verb. Compare on the § 142.

one hand *uṣaḫḫir mâtsu* 'I diminished his land' (Senhb. II 18. III 26), 'the gods *inârû ga-re-ia* subdued my foes' (V R 4, 49), *lâ iṣṣurû mâmît ilâni;* on the other *âla* (*âlâni*) *abbul akkur ina išâti ašrup*, *kullat mâtâtišunu ušeknišа,* (Assurn. I 23) and hundreds more. For the position of the object before the infinitive *v.* § 132; this position is much less frequent with the participle, *v.* § 131 note. Before we pass from the position of the object, I would mention here a characteristic Assyrian construction, which consists in short direct speeches being placed before the verb *ḳibû* 'to speak', without an introductory *umma.* Cf.: 'Ishtar *lâ tapallaḫ iḳbâ* said: "fear not"! (Assurb. Sm. 123, 47); 'whoever *eḳlu kî mu-lu-gi ul nadinma iḳabbû*' (1 Mich. II 17 f.), 'whoever *anâku lâ i-di iḳabbû* shall say, "I know not" (I R 27 No. 2, 82 f.), 'whoever *annâ mi-na iḳabû*' (Assurn. Balaw. rev. 18 f.). *e-ki-a-am i nilik iḳbûšu* "whither shall we go", they said to him' (IV R 34, 29 a), 'if a father say to his son *ul mârî atta iḳtabi* shall say: "thou art not my child", etc. (V R 25, where the same position of the words in the left column is alone sufficient to show that this 'Sumerian' text is no re-translation of an original Assyrian Semitic text).

b) Particular kinds of Sentences.

Negative declaratory sentences. The negative *lâ* serves for the negation of substantives and infinitives, of adjectives and participles, e. g. *emûḳ lâ nîbi* 'a countless army' (Senhb. Kuy. 2, 39), *ṣêni ša lâ nîbi* 'flocks without number' (Senhb. I 50), *lâ mi-na(m)*, *ana lâ ma-ni*, *ana lâ me-ni* or *mi-na(m)*, *ana' lâ ma-ni-e* (Tig. V 7. 53), rarely *ina lâ mèni*, 'without number, countless', *šarrûtu lâ šanân* (e. g. Senhb. I 10), 'he brought *umšikku ana la sapâḫ nagišu* that his land might not be laid waste' (Lay. 51 No. 1, 11), *mêsiru ša lâ naparšudi* 'a blockade which could not be run' (Assurb. Sm. 59, 88 b); *lâ pâdû* 'without mercy' (acc. *kakkašu lâ pa-da-a*, plur. *lâ pa-du-tum* IV R 5, 4 a), *lâ âdiru* 'not fearing' (cf. *la-(a-)di-ru* Assurn. I 20), *aḫu lâ kênu* etc. § 143.

While, according to the above, there can be no doubt that *lâ* is the most general negative (as opposed to all the other negatives, *ul* included), still it seems to me that the distinction between *lâ* and *ul* as employed in negative declaratory sentences has not yet been defined with sufficient precision. For my part, I must confine myself meanwhile to bringing together a few examples that are instructive in this connexion. Cf. for *lâ*: 'the edifice *lâ ussum* was not suited for the goddess to dwell in' (V R 34 col. III 17), *lâ uddâ uṣurâti* 'the walls were not recognizable' (Neb. Senk. I 16); *minâ lâ tîdi* 'what knowest thou not'? (IV R 7, 27. 29 a); *lâ iddin* 'he gave not' (K. 538, 25): *ša lâ iknuša, ša lâ kitnušu ana nîri'a, ša ana Ašûr lâ kanšu*, 'lands which *kanâša lâ i-du-û* knew not subjection' (Tig. III 75. IV 51) For *ul* cf.: *edu ul êzib*; *ul išemmû* 'they hear not', *nûru ul immarû; ul zi-ka-ru šunu ul zinnišâti šunu* 'they are not male neither are they female' (IV R 2 ,40 b). Is it the case that the use of *ul* is chiefly or even exclusively confined to principal clauses, while *lâ* is employed in principal and subordinate clauses indifferently?

§ 144. Prohibitive sentences. No negative can be joined to the imperative; prohibitions are expressed sometimes by *lâ* with the present, sometimes by *a-a* with the pret. (cf. § 87, c on p. 241), — for *ul* with the pres. *v.* § 134, 1 — *lâ* being found with the 3. and 2. pers. sing. and plur., *a-a*, on the other hand with the 3. pers. sing. and plur. and 1. singular. Examples: *lâ tasakip* 'cast not down' (thy servant, IV R 10, 36 b), *lâ taddara amêlu* 'shun no man' (M 55 col. I 19), 'upon another god *lâ tatakkil* rely not' (I R 35 No. 2, 12); *musarû šiṭir šumi'a lîmurma lâ unakkar* (V R 64, 45 c), *ḳâtsu lâ iṣabat* 'let him not take his hand, nor help him' (III R 43 col. IV 24),

‚my work *lâ uḫabbalûš* let them (the gods) not destroy' (S, 17). *lû* prefixed seems to denote greater urgency; e. g. K. 21, 20: *šarru lu la i-pa-laḫ* 'let the king fear not at all'. — *a-a itûr* or *itûrûni* 'let him (or them) not return', *ki-bi-ra a-a irši* 'burial shall he not receive' (V R 61 col. VI 55), *a-a illika* (Nimr. Ep. XI, 158), *a-a illikûni, a-a îrubûni* etc.; *idirtu a-a arši* 'into tribulation let me not fall' (IV R 64, 69 a), *a-a atûr ana arki'a* (III R 38 No. 2 rev. 57). We also find *a-a* employed with the second person, but curiously enough always under the form *ê*: *ê tašḫutî* (Nimr. Ep. 11, 10), *ê tannašir* (sic! IV R 13, 4 b), *ê têṣir* (IV R 17, 18 b), etc. The use of *a-a* in the declaratory sentence V R 7, 45 is quite exceptional: 'his corpse *a-a addin ana ki-bi-ri* I did not commit to burial.' *lâ* is found with the 2 pers. of the perm. in III R 15 col. I 8: *alik lâ ka-la-ta*; here, however, *lâ kalâta* is perhaps to be taken as a sort of circumstantial clause and to be translated: 'go without ceasing!'

Optative and cohortative sentences. For § 145. optative and cohortative sentences formed with the help of the adverb *lû* (§ 78 on p. 214) see above — so far as verbal and complex nominal sentences are concerned — § 93, 1 and 2, where a sufficient number of examples has been given of the precative and cohortative forms derived alike from the preterite and from the permansive. The 1 pers. plur. seems to have assumed a cohortative signification without any particle, so perhaps V R 1, 126: *mâta aḫennâ nizûz* 'let us divide'?; the more usual way, however, must have been to place the cohort. meaning beyond doubt by a prefixed *î* (*ê*), 'come now, go to!' *v.* § 78. In addition to the example cited in § 142, cf. K. 3437 rev. 3: 'arise (Tiâmat)! *anâku u kâši i ni-pu-uš šašma* thou and I, let us fight with each other'; ASKT 119, 23. 25: *al-kam i nillikšu i nillikšu, nînu ana âlišu i nillikšu* 'come now, let us go to him . . ., let us go to him to his city'; Nimr. Ep. 44, 68 and a few other passages. Examples of a simple nominal sentence expressing a wish are found in: *atta lû mu-ti-ma anâku lû aššatka* 'would that thou wert my husband and I thy wife' (Nimr. Ep. 42, 9), and in the greeting so common in the epistolary literature of the Assyrians and Babylonians, *lû šulmu ana šarri bêli'a* (with variations). In this formula, however, *lû* may be wanting. — Clauses expressing a wish are also repeatedly found depending on the verb of the principal clause, thus Tig. II 96 'I laid upon them the yoke of my sovereignty *šattišamma bilta u madatta ana maḫri'a littarrûni*' (. . . to bring before me). Cf. also Tig. II 67 (*ḳurâdê'a ša mitḫuṣ tapdê lipirdû*, where we have a precative in a relative clause) and many other passages.

Interrogative sentences. The examples of interrogative sentences given in § 79, γ, which were quoted to prove the existence of *û* as an enclitic interrogative particle, must meanwhile suffice. K. 522, 9 f. is the only additional illustration that need be given: *i-zir-tu-u ina libbi šaṭrat* 'is a curse (*izirtŭ*) written thereon?' § 146.

Attributive relative clauses. 1) Relative clauses introduced by *ša*, which is continued by a pronominal suffix in all cases where it has the force of a genitive, and in most cases where it has the force of an accusative or dative. Relative clauses, which, deprived of attributive signification, constitute nominal sentences, call for no remark. Cf. e. g.: *bêlum ša ana âlišu ta-a-a-ru* (K. 133 rev. 16), 'a woman with child *ša kirimmaša lâ išaru*' (K. 246 col. I 43), Verbal sentences possessing attributive signification are at once recognized as such by the fact that they always end in a vowel, mostly *u* (or *um*), more rarely *a*; cf. § 92. *a*) Pret. and pres.: *ša itbalu* 'who had carried off' (Esarh. II 47), 'Bel and Nebo *ša aptallaḫu ilûsun* whose divinity I worship' (Assurb. Sm. 103, 46), 'the land of Naïri *ša akšudu* which I had subdued' (Tig. VIII 14); 'the deity *ša taṣ(tiṣ)lit-tú imaḫarum* that heareth prayer' (V R 43, 47 c), 'he who never his ambassador *išpura lâ iš-a-lum šulum šarrûtišun* (Assurb. Sm. 289, 50, § 147.

for which in 292, etc.: *lâ išpuru lâ iš-a-lu*); *ša ikšuda* 'who conquered' (Assurn. I 39), 'Tammaritu *ša innabtu iṣbata šêpê'a*' (Assurb. Sm. 216, f). *b*) Perm.: 'who *lâ ḫassu* did not consider', *ša lâ kitnušu*, etc. etc. The 3. fem. perm. generally remains without the final vowel. We find, it is true: 'Tiglathpileser *ša* . . . *ḫaṭṭu ellitu nadnatašumma nišê* . . . *ultašpiru* on whom a brilliant sceptre was bestowed and who ruled the nations' (Tig. I 32 f.), 'the palace *ša eli maḫrîti ma'adiš šûturat ra-ba-ta u naklat*' (Senhb. VI 44 f.); but the usual form is: *ša ḳibîtsu maḫrat* (I R 35 No. 2, 2), *ša alaktaša lâ târat*, 'whose dwelling like an eagle's nest . . . *šitkunat* was situated' (Senhb. III 70). A pret. or a pres. without the final vowel in a relative sentence, such as *ša ištakkan* (V R 62 No. 1, 6), 'Darius *ša bîta agâ îpuš*' (Persepolis Inscr. B, 6), must be considered as a very rare exception. — A relative sentence introduced by *ša* occasionally precedes the subst. of which it is the attribute, e. g. K. 2867, 18: 'the heart of the great gods was not calmed, *ul ipšaḫ ša êzuzu kabitti bêlûtišunu* nor was soothed the angry spirit of their majesty'; V R 1, 133: *ṭâbti ḳâtuššun uba'ima ša êpussunûti dunḳu* 'my good deeds I demanded at their hand, the favour shown them by me'.

2) Relative clauses without *ša*. In these the final vowel of the verb is the only indication that

they are relative clauses. Examples: 'the four lions *ad-du-ku* (which) I had killed' (I R. 7 No. IX, A, 2), *ṭâbta êpušuš* 'the good (which) I did him' (V R 7, 86), *bîtu êpušu* 'the house (which) I built' (Neb. Grot. III 47); *ina isinni šaknuš* 'at the feast instituted in his honour' (K. 133 rev. 18). The relative pronoun is always wanting with the substantives *ma-la* and *ammar* discussed in § 58, when these signify 'as much, as many, as'; also with *ašar* signifying 'in the place where or whither' (cf. the Hebr. אֲשֶׁר־שָׁמָּה 'whither, but also אֲשֶׁר alone), cf. *ašar tallakî ittiki lullik* (Assurb. Sm. 125, 61), *ša narkabtu šû-a-tu ašar šaknata unakkaru* 'whoever shall attempt any change with the chariot in the spot where he is stationed' (IV R 12, 33), Senhb. VI 24, and other passages.

Conjunctional relative clauses. In these, § 148.
also, the verb must have a final vowel. 1) Conjunctional relative clauses introduced by special conjunctions (*v.* § 82). The most of these conjunctions are also found as prepositions; indeed they are all, strictly speaking, prepositions that have become conjunctions by the additon of *ša*. *ša* may, however, be dispensed with on occasion; in fact with some, such as *ištu* and *ultu* 'since', it is always wanting. Examples: *ištu ibnanni* 'since he (Merodach) created me' (Neb. I 23), *ultu êmedu mâtašu* 'after I had subdued his

land' (V R 2, 81), *ultu libbaša inuḫḫu* 'as soon as her heart shall be calmed' (Desct. rev. 16) cf. also for *ultu* as conj. III R 15 col. II 5. Senhb. VI 25; *ultu eli ša îmurûma* 'as soon as they saw, when they saw' (K. 10 obv. 21), *ultu eli ša Bîrat ḫipû u ilêšu abkû* 'since B. was destroyed and its gods carried off' (K. 509, 17); — *arki ša ana šarri atûru* 'after I became king' (Beh. 11); — *adi šamê u irṣitu bašû zêršu liḫliḳ* 'so long as heaven and earth endure, let his seed be destroyed'! (V R 56, 60); *a-du ana âli . . . tušêrabušûni* 'until thou bringest him into the city' (K. 650, 11), *adi allaku* 'till I come' (Assurb. Sm. 125, 67), 'they await me *adi eli ša anâku allaku ana Madâ* till I arrive in Media' (Beh. 47); — *ki-i aš-pu-ru* 'when I sent', *ki-i itbû* 'when they came' (K. 509) and many other examples in which the conj. *kî* presents the peculiarity of placing its subject, object and prepositional phrases before itself and its verb; — *aš-šú limuttum êpušu* 'because he had done evil' (Khors. 92, cf. also Esarh. II 48. IV 29), *aš-ša-a nittekiruš* 'because we have rebelled against him' (IV R 52, 27 a), 'I marched against Ba'al of Tyre, *šá* (var. *aš-šu*) *amât šarrûti'a lâ iṣṣuru* because he had not observed the commandment of my majesty, my royal command' (V R 2, 51) — is Nimr. Ep. XI, 113 also to be explained in this way? —, 'may the gods bless the king *ša mîtu anâku u šarru uballiṭanni* for I was dead and the king granted me my life' (K. 81, 12). 2) Conjunctional relative clauses attached to substantives and prepositional phrases, with or without *ša* as an indication of the attributive nature of the clause. Cf. e. g. *ištu rêši* with (S. 1046, 6) or without *ša* (K. 359, 3. 9) 'from the beginning' (such and such happened). To this category belongs, in particular, *i-nu*, *inum*, usually *e-nu-ma* (proply. a *or* the time) meaning 'at the time when, when, as': *i-nu Marduk . . . iḳbû* 'when M. . . . ordered' (V R 33 col. I 44; cf. Hamm. Louvre I 10 ff.), *inum Marduk rêši šarrûti'a ullûma* 'at the time when M. exalted my royal head' (lit. 'head of my royalty' Neb. I 40), *e-nu-ma ekallu ilabbirûma i-na-ḫu* (Esarh. VI 61). Cf. further the passage V R 6, 110 f. quoted in § 141, and the illustrations given in § 82 for 1) and 2) generally. 3) Conjunctional relative clauses without any special conj., without a governing subst. and at the same time without *ša*, so that the final vowel of the verb is the only cue to the proper understanding of the syntax. Cf. Assurn. Balaw. rev. 13 f.: 'future prince! *aširtu ši enaḫu narâ ta-mar-ma tašasû anḫûsa uddiš* should this temple come to ruin, thou wilt find the tablets, and shouldest thou read them then rebuild its ruin'. We can also understand how in the sentence Tig. VIII 50 ff.: 'may some future prince *e-nu-ma bîtu u sigurrâtu ušalbarûma e-na-ḫu anḫûsunu luddiš* when these buildings shall have become old and fallen to ruin, rebuild their ruins', *e-nu-ma* is wanting in one of the two duplicates; we may at least characterize this construction as harsh and not to be imitated. Cf. finally V R 64, 13 ff.: *ina palê'a kênim Sin . . . ana âli u bîti šâšu islimu iršû ta-a-a-ri ina rêš šarrûti'a dârîti ušabrû'inni šutti* 'during my well-established reign, when Sin turned towards that city and that house, took pity (upon them) — in the beginning of my lasting rule they (Sin und Marduk?) showed me a dream'. In this case the following translation is also admissible: 'during my reign Sin had turned towards that city', 'in the beginning of my reign he had shown me a dream' (new sentence beginning with l. 28: 'when the third year drew nigh'); for this construction of the verbs *islimu, iršû, ušabrû* as pluperfects see § 134, 2.

§ 149. Conditional clauses. On these we can, as yet, make only a few observations. In V R 25 1 ff. b, one of the so-called family laws, we read: *šumma aššata mussu izîrma ulmutî atta iḳtabi ana nâru inaddûšu* 'if a wife hates her husband and says: "thou art not my husband", let her be thrown into the river'; from this we are justified in inferring, first, that the verbs depending on *šumma* do not take on the final vowel (vocalic *auslaut*); secondly, that in such hypothetical protases of general application — not referring, that is, to a particular instance — the pret., not the pres., is the tense employed. Both inferences are confirmed by the law V R 25, 13 ff. b: 'if a householder *igurma imtût* hire a slave and the latter die etc.' The apodosis has in either case the present. If, on the other hand, the hypothetical clause has reference to a particular specified case — as, e. g., Desct. obv. 16: 'if thou dost not open the gate, I will smite the door in pieces' — then the protasis has likewise the present: *šumma lâ tapattâ bâbu amaḫḫaṣ daltum.* For the absence of the relative vowel cf. *šumma šarru iḳabbi* 'if the king thinks' (S. 1034, 14). A third observation is that in Assyrian, as in English, the hypothetical particle may be dispensed with altogether. Thus the text IV R 55 begins with the words: *šarru ana dîni lâ îgul* 'should the king not obey the laws' (his subjects will be destroyed, his land delivered over to ruin, *innammi* pres.); cf. Dicty. No. 63 (the reading *i-gul* there given is to be maintained as against Jensen's plausible emendation *i-zun* — the former being now found on the native tablets).

2) The joining together of several sentences.

a) *Copulative sentences.*

§ 150. Both nominal and verbal sentences are very often placed side by side without any connecting particle (*asyndeton*), as, for example, in the oft-recurring *abbul akkur ina išâti ašrup*; when, however, they are joined together by a copula, the latter is *u* in nominal sentences, or, more precisely in simple nominal sentences, and *ma* in verbal sentences and so-called complex nominal sentences, the latter particle being appended enclitically to the first verb (*v.* § 82). Cf. for the complex nominal sentences: *šunu liktûma anâku lum'id* 'let them perish, but let me increase' (K. 2455), *šî limûtma anâku lubluṭ* (IV R 66, 17 b); for the verbal sentences (which often consist entirely of a single verb): 'the troops *ina kakkê ušamkitma edu ul êzib* I cut down with the weapons (of war) and left none in life' (Senhb. I 57), '*arkânu ina adê'a iḫ-ṭi-ma ṭâbtî lâ iṣṣurma islâ nîr bêlûti'a* (Assurb. Sm. 284, 93 f.) 'the head *ikkisûnimma ana Ninâ ûbilûni*' (99, 13 f.), 'the palaces which in the course of years *umdašerâma ênaḫâma 'abtâ* had been forsaken and had fallen into decay and were now heaps of ruins' (Tig. VI 98). In cases like Senhb. I 26 f.: *ana ekallišu êrumma aptêma bît niṣirtišu*, the first *ma* is at most the copula, the second being added for emphasis (*v.* § 79, *a*); it is possible however that both are employed in the latter capacity, so that we should translate: 'into his palace I entered; I opened his treasure-chambers'. In compound verbal sentences like the above, it is very common to find the vowel *a* added to the first verb (with *ma: amma*); the second also ends occasionally in *a*. Examples: 'the horses etc. *ušêṣamma šallatiš amnu*' (Senhb. I 74), 'from Elam *innabtamma ana Ninâ illikamma unaššiḳ šêpê'a*' (Esarh. II 37 ff.), *tappuḫamma . . . tapti* 'thou didst come forward and didst open' (IV R 20 No. 2); *ana Ninâ išpuramma unaššiḳ(a) šêpê'a* (V R 3, 19), *illikamma . . . urriḫa kakkêšu* (Assurb. Sm. 175, 45).

For the occurrence side by side of permansive and preterite forms, in which there should be nothing to astonish us since states and events frequently succeed each other, see the passage Tig. VI 98, quoted above in § 150, also the words Tig. I 32 f. quoted in § 147, 1, b and there, in my opinion, explained for the first time. Cf. also for the permansive, followed by the preterite: 'the city moat *ša abtuma iprâti imlû*' (I R 28, 7 b); without a connective: *e-nu-ma aldâku abbanû anâku* 'since I was born, was created' (Neb. I 27). A present may, of course, also follow a permansive describing a condition in the present, without it being necessary for us to explain the clause con- § 151.

taining the former as a circumstantial clause like the cases discussed in § 152; e. g. Neb. Bab. I 19 ff. (similarly Nerigl. I 17 f.): *anâku ana Marduk bêli'a kânâk lâ baṭlâk* 'I cleave continually to Merodach, my lord, which pleaseth him well, every morning *i-ta-ma-am libbam* my heart reflects'. For the pret. and pres. followed by the perm. cf.: 'the house *ênaḫma 'abit*' (e. g. Tig. VIII 4); 'Nebuchadnezzar who the way of their divinity *išteni'û bitluḫu bêlûtsun* keeps in view, is full of reverence for their majesty' (Neb. I 9 f.), *arâmu puluḫti ilûtišunu pitluḫâk bêlûtsun* (I 38 f.).

b) Circumstantial Clauses.

§ 152. Should an event narrated by a preterite be accompanied by more precise qualifications, specifying in what state the subject was during the time of the action, what was the aim of the latter, or in what state another subject was during the same period, these more precise qualifications follow in the present; this tense, in such a case, is to be rendered in English by participles, participial phrases, and such like. Examples: *innabitma ibaḳam ziḳnâšu* 'he fled, tearing his beard' (K. 2674 obv. 15), 'every year to Nineveh *ilikamma unaššaḳa šêpê'a* he came to kiss my feet' (III R 15 col. II 26), *pâšu êpušma iḳabbi izakkara ana* 'he opened his mouth to speak, to announce to . . .'

(Nimr. Ep., passim), *uktammisma attašab abakki* 'I drew back, sitting down weeping' (Nimr. Ep. XI, 130), *innendûma šarrâni kilallân ippušû taḫâza* (V R 55, 29), *Êa mârašu issîma amâta ušaḫḫaz* 'Ea called his son, giving (him) commandment' (IV R 5, 57 b) — observe in all these examples the emphatic *ma* with the principal verb; *uptarriṣ iḳabbi umma* 'he lied, speaking thus' (Beh. 90—92), *il-si-ka Ištâr išakkanka ṭêmu* 'Ishtar called thee, giving thee commandment' *umma*, (Assurb. Sm. 124, 58), 'like Rammân *elišunu ašgum nablu elišunu ušazanin* (Assurn. II 106), 'my warriors, who through Kardunias did march (*ittanallakû*) *ukabbasû Kaldu* trampling on Chaldea' (Assurb. Sm. 171, 5). In all the illustrations now given the subject of the present is the same as that of the preterite. The subjects however may be different: cf. *ilûsa ušappâ illakâ di-ma-a-a* 'I melted (?) her divinity with tears' (Assurb. Sm. 120, 28), 'tribute etc. I laid upon him (*êmidsuma*) *išâṭ âbšâni*' (Senhb. II 64), 'so and so I set upon his throne (*ušêšibma*) *išâṭa abšâni*' (Esarh. II 54). The circumstantial clause may even precede the principal verb; cf. Nimr. Ep. 141. 143: 'the dove (swallow) flew hither and thither *manzazu ul ipaššimma* (var. *ipaššumma*) *issaḫra*, but as there was no place of rest she returned'. — Permansives may also be followed by circumstantial clauses with the present.

Examples: 'the inhabitants, who (*lâ sanḳû*) did not obey their viceroys *lâ inamdinû mandattu*' (V R 9, 117 f.), 'his numberless troops *kakkêšunu ṣandûma išaddiḫâ idâšu*' (V R 35, 16); cf. also the well-known: *šabrû utûlma inaṭal šutta,* V R 10, 4 b etc. The circumstantial clause may also precede the principal verb as in K. 3437 obv. 32: *Bêl inaṭalma eši mâlakšu* 'when Bel beheld it, his gait was troubled'; V R 3, 80 f.: *eliš ina šaptêšu itammâ ṭubbâti šaplânu libbašu ka-ṣir ni-ir-tu.* — Note finally a passage which is interesting from a syntactical point of view, Senhb. VI 9 ff.: 'the chariots *ša râkibušin dîkûma u šina muššurâma râmânuššin ittanallakâ* the charioteer of which had fallen, while they were forsaken and were careering about by themselves'.

PARADIGMATA.

A. Pronomen.

1. Pronomina personalia separata.

a) *cum vi nominativi.*

Singularis.		Pluralis.	
1. c.	*a-na-ku*, *ana-ku*	1. c.	*a-ni-ni*, *a-ni-nu*, *ni-(i-)ni*, *ni-nu*
2. m.	*at-ta*	2. m.	*at-tu-nu*
2. f.	*at-ti*	2. f.	
3. m.	*šú-ú*, *šú-u*	3. m.	*šú-nu*, *šu-nu*, *šun*
3. f.	*ši-i*	3. f.	*ši-na*, *šin*

b) *cum vi genitivi et accusativi.*

Singularis.		Pluralis.	
1. c.	*ia-(a-)ti*, *ia-a-tú*, *ia-a-ši*, *a-a-ši*, semel *a-ia-ši*	1. c.	*ni-ia-ti*, *ni-(i)a-šim* (uno adhuc loco repertum)
2. m.	*ka-a-tú*, *ka-a-ša*, *ka-a-ti*, *ka-a-ši*	2. m.	*ka-a-šu-nu*
2. f.	*ka-a-ti*, *ka-a-ši*		
3. m.	*šá-a-šú*, *ša-(a-)šú*, *ša-a-šu*, raro *šu-a-šú*, *šú-a-šum*	3. m.	*šá-a-šú-nu*, *ša-a-šu-nu*, *ša-a-šu-un*
3. f.	*ša-a-ša*, *ša-ši*		

2. Pronomina suffixa.

a) *nominalia.*

Singularis.		Pluralis.	
1. c.	*-î*, *-a* (forma orig. *ia*)	1. c.	*-ni*, raro *-nu*
2. m.	*-ka*, rarius *-ku*	2. m.	*-ku-nu*, *-ku-un*, *-kun*
2. f.	*-ki*	2. f.	
3. m.	*-šú*, *-šu*, *-š*	3. m.	*-šú-nu*, *šu-nu*, *šu-un*, *-šun*; rarius *-šu-nu-ti*, *-šu-nu-ú-te*
3. f.	*-ša*	3. f.	*-ši-na*, *-ši-in*

b) *verbalia.*

Singularis.		Pluralis.	
1. c.	*-a(n)-ni*, *-in-ni*; rarius *-ni*	1. c.	*-an-na-ši*, *-a-na-ši*, *-an-na-a-šu*
2. m.	*-ka*; *-ak-ka*, *-ak*, *-ik-ka*, raro *-ak-ku*	2. m.	*-ku-nu-ši*; *-ak-ku-nu-šu*
2. f.	*-ki*; *-ak-ki*, *-ik-ki*	2. f.	
3. m.	*-šú*, *-šu*, *-š*; *-aš-šu*, *-aš*	3. m.	*-šu-nu*, *-šú-nu-ú-ti*, *-šu-nu-ti*, *-šú-nu-ú-tu*, *-šu-nu-tú*, *-šu-nu-tu*, rarius *-šu-nu-ši*; *-aš-šu-nu*, *-aš-šu-nu-tú*
3. f.	*-ši*, *-š*; *-aš-ši*	3. f.	*-ši-na*, *-ši-na-a-tú*, *-ši-na-ši-im*, *-ši-na-(a-)ti*, *-ši-na-a-tim*; *-aš-ši-na-a-tú*, *-aš-ši-ni-ti*

3. Pronomina demonstrativa.

a) *šu'atu* ‚ille, is'.

(semper substantivo postponitur.)

Singularis.	Pluralis.
m. *šú-a-tu*, *šú-a-tú*, *šú-a-ti*, *šú-a-tum*, *šú-a-tim*, *šá-a-tu*, *ša-a-tu*, *šá-a-tim*, *ša-a-tú*, *šá-a-ti* (omnes formae cum vi cujuslibet casus)	m. *šú-a-tu-nu*, *šu-a-tú-nu*, *ša-(a-)tu-nu*, *ša-a-tú-nu*, *šá-tu-nu*
f. *ši-a-ti*	f. *šú-a-ti-na*, *ša-(a-)ti-na*, *šá-ti-na*

Vice earum formarum etiam hae usurpantur:

Singularis.	Pluralis.
m. *šú-u*, *šu-ú*, *šú-ú*, *šú*; raro *ša-a-šú*	m. *šú-nu*, *šu-nu*; *šú-nu-ti*, *šu-nu-ti*
f. *ši-i*	f. *ši-na-(a-)ti*, *ši-na-ti-na*

b) *annû* ‚hic, hoc', Fem. *annîtu* ‚haec, hoc'.

Singularis.	Pluralis.
m. N. *an-ni-ú* (etiam Acc.) G. *an-ni-i*, *an-ni-e*, *an-ni* A. *an-na-a*, *an-ni-a-am* (rarissime)	m. *an-nu-(ú-)tu*, *an-nu-(ú-)ti*, *an-nu-tú*, *an-nu-te*, *a-nu-te*
f. *an-ni-tu*, *an-ni-tú*, *an-ni-ti* (Gen.), *an-ni-ta* et *an-ni-tú* (Acc.)	f. *an-na-a-tú*, *an-na-a-ti*, *an-na-a-te*, *an-ni-tú*, *an-ni-ti*

c) *ullû* ‚ille, illud'.

Singularis.	Pluralis.
m. *ul-lu-ú* (Nom., Acc.), *ul-li-i* et *ul-li-e* (Gen.)	m. *ul-lu-ú-tu*

d) *agâ* (*agannu*) ‚hic',

vicem explens generis masculini, feminini et neutrius, atque omnium casuum et utriusque numeri.

a-ga-a, *a-ga*, *a-ga-'*

Speciatim vi

Singularis.	Pluralis.
	m. *a-gan-nu-tu* (Acc.), *a-ga-nu-te*(Acc.,Gen.)
f. *a-ga-ta*, *a-ga-a-ta* (Acc., Gen.)	f. *a-ga-ni-e-tú*, *a-ga-ni-e-tum* (Nom., Gen.)

Cfr. *agâšû* ‚hic, hoc'.

Sing. *a-ga-šú-ú*, *a-ga-šú-u* (Nom., Gen., Acc.)

Plur. *a-ga-šu-nu* (Gen.)

4. Pronomen relativum,

omnium casuum, generum et numerorum:

ša

Pron. rel. generale.

Masc., Fem. *ma*(*n*)-*nu* (*ša*) ‚quisquis'.

Neutr. *mi-na-a*; *man-ma* (h. e. probabilissime *min-ma* vel *mim-ma*) *ša*, *mi-im-ma* (*ša*), saepissime -*ma* (h. e. *mim-ma*) et (h. e. *mimma*) scriptum, *-mu-ú*, *-mu-u* (legendum *mim-mu-u*) ‚quidquid'.

Masc., Fem. et Neutr. *ma-la*, *mal*; *am-mar*.

5. Pronomina interrogativa.

Nonnisi substantive:

Masc., Fem. *man-nu* (Nom., Acc.) ‚quis? quem?'.

Neutr. *mi-nu(-ú)* (Nom., Acc.); *mi-ni(-i)*, *mi-ni-e*, (Gen.); *mi-na-a*, *mi-nam* (Acc.) ‚quid?'.

Substantive et adjective: *a-a-ú* ‚qui?'.

6. Pronomina indefinita.

Substantive et adjective:

Masc., Fem. omnium casuum: *ma-nu-man*, *man-ma-an*, *ma-am-ma-an*, *ma-am-man*, *ma-am-ma-na*, *ma-ma-na*; *ma-na-a-ma*, *ma-nam-ma*, *ma-na-ma*, *man-ma*, *ma-am-ma*, *ma-ma* ‚aliquis, aliqua', cum negatione *lâ* vel *ul* ‚nemo'. Saepe *-ma* () h. e. *mamma* scriptum.

Neutr. *mi-im-ma*, *mi-ma*, etiam *man-ma* (an legendum est *min-ma*, *mim-ma*?) ‚aliquid'. Saepissime *-ma* (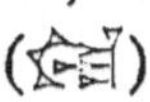) h. e. *mimma* scriptum.

Substantive et adjective: Masc. (Nom., Acc.) *a-a-um-ma*, *ia-um-ma*, *a-ia-um-ma*, *a-a-am-ma* (Acc.) ‚aliquis'.

B. Verbu

1. Verbun

inclusis verbis m

kašâdu ,expugnare, vincere'

		Praesens	Praeteritum	Imperativus
Sing.:				
I 1.	3.m.	*ikášad*; *išálal*	*ikšud***); *išlul*	
	3.f.	*takášad*	*takšud*	
	2.m.	*takášad*	*takšud*	*kušud*
	2.f.	*takášadî*	*takšudî*	*kušudî*
	1.c.	*akášad*	*akšud*	
Pl.:	3.m.	*ikašadû*(*ni*,rarius *nu*)	*ikšudû*(*ni*, *nu*)	
	3.f.	*ikašadâ*(*ni*)	*ikšudâ*(*ni*)	[*šudâ*
	2.m.	*takášadû*	*takšudû*	*kušudû* (etiam *ku-*
	2.f.	*takášadâ*	*takšudâ*	*kušudâ*(*ni*)
	1.c.	*nikášad*	*nikšud*	
II 1.		*ukaššad*	*ukaššid*, *ukéšid*	*kuššid*, *kaššid*
III 1.		*ušakšad*	*ušakšid*, *ušekšid*	*šukšid*
IV 1.		*ikkášad* (f. *takkášad*)	*ikkašid*	*nakšid*
I 2.		*iktášad*	*iktášad***)	*kitášad*, *kitšad*
II 2.		*uktaššad*	*uktaššid*, *uktéšid*	
III 2.		*uštakšad*	*uštakšid*, *uštekšid*	*šutakšid*
IV 2.		[*ittakšad*]	*ittakšad*	
I 3.		*iktanášad*	*iktanášad*	
IV 3.		*ittanakšad*	*ittanakšad* **)	

*) Formae Praesentis, Praeteriti et Permansivi I 1 extra dubitationei exemplis probari possint; reliquae autem formae omnes exemplis probatae sun

**) Aut *ipḳid* (Praes. *ipáḳid*, Imp. *piḳid*), *iṣbat* (Praes. *iṣábat*, Imp. *ṣabat*

trilitterum.*)

firmum

diae geminatae.

šalâlu ‚in servitutem redigere, diripere‘.

Participium	Permansivum		Infinitivus	
kâš(i)du; *šâ-* [*lilu*	*kašid*;	*šal*	*kašâdu*;	*šalâlu*
	kašdat	*šallat*		
	kašdât(a), *kašidât*	*šallât(a)*		
	kašdâti	*šallâti*		
	kašdâk(u)	*šallâk(u)*		
	kašdû(ni)	*šallû(ni)*		
	kašdâ	*šallâ*		
	kašdâtunu	*šallâtunu*		
	kašdâni (raro *nu*)	*šallâni*		
mukaššidu	*kuššud*;	*šul* (2. m. [*šullâta*)	*kuššudu*	
mušakšidu	*šukšud*		*šukšudu*	
mukkaš(i)du	*nakšud*		*nakšudu*;	*našlulu* et *našálulu*
muktaš(i)du	*kitšud*, raro *kitášud*		*kitášudu*, *kitšudu*,	*šitálulu* et *šitlulu*
muktaššidu	[*kutaššud*]		*kutaššudu*	
muštakšidu	*šutakšud*		*šitakšudu* [*šutakšudu*]	
muttakšidu			*itakšudu*;	*itašlulu*

positae sunt, quamvis non omnes in omnibus verbi firmi et infirmi generibus

— Praet. I 2 *iptêḳid*. — Cfr. Praet. IV 3: *ittanabriḳ*.

2. Verbum

naṣâru ‚servare, tueri‘;

		Praesens	Praeteritum		Imperativus
Singularis:					
I 1.	3.m.	*indṣar*; *inddin* *)	*iṣṣur*;	*iddin*	
	3.f.	*tandṣar tanddin*	*taṣṣur*	*taddin*	
	2.m.	*tandṣar tanddin*	*taṣṣur*	*taddin*	*uṣur*; *idin*
	2.f.	*tandṣarî* etc.	*taṣṣurî*	etc.	*id(i)nî*
	1.c.	*andṣar*	*aṣṣur*		
Pluralis:					
	3.m.	*indṣarû*	*iṣṣurû*	*iddinû(ni)*	
	3.f.	*indṣarâ*	*iṣṣurâ*	*iddinâ*	
	2.m.	*tandṣarû*	*taṣṣurû*		
	2.f.	*tandṣarâ*	*taṣṣurâ*		*uṣrâ*
	1.c.	*nindṣar*	*niṣṣur*		
II 1.		*unaṣṣar*	*unaṣṣir*		*nuṣṣir*
III 1.		*ušanṣar*, *ušaṣṣar*	*ušanṣir*		*šunṣir*
IV 1.		*inndṣar*	*innaṣir*;	*innadin*	
I 2.		*ittdṣar*	*ittdṣar*;	*ittddin*	
II 2.		*uttaṣṣar*	*uttaṣṣir*		
III 2.					
IV 2.					
I 3.		*ittand(n)dan*	*ittand(n)din* *)		
IV 3.		*ittandṣar*			

*) Et *iddan*, v. § 100.

rimae ב.

adânu ‚dare'.

Participium	Permansivum		Infinitivus	
nâṣiru; *nâdinu*	*naṣir*;	*nadin*	*naṣâru*;	*nadânu*
	naṣrat	*nadnat*		
	naṣrâta	*nadnâta*		
	etc.	etc.		

munaṣṣir		*nuṣṣuru*
mušanṣiru		*šuṣṣuru*, *šunṣuru*
	nanṣuru	*nanṣuru*
muttaṣiru		*itáṣuru*, *itṣuru*
	[*utaṣṣur*]	[*utaṣṣuru*]

3. Verbum

aḫâzu ‚capere, prehendere‘

	Praesens		Praeteritum		Imperativus
Singularis:					
I 1. 3.m.	*iḫḫaz* (rarius *i'áḫaz*);	[*irriš* (*erriš*)	*êḫuz*;	*êriš*	
3.f.	*taḫḫaz*	*tirriš*	*tâḫuz*	*têriš*	
2.m.	*taḫḫaz*	*tirriš*	*tâḫuz*	*têriš*	*aḫuz*
2.f.	*taḫḫazî*	*tirrišî*	*tâḫuzî*	*têrišî*	*aḫzî*
1.c.	*aḫḫaz*		*âḫuz*	*êriš***)	
Pluralis:					
3.m.	*iḫḫazû*		*êḫuzû*	*êrišû*	
3.f.	*iḫḫazâ*		*êḫuzâ*	*êrišâ*	
2.m.	*taḫḫazû*		*tâḫuzû*		*aḫuzû*
2.f.	*taḫḫazâ*		*tâḫuzâ*		*aḫuzâ*
1.c.	*niḫḫaz*		*nîḫuz*	*nîriš*	
II 1.	*uḫḫaz*		*u'aḫḫiz*, *uḫḫiz*		*uḫḫiz*
III 1.	*ušâḫaz*, *ušaḫḫaz*		*ušâḫiz*		*šûḫiz*
IV 1.	*innáḫaz*		*innaḫiz*		
I 2.	*itáḫaz*;	*etériš*	*itáḫaz* (3. f. *tâtá-ḫaz*); *etériš*		
II 2.	*uttaḫḫaz*		*u(t)taḫḫiz*		
III 2.	*uštâḫaz*, *uštaḫḫaz*		*uštâḫiz*		
IV 2.	*ittáḫaz* (*ittanḫaz*)		*ittáḫiz*		
I 3.			*etanáḫaz*		
IV 3.	*ittanáḫaz*(*ittananḫaz*)				

*) Cfr. stirpis אלל ‚splendere‘ Perm. Sing. 3. m. [*el*], f. *ellit*.

**) *Apâru* ‚vestire‘ format *âpir* (Sanh. V 56), fortasse forma antiqua.

primae $\aleph_1$.

rêšu ,cupere'.

Participium	Permansivum	Infinitivus
âḫizu	(')*aḫiz* *)	*aḫâzu*; *erêšu*
	aḫzat	
	aḫzâta	
	aḫzâti	
	aḫzâku	
	aḫzû(ni)	
	aḫzâ	
	aḫzâtunu	
	aḫzâni	
nu'aḫḫiz, *muḫḫiz*	*uḫḫuz*	*uḫḫuzu*
nušâḫizu		*šûḫuzu*
nunnaḫ(i)zu	*na'ḫuz*, *nâḫuz*, *nan-*[*ḫuz*	*na'ḫuzu*, *nâḫuzu*, [*nanḫuzu*
		itâḫuzu, *itḫuzu*
		[*utaḫḫuzu*] *utéḫuzu*
nuštâḫizu	*šutâḫuz*	*šutâḫ(u)zu*

4. Verbum

etêḳu ,movere';

	Praesens			Praeteritum		
Singularis:						
I 1. 3.m.	*ettiḳ*;	*eppuš* (*ippuš*);	*errub* (*irrub*)	*êtiḳ*;	*êpuš*;	*êrub*
3.f.	*tettiḳ*	*teppuš*	*terrub*	*têtiḳ*	*têpuš*	*têrub*
2.m.	*tettiḳ*	*teppuš*	*terrub*	*têtiḳ*	*têpuš*	*têrub*
2.f.	*tettiḳî*	*teppušî*	*terrubî*	*têtiḳî*	*têpušî*	*têrubî*
1.c.	*ettiḳ*	*eppuš*	*errub*	*êtiḳ*	*êpuš*	*êrub*
Pluralis:						
3.m.	*ettiḳû*	*eppušû*	*errubû*	*êtiḳû*	*êpušû*	*êrubû*
3.f.	*ettiḳâ*	*eppušâ*	*errubâ*	*êtiḳâ*	*êpušâ*	*êrubâ*
2.m.	*tettiḳû*	*teppušû*	*terrubû*	*têtiḳû*	*têpušû*	*têrubû*
2.f.	*tettiḳâ*	*teppušâ*	*terrubâ*	*têtiḳâ*	*têpušâ*	*têrubâ*
1.c.	*nittiḳ*	*nippuš*	*nirrub*	*nîtiḳ*	*nîpuš*	*nîrub*
II 1.	*uttaḳ*			*uttiḳ*; *uppiš*		
III 1.	*ušêtaḳ* etc.			*ušâtiḳ*, *ušêtiḳ* etc.		
IV 1.	*innéteḳ* (*innétiḳ*, *innitiḳ*)			*innitiḳ*, *innetiḳ*, *innipuš*		
I 2.	*etétiḳ*			*itátiḳ*, *itétiḳ*, *etétiḳ*; *itápuš*, *itépuš*, *etépuš**); *itérub*, *etárub*		
II 2.				*ut(t)attiḳ*, *ut(t)ettiḳ*		
III 2.				*uštêtiḳ* etc.		
IV 2.						
I 3.				*itenitiḳ*; *etanápuš*,		
IV 3.				[*etenépuš*		

*) 1. Pers. *etátiḳ*, *etêtiḳ*; *etápuš*, *etêpuš*, etiam *etápaš* (rarissime

imae ℵ₄.₅ (y).

šu ,facere'; *erêbu* ,intrare'.

Imperativus	Participium	Permansivum		Infinitivus
	êtiḳu; *êpišu*;	*etiḳ*;	*epuš*	*etêḳu*; *epêšu*;
	[*êribu*	(فَعَل)		[*erêbu*
		etḳit		
; *epuš*; *erub*		*etḳêt(a)*		
(*erba, ir-ba*)				
eṛbî (*ir-bi*)		*etḳêti*		
		etḳêku		
		etḳû		
		etḳâ		
		etḳêtunu		
		etḳêni		
				utluku
ḳ, *šêtiḳ*; *šûrib*	*mušêtiḳu* etc.	*šûtuḳ*		*šûtuḳu* etc.,
				[*šêtuḳu*
ʾḳ ; *itrub*	*mut(t)átiḳu*;			*itátuḳu, itétuḳu,*
	[*mutéribu*			[*etétuḳu*
				utétuḳu
	muštêtiḳu			*šutêpušu*
š).				

5. Verbu[m]

alâk

Singularis:	Praesens	Praeteritum
I 1. 3.m.	*illak*	*illik*
3.f.	*tallak*	*tallik*
2.m.	*tallak*	*tallik*
2.f.	*tallakî*	*tallikî*
1.c.	*allak*	*a(l)lik*
Pluralis:		
3.m.	*illakû*	*illikû(ni)*
3.f.	*illakâ*	*illikâ*
2.m.	*tallakû*	*tallikû*
2.f.	*tallakâ*	*tallikâ*
1.c.	*nillak*	*ni(l)lik*
III 1.		*ušâlik* (3.m., 1.c. Sing.)
Singularis:		
I 2. 3.m.	*ittâlak*	*ittâlak*
3.f.		*tattâlak*
2.m.		*tattâlak*
2.f.		*tattâlakî*
1.c.		*attâlak*
Pluralis:		
3.m.	*ittâlakû*	*ittâlakû*
1.c.	*nittâlak*	*nittâlak*
Singularis:		
I 3. 3.m.	*ittanâlak*(Plur.3.m. *ittanâlakû*)	*ittanâlak* (Plur. 3. m. *ittanâlakû*, f. *ittanâlakâ*)

rimae א₂ (ה).

re‘.

Imperativus	Participium	Permansivum	Infinitivus
	âliku		*alâku*
alik, *al-ka* *alkî*			
	mušâliku	*šûluk*,3.f.*šûlukat*, Plur. *šûlukâ*	*šûluku*
	muttâliku		*italluku*

6. Verbu

ma'âdu ,multum ess

	Praesens	Praeteritum
Singularis:		
I 1. 3.m.	*imâ'id*	*im'id*, *imid*; *iš'al*, *ibar*
3.f.	*tamâ'id*	*tam'id*
2.m.	*tamâ'id*	*tam'id*
2.f.	*tamâ'idî*	*tam'idî*
1.c.	*amâ'id*	*am'id* *abar*
Pluralis:		
3.m.	*imâ'idû*; *ibarrû*	*im'idû*, *imidû*; *iš'alû*
3.f.	*imâ'idâ*	*im'idâ*
2.m.	*tamâ'idû*	*tam'idû*
2.f.	*tamâ'idâ*	*tam'idâ*
1.c.	*nimâ'id*	*nim'id*
II 1.	*uma'ad*, raro *umâd* (Plur. *umaddû*)	*uma'id*
III 1.		*ušam'id*
IV 1.		
I 2.		*imtâ'id***) ; *ištâ'al*
II 2.		
III 2.		
IV 2.		
I 3.	*imtanâ'ad*, *imtanâd*	[*imtanâ'id*?]**) ; *ištanâ'al*
IV 3.		

*) Flexio verbi *râmu* (ר$א_3$ם) ,misericordem esse, amare' haec raro Praet. *irâm*, 1. c. *a-ri-im*; Imp. *rêm*, *rîm* (e. g. *rîmanni*); P

**) Cfr. *ittâ'id* ,extulit, glorificavit'.

...diae $א_1$ ($א_{2.3}$).*)

...*ilu* ‚interrogare'; *ba'âru* ‚extrahere'.

...erativus	Participium	Permansivum	Infinitivus
	mâ'idu	*ma'id* (*mâdi*)	*ma'âdu*, *mâdu*;
ša'al		*ma'idat*	[*ba'âru*, *bâru*
		ma'idât(*a*)	
		ma'idâti	
		ma'idâku, *mâdâku*	
		ma'idû	
		ma'idâ	
		ma'idâtunu	
		ma'idâni	
id	*muma'id*		*mu'udu*
...'*id*,*šumid*			*šum'udu*
šital	*mumta'idu*; [*muštâlu*		[*šita'ulu*] *šitûlu*

...s. *irâm*, *tarâm*, *arâm*, *irâmû*; Praet. *irêm* (cfr. *i-ri-en-šu*), *i-ri-im*, ...*nu*, *râmu*; Inf. *râmu*.

7. Verbu

bêlu (saepissime *pêlu* scriptur

	Praesens	Praeteritum	Imperativu
Singularis:			
I 1. 3.m.	*ibêl* (*izâkḳa, izêkḳu* Rel.)	*ibêl*	
3.f.			
2.m.			
2.f.			
1.c.		*abêl*	
Pluralis:			
3.m.		*ibêlû*(*ni*)	
3.f.			
2.m.			
2.f.			
1.c.			
II 1.	*uba'al*	*uba'il*	
III 1.*)	[*ušpêl*]	[*ušpêl*]	
I 2.		*ibtêl*	
III 2.*)	[*uštépêl*]		
I 3.		*ibtenêl*	

*) De formis angulatis uncinis inclusis *ušpêl*, *mušpêlu*, *uštépêl* e

ediae א$_4$.

mare, dominari'.

Participium	Permansivum	Infinitivus
bêlu	*bêl*	*bêlu*
	bêlit	
	bêlêt(a)	
	bêlêti	
	bêlêku	
	bêlû(ni)	
	bêlâ	
	bêlêtunu	
	bêlêni	
	bu'ul	
[*mušpêlu*]		[*šubêlu*]
mubtêlu		*bitêlu*

§ 85 et 106. — Stirpium IV 1—3. II 2 formas nondum adhuc inveni.

8. Verbu:

ma

	Praesens	Praeteritum	Imperativu
Singularis:			
I 1. 3.m.	*imáṣi*	*imṣi* *)	
3.f.	*tamáṣi*	*tamṣi*	
2.m.	*tamáṣi*	*tamṣi*	*miṣi*
2.f.	*tamáṣî*	*tamṣî*	
1.c.	*amáṣi*	*amṣi*	
Pluralis:			
3.m.	*imaṣû(ni, nu)*	*imṣû*	
3.f.	*imáṣâ*	*imṣâ*	
2.m.	*tamáṣû*	*tamṣû*	
2.f.	*tamáṣâ*	*tamṣâ*	
1.c.	*nimáṣi*	*nimṣi*	
II 1.	*umaṣṣi*	*umaṣṣi*	*muṣṣi*
III 1.		*ušamṣi* *)	
IV 1.		*immaṣi*	
I 2.	*imtáṣi*	*imtáṣi*	
II 2.		*umtaṣṣi*	
III 2.		*uštamṣi*	
IV 2.			
I 3.	*imtanáṣi*	*imtanáṣi*	
IV 3.	*ittanamṣi*		

*) Cum vocali *a*: *imṣâ*, *ušamṣâ*.

rtiae $א_1$.

venire'.

Participium	Permansivum	Infinitivus
mâṣû (*mâṣi*)	*maṣi*	*maṣû*
	maṣat (scrib. *ma-ṣa-at*)	
	maṣât(*a*)	
	maṣâti	
	maṣâku	
	maṣû(*ni*)	
	maṣâ(*ni*)	
	masâtunu	
	maṣâni	
		muṣṣû
mušamṣû, mušemṣû	*šumṣu*, 3. f. *šumṣat*	*šumṣû*
muštamṣû		

9. Verbum tertia

tebû (*tibû*) ‚venire‘

	Praesens		Praeteritum	
Singularis:				
I 1. 3.m.	*itábi*, *itébi*(*itébe*);	*ipáti*, *ipéti*(*ipéte*)	*itbi*, *itbe*;	*ipti*, *ipte**)
3.f.	*tatábi*, *tetébi*	*tepéti*	*tatbi*	*tapti*
2.m.	*tatábi*, *tatébi*, *tetébi*	*tepéti*	*tatbi*	*tapti*
2.f.	etc.	etc.	*tatbî*	*taptî*
1.c.	*atábi*, *atébe*		*atbi*	*apti*
Pluralis:				
3.m.	*itébû*		*itbû*(*ni*)	*iptû*(*ni*)
3.f.	*itébâ*		*itbâ*(*ni*)	*iptâ*
2.m.			*tatbû*	*taptû*
2.f.			*tatbâ*	*taptâ*
1.c.	*nitébi*		*nitbi*	*nipti*
II 1.		*u-pat-ta***)	*utabbi*, *utebbi*;	*upatti*
III 1.		*u-šap-ta***)	*ušatbi*;	*ušapti*
IV 1.	*ittábi*		*ittabi*, *ittebi*;	*ippeti*
I 2.			*ittábi*, *ittébi*;	*iptéti*
II 2.			*uttabbi*, *uttebbi*	
III 2.				
IV 2.				
I 3.			*ittenibi*	
IV 3.				

*) Cum voc. *a*: *itbâ*, *iptâ*.

**) Cum voc. *a*? v. § 109.

א$_{4.5}$ (ע) et א$_3$ (ח$_1$).

petû (*pitû*) ‚aperire‘.

Imperativus	Participium	Permansivum	Infinitivus
	têbû; *pêtû*	*tebi*; *peti*	*tebû*; *petû*
		tebat	
piti (*pitâ*)		*tebâta*	
pi-ti-e		*tebâti*	
		tebâku	
		tebûni	
tibâ		*tebâ*	
	mutabbû; *mupattû*,	*tubbu*	*tubbû*; *puttû*
šutbi, *šupti* [(*šuptâ*)	[*mupét*(*t*)*û*	*šutbu* f. *šutbat*	*šutbû*
titábe; *pitáte*			
			tutabbû

10. Verbum

banû ‚aedificare, procreare‘;

	Praesens	Praeteritum		Imperativus	
Singularis:					
I 1. 3.m.	*ibáni(ibéni)*	*ibni**)	*imnu*		
3.f.	*tabáni*	*tabni*	*tamnu*		
2.m.	*tabáni*	*tabni*	*tamnu*	*bini*;	*munu*
2.f.	*tabánî*	*tabnî*	*tamnî*	*binî*	
1.c.	*abáni*; *amá-* [*nu*	*abni*	*amnu*		
Pluralis:					
3.m.	*ibánû*	*ibnû*	*imnû*		
3.f.	*ibánâ*	*ibnâ*	*imnâ*		
2.m.	*tabánû*	*tabnû*	*tamnû*		
2.f.	*tabánâ*	*tabnâ*	*tamnâ*		
1.c.	*nibáni*	*nibni*	*nimnu*		
II 1.	*ubanni*	*ubanni**), *ubenni*		*bunni*	
III 1.	*ušabni**)	*ušabni*, *ušebni*		*šubni*(*šubnâ*)	
IV 1.	*ibbáni*	*ibbani*		*nabni*	
I 2.		*ibtáni*, *ibténi*; *imtáni*			
II 2.					
III 2.		*uštabni*, *uštebni*			
IV 2.	*ittabni*	*ittabni*, *ittebni*			
I 3.		*ibtanáni*			
IV 3.					

*) Cum voc. *a*: *ibnâ*, *ubannâ*, *ušabnâ*.
**) In propositione relativa *bunnû*, *šubnû*.

tertiae י et ו.

m a n û ‚numerare, aestimare'.

Participium	Permansivum	Infinitivus	
bânû (*bâni*, f. *bânîtu* [et *bântu*)	*bani*	*banû*;	*manû*
	banat		
	banât(a)		
	banâti		
	banâku		
	banû		
	banâ		
	banâtunu		
	banâni		
mubannû	*bunnu* **)	*bunnû*	
mušabnû	*šubnu***),3. f. *šub-* [*nat*	*šubnû*	
mubtánû, *mubténû*		*bitannû*, *bitnû*	
		butennû	
	šutabnu, *šutebnu*, [3. f. *šutebnat*	*šutabnû*	

11. Verbum

aš âbu ‚sedere, habitare‘

Singularis:	Praesens	Praeteritum	Imperativus
I 1. 3.m.	uššab	ûšib;	îšir
3.f.	tuššab	tûšib	tîšir
2.m.	tuššab	tûšib	tîšir šib
2.f.	tuššabî	tûšibî	etc.
1.c.	uššab	ûšib	
Pluralis:			
3.m.	uššabû	ûšibû(ni), ûšbûni	
3.f.	uššabâ(ni)	ûšibâ	
2.m.	tuššabû	tûšibû	
2.f.	tuššabâ	tûšibâ	
1.c.	nuššab	nûšib	

II 1.	u'aššab et uššab	uššib	
III 1.	ušâšab, ušeššab;	ušêšib*);	ušêšir šûšib, šêšib
	ušeššir, ušênak		
IV 1.			

I 2.	ittášab	ittášib**), ittûšib;	
II 2.		utaššib	[itášir
III 2.		uštêšir uštêšib, (ussîšib)*);	šutêšir
IV 2.			[uštêšir

I 3.	ittanášab
IV 3.	

---

*) Rarius ušâšib, uštâšib, mušâšibu.
**) Verbi arâdu (ורד) Praet. I 2 : ittárad.

primae ו et י.

išâru(?) ‚rectum esse'.

Participium	Permansivum	Infinitivus
âš(i)bu	*ašib*; cfr. *iši*	*ašâbu*
	ašbat	
	ašbâta	
	ašbâti	
	ašbâku: cfr. *išâku*	
	(')*ašbû*	
	ašbâ	
	ašbâtunu	
	ašbâni	
mu'aššibu	*uššub*; *uššur*	*uššubu*; *uššuru*
*mušêšibu**); *mušêširu*	*šûšub*	*šûšubu*, *šêšubu*
muttâšibu		*itaššubu*
		utaššubu
muštêšibu; *muštêširu*	*šutâšub*; *šutêšur*	*šutâšubu*; *šutêšuru*

12. Verbu

kânu ‚firmum esse', (*mât*

	Praesens		Praeteritum		Imperat.
Singularis:					
I 1. 3.m.	*ikân* et *ikunnu*;	*iṭâb* et	*ikûn*;	*iṭîb*	
3.f.		[*iṭibbu*	*takûn*	*taṭîb*	
2.m.		*taṭâb*	*takûn*	*taṭîb*	*kûn*; *ṭîb*
2.f.			*takûnî*	*taṭîbî*	*ṭîbî*
1.c.	*akân*	*aṭâb*	*akûn*	*aṭîb*	
Pluralis:					
3.m.	*ikânû* et *ikunnû*;	*iṭâbû*	*ikûnû(ni)*		
3.f.		[et *iṭibbû*	*ikûnâ*		
2.m.			*takûnû*		*kûnû* *ṭîb*
2.f.			*takûnâ*		
1.c.	*nikân*		*nikûn*		
II 1.	*ukân*;	*uṭâb*	*ukâin*, *ukên*, *ukîn*;	*uṭîb*	*kâin*, *kên*
					[f. *kinnî*
					ṭibb
III 1.**)	[*ušmât*]		[*ušmît*;	*ušṭîb*]	[*šumît*]
IV 1.					
I 2.			*iktûn*;	*iṭṭîb*	
II 2.			*uktên*, *uktîn*		
III 2.					
IV 2.					
I 3.	*iktanunnu*				
IV 3.					

*) Cfr. *dêk*, *dîk* ‚occisus est'.

**) De illis formis angulatis uncinis inclusis v. §§ 85 et 115.

CHRESTOMATHIA.

I.

Sardanapali expeditio contra Mannaeos.
(VR 2,126-3,26).

(Col.II, 126) [cuneiform text]
[cuneiform text] *(127)* [cuneiform text]
[cuneiform text] [cuneiform text]
[cuneiform text] *(128)* [cuneiform text]
[cuneiform text] *(129)* [cuneiform text]
[cuneiform text] *(130)* [cuneiform text]
[cuneiform text] *(131)* [cuneiform text]
(132) [cuneiform text]
[cuneiform text] *(133)* [cuneiform text]

---

1) *Par.* [cuneiform]. 2) [cuneiform]. 3) *Caret.* 4) [cuneiform]. 5) [cuneiform]. 6) [cuneiform].
7) *Caret.* 8) [cuneiform]. 9) *Caret.* 10) [cuneiform]. 11) [cuneiform]. 12) [cuneiform]. 13)
[cuneiform]. 14) [cuneiform].

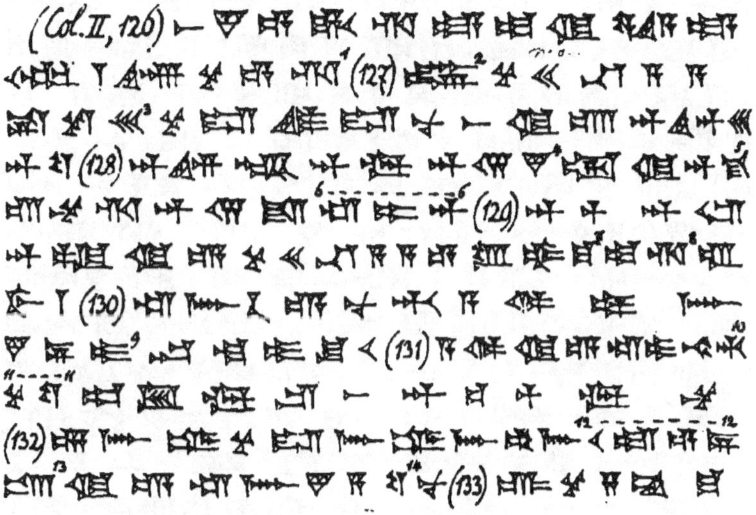

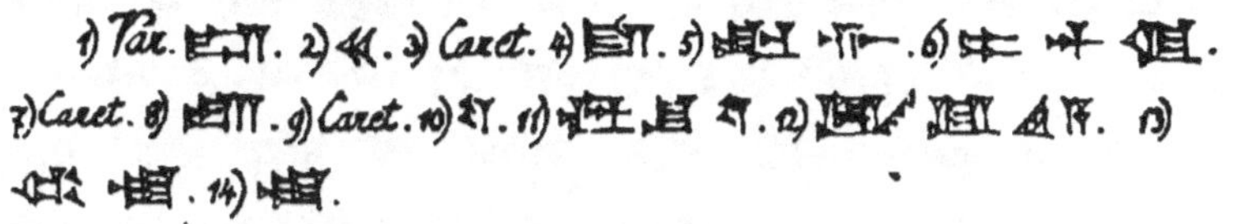

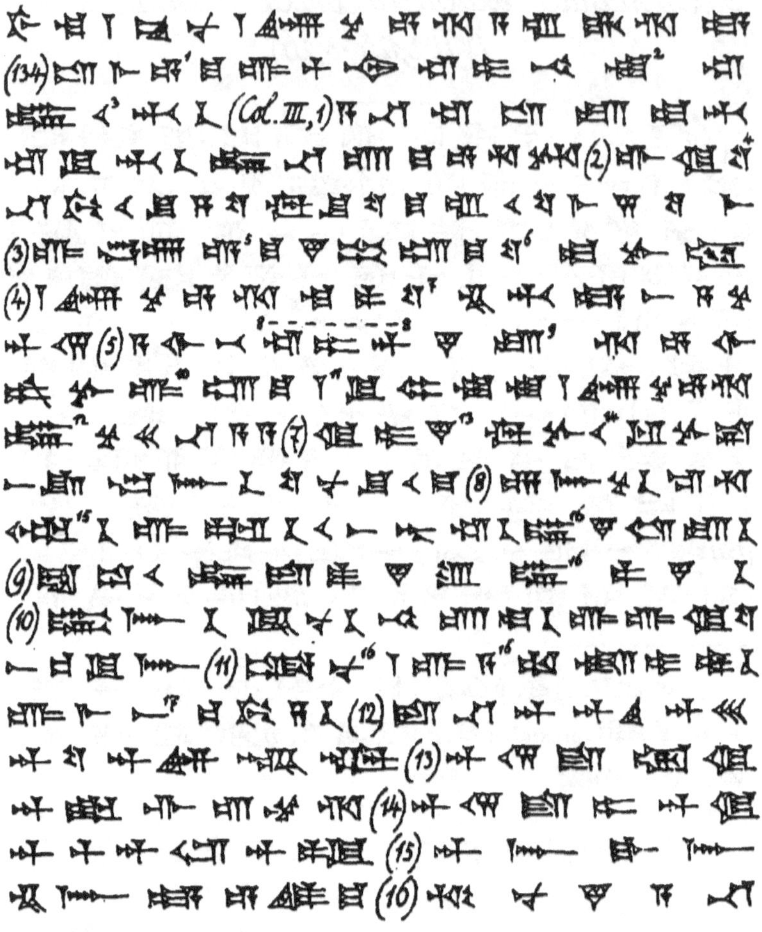

---

1) Caret. 2) [illegible]. 3) Caret. 4) [illegible]. 5) [illegible]. 6) [illegible]. 7) [illegible]. 8) [illegible]. 9) [illegible]. 10) [illegible]. 11) [illegible]. 12) [illegible]. 13) Caret. 14) [illegible]. 15) [illegible]. 16) Caret. 17) [illegible].

1) [illegible]. 2) [illegible]. 3) [illegible]. 4) [illegible]. 5) Caret. 6) [illegible]. 7) [illegible]. 8) Caret. 9) [illegible]. 10) [illegible]. 11) [illegible]. 12) Caret. 13) [illegible].

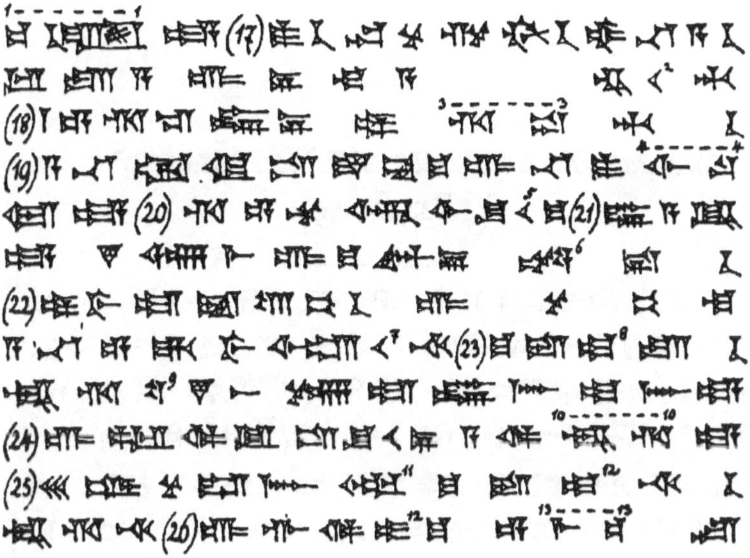

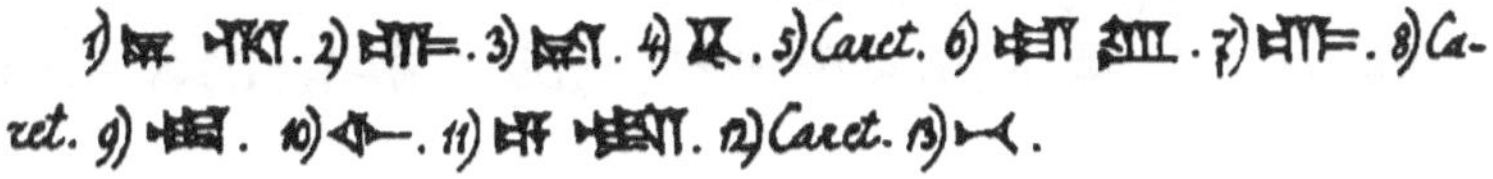

II.

Sancheribi expeditio contra Cossaeos.
(I R 37,63–38,26).*

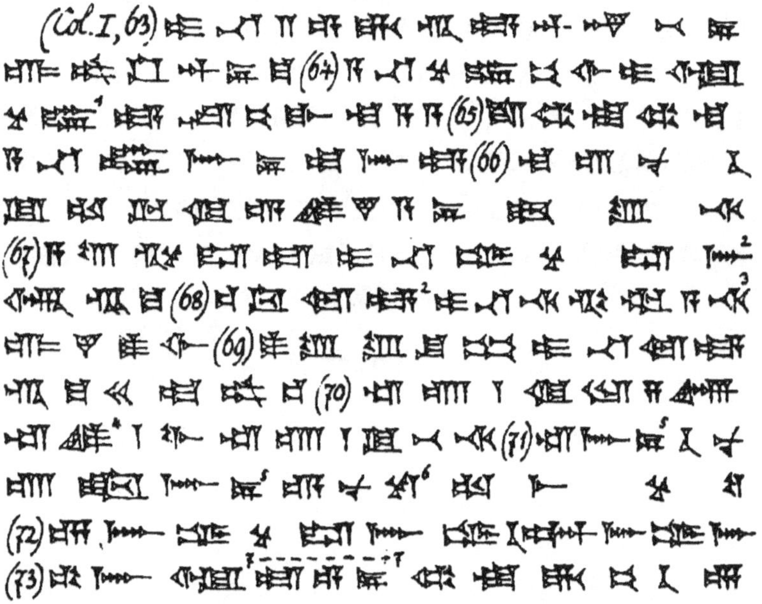

*) Vide linearum 37,63–38,7 translationem in libro meo, „Die Sprache der Kossäer", Leipzig 1884, pp. 2.3.

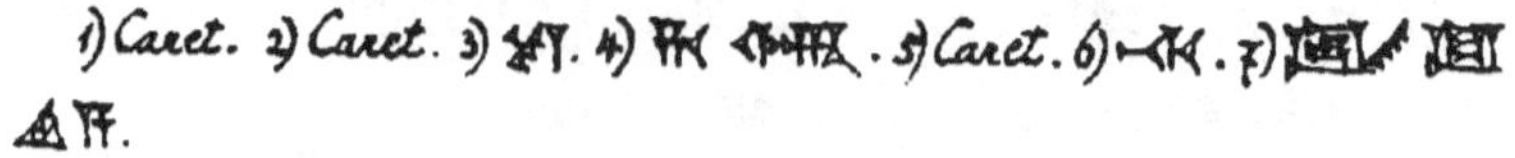

1) Caret. 2) Caret. 3) . 4) . 5) Caret. 6) . 7)
.

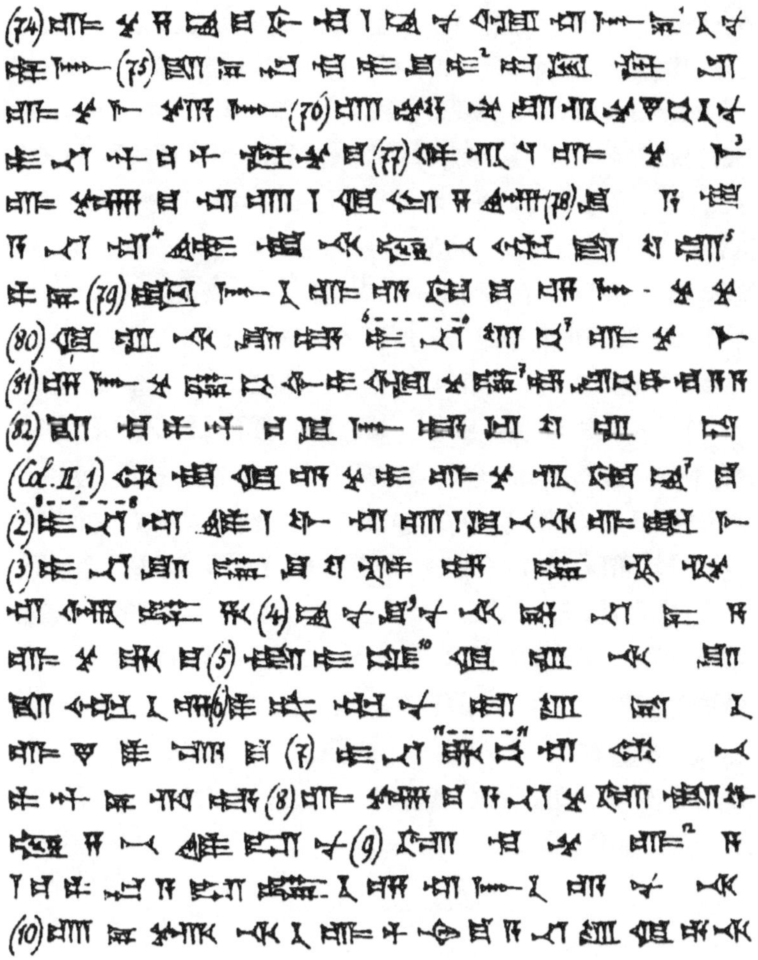

(74) [cuneiform] (75) [cuneiform] (76) [cuneiform] (77) [cuneiform] (78) [cuneiform] (79) [cuneiform] (80) [cuneiform] (81) [cuneiform] (82) [cuneiform]

(Col. II. 1) [cuneiform] (2) [cuneiform] (3) [cuneiform] (4) [cuneiform] (5) [cuneiform] (6) [cuneiform] (7) [cuneiform] (8) [cuneiform] (9) [cuneiform] (10) [cuneiform]

---

1) Caret. 2) [cuneiform]. 3) [cuneiform]. 4) Caret. 5) [cuneiform]. 6) [cuneiform]. 7) Caret. 8) [cuneiform]. 9) [cuneiform].
10) [cuneiform]. 11) [cuneiform]. 12) [cuneiform].

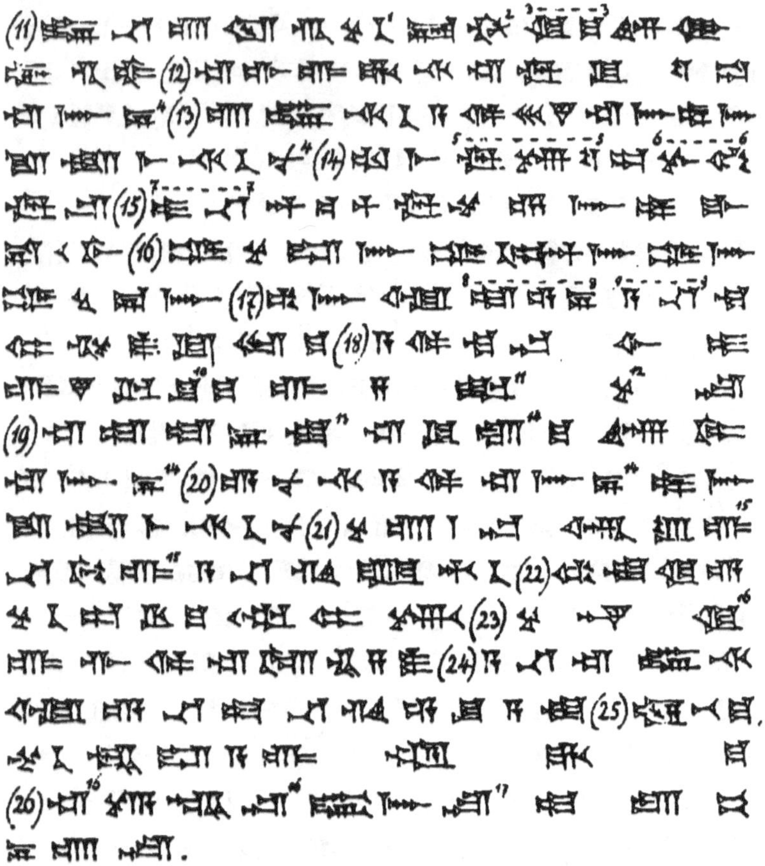

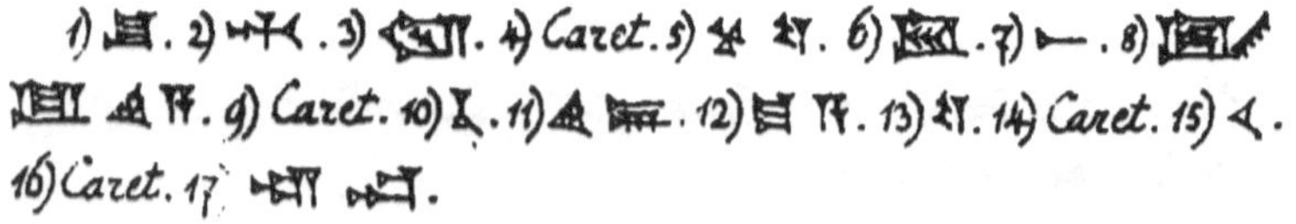

4) Caret.
9) Caret.
14) Caret.
16) Caret.

GLOSSARIUM.

א

(Animadverte notationes $א_1$ = hebr. א, $א_2$ = hebr. ה, $א_3$ = hebr. ח = arab. ح, $א_4$ = hebr. ע = arab. ع, $א_5$ = hebr. ע = arab. غ).

$א_2א_1$ל (?) *âlu* (ideogramma vid. § 9 num. 81) m. urbs. Plur. *âlâni* (de scriptione vid. § 23). *âl šarrûti* urbs regia. *âl tukulti* vid. תכל.

U'allî n. pr. m. filii Aḫšêri, regis Mannaeorum.

$א_1$בה *abû* (ideogr. § 9 num. 24) m. pater (§ 62, 1 extr.). Plur. *abê*. *bît abêšu* domus ejus paterna.

$א_1$בת IV 1 fugere (3 sing. praet. *innabit*).

$א_4$דה *adi* praep.: usque ad, cum (§ 81, a); *adi kirib* usque ad, *adi maḫri* ad, coram (§ 81, b).

אדר *Adar* n. pr. dei (ideogr. § 9 num. 60).

$א_1$ו *u* (*û*) copula: et (§ 82).

$א_1$ול *ellamu* (§ 65 num. 36) pars anterior, unde *ellamû'a* (§ 80, e) ante me.

Izirtu n. pr. urbis Mannaeorum.

$א_1$ח *aḫu* (ideogr. § 9 num. 165) frater. Plur. *aḫê*.

$א_1$חז *aḫâzu* (§102) capere, prehendere (3. m. sing. praet. *êḫuz*).

Aḫšêri (cf. אֲחִישָׁחַר) n. pr. m. regis Mannaeorum.

Akkuddu n. pr. urbis terrae Ellipi.

$א_1$ל *ilu* (ideogr. § 9 num. 60) m. deus, numen. Plur. *ilâni*.

$א_1$לה *ultu* (§ 81, a); *ultu kirib*, *ultu kirbi* (§ 81, b) praepp. ex, de. *ultu ullâ* antiquitus (§ 78). *ultu rêši* a primordio.

$א_4$לה *eli* praep.: super, de (victor de . . .), contra; ad (vi adjiciendi) (§ 81, b).

ullû, in *ultu ullâ* antiquitus.

$א_2$לך *alâku* (§§ 102. 104 extr.) ire, proficisci (1. sing. praet. *allik*).

I 2 idem (1. sing. praet. *attal(l)ak*).

ab-bul (*bu-ul*) vid. נבל. — *ib-bu-uš* legas *ip-pu-uš* et vid. אפש. — *ag-gur* legas *aḳ-ḳur*, נקר. — *id-du-ú* vid. נדה. — *u-dan-nin* vid. דנן. — *âlu* vid. אאל. — *ul-bat* (*mid* etc.) legas *ul-ziz* et vid. נזז. —

III 1 facere ut quis ad aliquem statum perveniat sive redigatur (1. sing. praet. *ušâlik*).

mâlaku, st. cstr. *mâlak*, via, iter.

Elenzaš n. pr. urbis regionis Bît-Barrû (vide id ipsum).

אלף$_1$ *alpu* (ideogr. § 9 num. 250) bos. Plur. *alpê*.

Ellipi (genitivus) n. pr. terrae prope Mediam sitae.

אמד$_4$ *emêdu* (§ 102) imponere (c. duplice accus., § 139) (1. sing. praet. *êmid*, c. pron. suff. *êmidsu*, cf. § 51, 1).

אמת *amâtu*, st. cstr. *amât*, vox, sermo.

אמה$_4$ III 1 parem facere, adaequare (1. sing. praet. *ušêmi*).

umma particula orationem directam introducens (§ 78).

ummânu (ideogr. § 9 num. 182) exercitus, plur. *ummânâte* et *ummânê* (§ 70, b) copiae.

אמר$_1$ *amâru* (§ 102) videre (3. m. sing. praet. *êmur*).

אמר$_3$ *imêru* (ideogr. § 9 num. 244) asinus (vid. § 65 num. 12 et § 32, α).

ana praep.: ad, in (c. accus.), contra, etiam nota dativi (§§ 81, a. 138).

ina praep.: in (c. ablat.), etiam de eo cujus ope aliquid efficitur (§ 81, a); *ina kirbi, ina kirib* in (§ 81, b). *ina ķibît* jussu (alicujus). *ina amât* convenienter ei quod quis pronuntiavit. *ina libbi* illic (§ 78).

אנך$_1$ *anâku* ego (§ 55, a).

Ispabâra n. pr. m. regis terrae Ellipi.

אבל *aplu* (vel *mâru*, ideogr. § 9 num. 139) filius. *apil ridûtišu* vid. רדה.

אפש$_4$? *epêšu* (§ 102) facere (1. sing. praes. *eppuš*).

III 1 faciendum curare (1. sing. praet. *ušêpiš*).

אקל$_3$ *eķlu* (ideogr. § 9 num. 1), st. cstr. *eķil*, ager, tractus, territorium (§ 65 num. 1).

ארב$_5$ *erêbu* (§ 102) intrare (1. sing. praet. *êrub*).

Arba'ilu vid. רבא$_4$.

ardu (incertae originis; ideogr. § 9 num. 226) servus.

ארן *arnu* peccatum. Plur. *arnâ* (§ 67, a, 4).

Erisinni n. pr. m. filii U'allî, filii Aḫšêri, regis Mannaeorum.

el-la-mu-u-a vid. אול. — *al-ur* legas *al-lik*, אלך. — *ul-tu* vid. אלה. — *am-nu* vid מנה. — *in-da-aš-ša-ru* vid. בשר. — *in-na-bit* vid. אבת. — *amêlu en-nam* vid. § 9 num. 116. — *aķ-ķur* vid. נקר. — *er-ba* vid. ערב. — *arkânu* vid. ארך. — *er ku-ti-šu* legas *âl tukulti-šu* et vid. תכל.

Arrapha n. pr. urbis et tractus, graece Ἀῤῥαπαχῖτις.

אשׁ$_1$ *išâtu* (ideogr. § 9 num. 60) ignis (cf. § 62, 2).

aššu praep.: causa (§ 81, c).

אשׁר$_1$ *ašru* locus.

Ašûr (de variis scriptionibus vid. § 9 num. 60 . 220) n. pr. summi dei Assyriorum.

Aššûr (ideogr. § 9 num. 220) n. pr. Assyriae.

Ištâr (ideogr. § 9 num. 60) n. pr. Veneris Assyriacae (cf. § 65 num. 40, a).

Ištatti n. pr. urbis Mannaeorum.

ב

באל$_4$ *bêlu* (ideogr. § 9 num. 62) dominus. Plur. *bêlê*. *be-ili* (sive *è-ni*) dominus meus (de valore syllabico *ili* qui signo *ni* convenit vid. S^a col. I 20).

Bêl (ideogr. § 9 num. 60) n. pr. dei Beli.

bêltu (ideogr. § 9 num. 256) domina.

bêlûtu dominium, majestas (de scriptione cf. § 23).

בטל III 1 abolere, abrogare (3. plur. praet. *ušabṭilû*).

בית *bîtu* domus. *bît ṣêri* vel *edini* domus deserti (voci *kultârê*, h. e. tentoria, vi determinativi praepositum). De usu vocis *bîtu* in *âlâni bît šarrûti* urbes regiae, *âlâni bît dûrâni* urbes moenibus cinctae, *âlâni bît niṣirti* urbes bene defensae vid. § 124.

Bît-Barrû n. pr. regionis terrae Ellipi.

Bît-Kubatti (cf. ^{mât} *Bît-ku-ba-tim* Neb. Grot. I 25) n. pr. urbis Cossaeorum.

Bît-Kilamzaḫ n. pr. urbis Cossaeorum.

בלט *balâṭu* vivere, st. cstr. *balâṭ*.

ברח *bîrtu* (cf. § 65 num. 2) arx, unde nom. abstr. *bîrtûtu*: *âla ana bîrtûti aṣbat* urbem, ut castelli vicem expleret, cepi.

בשׁה *bašû* (§ 108) esse (genit. *bašî*).

III 1 facere, creare, efficere, e. g. seditionem (3. plur. praet. *ušabšû*).

בתק *batâḳu* abscindere, sejungere (1. sing. praet. *abtuḳ*).

ג

גמל *gammalu* (tamquam ideogramma GAM. MAL scrip-

u-šib vid. ישׁב. — *u-še-bi-la* vid. יבל. — *u-še-me(mi)* vid. אמה; — *u-še-me* legas *u-še-šib* et vid. ישׁב. — *iš-me-e-ma* vid. שׁמא. — *u-še-piš* vid. אפשׁ. — *u-še-ṣa-am-ma* vid. יצא. — *u-ša-aš-ṭir* vid. שׁטר. — *uš-te-(eš-)še-ra* vid. ישׁר. — *at-ta-bi* vid. נבא. — *at-tag-giš* vid. נגשׁ. — *at-ta(l)-lak* vid. אלך. — *bîrtu* vid. ברח. — *be-ni* legas vel *be-ili* (vid. באל) vel *è-ni* (cf. *enu* dominus, § 62, 1). — *Bi-ši-i* legas *Kaš-ši-i*.

tum, praecedente determinativo § 9 num. 244) camelus.

גמר *gimru* universitas, totum. *gimri mâtišu* totam ejus terram (cf. § 72, a).

gimirtu idem.

גרר *girru* expeditio, e. g. *ina rebê girri'a* in quarta expeditione mea (cf. § 128, 1).

ד

dûru (ideogr. § 9 num. 239) m. murus. Plur. *dûrâni* . *âlâni bît dûrâni*, vid. בית.

דנן *danânu* robustum, firmum, munitum esse, potentem esse, de robore et potestate deorum, st. cstr. *danân*.

II 1 munire, fortificare (1. sing. praet. *udannin*).

dannu firmus, undique munitus. Plur. m. *dannûti*.

dannatu, st. cstr. *dannat*, arx, castellum.

דקא$_4$ *diḳû* (§ 108) conciere, congregare (copias). (1. sing. praet. *adḳi*).

ditallu (incertae lectionis atque derivationis) flamma; adv. *ditalliš* (§ 80, b, α).

ו

ובל (§ 111) III 1 facere ut ducatur, afferatur (3. sing. praet. *ušêbila*).

וצא$_1$ (§ 111) III 1 educere (1. sing. praet. c. copula *ušêṣamma*, cf. § 150).

ṣîtu exitus, exortus: *mârtu ṣît libbišu* filia ejus germana.

ורד (§ 111) III 1 facere ut quis descendat, deorsum portare (1. sing. praet. *ušêridamma*, cf. § 23 nota).

ורך *arkânu* (ideogr. § 9 num. 245, cum vel sine adjecto *nu*) adv. postea, posterius (§ 80, c).

ושב *ašâbu* (§ 111) sedere, considere, habitare (3. m. sing. praet. *ûšib*). Part. fem. st. cstr. *âšibat* incolens.

III 1 facere ut quis alicubi considat, assignare sedem (1. sing. praet. *ušêšib*).

mûšabu (§ 65 num. 31, a) sedes, habitaculum.

ז

זוא$_4$ *zû* (ideogr. § 9 num. 54) procella.

זכר *zikru* (ideogr. § 9 num. 94) virilis, vir (cf. § 65 num. 9).

זנש *zinništu* (ideogr. § 9 num. 212) muliebris, mulier.

זקר *zaḳru* altus, arduus, acuto cacumine eminens. Plur. m. *zaḳrûti*.

זרא$_4$ *zêru* (ideogr. § 9 num. 113), st. cstr. *zêr*, familia (cf. § 65 num. 1).

---

zir-ta-re legas *kul-ta-re*.

ח

חרב III 1 devastare (1. sing. praet. *ušaḫrib*).

Ḫardišpi n.pr. urbis Cossaeorum.

חרר *ḫarrânu* via; expeditio.

חרשׁ *ḫuršu* m. mons. Plur. *ḫuršâni* (§ 67, a, 2).

י

יום *ûmu* (ideogr. § 9 num. 26) m. dies. Plur. *ûmê* (de scriptione vid. § 23). *ûm(e) pâni* vid. פנה.

Ià-su-bi-gal-la-a-a n. pr. tribus montanae.

ירב (§ 111) multiplicare, augere (3. m. sing. praet. *er-ba*, etiam ideographice, § 9 num. 67, scriptum, vid. *Sinaḫêrba*).

ישׁה (§ 111) habere. *ša nîba lâ i-šú-u* innumerabilis (cf. נבא$_1$); scriptio *i-šú-i* (Sanh. I 75) error scribae est.

ישׁר (§ 111) III 2 dirigere (1. sing. praet. *uštêšera*, cf. §§ 113 et 36).

כ

kid-mu-ri (alias *ki-di-mu-ri*), fortasse nomen templi: *bêlit* vel *šarrat kid-mu-ri* cognomen deae Istar Niniveticae.

כי *kî*, sequente vel non sequente *ša*, conj.: quemadmodum, sicuti (vid. §§ 82 et 148, 1).

kîma praep.: instar (§ 81, c).

kakku (ideogr. § 9 num. 31), plur. *kakkê* m. arma.

Kum(m)aḫḫum n.pr. urbis terrae Ellipi.

כנשׁ *kanâšu* se subjicere, c. *ana* pers. vel rei, cui quis se submittit (3. m. sing. praet. *iknuša*).

I 2 idem. *ša lâ kitnušu* qui se non subjecerat (§ 89).

כסא$_1$ *kussû* (ideogr. § 9 num. 31) thronus.

Kar (vel *Kâr*, vid. § 9 num. 180) in n. pr. *Kar-Sinaḫêrba* vid. sub littera ק.

כרם *karmu* ager; *kar-miš* (*kar-meš*) adv. agri sive agrorum instar (§ 80, b, α).

Kašši n. pr. populi montani ad septentriones Babyloniae. *mât Kaššî* terra Cossaeorum.

כשׁד *kašâdu* expugnare, vincere (1. sing. praet. *akšud*; de variis scriptionibus vid. § 9 num. 176 et § 23 cum nota).

kišitti ḳâti victoria de aliquo reportata, etiam sensu concreto de ipso victo.

kuštâru, *kultâru* (§ 51, 3) tentorium (cf. § 65 num. 40, b). Plur. *kultârê* (vid. § 70, b).

ל

la in voce *la-pa-an* vid. פנה.

לא$_1$ *lâ* adv.: non (§§ 80. 143).

---

kultâru vid. *kuštâru*. — *ki-šit-ti* vid. כשׁד. — *kit-nu-šu* vid. כנשׁ.

לא₁ת *lêtu* potentia, victoria (cf. §§ 62, 1. 69 nota).

לבב *libbu* (ideogr. § 9 num. 259) cor, centrum, medium. *mârtu ṣît libbišu* vid. וצא₁. *ina libbi* illic (§ 78).

לו *lû*, particula affirmativa: certo, profecto (§ 78).

למה *lamû* (§ 108) obsidere (1. sing. praet. *al-me*).

limêtu circuitus, ditio, territorium urbis (§ 65 num. 9). De *ša* in *âlâni ṣiḫrûti ša limêtišunu* vid. § 123, 1.

מ

ma copula enclitice agglutinata (§§ 82. 150).

מא₂ר (§ 105) II 1 mittere (1. sing. praet. *uma'ir*).

מות *mîtûtu* status mortui, mors (§§ 64 et 65 num. 34).

מחר *maḫru* pars antica; *adi maḫri'a* (*maḫri* phonetice aut ideographice, § 9 num. 86, scriptum) coram me (§ 81, b). *maḫrû*, accus. *maḫrâ*, fem. *maḫrîtu*, prior.

מנה *manû* (§ 108) numerare, aestimare: *šallatiš amnu* spolii instar eos tractavi; *ina ḳât ... manû* in manum alicujus numerare h. e. ei tradere (3. f. sing. praet. *tamnu*; de *tamnušûma* cf. § 53, d).

mînu numerus (cf. § 65 num. 1); (*ana*) *lâ mînam* innumerabilis (§ 143).

Man-na-a-a (cf. § 13) n. pr. terrae Armeniacae (מִנִּי).

מצר *miṣru*, st. cstr. *miṣir*, regio certis finibus circumscripta.

מקת III 1 prosternere, interficere (3. m. plur. praet. *ušamḳitû*).

mâru vid. *aplu* filius. *mârtu* vel *bintu* (ideogr. § 9 num. 139) filia.

Marubišti n. pr. urbis terrae Ellipi.

מרץ *namraṣu* asperitas (de via laboriosa). Plur. *namraṣê*.

משר II 1 derelinquere, deserere, missum facere.

I 2 (?) abjicere, conculcandum tradere (3. m. plur. praes.?: *indaššarû*).

mâtu f. terra; *mâtsu*, *mâsu* (§ 51, 1) terram ejus. Plur. *mâtâti* (duplice ideogrammate KUR, § 9 num. 176, scriptum).

נ

נבא₁ I 2 nominare (1. sing. praet. *attabi*).

nîbu numerus (§ 65 num. 4); urbes parvae *ša nîba lâ i-šû-u* innumerabiles.

---

le-i-tu(m) vid. לא₁ת. — *madattu* vid. נדן. — *mi-tu-tu* vid. מות. — *nîbu* vid. נבא. —

nibittu (?), st. cstr. *nibit*, nomen; *nibitsu* nomen ejus.

Nabû (ideogr. § 9 num. 60) n. pr. dei Assyriorum.

נבל *nabâlu* destruere (1. sing. praet. *abbul*).

נגה *nagû* regio, provincia (§ 65 num. 6); genit. *na-gi-e* (cf. § 66 nota).

נגשׁ (cf. *igguš* = *illik*) I 2 conficere (viam peragrando) (1. sing. praet. *attaggiš*).

נדה *nadû* (§ 108) jacere, conjicere (3. m. plur. praet. *iddû*).

נדן *madat(t)u* (cf. § 49, b) tributum.

נזז III 1 statuere, erigere, e. g. cippum (1. sing. praet. *ulziz*, vid. §§ 37 extr. et 51, 3).

Nînua, *Nînâ* (ideogr. § 9 num. 237) n. pr. capitis Assyriae.

ניר *nîru* (ideogr. § 9 num. 31) jugum.

נכר II 1 mutare, ἀλλοιοῦν (1. sing. praet. *unakkir*).

Nusku (ideogr. § 9 num. 60) n. pr. dei Assyriorum.

נפשׁ *napištu* (ideogr. § 9 num. 28) anima, vita; genit. c. pron. suff. *napištimšu* (vid. § 74, 1 nota).

נצר *niṣirtu* custodia, protectio. *âlâni bît niṣirti* vid. בית.

נקר *nakâru* destruere, devastare (1. sing. praet. *akkur*).

Nergal (ideogr. § 9 num. 60) n. pr. dei Assyriorum.

נרה *narû* (ideogr. § 9 num. 151) m. lapis monumentalis, qui facta inscriptione erigebatur.

nišu (ideogr. § 9 num. 63) populus, plur. *nišê* homines, incolae.

נשׂא₁ *našû* afferre, e. g. tributum (3. m. plur. praet. *iššûni*).
III 1 portandum curare (1. sing. praet. *ušašši*).

נשׁק II 1 osculari et pedes quidem, de eo qui ultro se subjicit (3. m. sing. praet. *unaššiḳ(a)*).

ס

סוק *sûḳu* (ideogr. § 9 num. 105) platea sive latior sive angustior.

סחה (§ 108) *si-ḫu* seditio.

סחף *saḫâpu* prosternere (1. sing. praet. *asḫup*).

Sin (*Sîn*? ideogr. § 9 num. 60) n. pr. dei Luni.
Sin-aḫê-er-ba (h. e. Sin fratres multiplicavit) in n. pr. urbis *Kâr-Sinaḫêrba* (vid. sub littera ק).

sîsû (ideogr. § 9 num. 244) equus. Plur. *sîsê*.

פ

פגר *pagru*, st. cstr. *pagar*, cadaver (cf. § 74, 1, a).

פחה *paḫâtu* vel *piḫâtu* (ideogr.

---

namraṣu vid. מרץ.

§ 9 num. 116) praefectus, regis vicarius.

פלח *palâḫu* metuere, revereri. Part. m. st. cstr. *pâliḫ*.

פנה *pânu*, st. cstr. *pân*, pars anterior; *eli ša ûm* (vel *û-me*) *pâni* magis quam antehac. *la-pa-an* ante (§ 81, b).

פרה *parû* (ideogr. § 9 num. 244) bos juvencus. Plur. *parê*.

פרשד (§ 117, 1) IV 1 fugere, fugam capessere (3. m. plur. praet. *ipparšiddû*, cf. § 53, c).

פשק *šupšuḳu* arduus, ascensu difficilis ac paene inaccessus (cf. § 65 num. 33 extr. et § 88, b).

פתא$_3$ *pitû* (§ 108) aperire, manifestare, confiteri (peccata) (3. m. sing. praet. *iptû*, cf. § 92).

צ

צא$_1$ן *ṣênu* nomen gen. ovium et caprarum (cf. § 65 num. 1).

צא$_2$ר *ṣîru* (*ṣêru* § 65 n. 1) dorsum, deinde id quod supra est, pars supera; *ṣîruššu* (*ṣîru* etiam ideographice, § 9 num. 240, scriptum) super eo (§ 80, e).

צבת *ṣabâtu* capere, sumere, de via: deligere et ingredi (1. sing. praet. *aṣbat*).

I 2 idem (1. sing. praet. *aṣṣabat*, cf. § 48).

צחר II 1 imminuere (1. sing. praet. *uṣaḫir*).

ṣaḫru et *ṣiḫru* (ideogr. § 9 num. 139) parvus (§ 65 num. 7 nota). Plur. m. *ṣiḫrûti*. *ṣiḫir rabû* parvos magnosque (cf. § 127).

צלח II 1 rogare, implorare (3. m. sing. praet. *uṣallâ*).

Ṣiṣirtu n. pr. urbis terrae Ellipi.

ק

קבא$_4$ *ḳibû* fari, dicere (3. f., 1. sing. praet., mod. relat. *taḳbû*, *aḳbû*, cf. §§ 92. 147. 148). *ḳibîtu*, st. cstr. *ḳibît*, effatum, jussum (§ 65 num. 11).

קמה *ḳamu* (§ 108) comburere (1. sing. praet. *aḳmu*).

קנן *ḳinnu* familia.

kâru in n. pr. urbis *Kar-Sin-aḫê-êrba* (var. *er-ba*), probabiliter legendum *ḳâru*, agger, deinde oppidum munitum.

קרב *kirbu* (vid. § 19), st. cstr. *kirib*, id quod intus est; *kirib*, *ina kirib*, *ina kirbi* praep.: in; *ultu kirib*, *ultu kirbi* ex; *adi kirib* usque ad (§ 81, b).

ḳâtu manus. *ina ḳât* . . . *manû* vid. מנה. *kišitti ḳâti* vid. כשד.

ר

רא$_1$ם *rîmu* bos sylvestris, unde adv. *rîmâniš* boum ferorum instar (§ 80, b, *α*).

רא$_3$ם *rêmu* misericordia (§ 65 num. 1 et cf. § 29).

רא$_3$ק *rûḳu* longinquus, plur. fem.

rûḷêti loca longinque dissita (cf. §§ 32, γ et 70, a, nota).

ראשׁ₁ *rêšu* initium (§ 65 num. 1); *ultu rêši* inde ab initio.

רבא₄ *arba'u* quattuor (§ 75), unde n. pr. urbis Assyriacae *Arba'ilu* Arbela (de ideogrammate vid. § 9 num. 234 et 60).

rebû quartus (§ 76); IV-*e* legas *rebê* (genit.).

רבה *rabû* (ideogr. § 9 num. 169) magnus. Plur. m. *rabûti*.

רדה *radû, ridû* (§ 108) ire, fluere, unde

ridûtu (phonetice vel ideographice, § 9 num. 94, scriptum) effusio (sc. seminis): *apil ridûtišu* filium ab ipso genitum.

ירד II 1 addere, c. *eli* rei cui aliquid adjicitur (1. sing. praet. *uraddi*, c. copula: *uraddîma*, § 53, d).

רכב *rakâbu* conscendere, e. g. equum, c. *ina* jumenti quo aliquis vehitur (1. sing. praet. *arkab*).

narkabtu (ideogr. § 9 num. 31) vehiculum, currus (§ 65 num. 31, a); *narkabat sêpê'a* vehiculum pedum meorum, essedum meum (?).

רמה (§ 108) III 1 facere ut quis alicubi domicilium figat (1. sing. praet. *ušarme*).

רמם *Rammân* (ideogr. § 9 num. 60) n. pr. dei Assyriorum.

רפשׁ *rapšu* (ideogr. § 9 num. 247), fem. *rapaštu, rapaltu*, latus, amplus (§ 65 num. 6).

רשׁה *rašû* (§ 108) capere, spec. gratiam (clementiam) h. e. ea commoveri in aliquem (cf. 1. sing. praet. *rêmu aršišûma*).

שׁ

ša pron. relat. (§§ 58. 147); nota genitivi (§§ 58. 123).

šû-a-tu, plur. *šâtunu*, pron. demonstr. (§ 57, a).

שׁדה *šadû* (ideogr. § 9 num. 176), genit. *šadî* (cf. § 23), mons.

šú-ud-šakû, c. determ. *amêlu*, praefectus militum superior.

שׁוף *šêpu* (ideogr. § 9 num. 261) pes (de suffixo *-ia* vid. § 74, 1, b).

שׁטר III 1 scribendum curare (1. sing. praet. *ušašṭir*).

שׁכן I 2 parare, facere, acquirere (potestatem), reportare (victoriam de aliquo) (1. sing. praet., mod. relat., *aštakkanu*).

שׁלט *šalṭiš* adv. victoriose.

שׁלל *šalâlu* spoliare, captivum abducere (1. sing. praet. c. copula: *ašlulamma*, cf. § 150).

---

ru-šú-ḳu legas *šup-šú-ḳu* et vid. פשׁק.

šallatu praeda, spolia, unde adv. *šallatiš* (vid. מנה).

שלם *šulmu* pax.

šalamtu, c. determ. *amêlu* vel sine determ., cadaver.

שם *šumu* (ideogr. § 9 num. 52) nomen (§ 62, 2).

שמע$_4$ *šemû* audire (3. m. sing. praet. *išmi*, c. copula: *išmêma* vid. §§ 53, d et 32, γ).

שמש *Šamaš* (ideogr. § 9 num. 60) n. pr. dei Solis.

שנה *šanû* secundus (§ 76); II-e legas *šanê* (genit.).

שפר *šapâru* mittere (3. m. sing. praet. c. copula: *išpuramma*, cf. § 150).

apil šipri (ideogr. § 9 num. 1 et 74) filius missionis (epistolae) h. e. nuntius; *apil šipri'a ša šulmi* nuntium pacis meum (cf. § 123).

שקם *šaḳummatu* (§ 65 num. 23) cruciatus, miseria.

שרר *šarru* (ideogr. § 9 num. 238 et 203) m. rex. Plur. *šarrâni*.

šarrûtu (de scriptione vid. § 23) regalis dignitas et dominatio. *âl šarrûti* urbs regia.

šarratu, st.cstr. *šarrat*, regina.

ת

תבך *tabâku* effundere (1. sing. praet. *atbuk*).

תור II 1 vertere, mutare, reddere, facere (1. sing. praet. *utîr*).

תכך *tikkatu* funis. Plur. *tikkâti*.

תכל II 1 confidentem et fortem facere, fiducia implere, corroborare (3. m. sing. praet. *utakkil*).

tukultu (ideogr. § 9 num. 41) praesidium, auxilium; *âl tukultišu* urbs praesidii sui h. e. qua prae aliis nixus est. Quomodo ideogramma § 9 num. 265, quod cum ideogrammate num. 41 ejusdem valoris est, enuntiandum sit, signo sexus muliebris (§ 9 num. 212) antecedente, nondum liquet; at certum est, inesse vim copulae carnalis sive concubitus itemque vocabulum assyriacum, quod eo ideogrammate indicatur, in terminationem fem. abstractivam — *ûtu* exisse.

תרץ *ina tirṣi* aetate, e. g. majorum meorum (§ 81, b).

LITTERATURA.

A. DE INVENTIONE ATQUE EFFOSSIONE MONUMENTORUM CUNEATORUM*):

a) monumentorum persicorum

(plerumque trilingium: persico-susiano-babylonicorum).

1 *Garcia de Silva y Figueroa.* De rebus Persarum epistola. V. Kal. an. MDCXIX Spahani exarata ad Marchionem Bedmarii etc. Antverpiae 1620. — Cf.: L'ambassade de Don *Garcia de Silva y Figueroa* en Perse ... traduite de l'Espagnol par M. *de Wicqfort.* Paris 1667.

2 Viaggj di *Pietro della Valle* il pelegrino. Descritti da lui medesimo in 54 Lettere familiari (1614—1626). 2. impressione. Roma 1662 (prima prodiit 1650). 4. (Parte II: La Persia). [Exstant translationes in linguam germanicam (Genff, Joh. Herm. Widerhold, 1674), gallicam, anglicam et batavicam.]

3 Les six voyages de *J. B. Tavernier,* 2 vols. Paris 1676—1679.

4 Voyages de Monsieur le Chevalier *Chardin,* en Perse, et autres lieux de l'Orient. Tome III. Amsterdam 1711.

5 *Engelbertus Kaempferus.* Amoenitatum exoticarum politico-physico-medicarum fasciculi V, quibus continentur variae relationes, observationes et descriptiones rerum Persicarum et ulterioris Asiae. Lemgoviae 1712. 912 pp. 4.

6 *Cornelis de Bruin.* Reizen over Moskovie, door Persie en Indie: verrykt met 300 kunstplaten .... voor al ... van Persepolis. t'Amsteldam 1714. fol. [Exstant translationes in linguam gallicam (*Corneille Le Brun.* Voyages etc. Amsterd. 1718) et anglicam.]

7 *Carsten Niebuhr.* Reisebeschreibung nach Arabien und andern umliegenden Ländern. Bd. II. Kopenhagen 1778. 479 pp. 4. [Exstant translationes in linguam gallicam et batavicam.]

---

*) Animadverte compendia: Ac = Academy. Ath = Athenaeum. CR = Comptes rendus de l'Académie des Inscriptions et Belles-lettres. GGA = Göttingische gelehrte Anzeigen. JA = Journal Asiatique. JRAS = Journal of the Royal Asiatic Society. RA = Revue archéologique. RC = Revue critique. TRIA = Transactions of the Royal Irish Academy (Dublin). ZDMG = Zeitschrift der Deutschen Morgenländischen Gesellschaft.

8*James P. Morier.* A Journey through Persia, Armenia and Asia Minor etc. London 1812. 4.

9*Sir William Ouseley.* Travels in Various Countries of the East; more particularly Persia, etc. 3 Vols. 4. London 1819—1823.

10*Robert Ker Porter.* Travels in Georgia, Persia, Ancient Babylonia etc., during the years 1817, 1818, 1819 and 1820. Vol. II. London 1822. 4.

11*Flandin et Coste.* Voyage en Perse de MM. *Eugène Flandin*, Peintre, et *Pascal Coste*, Architecte, attachés à l'Ambassade de France en Perse, pendant les années 1840 et 1842, entrepris par Ordre de M. le Ministre des Affaires Etrangères, d'après les instructions dressées par l'Institut. 2 vols.: Relation de voyage par *E. Flandin* (Paris 1851. 8. fr. 15. 15 s. (Trübner)); Atlas de 6 vols. in folio, contenant 260 planches gravées, 100 planches lithographiées, et un texte archéologique. Paris 1843—1854. (Publié à fr. 1460).

12Persepolis. Die achaemenidischen und sasanidischen Denkmäler und Inschriften von Persepolis, Istakhr, Pasargadae, Shâpûr zum ersten Male photographisch aufgenommen von *F. Stolze* im Anschluss an die epigraphisch-archaeologische Expedition in Persien von F. C. Andreas. Herausgegeben auf Veranlassung des fünften internationalen Orientalisten-Congresses zu Berlin mit einer Besprechung der Inschriften von *Th. Nöldeke.* 150 Lichtdruck-Tafeln. Berlin 1882. 2 Bände. fol. M. 250.

b) monumentorum babylonicorum et assyriacorum.

13*Joseph Hager.* A Dissertation on the newly discovered Babylonian Inscriptions. London 1801. XXIII, 62 pp. 4. 4 tabulae. 12 s. 6 d. [Germanice edidit *Klaproth*: Über die vor kurzem entdeckten Babylonischen Inschriften. Weimar 1802. 110 pp. 8. 6 tabulae.]

14*A. L. Millin.* Déscription d'un monument persépolitain, qui appartient au Muséum de la Bibliothèque Nationale: Monuments antiques inédits. Paris 1802. pp. 58—68. [Monumentum de quo agitur est id quod Caillou de Michaux vocatur.]

15*Claudius James Rich.* Memoir on the Ruins of Babylon. Third Edition. With three plates. London 1818. IV, 67 pp. 8. (First Edition, 1815).

16*Idem.* Second Memoir on Babylon: containing an Inquiry into the Correspondence between the Ancient Descriptions of Babylon and the Remains still Visible on the Site. Suggested by the "Remarks" of Major Rennell published in the *Archaeologia.* London 1818. 58 pp. 8. — Cf.:

[17]Narrative of a Journey to the Site of Babylon in 1811. Memoir on the Ruins. Remarks on the Topography of Ancient Babylon by Major Rennell in Reference to the Memoir. Second Memoir on the Ruins in Reference to Major Rennell's Remarks. With Narrative of a Journey to Persepolis. By the late *C. J. Rich.* Edited by his widow. With 26 plates and plans. London 1839. XLVII, 324 pp. M. 12.

[18]*C. J. Rich.* Narrative of a Residence in Koordistan, and on the Site of Ancient Niniveh, with Journal of a Voyage down the Tigris to Bagdad, and an Account of a Visit to Shiraz and Persepolis. Edited by his widow. London 1836.

[19]*P. E. Botta.* Lettres de M. Botta sur ses découvertes à Ninive. A M. *J. Mohl* à Paris: JA. IV Sér., II, 1843, 61—72. 201—214. III, 1844, 91—103. (... sur ses découvertes près de Ninive) 424—435. IV, 1844, 301—314.

[20]Monument de Ninive, découvert et décrit par M. *P. E. Botta*; mesuré et dessiné par M. *E. Flandin.* Ouvrage publié par Ordre du Gouvernement sous les auspices de S. Exc. M. le Ministre de l'Intérieur, et sous la direction d'une commission de l'Institut. 5 vols. Paris 1847—1850. 400 tabulae. fol. (fr. 1800). £ 45 (Trübner).

[21]*Victor Place.* Ninive et l'Assyrie; avec des essais de restauration par *Félix Thomas.* 3 vols: 2 vols. de texte et un atlas de 82 planches. Paris 1866—69. fol. (fr. 850). fr. 500. M. 300 (Joseph Baer)—350.

[22]*Austen Henry Layard.* Nineveh and its Remains: with an Account of a Visit to the Chaldaean Christians of Kurdistan, and the Yezidis, or Devil-Worshippers; and an Enquiry into the Manners and Arts of the Ancient Assyrians. 2 Vols. London 1849. (6., ultima, editio London 1854). XXX, 399 et 491 pp. 8. M. 22—30. £ 1 4 s. (Trübner).

Idem. Niniveh und seine Überreste. Deutsch von *N. N. W. Meissner.* Leipzig 1850. Neue Ausgabe, 1854. 8. M. 18.

[23]*Idem.* A Popular Account on the Excavations of Nineveh. London 1851.

Idem. Populärer Bericht über die Ausgrabungen zu Niniveh. Nebst der Beschreibung eines Besuches bei den chaldäischen Christen in Kurdistan und den Jezidi oder Teufelsanbetern. Nach dem grösseren Werke von ihm selbst abgekürzt. Deutsch von *N. N. W. Meissner.* Leipzig 1852. XII, 228 pp. 8. M. 2.50 — 4.50. 4 s. 6 d. (Trübner).

[24]*Idem.* Discoveries in the Ruins of Nineveh and Babylon, with Travels in Armenia, Kurdistan, and the Desert: being the Result of a Second Expedition undertaken for the Trustees of the British

Museum. London 1853. 8. With Maps, Plans and Illustr. M. 16—22. £ 1 1 s.

Idem. Nineveh und Babylon. Nebst Beschreibung seiner Reise in Armenien, Kurdistan und der Wüste. Übersetzt von *J. Th. Zenker.* Leipzig 1856. VIII, 526 pp. 8.

25 The Monuments of Nineveh, illustrating Mr. *Layard's* First Expedition to Assyria, from Drawings made on the Spot. London 1849 (100 plates. fol.); a Second Series of the Monuments of Nineveh, including Basreliefs from the Palace of Sennacherib and Bronzes from the Ruins of Nimroud, from Drawings made on the Spot, during a Second Expedition to Assyria, by *Austen Henry Layard.* London 1853 (71 plates. fol.). (£ 21). £ 10 10 s. (Trübner). M. 250.

26 *Fulgence Fresnel.* Lettre à M. Jules Mohl, écrite de Hillah, en décembre 1852, sur les antiquités babyloniennes: JA. V Sér., I, 1853, 485—548. II, 1853, 5—78.

27 *Sir Henry C. Rawlinson.* Babylonian Discoveries (of M. Taylor): Ath 1854, pp. 341 ff. 465 f. 525. 556 f. 654.]

28 *J. E. Taylor.* Notes on the Ruins of Muqeyer: JRAS XV, 1855, 260—276. Notes on Abu Shahrein and Tel el Lahm: ibid., 404—415.

29 *Sir Henry C. Rawlinson.* On the Birs Nimrud, or the Great Temple of Borsippa (read Jan. 13, 1855): JRAS XVIII, 1861, 1—34. 6 s.

30 *William Kennett Loftus.* Travels and Researches in Chaldaea and Susiana; with an Account of Excavations at Warka, the "Erech" of Nimrod, and Shúsh, "Shushan the Palace" of Esther, in 1849 —1852, under the Orders of Major-General Sir W. F. Williams of Kars, and also of the Assyrian Excavation Fund in 1853—4. London 1857. XVI, 436 pp. 8. 12 s.

31 *Idem.* Warkah: its Ruins and Remains: Transs. of the Royal Soc. of Litterature, VI, 1859, 1—64. 4 s. 6 d.

32 Expédition scientifique en Mésopotamie, exécutée par Ordre du Gouvernement de 1851 à 1854 par MM. *Fulgence Fresnel, Félix Thomas* et *Jules Oppert,* publiée sous les auspices de son Excellence M. le ministre de l'État par *Jules Oppert.* Tome I: Relation du voyage et résultats de l'expédition. Paris 1863. III, 370 pp. 4. Tome II vid. num. 84. Atlas de 21 planches. fol. Tome I, II et Atlas fr. 125. £ 7 10 s. (Trübner).

33 *George Smith.* Assyrian Discoveries; an Account of Explorations and Discoveries on the Site of Nineveh, during 1873 and 1874. With Illustrations. London 1875. XVI, 461 pp. 8. M. 12—20. 18 s. (Trübner).

34 *Hormuzd Rassam.* Excavations and Discoveries in Assyria (read 4. Nov., 1879): TSBA VII, 1882, 37—58. (Etiam seorsum). — Cf. num. 108.

35 *Idem.* Recent Assyrian and Babylonian Research: being a Paper read (on February 2nd, 1880) before the Victoria Institute, or Philosophical Society of Great Britain. London. Seventh edition. 38 pp. 8.

36 *Idem.* Recent Discoveries of Ancient Babylonian Cities: TSBA VIII, 1885, 172—197.

37 *Theo. G. Pinches.* The Antiquities found by Mr. H. Rassam at Abu-Habbah (Sippara): TSBA VIII, 1885, 164—171.

38 *Delauney.* Les fouilles de M. de Sarzec dans la Mésopotamie: Journal officiel 1881.

39 *Léon Heuzey.* Les fouilles de Chaldée. Communication d'une lettre de M. de Sarzec: RA XLII, 1881, novembre. (Seorsum: Paris 1882. 18 pp. 8). Cf. ibid. 1881, juillet, p. 56.

40 *George Perrot.* Les fouilles de M. de Sarzec en Chaldée: Revue des deux Mondes, 1er octobre 1882, LIII, 525—565.

Vide etiam num. 117.

41 *W. St. Chad Boscawen.* The Monuments and Inscriptions on the Rocks at Nahr-el-Kelb: TSBA VII, 1882, 331—352.

42 *Eberhard Schrader.* Die Keilinschriften am Eingange der Quellgrotte des Sebeneh-Su: Abhh. d. K. Preuss. Acad. d. Wiss. zu Berlin 1885. (Seorsum: Berlin 1885. 31 pp. 4. Mit 1 Tafel. M. 3).

43 *Francis Brown.* The Wolfe Exploring Expedition to Babylonia: Presbyterian Review 1886 (Jan.), 155—159.

44 The American Expedition to Mesopotamia: Ac 1886 (Nr. 736), 421—422.

45 *Joachim Ménant.* L'expédition Wolfe en Mésopotamie: RA VIII, 1886, 233—238.

46 *William Hayes Ward.* Report on the Wolfe Expedition to Babylonia 1884—85. Boston (Archaeological Institute of America) 1886. 33 pp. 8.

47 *Idem.* On Recent Explorations in Babylonia: Johns Hopkins University Circulars Nr. 49, May 1886.

48 *Ad. Erman.* Der Thontafelfund von Tell-Amarna: Sitzungsberr. der Kgl. Preuss. Ak. d. Wiss. zu Berlin, XXIII, 1888. 7 pp.

Cf.:

49 *Theo. G. Pinches.* Assyrian Antiquities. Guide to the Kouyunjik Gallery. With four Autotype Plates. Printed by Order of the Trustees. British Museum, London 1883. IV, 199 pp. 8. (1 s. 6 d., nunc) 4 d.

50 *Idem.* Assyrian Antiquities. Guide to the Nimroud Central Saloon. Printed by Order of the Trustees. British Museum, London 1886. XI, 128 pp. 8. 4 d.

B. DE INITIIS AC PROGRESSIBUS EXPLICATIONIS:

a) *scripturae cuneatae monumentorum persicorum.*

51 *Georg Friedrich Grotefend.* Praevia de cuneatis quas vocant inscriptionibus persepolitanis legendis et explicandis relatio [praelecta est 4. Sept. 1802]: GGA 1802, 1481—87. — Cf.:

52 *Idem.* Über die Erklärung der Keilschriften, und besonders der Inschriften von Persepolis: Beilage I der 1. Abth. des 1. Bandes von *A. H. L. Heeren.* Ideen über die Politik, den Verkehr und den Handel der vornehmsten Völker der alten Welt. 3. Aufl. Göttingen 1815. S. 564—603.

53 *Eug. Burnouf.* Mémoire sur deux inscriptions cunéiformes trouvées près d'Hamadan. Paris 1836. VII, 198 pp. 4. Cum 5 tabulis. 12 s. (Trübner).

54 *Christian Lassen.* Die altpersischen Keil-Inschriften von Persepolis. Entzifferung des Alphabets und Erklärung des Inhalts. Nebst geographischen Untersuchungen über die Lage der im Herodoteischen Satrapien-Verzeichnisse und in einer Inschrift erwähnten altpersischen Völker. Bonn 1836. Mit 2 Inschriftentaff. 8. M. 2—4.

55 *G. F. Grotefend.* Neue Beiträge zur Erläuterung der persepolitanischen Keilschrift nebst einem Anhange über die Vollkommenheit der ersten Art derselben. Mit 4 Steintafeln. Hannover 1837. 48 pp. 4.

56 Major *H. C. Rawlinson.* The Persian Cuneiform Inscription at Behistun decyphered and translated; with a Memoir on Persian Cuneiform Inscriptions in general, and on that of Behistun in particular: JRAS X, 1847, LXXI, 349 pp. 8. With 8 folding Plates. £ 2 10 s. (Trübner).

57 *Edward Hincks.* On the First and Second Kinds of Persepolitan Writing (read June 9th, 1846): TRIA XXI, 1848. Polite Lit., 114—131.

58 *H. C. Rawlinson.* Note on the Persian Inscriptions at Behistun: JRAS XII, 1850, I—XXI.

59 *Theodor Benfey.* Die persischen Keilinschriften mit Übersetzung und Glossar. Leipzig 1847. 97 pp. 8.

60 *J. Oppert.* Das Lautsystem des Altpersischen. Berlin 1847. 56 pp. 8. 8 s. (Trübner).

61 *Idem.* Mémoire sur les inscriptions achéménides [etiam: des Achéménides], conçues dans l'idiome des anciens Perses: JA. IV Sér., XVII, 1851, 255—296. 378—430. 534—591. XVIII, 1851, 56—83. 322—366. 553—584. XIX, 1852, 140—215.

62*Friedrich Spiegel.* Die altpersischen Keilinschriften. Im Grundtext mit Übersetzung, Grammatik und Glossar. 2. vermehrte Auflage. Leipzig 1881. VIII, 246 pp. 8. M. 9. (pp. 133—148: Kurze Geschichte der Entzifferung). (1. Aufl. Leipzig 1862).

Cf.:

63Inscriptiones Palaeo-Persicae Achaemenidarum, quot hucusque repertae sunt ad apographa viatorum criticasque Chr. Lassenii, Th. Benfeyi, J. Oppertii nec non Fr. Spiegelii editiones archetyporum typis primus edidit et explicavit, commentarios criticos adjecit glossariumque comparativum Palaeo-Persicum subjunxit *Cajetanus Kossowicz.* Petropoli 1872. 8. fr. 40. £ 3 (Trübner).

64*Joachim Ménant.* La stèle de Chalouf. Essai de restitution du texte perse: Recueil de travaux relatifs à la philologie et à l'archéologie égyptiennes et assyriennes IX, livr. 3/4. (Seorsum: Paris 1887. 27 pp. Cum 1 tabula).

b) scripturae cuneatae monumentorum babylonicorum et assyriacorum.

65*Isidore Loewenstern.* Essai de déchiffrement de l'écriture assyrienne pour servir à l'explication du monument de Khorsabad. Paris 1845. 36 pp. 8. Cum 3 tabulis. fr. 5.

66*Idem.* Exposé des éléments constitutifs du système de la troisième écriture cunéiforme de Persépolis. Paris et Leipsic 1847. 101 pp. 8. (fr. 10). M. 5. 7 s. 6 d. (Trübner).

67*H. A. P. de Longpérier.* Lettre à M. Isidore Loewenstern sur les inscriptions cunéiformes de l'Assyrie (20. sept. 1847): RA IV. année, 2. partie (oct. 1847—mars 1848), 501—507.

68*E. Hincks.* On the three Kinds of Persepolitan Writing, and on the Babylonian Lapidary Characters (read 30. Nov., and 14. Dec., 1846): TRIA XXI, 1848. Polite Lit. 233—248. (Seorsum: Dublin 1847).

69*Idem.* On the Third Persepolitan Writing, and on the Mode of expressing Numerals in Cuneatic Characters (read 11. Jan., 1847): TRIA XXI, 1848. Polite Lit., 249—256.

70*P. E. Botta.* Mémoire sur l'écriture cunéiforme assyrienne: JA. IV Sér., IX, 1847, 373—391. 465—505. X, 1847, 121—148. 207—229. 296—324. 444—472. XI, 1848, 242—273. (Seorsum: Paris 1848. 197 pp. 8. fr. 5. M. 3.50).

71*F. de Saulcy.* Recherches sur l'écriture cunéiforme du système assyrien [vel: .... cunéiforme assyrienne]. Inscriptions des Achéménides. Mémoires autographiés (14. Sept. et 27. Nov. 1849). Paris 1849. 44 et 61 pp. 4.

72*Idem*. Sur les inscriptions assyriennes de Ninive. (Khorsabad, Nimroud, Koioundjouk): RA VI. année. (Seorsum: Paris 1850. 23 pp. 8. Cum 2 tabulis).
73*E. Hincks*. On the Khorsabad Inscriptions (read 25. June 1849): TRIA XXII, Part II, 1850. Polite Lit., 3—72. (Seorsum: Dublin 1850. 72 pp. 4. 12 s.).
74*H. C. Rawlinson*. A Commentary on the Cuneiform Inscriptions of Babylonia and Assyria, including Readings of the Inscription on the Nimrud Obelisk, and a Brief Notice of the Ancient Kings of Nineveh and Babylon. London 1850. 83 pp. 8. Cf.: Notes on the Inscriptions of Assyria and Babylonia (read on 19th January and 16th February 1850): JRAS XII, 1850, 401—483. 2 s. 6 d. (Trübner).
75*Idem*. Memoir on the Babylonian and Assyrian Inscriptions: JRAS XIV, Part I, 1851. CIV, 32 pp. and 16 folding Sheets. 6 s. (Trübner). [Partes hujus commentationis inscriptae sunt: Inscriptions of Behistun and detached Inscriptions at Nakhsh-i-Rustam; Indiscriminate List of Babylonian and Assyrian Characters; (pp. I—CIV:) Analysis of the Babylonian Text at Behistun.]
76*G. F. Grotefend*. Bemerkungen zur Inschrift eines Thongefässes mit babylonischer Keilschrift. Nebst zwei Steindrucktafeln [continentes textum originalem ejus inscriptionis Nebucadnezaris quae Neb. Grot. signatur]. Göttingen 1848. 18 pp. 4. (Aus dem IV. Bd. der Abhh. d. Kgl. Ges. d. Wiss. zu Göttingen).
77*Idem*. Bemerkungen zur Inschrift eines Thongefässes mit ninivitischer Keilschrift. Nebst 3 Steindrucktafeln: Abhh. der Kgl. Ges. d. Wiss. zu Göttingen, IV, 1850. Cf.: Nachträge zu den Bemerkungen über ein niniv. Thongefäss, ibid. 1850.
78*E. Hincks*. On the Assyro-Babylonian Phonetic Characters (read 24. May, 1852): TRIA XXII, Part IV, 1853. Polite Lit., 293—370. (Etiam seorsum: A List of Assyro-Babylonian Characters with their Phonetic Values. Dublin 1852. 4.).
79*G. F. Grotefend*. Erläuterung der Keilinschriften babylonischer Backsteine mit einigen anderen Zugaben und einer Steindrucktafel. Hannover 1852. 4. Mit 1 Tafel. M. 1.
80*Idem*. Die Tributverzeichnisse des Obelisken aus Nimrud nebst Vorbemerkungen über den verschiedenen Ursprung und Charakter der persischen und assyrischen Keilschrift und Zugaben über die babylonische Current- und medische Keilschrift. Mit 2 lithogr. und 3 gedr. Tafeln: Abhh. d. Kgl. Ges. d. Wiss. zu Göttingen, V, 1852. 94 pp. 4. M. 2.
81*Idem*. Erläuterung einer Inschrift des letzten assyrisch-babylonischen Königs aus Nimrud, mit 3 anderen Zugaben und einer Steindrucktafel. Hannover 1853.

82 *Idem.* Erläuterung der babylonischen Keilinschriften aus Behistun. Göttingen 1853. 4. Cum 1 tabula. M. 1.

83 *F. de Saulcy.* Traduction de l'inscription assyrienne de Behistoun: JA. V Sér., III, 1854, 93—160.

84 *Jules Oppert.* Expédition scientifique en Mésopotamie (vid. num. 32). Tome II: Déchiffrement des inscriptions cunéiformes. Paris 1859. II, 366 pp. 4. Compendiose scribimus: *E. M.* II.

85 *Joachim Ménant.* Les noms propres assyriens. Recherches sur la formation des expressions idéographiques. Paris 1861. 64 pp. 8. M. 4.

86 *E. Hincks.* On the Polyphony of the Assyrio-Babylonian Cuneiform Writing. A Letter to Professor Renouf. Dublin 1863. 58 pp. 8. (From the Atlantis, Vol. IV).

Cf. ad B, a et b:

87 *J. Ménant.* Les écritures cunéiformes. Exposé des travaux qui ont préparé la lecture et l'interprétation des inscriptions de la Perse et de l'Assyrie. 2. édit. 2 parties. Paris 1864. 310 pp. 8. (fr. 30). fr. 15. 15 s.

88 *Idem.* Leçons d'épigraphie assyrienne, professées aux cours libres de la Sorbonne pendant l'année 1869. Paris 1873. VIII, 115 pp. 8. fr. 6.

89 *Fr. Spiegel.* Geschichte der Entzifferung der Keilschrift: Ausland 1865 (Nr. 18, 6. Mai), 409—420.

90 *Wellhausen.* Über den bisherigen Gang und den gegenwärtigen Stand der Keilentzifferung: Rhein. Mus. f. Phil., N. F., XXXI, 1876, 153—175.

Cf. ad A et B:

91 *Fr. Kaulen.* Assyrien und Babylonien nach den neuesten Entdeckungen. 3. Aufl. Mit Titelbild, 78 in den Text gedruckten Holzschnitten, 6 Tonbildern, einer Inschrifttafel und zwei Karten. Freiburg im Breisgau 1885. X, 266 pp. 8. M. 6. (pp. 19—132).

92 *Fritz Hommel.* Geschichte Babyloniens und Assyriens. Mit Abbildungen und Karten. Berlin 1885 ff. pp. 58—134.

93 *J. Ménant.* Les langues perdues de la Perse et de l'Assyrie. Rouen: Perse, 1885. XI, 172 pp. Assyrie, 1886. XVI, 340 pp. 8.

c) collectiones signorum quibus scriptura utitur.

94 *George Smith.* The Phonetic Values of the Cuneiform Characters. London 1871. 23 pp. 8.

95*J. Ménant.* Le Syllabaire Assyrien. Exposé des éléments du système phonétique de l'écriture anarienne. (Extr. du tome VII, I Sér., 1re et 2e partie, des Mémoires présentés par divers savants à l'Académie des Inscriptions et Belles-lettres). Paris: I. partie, 1869. IV, 455 pp. II. partie, 1873. IV, 462 pp. 4. (fr. 60). M. 25.

96a*Ed. de Chossat.* Essai d'une classification du syllabaire assyrien: Moderne-archaïque, Babylonien-Ninivite. Paris 1873. 93 pp.

96b*Idem.* Classification des caractères cunéiformes, babyloniens et ninivites. Paris [sine anno]. 261 pp. 4.

97*Idem.* Répertoire assyrien. Traduction et lecture. Lyon 1879. VIII, 184 pp. et 204 pp. lithogr. 4. M. 25.

98*Idem.* Répertoire sumérien (accadien). Lyon 1882. VI, 217 pp.

99*Eb. Schrader.* Assyrisches Syllabar für den Gebrauch in seinen Vorlesungen zusammengestellt. Mit den Jagdinschriften Asurbanipals in Anlage. Berlin 1880. 8 pp. 4. M. 1.50.

Vide etiam num. 110. 112. 127 et 143.

100*A. Amiaud* et *L. Méchineau.* Tableau comparé des écritures babylonienne et assyrienne, archaiques et modernes, avec classement des signes d'après leur forme archaïque. Paris 1887. XVI, 148 pp. 8. (fr. 15). fr. 12.75.

101*Rudolph E. Brünnow.* A classified List of all Simple and Compound Cuneiform Ideographs occurring in the Texts hitherto published, with their Assyro-Babylonian Equivalents, Phonetic Values etc. Leyden: Part I. II. 1887. 400 pp. 4.

Cf.:

102*W. Houghton.* On the Hieroglyphic or Picture Origin of the Characters of the Assyrian Syllabary: TSBA VI, 1879, 454—483.

C. EDITIONES TEXTUUM.

Vide num. 75 et 84.

103*P. E. Botta.* Monument de Ninive (vid. num. 20). Voll. III. IV: Inscriptions. Paris 1849.

104Inscriptions in the Cuneiform Character, from Assyrian Monuments, discovered by *A. H. Layard.* London, printed by Harrison and Son, 1851. 98 plates. fol. M. 20. Compendium: **Lay.**

105The Cuneiform Inscriptions of Western Asia. London. 5 Vols. Vol. I. A Selection from the Historical Inscriptions of Chaldaea, Assyria, and Babylonia. Prepared for publication by Major-General *Sir H. C. Rawlinson*, assisted by *Edwin Norris*; lithographed by *R. E. Bowler.* 1861. 70 tabulae. [Non jam venale].

Vol. II. A Selection from the Miscellaneous Inscriptions of Assyria. Prepared for publication, under the Direction of the Trustees of the British Museum, by Major-General *Sir H. C. Rawlinson*, assisted by *Edwin Norris*; lithographed by *R. E. Bowler*. 1866. 70 tabulae. M. 20. Vol. III. .... assisted by *George Smith* .... 1870. 70 tabulae. Vol. IV. 1875. [Initio anni 1889 denuo edetur]. Vol. V. .... assisted by *Theophilus G. Pinches*; lithographed by *J. Jankowsky*. 1880 (tabulae 1—35). [Non jam venale.] 1884 (tabulae 36—70). M. 10.60. Compendium: **I R, II R** etc. [secundum alios: W. A. I.]

106 *J. Oppert* et *J. Ménant*. Les Fastes de Sargon, roi d'Assyrie (721 à 703 av. J.-Ch.), traduits et publiés d'après le texte assyrien de la grande inscription des salles du palais de Khorsabad. Paris 1863. fol. (fr. 15). M. 20. £ 1 10 s. (Trübner). (Extr. du JA. VI Sér., I, 1863, 5—26. II, 1863, 475—517. III, 1864, 5—62. 168—201. 209—265. 373—415): *O.* et *M.* Grande inscription du palais de Khorsabad, publiée et commentée. 8. 15 s. (Trübner). Compendium: **Khors.**

107 *François Lenormant*. Choix de textes cunéiformes inédits ou incomplètement publiés jusqu'à ce jour. 3 fasc. Paris 1873—1875. 270 pp. 4. fr. 15. M. 12.

108 *Theo. G. Pinches*. The Bronze Gates discovered by Mr. Rassam at Balawat (read 5. Nov., 1878): TSBA VII, 1882, 83—118.

109 The Bronze Ornaments of the Palace Gates of (vel: from) Balawat. (Shalmanaser II., B. C. 859—825.) Edited, with an Introduction, by *Samuel Birch*, with Descriptions and Translations by *Theophilus G. Pinches*. Parts I—IV. London 1880—1882. 72 tabulae. fol. £ 1 10 s. each part. M. 120.

110 *Paul Haupt*. Akkadische und sumerische Keilschrifttexte nach den Originalen im Britischen Museum copirt. 4 Lieferungen. Leipzig 1881—1882. 220 pp. 4. M. 36. [Fasciculus quintus nondum editus est.] (Assyriologische Bibliothek, hrsgn. von Friedr. Delitzsch und Paul Haupt, Bd. I). Compendium: **ASKT.**

111 *Eb. Schrader*. Die Sargonsstele des Berliner Museums: Abhh. d. Kgl. Akad. d. Wiss. zu Berlin 1881. Mit 2 Tafeln. (Seorsum: Berlin 1882. 36 pp. 4. M. 3).

112 *Theo. G. Pinches*. Texts in the Babylonian Wedge-Writing, autographed from the Original Documents. With a List of Characters and their Meanings. Part I. Texts in the Assyrian Language only, from the Royal Library at Nineveh. London 1882. V, 20 pp. 8. 4 s. 6 d. Compendium: **Pinches, *Texts*.**

113 *Carl Bezold*. Die Achämenideninschriften. Transcription des babylonischen Textes nebst Übersetzung, textkritischen Anmerkungen und einem Wörter- und Eigennamenverzeichnisse. Mit

dem Keilschrifttexte der kleineren Achämenideninschriften, autographirt von *Paul Haupt*. Leipzig 1882. XVI, 96 pp. 4. M. 24. (Assyriol. Bibl., Bd. II).

114*J. N. Strassmaier*. Die altbabylonischen Verträge aus Warka. (Mit einer autographischen Beilage): Verhandlungen des V. internationalen Orientalisten-Congresses, gehalten zu Berlin im Sept. 1881. Zweiter Theil, I. Hälfte. Berlin 1882, 315—364, nebst 144 autographirten pp. (Etiam seorsum. M. 4).

115*D. G. Lyon*. Keilschrifttexte Sargon's, Königs von Assyrien (722—705 v. Chr.). Nach den Originalen neu herausgegeben, umschrieben, übersetzt und erklärt. Leipzig 1883. XVI, 93 pp. 4. M. 24. (Assyriol. Bibl., Bd. V).

116*Paul Haupt*. Das babylonische Nimrodepos. Keilschrifttext der Bruchstücke der sog. Izdubarlegenden mit dem keilinschriftlichen Sintfluthberichte nach den Originalen im Britischen Museum copirt und herausgegeben. Abth. I, den Keilschrifttext der ersten 10 Tafeln enth. Leipzig 1884. 78 pp. 4. M. 20. (Assyriol. Bibl., Bd. III, 1). Compendium: **Nimr. Ep.**

117*Ernest de Sarzec*. Découvertes en Chaldée: Ouvrage accompagné de planches. Publié par les soins de *Léon Heuzey*. Sous les Auspices du Ministère de l'Instruction publique et des Beaux-Arts. Paris: 1. livraison 1884. 2. livr. 1887.

118*J. N. Strassmaier*. Die babylonischen Inschriften im Museum zu Liverpool nebst anderen aus der Zeit von Nebukadnezzar bis Darius: tiré du Vol. II des Travaux de la 6e session du Congrès international des Orientalistes à Leide. Leide 1885. 56 + 176 pp. 8. M. 18. Compendium: **Str. I.**

119Collection de Clercq. Catalogue méthodique et raisonné. Antiquités assyriennes. Cylindres orientaux, cachets, briques, bronzes, bas-reliefs, etc. publiés par M. *de Clercq* avec la collaboration de M. *J. Ménant*. 3 livraisons. Paris 1885 ss. fol. fr. 60.

120*J. F. X. O'Conor*. Cuneiform Text of a recently discovered Cylinder of Nebuchadnezzar. With 12 plates of Cuneiform Text. With Transcription and Translation. Woodstock 1885. 53 pp. M. 7.50.

121*J. A. Craig*. Throne-Inscription of Salmanassar II.: Hebraica II (Nr. 3, April 1886), 140—146. Vide num. 191.

122*H. Pognon*. Les inscriptions babyloniennes du Wadi Brissa. Ouvrage accompagné de 14 planches. (Bibliothèque de l'École des hautes études, 71. fasc.). Paris 1887. II, 199 pp. 8. (fr. 12). fr. 9.60. M. 10.

123*Samuel Alden Smith*. Die Keilschrifttexte Asurbanipals, Königs von Assyrien (668—626 v. Chr.) nach dem in London copirten Grundtext mit Transcription, Übersetzung, Kommentar und vollständigem Glossar. Heft II. Neue Bautexte, unveröffentlichte

Briefe und Depeschen mit Originaltextausgabe u. s. w. Leipzig 1887. IV, 99 pp. 8. Mit 23 Seiten Keilschriftdruck. M. 12. Compendium: **Asurb. S. A. Sm. II.**

124*Idem.* Miscellaneous Assyrian Texts of the British Museum, with Textual Notes. Leipzig 1887. VII, 16 pp., 28 tabulae. 8. M. 7.

125*J. N. Strassmaier.* Babylonische Texte. Inschriften von Nabonidus, König von Babylon (558—538 v. Chr.), von den Thontafeln des britischen Museums copirt und autographirt. Enthaltend 1134 Inschriften mit 5 Registern. Leipzig 1889. (Heft I. II 1887. III 1888. IV 1889). X, 68 + 640 pp. (M. 48). M. 43.20. Compendium: **Str. II.**

126*Theo. G. Pinches.* The Babylonian Chronicle: JRAS. N. S., XIX, 1887, 655—681.

Cf.:

127*Friedrich Delitzsch.* Assyrische Lesestücke nach den Originalen theils revidirt, theils zum ersten Male herausgegeben nebst Paradigmen, Schrifttafel, Textanalyse und kleinem Wörterbuch zum Selbstunterricht wie zum akademischen Gebrauch. 3., durchaus neu bearbeitete Auflage. Leipzig 1885. XVI, 148 pp. kl. fol. M. 30. (2. Aufl. 1878. VIII, 107 pp. M. 24). Compendium: AL³.

Vide etiam num. 143. 148. 157.

D. LIBRI GRAMMATICI ET COMMENTATIONES GRAMMATICAE.

128*E. Hincks.* On the Personal Pronouns of the Assyrian and other Languages, especially Hebrew (read 26. June, 1854): TRIA XXIII, Part II, 1859. Polite Lit., 3—10.

129*Idem.* On Assyrian Verbs: Journal of Sacred Literature and Biblical Record. Nr. II, July 1855, 381—393. Nr. III, Oct. 1855, 141—162. Nr. V, April 1856, 152—171. July 1856, 392—403. London 1855—1856.

130*J. Oppert.* Éléments de la grammaire assyrienne. Paris 1860. (Extr. du JA. V Sér., XV, 97—130. 338—398). — Duppe Lisan Assur. Éléments de la grammaire assyrienne. Seconde édition considérablement augmentée. Paris 1868. XXII, 126 pp. 8. (fr. 6). fr. 3.35.

131*J. Olshausen.* Prüfung des Charakters der in den assyrischen Keilinschriften enthaltenen semitischen Sprache: Abhh. der Kgl. Akad. d. Wiss. zu Berlin 1864, 475—496. (Seorsum: Berlin 1865. 4. M. 0.80).

132 *E. Hincks.* Specimen Chapters of an Assyrian Grammar: JRAS. N. S. II, 1866, 480—519. (Seorsum: London 1866. 40 pp. 8. 1 s.).

133 *J. Ménant.* Exposé des éléments de la grammaire assyrienne. Imprimé par Ordre de S. M. L'empereur à l'Imprimerie Impériale. Paris 1868. IV, 392 pp. 8. (fr. 15). M. 8—15. fr. 10 (Welter).

134 *Eb. Schrader.* Die assyrisch-babylonischen Keilinschriften. Kritische Untersuchung der Grundlagen ihrer Entzifferung: ZDMG XXVI, 1872, 1—392. (Etiam seorsum: Leipzig 1872. £ 1. (Trübner)). Compendium: **ABK.**

135 *A. H. Sayce.* An Assyrian Grammar for Comparative Purposes. London 1872. XVI, 188 pp. 8. 7 s. 6 d. (Trübner).

136 *Idem.* An Elementary Grammar; with Full Syllabary and Progressive Reading Book, of the Assyrian Language in the Cuneiforme Type. London 1875. VI, 129 pp. 4. 9 s.

137 *Idem.* Lectures upon the Assyrian Language and Syllabary. London 1877. VIII, 157 pp. 4. 9 s. 6 d. (Trübner).

138 *Idem.* The Tenses of the Assyrian Verb: JRAS. N. S., IX, 1877, 22—58.

139a *Eb. Schrader.* Über die Aussprache der Zischlaute im Assyrischen: Abhh. der Kgl. Akad. d. Wiss. zu Berlin, vom 5. März 1877. — Cf. ZDMG XXVI, 195 f. Jenaer Literaturzeitung 1874, Nr. 15; *B. Stade.* Erneute Prüfung des zwischen dem Phönikischen und Hebräischen bestehenden Verwandtschaftsgrades, p. 181 ff. Anm. in: Morgenländische Forschungen, Leipzig 1875; *F. Philippi.* Das Zahlwort zwei im Semitischen: ZDMG XXXII, 21 ff. (24—32).

139b *Idem.* Zur Frage nach der Aussprache der Zischlaute im Babylonisch-Assyrischen: ZK I, 1884, 1—18. — Cf. *St. Guyard.* Quelques remarques sur la prononciation et la transcription de la chuintante et de la sifflante en Assyrie: ibid. 27—31.

140 *Fritz Hommel.* Zwei Jagdinschriften Asurbanibal's nebst einem Excurs über die Zischlaute im Assyrischen wie im Semitischen überhaupt. Mit einer photolithographischen Abbildung. Leipzig 1879. VIII, 63 pp. 8. (M. 5.60). M. 3—3.50. Cf. *Fr. Philippi* Zeitschr. f. Völkerpsychol. u. Sprachw. XIII, 143—165. *Paul Haupt* ZDMG XXXIV, 1880, 757—763.

141 *Paul Haupt.* The Oldest Semitic Verb-Form: JRAS. N. S., X, 1878, 244—252.

142 *Idem.* Die sumerischen Familiengesetze in Keilschrift, Transcription und Übersetzung, nebst ausführlichem Commentar und zahlreichen Excursen. Eine assyriologische Studie. Leipzig 1879. VIII, 75 pp. 4. M. 12. Compendium: **SFG.**

Vide etiam 178.

143 *J. Ménant.* Manuel de la langue assyrienne. I. Le syllabaire. II. La grammaire. III. Choix de lectures. Imprimé par

Autorisation du Gouvernement à l'Imprimerie Nationale. Paris 1880. V, 383 pp. 8. 18 s. (Trübner).

144 *Theo. G. Pinches.* Papers upon Assyrian Grammar: PSBA (Nov. 7, 1882) V, 1883, 21—31. (Jan. 8, 1884) VI, 1884, 62—67.

145 *P. Haupt.* Beiträge zur assyrischen Lautlehre: Nachrichten v. d. Kgl. Ges. d. Wiss. und der Georg-Augusts-Univ. zu Göttingen 1883, 25. April, Nr. 4, 85—115.

146a *Idem.* Assyrian Phonology, with Special Reference to Hebrew: Hebraica I, 1885, 175—181.

146b *Idem.* Wâteh-ben-Hazael, Prince of the Kedarenes about 650 B. C.: Hebraica I, 1885, 217—231. (Seorsum: Chicago 1885).

146c *Idem.* On the Etymology of *Mûtnînû*: Hebraica II (Nr. 1, Oct. 1885), 4—6.

147 *J. F. McCurdy.* The Semitic Perfect in Assyrian: Travaux de la 6e session du Congrès international des Orientalistes à Leide I, 507—534. (Seorsum: Leiden 1885. 25 pp. M. 1.50).

Vide etiam num. 122.

148 *D. G. Lyon.* An Assyrian Manual for the Use of Beginners in the Study of the Assyrian Language. Chicago 1886. XLV, 138 pp. 8. 21 s.

149 *E. Müller.* Grammatische Bemerkungen zu den Annalen Asurnaṣirpals: ZA I, 1886, 349—379.

150 *P. Haupt.* On the Etymology of *nekasim*: Hebraica III (Nr. 2, Jan. 1887), 107—110.

151 *Idem.* On the Pronunciation of *tr* in Old Persian: Johns Hopkins University Circulars, Nr. 58, Aug. 1887.

152 *Idem.* Über den Halbvocal *ṷ* im Assyrischen: ZA II, 259—286.

153 *Idem.* The Assyrian *e*-Vowel. A Contribution to the Comparative Phonology of the Assyro-Babylonian Language: Americ. Journ. of Phil. VIII, 1887, 265—291. (Seorsum: Baltimore 1887. 29 pp. 8.). [Hac commentatione nituntur quae in §§ 32—35 exposuimus.]

154 *J. Barth.* Das Nominalpräfix *na* im Assyrischen: ZA II, 1887, 111—117.

155 *Idem.* Das semitische Perfect im Assyrischen: ZA II, 375—386.

156 *Idem.* Verschiebung der Liquidae im Assyrischen: ZA III, 57—61.

157 *Brutto Teloni.* Crestomazia assira con paradigmi grammaticali: Publicazioni della Società Asiatica Italiana. Vol. I. Roma-Firenze-Torino 1887. IV, 144 pp. 8. L. 10. M. 9.

158 *Eb. Schrader.* Zur Aussprache der Zeichen *a-a* und *ia* im Babylonisch-Assyrischen: ZA III, 1—16.

159 *George Bertin.* Abridged Grammars of the Languages of the Cuneiform Inscriptions containing I. A Sumero-Akkadian Gram-

mar (pp. 1—26). II. An Assyro-Babylonian Grammar (pp. 27—69). III. A Vannic Grammar. IV. A Medic Grammar. V. An Old Persian Grammar. London 1888. VIII, 117 pp. 8. 5 s.

E. TRANSLATIONES ET INTERPRETATIONES TEXTUUM.

Vide num. 81.

160 *J. Oppert.* Études assyriennes. Inscription de Borsippa, relative à la restauration de la Tour des langues, par Nebuchodonozor: JA. V Sér., IX, 1857, 125—209. 490—548. X, 1857, 168—226.

161 Comparative Translations, by *W. H. Fox Talbot, E. Hincks, Oppert,* and *Sir Henry C. Rawlinson,* of the Inscription of Tiglath Pilesar I: JRAS XVIII, 1861, 150—219. (Seorsum: Inscription of Tiglath Pileser I., King of Assyria, B. C. 1150, as translated by *Sir H. Rawlinson, Fox Talbot,* Dr. *Hincks,* and Dr. *Oppert.* London. Published by the Royal Asiatic Society. 73 pp. 8. 2 s.).

162 *J. Oppert.* Les inscriptions assyriennes des Sargonides et les fastes de Ninive: Versailles 1862. 60 pp. 8. fr. 1.50. (Extr. des Annales de philosophie chrétienne, V Sér., VI, 1862).

Vide etiam num. 32 (tome I).

163 *J. Ménant.* Inscriptions de Hammourabi, roi de Babylone (XVIe siècle avant J.-C.), traduites et publiées avec un commentaire à l'appui. Paris 1863. 12 tabulae, 80 pp. 8. fr. 10. M. 7—10.

164 *J. Oppert.* Grande inscription de Khorsabad. Commentaire philologique. Supplément. Paris 1866. 8. 6 s. (Trübner)). Cf. num. 106.

165 *Idem.* Histoire des Empires de Chaldée et d'Assyrie d'après les monuments, depuis l'établissement définitif des Sémites en Mésopotamie (2000 ans avant J.-C.) jusqu'aux Séleucides (150 ans avant J.-C). Versailles 1865. 144 pp. 8. M. 2.25. 4 s. (Trübner). (Extr. des Annales de philos. chrét., V Sér., XI, 1865, 81—112. 165—186).

166 *J. Ménant.* Inscriptions de revers de plaque du palais de Khorsabad, traduites sur le texte assyrien. Paris 1865. 23 pp. fol. (Texte, transcription et traduction). fr. 10. (Extr. du Journal de la Société des Antiquaires, 1865).

167 *J. Oppert.* Les inscriptions commerciales en caractères cunéiformes. Paris 1866. 9 pp. 8. fr. 2. (Extr. de la Revue orientale et américaine, tome VI, 333—341).

168 *Idem.* Les inscriptions de Dour-Sarkayan (Khorsabad); provenant des fouilles de M. Victor Place, déchiffrées et interprétées. Paris 1870. 39 pp. fol. (fr. 30). M. 16.

169 *George Smith.* History of Assurbanipal, translated from the Cuneiform Inscriptions. London 1871. IV, 384 pp. 8. M. 60. £ 2 10 s. (Trübner). Compendium: **Asurb. Sm.**

Vide etiam num. 33 (p. 165 ss.).

170 *J. Ménant.* Annales des rois d'Assyrie traduites et mises en ordre sur le texte assyrien. Paris 1874. XII, 312 pp. 8. fr. 15.

171 *Idem.* Babylone et la Chaldée. Paris 1875. VII, 303 pp. 8. fr. 15.

172 *Eb. Schrader.* Die Höllenfahrt der Istar. Ein altbabylonisches Epos. Nebst Proben assyrischer Lyrik. Text, Übersetzung, Commentar und Glossar. Giessen 1874. 153 pp. 8. (M. 4.) M. 2.80—3.

173 *J. Oppert.* L'immortalité de l'âme chez les Chaldéens. Traduction de la Descente de la déesse Istar (Astarté) aux enfers. Paris 1875. 28 pp. 8. fr. 1.50. (Extr. des Annales de philos. chrét., VIII, 1874).

174 *J. Oppert* et *J. Ménant.* Documents juridiques de l'Assyrie et de la Chaldée. Paris 1877. VIII, 366 pp. 8. fr. 20.

175 *G. Smith.* History of Sennacherib, translated from the Cuneiform Inscriptions. Edited by *A. H. Sayce.* London 1878. IV, 182 pp. 4. Compendium: **Sanh. Sm.**

176 *Reinhart Hörning.* Das sechsseitige Prisma des Sanherib in Grundtext und Übersetzung, nebst Beiträgen zu seiner Erklärung. Leipzig 1878. 32 pp. 4. (Diss.).

177 *A. Delattre.* Les inscriptions historiques de Ninive et de Babylone. Aspect général de ces documents, examen raisonné des versions françaises et anglaises. Paris 1879. 90 pp. 8. 3 s. (Trübner).

178 *H. Pognon.* L'inscription de Bavian. Texte, traduction et commentaire philologique avec trois appendices et un glossaire. Paris 1879—1880. 221 pp. 8. (Trente-neuvième et quarante-deuxième fascicule de la Bibliothèque de l'école des hautes études, publiée sous les auspices du Ministère de l'instruction publique. Sciences philologiques et historiques). (fr. 12). fr. 8.75.

179 *Wilhelm Lotz.* Die Inschriften Tiglathpileser's I. in transscribirtem assyrischem Grundtext mit Übersetzung und Kommentar. Mit Beigaben von *Friedrich Delitzsch.* Leipzig 1880. XVI, 224 pp. M. 20.

180 *Ernest A. Budge.* The History of Esarhaddon (Son of Sennacherib), King of Assyria, B. C. 681—668, translated from the Cuneiform Inscriptions upon Cylinders and Tablets in the British Museum Collection, together with Original Texts, a Grammatical Analysis of each Word, Explanations of the Ideographs by Extracts from the Bi-lingual Syllabaries, and List of Eponyms, etc. London 1880. XII, 163 pp. 8. 10 s.

Vide etiam num. 108. 109. 111. 113. 115.

181 *J. Halévy.* Documents religieux de l'Assyrie et de la Babylonie. Ire partie (seule parue): Texte assyrien (en caractères hébreux), traduction et commentaire. Ire partie contenant le texte complet

et une partie de la traduction et du commentaire. Paris 1882. 144 + 200 pp. 8. M. 8.50.

182 *Hermann Hilprecht.* Freibrief Nebukadnezar's I, Königs von Babylonien (c. 1130 v. Chr.), zum ersten Mal veröffentlicht, umschrieben und übersetzt. Leipzig 1883. XVI, 9 pp. 4. (Diss.).

183 *Johannes Flemming.* Die grosse Steinplatteninschrift Nebukadnezars II. in transscribiertem babylonischen Grundtext nebst Übersetzung und Commentar. Göttingen 1883. VIII, 61 pp. 8. (Diss.). — Cf. *J. Oppert* GGA, 1884, 329—340.

184 *H. Pognon.* Inscription de Mérou-nérar Ier, roi d'Assyrie: JA. VIII Sér., II, 1883, 351—431. III, 1884, 293—335.

185 *P. Jensen.* De Incantamentorum sumerico-assyriorum seriei quae dicitur „*šurbu*" tabula sexta (commentatio philologica): ZK I, 1884, 279—322. II, 1885, 15—61. (Revidierter Separatabdruck: Monachii 1885. 91 pp. 8.).

186 *J. Oppert.* Le poème chaldéen du déluge. Traduit de l'assyrien. Paris 1885. 13 pp.

187 *Idem.* Inscription d'Antiochus I Soter: Mélanges Renier. Recueil de travaux publiés par l'école pratique des hautes études en mémoire de son président Léon Renier. Paris 1886, 217—232. — Cf. *Idem.* L'inscription babylonienne d'Antiochus Soter: Revue d'Assyriologie et d'Archéologie orientale I, 1885, 102—105.

188 *Heinrich Zimmern.* Babylonische Busspsalmen, umschrieben, übersetzt und erklärt. Leipzig 1885. X, 120 pp. 4. M. 30. (Assyriol. Bibl., Bd. VI).

189 *P. Haupt.* The Battle of Halûle, 691 B. C.: Andover Review 1886 (May), 542—547.

190 *H. Winckler.* De inscriptione Sargonis regis Assyriae quae vocatur Annalium. Berolini 1886. 62 pp. 8. (Diss.).

191 *James A. Craig.* The Monolith Inscription of Salmaneser II. (860—824 B. C.) collated, transcribed, translated and explained, together with Text, Transcription, Translation and Explanation of the Throne-Inscription of Salmaneser II. New Haven, Conn., 1887. 32 + 7 pp. 8. (Diss. Lips.).

192 *Victor* et *Eugène Revillout.* Sur le droit de la Chaldée au XXIIIe siècle et au VIe siècle avant notre ère. Appendice du livre: *Eugène Revillout.* Les obligations en droit égyptien comparé aux autres droits de l'antiquité. Paris 1886. pp. 275—530.

193 *Alfred Jeremias.* Die babylonisch-assyrischen Vorstellungen vom Leben nach dem Tode. Nach den Quellen mit Berücksichtigung der alttestamentlichen Parallelen dargestellt. Leipzig 1887. 126 pp. 8. M. 6.

Vid. etiam num. 122.

194 *Robert Francis Harper.* Cylinder A of the Esarhaddon Inscriptions, transliterated and translated, with Textual Notes, from the

Original Copy in the British Museum; together with the hitherto unpublished Texts of Cylinder C. New Haven 1888. IV, 35 pp. 8. (Diss. Lips.).

195*Theo. G. Pinches.* Inscribed Babylonian Tablets in the Possession of Sir Henry Peek, translated and explained. London 1888. VIII, 36 pp. 4. 3 s.

(196Cf.: Records of the Past, being English translations of the Assyrian and Egyptian Monuments. Vol. I. III. V. VII. IX. XI. London 1873—1878. (11 vols. fr. 50.)). [Nova editio propediem prodivit.]

F. LEXICOGRAPHIA.

197*F. de Saulcy.* Lexique de l'inscription assyrienne de Behistoun: JA. V Sér., tome V, 1855, 109—197.

198*H. Fox Talbot.* Contributions toward a Glossary of the Assyrian Language: JRAS. N. S.: Part. I: Vol. III, 1868, 1—64. Part. II: Vol. IV, 1870, 1—80.

199*Edwin Norris.* Assyrian Dictionary, intended to further the Study of the Cuneiform Inscriptions of Assyria and Babylonia. London: Part I. 1868. Part II. 1870. Part III. 1872. 1068 pp. 8. (£ 4 4 s.). M. 60. [Opus nonnisi ad NȘT perductum.]

200*Friedr. Delitzsch.* Assyrische Studien. Heft I. Assyrische Thiernamen mit vielen Excursen und einem assyrischen und akkadischen Glossar. Leipzig 1874. VIII, 190 pp. M. 8.

201*François Lenormant.* Études sur quelques parties des syllabaires cunéiformes. Essai de philologie accadienne et assyrienne. Paris 1876. XXIV, 329 pp. 8. (fr. 18.) M. 11.

202*Idem.* Études cunéiformes. Fasc. I—IV. Paris 1878—1879. 64. 56. 111. 150 pp. 8. (Extr. du JA. VII Sér., XI, 1878, et XII, 1879). à fr. 2.50. (IV. fasc. 4 s. (Trübner)).

Vide etiam num. 113. 115. 179.

203*Stanislas Guyard.* (Mélanges d'Assyriologie:) Notes de lexicographie assyrienne, suivies d'une étude sur les inscriptions de Van Paris 1883. II, 144 pp. 8. M. 5.

204*Idem.* Nouvelles notes de lexicographie assyrienne (§ 1—19): JA. VIII Sér., II, 1883, 184—198.

205*Idem.* Une nouvelle racine assyrienne: *barû*: JA. VIII Sér., III, 1884, 499—517.

206*Eb. Schrader.* Die Keilinschriften und das Alte Testament. Mit einem Beitrage von *Paul Haupt.* 2. umgearbeitete und sehr vermehrte Auflage. Nebst chronologischen Beigaben, zwei Glossaren, Registern und einer Karte. Giessen 1883. VII, 618 pp. 8. M. 16. Compendium: KAT.

Vide etiam num. 127.

207 *J. Halévy.* Notes de lexicographie assyrienne: ZK I, 75—78. 180—184. 262—269.

208 *J. N. Strassmaier.* Alphabetisches Verzeichniss der assyrischen und akkadischen Wörter der Cuneiform Inscriptions of Western Asia Vol. II sowie anderer meist unveröffentlichter Inschriften mit zahlreichen Ergänzungen und Verbesserungen, und einem Wörterverzeichniss zu den in den Verhandlungen des VI. Orientalisten-Congresses zu Leiden veröffentlichten babylonischen Inschriften. Leipzig 1886. IV, 1144 + IV, 66 pp. 4. M. 150. (Assyriol. Bibl., Bd. IV). Compendium: **Strassm.** — Appendix hujus operis etiam seorsum sub titulo:

209 *J. N. Strassmaier.* Wörterverzeichniss zu den babylonischen Inschriften im Museum zu Liverpool nebst anderen aus der Zeit von Nebukadnezar bis Darius, veröffentlicht in den Verhandlungen des VI. Orientalisten-Congresses zu Leiden. Leipzig 1886. IV, 66 pp. 4. M. 8.

210 *Friedr. Delitzsch.* Prolegomena eines neuen hebräisch-aramäischen Wörterbuchs zum Alten Testament. Leipzig 1886. IX, 218 pp. 8. M. 8. Compendium: **Proll.**

Vide etiam num. 122. 148.

211 *Friedr. Delitzsch.* Assyrisches Wörterbuch zur gesammten bisher veröffentlichten Keilschriftliteratur unter Berücksichtigung zahlreicher unveröffentlichter Texte. I. und II. Lieferung. Leipzig 1887—1888. 328 pp. 4. M. 61.50. Compendium: **WB.**

G. SCRIPTIONES PERIODICAE ET COLLECTANEA.

The Athenaeum.

Journal Asiatique.

Journal of the Royal Asiatic Society of Great Britain and Ireland. London: I Ser. 1834—1863 (20 vols.). New Series 1865—1887 (19 vols.).

Journal of Sacred Literature.

Revue Archéologique ou Recueil de documents et de mémoires relatifs à l'étude des monuments, à la numismatique et à la philologie de l'antiquité et du moyen age, publiés par les principaux archéologues français et étrangers. Paris 1844 ss.

Transactions of the Royal Irish Academy.

Transactions of the Royal Society of Litterature of the United Kingdom. London: I Ser. 1827—1842 (3 vols. 4.). II Ser. 1843—1874 (10 vols. 8). [Vol. VII, 1863, et VIII, 1866, continent translationes quas *Talbot* confecit.]

Zeitschrift der Deutschen Morgenländischen Gesellschaft.

Praeter haecce acta commemorentur:

212 Recueil de travaux relatifs à la philologie et à l'archéologie égyptiennes et assyriennes, pour servir de bulletin à la mission française du Caire, publié sous la direction de *G. Maspero.* Vol. I—IX. Paris 1870—1887. 4.

213 Transactions of the Society of Biblical Archaeology. Vol. I—IX. London 1872—1887. [Continent commentationes virorum eruditorum *George Smith, Talbot, Sayce, Lenormant, Pinches, Boscawen, Ernest A. Budge, George Bertin,* aliorum.] Compendium: **TSBA.**

214 Proceedings of the Society of Biblical Archaeology. Vol. I—X. London 1879—1888. Compendium: **PSBA.**

215 Assyriologische Bibliothek, herausgegeben von *Friedrich Delitzsch* und *Paul Haupt.* Bd. I—VI. Leipzig 1881—1885. Vid. num. 110. 113. 116. 208. 115. 188.

216 Mélanges d'Archéologie égyptienne et assyrienne, publiés sous la direction de M. *Mariette Bey.* Paris 1876 ss.

217a Zeitschrift für Keilschriftforschung und verwandte Gebiete, unter Mitwirkung der Herren A. Amiaud und E. Babelon in Paris, G. Lyon in Cambridge-Mass. und Theo. G. Pinches in London herausgegeben von *Carl Bezold* und *Fritz Hommel.* Leipzig: Bd. I. 1884. 365 pp. II. 1885 (Zeitschr. für Keilschriftforschung etc., begründet von *Fritz Hommel,* etc., herausgegeben von *Carl Bezold*). 434 pp. Compendium: **ZK.**

217b Zeitschrift für Assyriologie und verwandte Gebiete in Verbindung mit J. Oppert in Paris, A. H. Sayce in Oxford, Eb. Schrader in Berlin, und Anderen herausgegeben von *Carl Bezold.* Bd. I. 1886. 464 pp. II. 1887. 464 pp. III. 1888. Compendium: **ZA.**

218 *J. Oppert* et *E. Ledrain.* Revue d'Assyriologie et d'Archéologie orientale. Paris: I. 1884—1886. II. 1888.

219 The Babylonian and Oriental Record: a Monthly Magazine of the Antiquities of the East. Director: Prof. *T. de Lacouperie.* Consulting Committee: *Theo. G. Pinches, Wm. C. Capper, W. St. Chad Boscawen,* and Dr. *C. de Harlez.* Assistant Editor: *H. M. Mackenzie.* London: Vol. I (Nr. 1—12), 1887. 210 pp. II, 1888. 244 pp. (Nr. 1—10). 4. Single Numbers 1 s. 6 d., Annual Subscription 12 s. 6 d. [Continet multas commentationes quas *Pinches* scripsit.]

220 *Friedr. Delitzsch* und *P. Haupt.* Beiträge zur Assyriologie und vergleichenden semitischen Sprachwissenschaft. I. Band. Heft 1. Leipzig 1889.

APPENDIX.

a) *Litteratura ad linguam quam vocant sumerico-accadicam.*

221*A. H. Sayce.* On Accadian Grammar: Journal of Philology, 1870.

222*Idem.* On an Accadian Seal: ibid. III, 1871.

223*J. Grivel.* Le plus ancien dictionnaire: Revue de la Suisse catholique 1871 (août). 17 pp. 8.

224*Fr. Lenormant.* Lettres assyriologiques. II Sér.: Études accadiennes. Tome I. Paris 1873. (1. partie: Introduction grammaticale. 207 pp. 2. partie: Restitution des paradigmes. 143 pp. 3. partie: Répertoire des caractères avec leurs valeurs accadiennes. 151 pp.). 4. fr. 15. Tome II. Paris 1874. (1. partie: Choix de textes avec traduction interlinéaire). 382 pp. 4. fr. 20. Tome III. Paris 1879. (1. livraison: Choix de textes bilingues formant une chrestomathie accadienne. 2. livr., 1880: Glossaire assyrien des mots compris dans les textes qui précèdent). 292 pp. 4. [Opus ab auctore non ad finem perductum.]

Vide num. 201. 202.

225*J. Oppert.* Études sumériennes. Article II. Sumérien ou rien: JA, may-juin 1875, 442—500. (Seorsum: Paris 1875. 3 s. 6 d. (Trübner)).

226*Idem.* Sumérien ou Accadien? Paris 1876. 8 pp. 8. fr. 1.

227*A. H. Sayce.* Accadian Phonology. London 1877. 20 pp.

228*F. Hommel.* Die neueren Resultate der sumerischen Forschung: ZDMG XXXII, 1878, 177—186.

Vide num. 142.

229*P. Haupt.* Über einen Dialekt der sumerischen Sprache: Nachrichten v. d. Kgl. Ges. d. Wiss. und der G. A.-Univ. zu Göttingen 1880, 3. Nov., Nr. 17, 513—541.

230a*Idem.* Die sumerisch-akkadische Sprache: Verhandlungen des V. internationalen Orientalisten-Congresses, gehalten zu Berlin im Sept. 1881. Zweiter Theil, I. Hälfte, 249—287. (Seorsum: Berlin 1882).

230b*Idem.* Die akkadische Sprache. Vortrag, gehalten auf dem V. internationalen Orientalisten-Congresse zu Berlin. Mit dem Keilschrifttexte des fünfspaltigen Vocabulars K. 4225 sowie zweier Fragmente der babylonischen Sintflutherzählung und einem Anhange von *O. Donner* über die Verwandtschaft des Sumerisch-Akkadischen mit den ural-altaischen Sprachen. Berlin 1883. XLIV, 48 pp. 8.

231 *Idem.* The Babylonian „Woman's Language": Americ. Journal of Phil., V, 1, 68—84. Cf. Johns Hopkins University Circulars Vol. III, 1884, Nr. 29, p. 51.

232 *Theo. G. Pinches.* Observations upon the Languages of the Early Inhabitants of Mesopotamia: JRAS. N. S., XVI, 1884, 301—324. (Etiam seorsum: 24 pp.).

Vide etiam num. 185. 188. 159.

233 *A. Amiaud.* L'inscription A de Gudea: ZK I, 1884, 233—256.

234 *Idem.* L'inscription H de Goudêa: ZA II, 1887, 287—298. —

235 *Fr. Lenormant.* Les principes de comparaison de l'Accadien et des langues touraniennes. Paris 1875. Réponse à une critique. 24 pp. 8. fr. 1.50.

236 *F. Hommel.* Die sumero-akkadische Sprache und ihre Verwandtschaftsverhältnisse: ZK I, 1884, 161—178. 195—221. 323—342. (Seorsum: 1884. 70 pp.). — Cf. *J. Halévy* RC 1885, 45—49.

b) *Ad quaestionem an revera existat lingua sumerica.*

237 *Joseph Halévy.* Observations critiques sur les prétendus Touraniens de la Babylonie: JA. VII. Sér., III, 1874, 461—536. (Etiam seorsum).

238 *Eb. Schrader.* Ist das Akkadische der Keilinschriften eine Sprache oder eine Schrift: ZDMG XXIX, 1875, 1—52.

239 *Fr. Lenormant.* La langue primitive de la Chaldée et les idiomes touraniens. Étude de philologie et d'histoire, suivie d'un glossaire accadien. Paris 1875. VII, 455 pp. et 2 planches. 8. fr. 25.

240 *J. Halévy.* La prétendue langue d'Accad est-elle touranienne? Réplique à M. Fr. Lenormant. Paris 1875. 31 pp. 8. 2 s. (Trübner).

241 *Idem.* Recherches critiques sur l'origine de la civilisation babylonienne. Paris 1876. 268 pp. 8. fr. 18. (Extr. du JA, années 1874 et 1876). — Cf. *Schrader*, Jenaer Literaturzeitung 1879 Art. 272.

242 *Idem.* La nouvelle évolution de l'accadisme. Paris 1876. 16 pp. II. partie 1878. 24 pp. 8. fr. 1.

243 *Idem.* Étude sur les documents philologiques assyriens: Mélanges de critique et d'histoire relatifs aux peuples sémitiques, Paris 1883, 241—364.

244 *St. Guyard.* Bulletin critique de la religion assyro-babylonienne. La question suméro-accadienne: Revue de l'histoire des religions, III. année, tome V, 252—278. (Seorsum: Paris 1882. 26 pp. 8).

245 *Idem.* Questions suméro-accadiennes: ZK I, 1884, 96—114.

246 *J. Halévy.* Les nouvelles inscriptions chaldéennes et la question de Sumer et d'Accad: Mélanges de critique et d'histoire, p. 389—409.

247 *Eb. Schrader.* Zur Frage nach dem Ursprung der altbabylonischen Cultur: Abhh. d. k. Preuss. Akad. d. Wiss. zu Berlin 1883.

(Seorsum: Berlin 1884. 49 pp. 4. M. 3). — Cf. *J. Halévy* RC 1884, 41—48. 61—77.

248 *J. Halévy*. Aperçu grammatical de l'allographie assyro-babylonienne: tiré du Vol. II des Travaux de la 6e session du Congrès international des Orientalistes à Leide. Leide 1884. 34 pp. 8. M. 2.

249 *Idem*. Les monuments chaldéens et la question de Sumir et d'Accad: CR. IV Sér., X, Avril-Juin.

250 *Idem*. La religion des anciens Babyloniens et son plus récent historien M. Sayce: Revue de l'histoire des religions, IX. année, XVII, 169—218. (Seorsum: Paris 1888. 51 pp.).

Corrigenda.

Page 41 line 6 from below: the expression 'but rarely' will have to be modified after what has been said on p. 302.

P. 84, lines 7—10: the ordinals *rebû*, *sebû*, *seššu* fall more appropriately under § 34, *b* (*vid.* § 76).

P. 94, l. 7 from below: delete *têziz* (= *itêziz*). The original has *itêziz*; *vid.* Haupt in Schrader's *Keilinschriften und das alte Testament* (KAT2) p. 60, note 1.

P. 113, l. 12, read: *seššu* (= *sedšu*, *sad(u)šu*); acc. to §§ 75, 76.

P. 117, l. 7 from below: should 'Iftaal (?): *itappuṣu*' be amended as laid down in §§ 88 and 101?

P. 122, l. 5: for § 101 read § 100 p. 278.

P. 132, l. 12: for 'equally' read 'by no means'.

P. 171, l. 8: delete *in-di-ru* 'threshing-floor'; K. 6 l. 22 has not *in-di-rim* but, as my recent inspection of the original has shown me, *in-di pû*.

A few other trifling corrections require no special notice.

Addenda.

P. 26, No. 72: that *rik* is not so very rare as a syllabic value of the sign *ṣu* is shown by Peiser in the *Zeitschrift für Assyriologie* II, 447 f.

P. 29, No. 111 and p. 30, No. 121: with the syllabic values there indicated compare the remarks made in § 117, 1 under III 1 (pres.), IV 1 (inf.), and IV 2 (pret.)

P. 86, § 34, *β*: observe also the infinitives *piḫû*, *ṭaḫû* and *ṭeḫû* mentioned in § 110 (p. 305).

P. 87, § 34, *δ*: to the "other miscellaneous cases" — besides the infinitives *peḫû* (*piḫû*) etc., just referred to, and the ordinals *rebû* etc. to be transferred to this section from p. 84 lines 7—10 — we may add adjectives like *ṣiḫru*, *limnu* (= *ṣeḫru*, *lemnu*, *v.* § 65 Nos. 7 and 8, notes), permansives like *nekisi* (*nikisi*), and *ṣebâku* (*ṣibâku*, *v.* § 97 on p. 268 and § 110 on p. 304); also presents like *inêruṭ* (= *inâruṭ*, *v.* §§ 98 and 101 under I 1).

P. 88. The form *asikin* (= *aštakan*,*assakan*, *assekan*, *assikin*) mentioned incidentally on p. 225 might be added with equal propriety to § 34 *δ* and to § 35.

P. 91, the following is to be added as *d*); Syncope of accented *a* and *e*: *šitkunu* infin. from and alongside of *šitákunu*, *itkulu* from and alongside of *itákulu*; *pitlaḫ* imp. from and alongside of *pitálaḫ*, *itrubî* (fem.) from *itérubî*, and others; *v.* § 88, b. 94.

P. 115, note: with reference to the interchange of *m* and *g* observe the interesting form *išakkanga* (K. 81, 27) = *išakkamma*; details will be given in the "*Beiträge zur Assyriologie und vergleichenden Sprachwissenschaft*" Heft I.

P. 256. As contrasted with *ḳuṣṣupâkunu* and as supporting *banâtunu* the permansive *limnêtunu*, adduced p. 165 on Pinches' authority, is worthy of notice.

P. 275, l. 8: the *u* here inferred as the vowel of the present of סחר has since been confirmed by ***isahurûni*** K. 113, 11 (PSBA X, part 3, plate I).

Attention should here be drawn to the fact that, in accordance with § 16, every *ú* in the beginning of a word has been transcribed simply as *u*; had the sign for *u* given as No. 5 in § 9 been ever used in the beginning of a word, I would have expressly said so.

That many more 'addenda' might still be given I am fully aware: cf., for example, to § 43 the interchange of *ṭa* (*ṭâ*) with *ṭâb* (*ṭâ*ʃ) in the contract tablets; to § 55 b, the forms *kâšu* and *kâtunu* of the second person; to § 55, a *šûtu* = *šû* 'he'; to § 96 certain pres. and pret. forms occurring in Assyro-Babylonian letters such as ***i-pa-lu-hu*** (R^M 77, 28) ***i-šak-ku-nu*** (K. 183, 19) ***lišparûni*** 'let them send' (R^M 77, 19) or ***lirpiš*** 'let . . . extend', pres. ***irâpiš*** (K. 479, 33. 35). Finally to §§ 78—82 which treat of the particles might be added a series of adverbs etc., which have as yet been found only in letters and contracts, such as ***me-meʾni*** 'somehow', the prep. and conj. ***bi-id*** and many others, some of which will be discussed in the first Heft of the "*Beiträge zur Assyriologie*" *etc.* We must first enquire, however, how much of all this is suitable for adoption into this grammar, which, notwithstanding its comparatively large size, ought to be and is meant to be a Porta linguae Assyriacae.

www.ingramcontent.com/pod-product-compliance
Lightning Source LLC
Chambersburg PA
CBHW022018110726
47901CB00006B/1576
* 9 7 8 3 3 3 7 2 2 7 7 9 1 *